Discovering Public Relations

To Mom, Dad, Kristin, Karla, Scott, and Marcus. My family who has supported me throughout the years.

To my students (current and former) at the University of Louisville and WVU. You are the reason why I do what I do. This book and how it came about is for you as you embark in this new journey into the PR field.

To Ronnie and Rosie. Thank you for trying to contribute to this book with dedicated focus, paws on the keyboard, and barks to get me moving on my deadlines.

To Starbucks coffee. You powered me through creating this book!
#ThisProfRunsOnCoffee

Sara Miller McCune founded SAGE Publishing in 1965 to support the dissemination of usable knowledge and educate a global community. SAGE publishes more than 1000 journals and over 800 new books each year, spanning a wide range of subject areas. Our growing selection of library products includes archives, data, case studies and video. SAGE remains majority owned by our founder and after her lifetime will become owned by a charitable trust that secures the company's continued independence.

Los Angeles | London | New Delhi | Singapore | Washington DC | Melbourne

Discovering Public Relations

An Introduction to Creative and Strategic Practices

Karen Freberg
University of Louisville

Los Angeles | London | New Delhi
Singapore | Washington DC | Melbourne

FOR INFORMATION:

SAGE Publications, Inc.
2455 Teller Road
Thousand Oaks, California 91320
E-mail: order@sagepub.com

SAGE Publications Ltd.
1 Oliver's Yard
55 City Road
London, EC1Y 1SP
United Kingdom

SAGE Publications India Pvt. Ltd.
B 1/I 1 Mohan Cooperative Industrial Area
Mathura Road, New Delhi 110 044
India

SAGE Publications Asia-Pacific Pte. Ltd.
18 Cross Street #10-10/11/12
China Square Central
Singapore 048423

Printed in Canada

ISBN: 9781544355375

Acquisitions Editor: Lily Norton
Content Development Editor: Jennifer Jovin-Bernstein
Editorial Assistant: Sarah Wilson
Production Editor: Bennie Clark Allen
Copy Editor: Melinda Masson
Typesetter: Hurix Digital
Proofreader: Sarah Duffy
Indexer: Integra
Cover Designer: Scott Van Atta
Marketing Manager: Vicky Velasquez

This book is printed on acid-free paper.

20 21 22 23 24 10 9 8 7 6 5 4 3 2 1

BRIEF CONTENTS

DETAILED CONTENTS

PART I: FOUNDATIONS

Chapter 2. Historical Contexts and Today's Practices   22

PART II: APPLICATIONS

PREFACE AND ACKNOWLEDGMENTS

Once upon a time, there was a young girl growing up in California who wanted to make a difference in the world. She had a vision of making an impact, especially in her field. With ambition in one hand and a coffee cup in another, she set forth on her epic journey, saying, "I'm going on an adventure," just like Bilbo Baggins does in *The Hobbit*.

This girl was not going to be battling Smaug (even though she would have loved to meet Benedict Cumberbatch!), traveling through the many highs and lows to Mordor, or joining the Force among the Jedi (wait a minute—wrong franchise!). No, she also did not have her Lord of the Rings or Seven Dwarfs to help her accomplish her goals and dreams (sorry, Disney!).

The overall lesson here, to cut to the chase, is simple: Life is too short to miss going on a little adventure to find yourself and find out how you can make an impact in your field.

And this is my story, of how this book came about and why I hope it will influence the future of the PR profession.

A Shift in the PR Field

Ever since I started teaching strategic communications at the University of Louisville in 2011, I have had a thought in the back of my mind that something is missing in the PR field. Each year, as I was teaching strategic communications and seeing what the PR field was doing, I was growing more and more frustrated.

Why was I frustrated? I was frustrated with the lack of innovation and forward thinking about the PR field provided for the classroom. The textbooks were the same, the case studies highlighted were the same, and everything was focused on what the PR field has done in the past and what it is doing presently. I was seeing in real time how big the gap was between industry and academia, and it was scary. As a professor, my goal has always been to make sure my students are prepared with the skills, knowledge, and experience to be successful in their future ventures—whether in pursuing graduate studies or going into industry.

In addition, there was no discussion about the future of public relations. Limited discussions took place about how public relations is integrated within marketing and advertising and other related disciplines as a hub, but we have the potential to do so much more. Public relations as a profession was getting swamped by related disciplines, such as English in the area of social media strategy and digital storytelling. We were being cannibalized as a profession by other disciplines, a huge risk for the future of our profession.

I was also frustrated by how certain practices in public relations were being high-lighted above others. One of the things that I realized very early on in my career is how politics and certain professional alliances are not just what you see happening in Washington, DC, but they are very much apparent and at the forefront of what we are doing in public relations. Traditional backgrounds for research agendas and schools of thought were highly valued, and I was entering the field as a complete outsider. My background in many ways is colorful, but I blended experience and educational pro-grams that balanced research and integrated practices of public relations. This is what I think the PR field needs to have, but of course as I entered the field, I was told otherwise.

This is where I was at a crossroads of my career. There was a fork in the road for where I was going in my professional career, and I had to make a choice. On the left was the path to accepting the status quo of the PR field. I would have to bow down to the current and traditional practices that have always been in place, and let self-appointed leaders determine the course of this field. This would have been a safe route to go, and many other professors, scholars, and practitioners have gone this route because they do not want to be singled out. However, the right path was uncharted—one filled with possibilities and new adventures, but also a lot of work to clear the field and road ahead for others to follow. It is always difficult and challenging to be the first in doing anything. A lot of mistakes will be made along the way, and some things that you decide to do may fail. Some people are afraid of change, and even more are afraid of failure.

Trying out new things and seeing if they work is very stressful. If you put yourself out there for the world to see and something does not go well, people will judge you. They will make comments and say, "Poor you—you failed in what you tried to accomplish." My response is always this: "At least I tried and learned something from the experience."

We need more PR professionals to push the envelope just a bit more. If we are satisfied with everything that has been done in the past, how are we going to evolve? The PR field for decades has been running around like a hamster in a hamster wheel—circling around doing the same things, discussing the same ideas, citing the same research articles, and discussing the same cases over and over again. This is not a model that supports or encourages innovation.

Sometimes we have to take a lesson from Daenerys Targaryen of *Game of Thrones* and break the wheel. I'm not saying to take your dragons and set ablaze the entire field of public relations. That would be a bit drastic. But I *am* saying that sometimes to make a field stronger, we have to break the mold and what we've always known it to be.

Ultimately, to make change happen in the field, you have to do it yourself. The time is now for the field to finally move forward in a new and innovative direction. Looking at the profession, I knew that something had to be done.

How This Book Came About

How did this book come about? Well, the process was pretty straightforward and very fast, to be perfectly honest. I had just finished writing my *Social Media for Strategic Communication* book for SAGE when I met with my team at SAGE to discuss another project, writing another book. I was excited to be able to write another book with a great team at SAGE because of the positive experiences that I had with my first solo published book. I remember sitting down with the team, and they asked me to write an introduction for the PR book. Of all the different book markets out there in public relations, the "introduction to public relations" set features the most established books. Some I even used as an undergraduate student at the University of Florida back in 2002. That will give you an idea of how established but also how tough the market is. The team did not sugarcoat things with me at all—they were very blunt but very honest in terms of their expectations. They said that customer research has shown that there is a need for an introduction to public relations book to talk about not just the past or where we are presently but where we need to go as a field. The team also said that most of the other books do not integrate new perspectives or specialized areas (e.g., social media) in a way that reflects the market and industry expectations.

Among people who know me and who've seen my career evolve, I may be known for my social media teaching and research in the PR field, but first and foremost, public relations is where my professional roots are as a scholar, researcher, and consultant in the industry. When I wrote my social media book, I viewed it through a strategic communications lens and integrated PR process.

It should not be a surprise that I would write a PR book as well. Also, if I had to write a book on public relations, it would be for an introduction to public relations course. First, this is a class that I have insisted on teaching every semester at the University of Louisville. Second, ever since I stepped into my first intro to public relations course at the University of Florida, I have had a soft spot for that class. This was the class where I found my calling and fell in love with a profession that I have been a part of for nearly 20 years. It is also one of the most important courses in our profession. Why do you think this is the case? The introduction course is where you introduce and show what the field is all about to new students who may eventually decide they want to be part of our community. It is a chance for PR professionals to show the dynamic aspect of our field and what our industry has to offer that is different from related disciplines like advertising, journalism, and marketing. This class also is the gateway to future classes in the profession. This class cannot be uninteresting, boring, or, worst-case scenario, out of date. If we do any of these things, we have failed our students. We have failed to be the best advocates for our profession, and we have done our profession a disservice.

So, I signed another contract with SAGE, received my schedule, and was off to the races. I had eight months to write a new book with new material presenting a new perspective on public relations. No big deal, right? Bring it on.

About the Book

The goal of *Discovering Public Relations: An Introduction to Creative and Strategic Practices* is to provide students with an integrated, engaging, and strategic focus of the future of public relations as a profession and an industry. While most books cover what has been done in the past in public relations or what is happening now, this book highlights where the field is going in the future, making sure to discuss how public relations is embracing the ever-changing media and digital landscape with creative evidence-based practices that will never go out of style.

Chapters

The chapters are broken into different sections and focus areas. The first seven chapters build on PR's foundation and history as a profession. **Chapter 1** discusses the current state of public relations. This is where you look at the rising expectations that are needed for PR professionals to be successful in the industry. **Chapter 2** focuses on the evolution of the field by looking at where public relations started and at the key figures who helped shape the field to where it is today. **Chapter 3** focuses on the ethical and legal considerations that are necessary to understand in operating public relations.

Understanding the importance of representation and inclusivity within PR practices is a key element for us to practice. **Chapter 4** offers a thorough overview of the issue of diversity inclusion and public relations. This chapter discusses some of the main issues in areas of diversity inclusion that need to be taken into consideration and acknowledged in our day-to-day practices. **Chapter 5** outlines the core principles of research in public relations, as well as the current and future traditional research methods that are implemented to help PR professionals better gather research, create and discuss insights, and apply these insights into actionable strategies. **Chapter 6** focuses on personal branding and outlines why a strong personal brand is essential for PR professionals to master and apply for their clients and for themselves. **Chapter 7** explores writing for public relations and describes the essential components and principles needed to construct effective PR assets. This chapter identifies different traditional forms of content creation for public relations such as news releases, press releases, media kits, brochures, websites, blogs, and social media.

The second part of the book focuses on the application of the principles introduced in the first part. **Chapter 8** describes the strategic planning framework for PR campaigns and ideation. It is important to know the different formats and models that are used to make up a PR campaign. Audience and relationship management is the primary focus for **Chapter 9**. Relationship management is a core part of what makes public relations a field and profession. **Chapter 10** describes content creation, content curation, content amplification, and content strategy. These are principles commonly found in social media practices, but are linked strategically within PR practices. **Chapter 11** addresses a much-needed topic according to the Commission on Public Relations Education: management and business acumen. This chapter discusses the various components and where public relations is compared to related disciplines using this perspective. **Chapter 12** focuses on measurement and evaluation for public relations. **Chapter 13** discusses the working field of public relations, including the components and skills that are necessary, such as internships, fellowships, personal branding, and study abroad. The second part of the book builds upon these foundations in public relations. **Chapter 14** introduces us to the various specializations within public relations. Each of these specializations could fill its own chapter, class, or degree program.

Finally, in the summary part of the text, **Chapter 15** evaluates public relations as a field today and in the future, and discusses best practices for working and moving forward in the field.

Pedagogical Features

Game Changer. Each chapter (except for Chapter 14, which highlights several of these) has a Game Changer feature. These interviews feature individuals who are essentially changing the game in their respective areas of public relations. Many different areas of specialization and roles are showcased here, showing diversity in experience, perspectives, background, gender, and race. I would like to thank all of the great professionals who took the time to answer my questions and share their wisdom for the future generation of PR scholars.

Building Your Brand. In chapters 4 through 15 there is an activity for applying your insights and knowledge from what you are learning in each book chapter to your own personal brand. The most important client you will ever have is yourself—and you can easily apply each of these client, agency, and brand strategies and practices to market yourself for a future job, internship, or professional opportunity. These exercises will provide a guide for how to accomplish these tasks for building your own personal brand.

Building Your Portfolio. Public relations is an applied field, and professionals in the industry are looking for future employees who know what they are talking about and can show that they can apply insights and skills. These activities will provide you with some real-world and applicable exercises that can be added to your digital or physical portfolio of work to show future employers or internship coordinators. The more experience and hands-on work you are able to provide to showcase your understanding in public relations, the better.

Acknowledgments to #TeamFreberg

To be successful in life, we have to have a team behind us supporting us in every challenge and opportunity we face. The same can be said about writing a book. Writing a book takes a lot of time and energy and resources that could be spent doing other things. This textbook took a lot of my time. I was writing at every free moment I could gather for about eight months. I was writing at desks, on planes, in airports while waiting for my flights to take off, on the beach (the French Riviera, in fact, after finishing the Cannes Lions Educators Summit), at coffee shops, in my office, on planes, and at home. I was writing my book everywhere.

I could not have done it without the support and help of family and friends. I guess you could say that these were my group of Avengers, or people I consider to be part of my #TeamFreberg. My friends and family were able to help me in all aspects of working on this book by sending me encouraging messages, getting me coffee to fuel my typing skills, and giving me advice about whether I was on the right track with certain chapters. I dedicate this book to my family, who have been there for me each and every step of the way. I would like to thank Mom and Dad for their continued support and encouragement as I was writing the second book after immediately finishing my social media book. Mom and Dad are two great role models that I had in my life who have helped me become the professional that I am today as well as the person I am in and out of the classroom. I am indebted to their mentorship, kindness, and motivation to be all I can be. I would like to thank my two sisters, Kristin and Karla, for their continued love and support and encouragement along the way in this journey. I would like to thank my brother-in-law, Scott, and my nephew, Marcus, for the encouragement along the way. Love you all!

I would like to give a special shout-out to my younger sister Karla for creating the inspiration behind the book cover design. Karla, who is on the autism spectrum, is one of the best and most talented artists I've ever known. When I told my family I was writing a new book, Karla asked me if she could create a drawing to be considered for part of my book cover design. I was truly honored because I think Karla's artistic talent is unprecedented, and I was super excited to see what she came up with. So what you see here for the book cover was inspired by my sister Karla. Thank you, Karla, for sharing your talents with the world and showing everyone how wonderful and what a talented artist you are.

Of course, I have to thank our family Australian Shepherds, Ronnie and Rosie, my honorary puppy co-authors and constant supporters throughout my social media book. Ronnie would try to help me write my PR book, but instead of writing about public relations, she would want to bark and bark or say, in translation, "Human, you need to give me a Milk-Bone® cookie and take me out for a walk!"

I have to give special thanks to the amazing team at SAGE (Lily, Jen, Ellen, Sarah, and Melinda) for working with me to make this project happen. You all are the best team of collaborators to work for, and I thank you for giving me the opportunity to write this book.

I would also like to dedicate this to fellow professors who have shifted and changed the field in their own ways and who have inspired me to contribute this book to our growing field. These PR professionals inspire me each and every day with the innovations they showcase in their classes. They are the real deal, some of the best, brightest, and most amazing professors and educators that I know who are teaching where the field is going in public relations. Thank you to Sabrina Page, Carolyn Mae Kim, Amanda Weed, Karen Sutherland, Emily Kinsky, Geah Pressgrove, Leo Morejon, Matt Kushin, Dustin Supa, Brandon Boatwright, and many in the #PRprofs community.

I would also like to thank all of the amazing professionals and industry leaders who have been super supportive and helpful by including me in their professional activities and projects. These professionals have been wonderful to work with on industry projects, influencer campaigns, and certification projects. Special thanks to Sebastian Distefano (Adobe), Mark Boothe (Adobe Insiders), Rani Mani (Adobe Insiders), Monica Grant (Adobe), Nicole Goldstein (Facebook), David Vogt (Facebook), Mark Zeller (Facebook), Keith Anderson (Facebook), Corinna Kong (Facebook), Jordan Ames (HubSpot), Stu Draper, Trevor Erikson and the entire student team, and Steve Latham (Cannes Lions and Cannes Lions Educators Summit).

I would also like to thank all of the great professionals who took time to interview with me for the Game Changers features. Special thanks to Stephen Waddington, David Armano, Jason Falls, Deirdre Breakenridge, Goldie Chan, Kara DeLost, Shahbaz Khan, Rani Mani, Leo Morejon, David Remund, Leah Schultz, Dennis Yu, Amir Zozoni, Ty Rogers, Albane Flamant, Chris Strub, and Brian Solis. I really do appreciate each and every one of you for taking the time to share your stories, insights, and expertise with us. Special thanks to my former students Abbie Chambers, Candice Champlin, Megan Richardson, and Michael Jester for also sharing your thoughts about what it takes to be successful in modern-day PR practices as a young professional.

Last but not least, I would like to thank certain professors in my career who have shaped me to be the PR professional, researcher, and author that I am today. You have provided constructive feedback and support throughout my journey from a student in public relations to an author writing books in the field. I would like to thank all of my professors that I had at the University of Florida, University of Southern California, and University of Tennessee for always making sure to push me to the next level in my work. I would like to give a special shout-out to a few professors.

- To Dr. Craig Carroll, who made quite the first impression in my first graduate research class, saying that going to the University of Florida would not help me in his class at the University of Southern California. This definitely made me feel that the bar had been set pretty high for me to basically make a good impression. Craig has been not only a great mentor over the years but a great friend.

- I would also like to thank Jennifer Floto, who was my thesis advisor at the University of Southern California. She provided me with great insights on what to keep in mind always when combining research with practice expectations. My time at the University of Southern California, of course, was very short since it was a two-year master's program, but the lessons I learned have continued to help me in my career many years later.

- I would also like to thank my dissertation advisor at the University of Tennessee, Dr. Michael Palenchar. It was at Tennessee and working with Dr. Palenchar when I had the chance to see the vast amount of research opportunities in crisis communications, and to get guidance in my dissertation work in social media and crisis communications. Thank you for your dedication and due diligence in making sure I always considered theory and research applications in my work.

- I would also like to say a special thank-you and shout-out to Dr. Tim Coombs. Tim is one of the prominent thought leaders in our field, especially in the PR crisis communication arena. Tim is someone with whom you can talk about the latest crisis communication theory and research developments, and then the next minute switch to talk about what happened at Comic-Con and when the next Star Wars races are going to be at Disney. If you want to see "Professor Goals" status, I think Tim has accomplished this. Tim has been a mentor of mine ever since I became an academic, and I am very grateful for his friendship and support over the years.

- I would like to give another special shout-out to my colleague at the University of Louisville, William Thompson, aka "Thompson." William started the PR program at the University of Louisville, and has been a dear friend and supporter and mentor of mine ever since I arrived in 2011. William was the one who helped me get my first book contract at SAGE, and I feel it is appropriate to give him acknowledgement and praise for his continued support of my work in our industry.

- Last but not least, I would like to thank my students at the University of Louisville and West Virginia University. I have had the honor of being able to have hundreds of students walk through my doors or check in online for my classes. These students could have chosen any other section or another course to take during their studies, but they all chose to take my class in public relations. I am forever grateful to be able to make an impact on the lives of these great young professionals. I've had the opportunity to meet some incredible people with amazing stories and to see them flourish in our field successfully and make a difference. There is no better reward. I am forever grateful for the fact that our paths aligned and have crossed. This is why I teach, and this is why this book is for them.

In order to ensure that *Discovering Public Relations* meets the needs of both students and instructors, many scholars devoted their time to provide constructive feedback on this book throughout its development. Thanks to the following individuals for their helpful comments:

LiRon Anderson-Bell, Temple University; Clover Baker-Brown, Prince George's Community College; Courtney A. Barclay, Jacksonville University; Melinda A. Booze, Evangel University; Brett A. Borton, University of South Carolina Beaufort; Lois A. Boynton, University of North Carolina at Chapel Hill; Charles F. Byers, Santa Clara

University; L. Simone Byrd, Alabama State University; William L. Cowen, Villanova University; Rochelle R. Daniel, Bowie State University; Josie DeAngelis, Western New England University; Mary E. Donato, Buena Vista University; Colleen A. Fitzpatrick, Saint Mary's College; Elizabeth Avery Foster, University of Tennessee; S. Catherine Foster, Canisius College; Terry L. Hapney Jr., Marshall University; Denise Herd, Indiana University–Purdue University Indianapolis; Laura Hester, Lander University; Marcie Hinton, Murray State University; Katherine Coffey Irwin, Columbus State University; Rachel E. Kaitz, Lewis-Clark State College; Yahya R. Kamalipour, North Carolina A&T State University; Jason Karpf, Southern New Hampshire University; Kate S. Kurtin, California State University, Los Angeles; Linda Lockhart, Marietta College; Dylan McLemore, University of Central Arkansas; Christopher J. McCollough, Columbus State University; Scott A. Morton, Catawba College; Robert Nanney, The University of Tennessee at Martin; Klive Oh, Pepperdine University; Maxey Parrish, Baylor University; Anna Popkova, Western Michigan University; Richard A. Pozniak, Middlesex Community College and Merrimack College; Claire M. Regan, Wagner College; Jennifer Robinette, Marist College; Jean Kelso Sandlin, California Lutheran University; Tracy Sereda, Glendale Community College; Efe Sevin, Reinhardt University; Ann Strahle, University of Illinois Springfield; Matthew P. Taylor, Middle Tennessee State University; Natalie T. J. Tindall, Lamar University; Mimi Tsui, Seneca College; Ying Wang, Youngstown State University; Jamie Ward, Eastern Michigan University; Kirsten Whitten, Stonehill College; Erin Wilgenbusch, Iowa State University Greenlee; Cessna Winslow, Tarleton State University; Travis C. Yates, Quincy University; Angela Zhang, Kansas State University and University of Oklahoma.

Summary

So you can see there's a lot of thought, hard work, and dedication that has gone into this book. I hope you enjoy the range of chapters that follow, and I hope that this will provide you with a clear overview of not only where public relations has been but ultimately where public relations is going in the future.

At the end of this textbook, you will have a pretty good idea of where you stand in the field, and what next steps you need to take to be successful. I wish you all the very best as you venture out in this new journey. I love public relations as a field. It is the best industry, the opportunities are endless, and the future is bright and full of potential possibilities. We need individuals who are willing to discover the possibilities in our field to help us move forward as a profession.

Have you chosen to accept your mission? Are you ready to go on an adventure?

Let's go, then, on this incredible adventure with Gandalf. Assemble your PR Avengers. Engage, Mr. Sulu!

Best Wishes,
Karen

ABOUT THE AUTHOR

Karen Freberg (@kfreberg) is an associate professor in strategic communications at the University of Louisville. She is also an adjunct faculty member for the West Virginia University graduate online program in integrated marketing communications. Freberg has presented at several U.S. and international research conferences, including ones in Australia, Brazil, China, Ireland, Greece, Italy, Slovenia, Spain, Sweden, the Netherlands, and the United Kingdom. In 2019, she was appointed associate adjunct instructor during her sabbatical to Australia at the University of the Sunshine Coast.

In addition to academic conferences, Freberg has presented at professional and trade conferences such as the Public Relations Society of America (PRSA), Social Media Strategies Summit, Adobe Creative Campus, SXSW EDU®, and Cannes Lions, as well as been invited to do industry workshops and talks with the Dallas Mavericks, USA Football, Kentucky Organ Donor Affiliates, and Signature HealthCARE on social media trends and strategies.

Freberg is also a research consultant in social media and crisis communications and has worked with several organizations and agencies such as Firestorm Solutions, Hootsuite, Kentucky Derby Festival, IMC Agency, the U.S. Department of Homeland Security (DHS), the Centers for Disease Control and Prevention (CDC), the National Center for Food Protection and Defense (NCFPD), Kentucky Organ Donor Affiliates, and Colorado Ski Country USA. This experience led her to be a 2015 Plank Center Fellow for General Motors (GM), where her responsibility was to work with the PR and social media teams forming best practices and recommendations on social media measurement strategies and influencer marketing practices.

Freberg has coordinated and advised various companies on the areas of social media pedagogy and certification programs, such as Hootsuite (Advanced Social Media Strategy certification and #HootAmb), Meltwater (certification program and contributor), Adobe (EDUMax Thought Leader), HubSpot (education program and podcast), and Facebook Blueprint (subject matter expert).

Along with her teaching, Freberg's research has been published in several book chapters and in academic journals such as *Public Relations Review*, *Media Psychology Review*, *Journal of Contingencies and Crisis Management*, and *Health Communication*. She also serves on the editorial board for *Psychology of Popular Media Culture*, *Corporate Communications*, *Marketing Education Review*, *Journal of Public Relations Research*, and *Case Studies in Strategic Communication* (CSSC).

In addition to academic publications, Freberg has been interviewed for popular press publications such as *USA Today*, *USA Today College*, and *Forbes*. Freberg is also professionally active serving on the executive committee for the PRSA Entertainment and Sports Section and is on the Technology Chapter Committee for the Commission on Public Relations Education (CPRE). Freberg is also a regular contributor and a young professionals award judge for Front Office Sports.

Before coming to the University of Louisville, Freberg earned a PhD in communication and information at the University of Tennessee in May 2011, and a master's degree in strategic public relations at the Annenberg School for Communication and Journalism at the University of Southern California in August 2007. Freberg received her bachelor's of science degree in public relations at the University of Florida in August 2005.

FOUNDATIONS

PART I

CHAPTER 1

AN INTRODUCTION TO PUBLIC RELATIONS

LEARNING OBJECTIVES

- Define public relations.

- Identify key areas within public relations.

- Distinguish between public relations and similar disciplines.

- Understand the influences of other disciplines on public relations.

Introduction

What do you think of when you hear the term *public relations*? Take a moment and jot down your first impressions. After reading this chapter, reflect back on your notes and see what has or has not changed in your thinking about the field.

In the mind of the general public, our field is often associated with fictional characters such as Samantha Jones in *Sex and the City* or Olivia Pope in *Scandal*. Some even refer to us derogatively as "spin doctors," meaning that our job is to make something seem better than it is. Yes, it is true that planning events in the entertainment industry and managing crisis communications are important parts of what we do. However, our field is so much more. In contrast to the "spin doctor" stereotype, we are bound by carefully constructed ethical guidelines, as will become clear in this book.

PR practitioners, or those of us who work in the field, look at public relations from various perspectives. Some focus on the duties of PR professionals, such as media pitching, creating press releases, and formulating media kits, while others focus on specializations within the field, such as event planning and crisis communications, as well as media campaigns, or reputation management, and we will explore these perspectives in depth. An example of these efforts includes the campaign that brought together McDonald's and Burger King. Both are competitors in the marketplace with their own reputations to manage and oversee, but for the purpose of a good cause, the two brands came together in a media campaign to fight the battle against cancer.

Burger King and McDonald's had not partnered on previous campaigns due to the fact they are competitors in the same market in the fast-food industry. However, the purpose of this campaign focused on a good cause that affects all audiences, even the brands' own customers. They took off their competitors' hats (or, in this case, gloves) to partner together to raise awareness and drive donations to support the cause to fight cancer. This resulted in positive media coverage and acknowledgment for their efforts, which shows you can collaborate and support a good initiative even with your biggest competitor. Some things are bigger than selling burgers, and this is what Burger King and McDonald's did with this partnership.

As we will discover in this chapter, public relations is in a state of transition. We face new challenges every day, and we need to have the right tools, resources, and insights to best meet these challenges. This chapter explores what public relations is and how it functions, what PR professionals do, and how the field differs from, and collaborates with, related disciplines.

Burger King and McDonald's join hands to fight cancer.
GritDaily

Finally, this chapter summarizes how public relations today is more than just press releases and working with the media—ours is a field that is evolving, combining the use and application of data, stories, marketing, advertising, and social and digital components to foster and sustain mutually beneficial relationships across audiences and channels. Using conversation, storytelling, and the development of sustainable communities, we can connect with related disciplines using our relationship management practices.

What Is Public Relations?

Everyone has a different perception and definition of what public relations is, and it is important to know how the parties involved, from academics to practitioners, define the field.

How Academics Define Public Relations

Academic scholars have defined **public relations** as "the planned effort to influence opinion through socially responsible and acceptable performance based on mutually satisfactory two-way communication" (Cutlip & Center, 1971, p. 4). Broom and Dozier (1983) further defined public relations as being "concerned with relations with numerous publics, that like consumers, affect organizational survival and growth" (p. 6). Coombs (2001, p. 106; see also Health, 2000) defined public relations as "the use of communication to manage the relationship between an organization and its stakeholders."

How Practitioners Define Public Relations

As practitioners, we have our own view of the field. The Public Relations Society of America (PRSA), our largest professional organization, defines public relations as a "strategic communication process that builds mutually beneficial relationships between organizations and their publics" (Public Relations Society of America, 2020). Lewis, a PR firm, describes public relations as the "seamless integration across multiple channels. Successful brands know there is a multiplier effect when public relations and digital marketing work hand in hand, ensuring continuity across channels and around the world"

(Tannahill, 2015). What this means is, for public relations to work, there has to be an effort in making sure all channels, audiences, and content are coordinated together for the right place, time, and location.

There are similarities between academic and practitioner perspectives when it comes to the conceptualization of public relations. First, both academics and practitioners recognize that public relations has a core focus on relationship management (understanding the dynamics of the needs and expectations from each party involved) and that this impacts the dynamics between an organization and its key publics. Key publics are individuals who have a clear relationship with the client and will be the primary targets for the message strategies being implemented in a PR campaign. Second, academics and practitioners alike argue that for these relationships to work, they have to offer a win-win situation for both parties, not just one.

Yet there are some differences between academic and practitioner perspectives. Academic scholars focus on how public relations is conceptualized based on theoretical perspectives (discussed in Chapter 2), whereas practitioners look at public relations as a strategic element and a process for accomplishing mutually beneficial relationships. Mutually beneficial relationships focus on creating a win-win situation for both parties involved. The strategic element is an important one to add here because the field relies on research, planning, and the creative execution of these efforts.

How Do We Build Relationships in Public Relations?

Why do we use the term *public relations* to describe our field? The first word, *public*, refers to the key audiences with whom we want to engage in conversation for the ultimate purpose of creating a strong connection that is sustainable for the long term. *Relations* refers to the connection we forge with our audiences (or publics), based on common ground. So, in sum, the term *public relations* literally refers to engaging in an ongoing dialogue with individuals or groups in a win-win situation. For example, in the case of the McDonald's and Burger King collaboration to fight against cancer, both brands gained positive media coverage for uniting to help address a global health issue, and at the same time, audiences and those impacted by these efforts benefited in knowing two global brands are doing their part in helping address this cause for them, which creates a win-win situation for everyone involved.

We Identify Publics

Our audiences usually have relevant age cohort (otherwise known as age generational cohorts, similar to baby boomers, Generation Z, millennials, etc.), demographic, and psychographic (core lifestyle, attitude, behavior, and opinion attributes) characteristics that may be important to keep in mind when planning particular initiatives and activities. For example, the age cohort of boomers (born between 1946 and 1964) may respond to a PR campaign differently than millennials (born between 1981 and 1996) do. Some brands (products or items that are created and produced by a parent company like General Motors and Chevrolet) aim for engagement with members of a particular demographic, such as a socioeconomic group. For example, manufacturers of affordable or luxury cars take their audience's respective needs into account. PR campaigns also target particular psychographic segments of their audience, such as people interested in fitness, food, or home improvement. One of the cardinal sins for PR practitioners is to state "we want to target the general public." This means you want to target everyone, which may be neither realistic nor achievable within the scope of a campaign. Targeting the general public—essentially capturing the 8 billion people who are part of the global society—is usually not the best way to approach things.

Publics is a common term in public relations, one that helps us identify audiences who will be the focus of a campaign. These are individuals whose shared characteristics mean it makes sense to group them together. For example, if Starbucks were going to explore its publics, it might separate publics who are avid coffee drinkers from publics who are tea drinkers (or, heaven forbid, decaf drinkers!). The key for PR professionals is to make sure publics are categorized by specific attributes. By doing this, PR professionals are able to group and focus on certain audiences during a campaign, which is far more practical than trying to reach every person on the planet.

We Focus on Stakeholders

A special kind of public is known as a **stakeholder**, an individual who has a vested interest in the organization. Stakeholder theory, which helps us understand the behavior of stakeholders, has been an important part of PR research for decades (Laplume, Sonpar, & Litz, 2008). Stakeholders come in many different ways, but those who have an invested interest financially or emotionally are those who are considered to be stakeholders. For example, college students are key stakeholders for the university since they (1) are invested in their education financially and (2) want their university to do well for their reputation and the prestige of their degree. Freeman (1984, p. 25) was the first scholar to operationalize what stakeholders are by defining them as "any group or individual who can affect or is affected by the achievement of the firm's objectives." Clarkson (1995, p. 106) defined stakeholders similarly by stating that they "have, or claim, ownership, rights, or interests in a corporation and its activities, past, present, or future." Grunig and Repper (1992) defined stakeholders as publics, implying they are a broader group comprised of anyone an organization needs to be aware of for its well-being. Stakeholders want to work with organizations that practice ethical behavior and maintain a positive and proactive relationship with them for the long term (Brass, Butterfield, & Skaggs, 1998).

More contemporary scholars view the management of stakeholders as more "network-based, relational, and process-oriented" (Andriof & Waddock, 2002, p. 19), meaning that stakeholders are not working or operating in silos, but are connected to each other based on mutual contacts, experiences, and even online communities. We are all "six degrees of Kevin Bacon" related! Organizations that are effective in managing relationships with stakeholders can enhance their overall strategies and reputation among their stakeholders for the long term while separating themselves from their competitors (Hillman & Keim, 2001). One of the main reasons that corporations and other large entities focus on their communication and business practices in relation to stakeholders is that such a focus increases the positive perception of a corporation (Argenti, 1996).

We Manage Relationships Between Publics and Brands

Besides exploring population data (demographics) and attitudes and opinions (psychographics), we will look at other attributes that define the publics of public relations. The current relationship that a public has with a brand or an organization is a key factor. **Engagement**—the actions

Nike ✓
@Nike

You can take the superhero out of her costume, but you can never take away her superpowers. #justdoit

You can take the superhero out of her costume, but you can never take away her superpowers.

Just do it.

12:34 AM - 25 Aug 2018

124,474 Retweets **295,587** Likes

👤 Serena Williams

💬 2.5K   🔁 124K   ♡ 296K   ✉

Nike and Serena Williams
Nike, via Twitter

taken in response to a content or message strategy of an organization—is a focus of PR practitioners and researchers. PR researchers need to recognize not only the power of engagement in traditional circumstances, but also the importance of engaging with audiences online, both digitally and socially (Dhanesh, 2017).

By connecting at the online spaces our audiences gravitate to, we can form relationships. Some audiences will have a positive relationship with a brand or organization, while others will not. We describe a public's relationships with brands as positive, neutral (not engaged yet), or negative. These various relationships are evident in recent cases. For example, Nike received positive feedback from its customers when it released an ad supporting tennis player Serena Williams after the French Open president said she couldn't wear her catsuit during competition because it was "too revealing." The way that Nike responded, supporting Williams, sparked positive feelings among key publics because Nike's actions aligned with the public's expectations of the brand. This alignment is a key factor that can help contribute to the overall relationship that a public has with a brand. Because of this, more brands are willing to stand for a viewpoint, perspective, or issue that is tied to their brand and those that are associated with it. This practice is bringing forth a new advocacy wave for brands to take on. Audiences, especially those in Generation Z, want organizations and others to stand for various issues—social, environmental, race, global, and so on—that are tied to their corporate values and community-based expectations. REI did this for its #OptOutside campaign to encourage its customers, employees, and others to go outside instead of shopping during Black Friday sales. And brands such as Dick's Sporting Goods and Walmart have taken the initiative to not sell guns and other firearm products in their stores to address the gun control issue. When implemented, the reactions from brands on these various issues have been both positive and negative, depending on the response from the brand's key audiences and the brand's own view of its actions. As will be discussed later in this book, advocacy messaging, such as that accomplished by Nike, can bring forth both praise and resistance, even to the point of boycotts and outrage from key audiences. An example of this was the recent Gillette commercial (discussed in Chapter 2) in which the corporation, for the sake of its brand, took advantage of the growing trends in advocacy advertising. This new approach is especially relevant to longer-term audiences (such as Generation Z and future generations).

Let's look at another example of relationship management. In 2017, United Airlines faced a brand crisis when a live video of a passenger went viral on social media; the content of the video did not do any favors for the brand's reputation. In this case, a passenger was dragged from a United flight, which resulted in a damaging onslaught of media coverage of the airline. Customers who saw the video responded negatively toward the brand; it had damaged their relationships with United. Subsequently, the airline noted the response and adjusted its messaging strategies to try to restore its relationships with customers. While the brand will always have to bear the incident and its fallout as part of the company's history, United strategists are making efforts to restore customer trust and improve relationships with the airline's key audiences.

Where Do We Find Public Relations in Action?

The work we do takes place across a wide spectrum of industries and sectors. Avidar (2017) notes that public relations functions in public and government sectors, private business sectors, and social nonprofit sectors. In addition to these three traditional areas, new contexts for PR specialty areas (social media, technology, etc.) and roles (consultants, entrepreneurship, and freelancing) are emerging. The lines between related disciplines are blurring. For example, today's PR professional is expected to be competent in advertising and paid media, responsibilities that used to exist outside the domain of the PR professional.

The work we do is not always recognized as "public relations." Jobs for PR professionals are listed in various and different terms. For example, for some organizations, PR functions are listed as part of "corporate communications." This model is used by General Motors, Brown-Forman, Yum! Brands, and many other large organizations. In these cases, our responsibilities and work are focused internally, within the corporate setting. Many corporations and their brands list corporate communications in job titles, yet the individuals in these positions supervise other departments of specialization such as employee advocacy, public affairs, investor relations, social media strategy, and community outreach and relations. In organizations such as the military or nonprofit groups, a public affairs or public information officer may be described with terms that we associate with PR professionals.

The profession of public relations is practiced worldwide. Public relations has a significant global presence, and practices differ from country to country (Verčič, van Ruler, Bütschi, & Flodin, 2001). Many brands maintain a global presence, requiring consistent messages that we create and share. At the same time, brands need to tailor messages to unique local circumstances.

What Do We Do as PR Professionals?

As PR professionals, we are often assigned to the following functions:

- serve as the trusted counsel of an organization (which means being proactive in making sure the team knows all of the different perspectives, options, and challenges they could face and how messaging strategies could help address this)

- engage with internal audiences (building team advocates internally with employees and staff members could help address any challenges that come from external audiences)

- serve as the contact point for the media (being the face of the organization in the media allows the messaging to be consistent across channels and situations)

- implement community initiatives (which means leading the way to advocate for community efforts to support those who are impacted by our efforts)

- manage expectations and perceptions before, during, and after a crisis (which means making sure to address all concerns, questions, and preparations for when a crisis hits)

- advocate for audiences internally and externally (public relations serves as an advocate for our client for all audiences, inside and out, and it is important to make sure to communicate consistently across all audiences)

In addition to this list of our traditional responsibilities, our field is growing and developing new areas of specialization. For example, we might be expected to manage social media, augmented reality (AR), and virtual reality (VR) message strategies. Social media messages come from all platforms and channels, which means we must be able to create, curate, and analyze content, making sure it reflects our brand's voice, community, and values. AR and VR are still relatively new media for us, but through experience—immersing ourselves into virtual worlds (through VR) and adding in additional layers of information (through AR)—we can make stronger connections between our audiences and brands.

On the job, we must be able to write, research, think creatively, and function in a business setting.

We Write

Writing in many different formats and in different media is one of our biggest responsibilities (see Chapter 7 for coverage of writing). Among the items we produce are

- press releases;

- news releases, or formatted stories that follow the journalism structure of a news article in the style of the Associated Press, which allows journalists and media professionals a way to review this story to determine if they want to cover it in their own publication or media outlet;

- fact sheets;

- backgrounders, which focus on providing an overview of the brand, key parties, and the campaign for the media in order for them to write a thorough and complete story for their media outlet;

- memos and pitches, which are persuasive statements and points directed to media professionals to persuade them to cover the story about your client and can come via phone, email, or social media channels;

- speeches;

- question-and-answer sessions;

- scripts for public service announcements (PSAs);

- feature stories;

- strategic briefs and plans, from creating a brief overview of an idea you have for a campaign to launching a full comprehensive PR plan to execute; and

- social media content to be distributed across vast array of channels.

Because of changes happening in the industry, we are performing new tasks and creating new kinds of writing. Some of the shifts in the industry are the result of new platforms and tools (e.g., social media), the blurring of the lines between industries (e.g., ads for advertising campaigns), and new content for new channels (e.g., AR, VR). These new tasks and types of writing require that we

- update social media;

- create storyboards for advertisements and social media content pieces (visual layouts of each scene that will be created);

- listen to and monitor reports from traditional, digital, and social media;

- perform influencer audits (evaluating which influencer to work with based on certain criteria);

- create white papers and ebooks;

- conduct walk-throughs for VR experiences;

- create briefs to launch new AR features to provide information and generate awareness on issues and knowledge;

- compose ads;

- create content calendars (outlined dates and schedules for when content will be pushed and executed across different channels);

- write analytics reports from social and digital media campaigns; and

- create visual storyboards for stories on specific platforms.

We Conduct Research

Conducting research, setting forth objective predictions, systematically collecting information, and working with numbers are key skills that we must have. Yes, we *do math*: The days of simply sharing data with marketing research firms and asking them to calculate the numbers are over. Identifying trends, current expectations, and early warning signs of possible issues that could translate into a bigger crisis for the brand helps us understand what is happening in the field.

Research skills not only allow us to uncover data and interpret results; they help us to apply what we learn. To apply our insights, we outline and discuss our findings through a strategic lens and evaluate them in terms of their relevance using the plan we have in place. We develop strategic plans, analytical reports, and SWOT analyses (understanding the strengths, weaknesses, opportunities, and threats for an organization or client in question), and we listen to and report further insights gained.

Many PR firms and university programs are well known based on the research they share with the community. For example, over the past 12 years, the communications firm Edelman has established itself through research that explores trends in consumer trust. Further, every two years, the University of Southern California produces the Communication and Public Relations Generally Accepted Practices (GAP) Study, a comprehensive study focused on identifying new trends related to the industry, emerging skills among practitioners, and the current industry landscape.

We Think Creatively

Creativity and creative thinking are essential skills for the PR professional. Other disciplines such as marketing and advertising may lay claim to the creative hat, but no one discipline "owns" creativity. As PR professionals, we are in an optimal position to bridge the science and art of persuasive messaging. We help amplify our clients' stories to invite audience connection. With the help of integrated research practices, strong audience insight analysis, and an understanding of the nature of sustainable relationship- and community-building practices, public relations can become the hub that connects various disciplines together in the integrated marketing communication spectrum. We are creative in how we approach and build bridges between the insights gathered from research and how they can be executed and applied through messaging, content creation, and storytelling. Public relations is as much of an art as it is a science.

We Understand Business Practices

As PR professionals, we must have and be able to exercise an understanding of business. We must be ready to go into a boardroom with a solid background in finance, accounting, marketing research, and business communication practices. Most PR departments report to a chief marketing officer (CMO) or marketing department. Like public relations, business has its own language, terms, and practices. To be effective, we must be able to work hand in hand with professionals from various departments in our organizations.

We Meet Emerging Expectations

As mentioned earlier, being skilled in writing, research, creativity, and business are key elements for us to have in our tool kits. To cope with a rapidly changing industry landscape, we must be adaptive and agile and able to bring new capabilities to the table. Already, academic disciplines such as marketing, advertising, and English are becoming more adaptive, and we PR students and professionals must work to stay ahead of these trends.

Among the newer roles and expectations for PR practitioners are the following:

- *Forecasters.* Forecasters anticipate concerns about issues such as the environment. An example of an award-winning environmental campaign is the Cannes Lions "Trash Isles" campaign. This was a campaign that advocated action to make sure we are not polluting our oceans anymore as a planet.

- *Reputation managers.* Reputation managers understand how to manage, build, and rejuvenate a brand image when it is in crisis, and to protect it in case something further goes wrong. Examples of recent reputation management are the handling of the Papa John's case, Aflac's reputation deficit, and Prince Harry and Meghan Markle's move to no longer be part of the Royal Family. In addition,

Carnival is battling to overcome reputation and crisis challenges (as discussed in the next point) in how it handled sick passengers on its cruise ships in light of the coronavirus epidemic. In these cases, owning the narrative and being mindful of the long-term effects could be factors to discuss and strategize from a PR standpoint.

- *Crisis communicators.* Crisis communicators manage major problems that cannot necessarily be anticipated. For example, the "Crock-Pot® Killed Jack" campaign that refers to the popular character from the show *This Is Us* sparked a lot of discussion on how to manage a PR crisis. When the character Jack Pearson died because of a fire that was caused by a Crock-Pot during one of the episodes on the show, Crock-Pot as a brand had to respond to the outrage emerging from the fans of the show online and in the press.

- *Creators.* Creators, such as Nike and Serena Williams, understand how to create new stories from perspectives not showcased in previous efforts in public relations. For example, the brand Nike took a stand, in collaboration with Williams, to empower athletes to have their own voices, not only in its product but through its branding. This happened after the French Open, where Williams was not allowed to wear a catsuit or a tutu while competing.

- *Digital and social media experts.* Such experts know how to engage the public through their brand and how to stand out with brand messaging on social media. One example is the Mr. Peanut campaign created for the 2019 Super Bowl. The experts who created the campaign connected with Super Bowl audiences through real-time interactions and contests.

- *Storytellers and storymakers.* Storytellers provide an opportunity for audiences to engage and relate more to a brand or organization on an emotional level. Examples of expert stories include the "Here to Create" campaign with Billie Jean King and Adidas at the U.S. Open, DiGiorno, and the tribute Nike provided to the late basketball star Kobe Bryant and his family. Stories come in all shapes and sizes, and each has a unique tone. Some spark happiness, some sadness, but overall, the goal is to spark an emotional connection with audiences that resonates with them.

- *Advocates.* Advocates spark change and raise awareness. One example is the animal crackers campaign by People for the Ethical Treatment of Animals (PETA).

- *Cause evangelists.* So-called cause evangelists advocate for action to be taken to make an impact on society to think or act differently to address an ongoing issue. An excellent example of this is the Dove "Real Beauty" initiative, which focused on addressing the idea that beauty is everywhere, and we are all beautiful inside, to address the pressure of certain standards of beauty that were presented only in the mass media.

- *Strategists.* Strategists provide connections to creative ideas and strategic executions. An example of an excellent strategy is the campaign "Nothing Beats a Londoner" by Nike. This campaign took a new innovative idea and, with the help of research and being able to determine what has been done in the industry already, creatively executed this experience for London residents to be a part of and share with others.

How Do We Work With Professionals in Related Fields?

What differentiates public relations from related fields, such as journalism, advertising, and marketing?

Those who may underestimate or misinterpret public relations as a profession may not understand our responsibilities. Our field is sometimes viewed inaccurately as a subfield of marketing or tied to limited specializations such as event planning and publicity. Public relations may not be taken seriously by some because it "only" focuses on managing relationships. This is in spite of the fact that social psychologists view managing relationships as one of the most challenging functions of the human mind (Caccioppo & Freberg, 2019). Our field may not be considered to be truly scientific because, as practitioners, we deal with intangible assets, such as attitudes and opinions.

In fact, to achieve optimal outcomes for our organizations and publics, our activities must be integrated with those carried out by professionals in marketing, advertising, journalism, and other related fields: Public relations can be the bridge that connects these disciplines together. To this end, it is important that we advocate for our discipline and correct any misinterpretations or misunderstandings of what we do and how we do it.

For decades, professors of advertising and marketing and professors of public relations distinguished between the fields based on "paid" versus "earned" mentions in the media. Advertising agencies, responsible for placing paid content in media sources, were separate entities from PR agencies that pursued strong relationships with journalists and used persuasive strategies. The emergence of digital media blurred the lines between paid and earned. In response, Gini Dietrich (2020) developed the PESO model, which distinguishes between paid, earned, shared, and owned media.

As PR professionals, we are on the same team as those in journalism, advertising, and marketing. We no longer work in discipline-related silos within our organizations but must take an integrated interdisciplinary approach to succeed. To be effective, we need to be aware of what our colleagues in public relations and related disciplines are doing and how to best work together.

We Work With Journalism Professionals

There are many professions that are aligned and work well together, and then there are those that do not get along so well. Welcome to the relationship between public relations and journalism.

Most PR programs in colleges and universities around the world are found within journalism programs, and the relationship is somewhat "complicated." Public relations is sometimes viewed as the "stepchild" of journalism, and journalists claim they are the "real storytellers" for the profession. Now, we are capable of working together—and we need to do so. Journalism programs, along with PR programs, are adapting and changing together.

However, the market speaks differently to the disciplines. While media outlets lay off reporters and journalists, the number of PR jobs continues to grow. According to *PR Daily*, in 2018 PR professionals outnumbered journalists by 6 to 1 (Schneider, 2018). Many times, journalists come to the "dark side" of public relations after their careers in journalism stall. That's okay—we have coffee and cookies. In all seriousness, journalists have a job: to find facts, to report news, and to capture and create stories that are relevant for their publication or outlet. Of course, PR professionals need to get exposure for their stories as well. This is not just a conversation taking place in the United States; it's happening on a global scale (Tkalac Verčič, Lalić, & Vujičić, 2017). The relationship

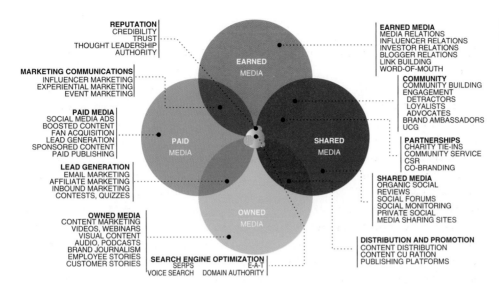

PESO model 2.0 by Gini Dietrich

SpinSucks

between journalism and public relations is the subject of a global discussion in which both parties have different views and expectations for the other.

Here are some ways in which journalists and PR professionals interact with each other today:

- *We embrace experiential media to tell stories.* Journalists are all about using new ways to tell stories, whether to explore through VR what it is like to be in Syria during the country's civil war or to see the Weather Channel integrate AR to show the potential damage caused by Hurricane Florence, a storm that hit the Carolinas in 2018. PR professionals can work with journalists on these types of stories to help audiences experience what it is like to be in particular circumstances—whether it is for a movie promotion (such as *Tomb Raider* and VR) or for providing new services (such as Lowe's and its VR showroom). Any integration for experiences through these new emerging media can help journalism and PR professionals come together. Every experience is a story, and that's what journalists are always after.

- *We build a content marketing initiative through owned media (media that is controlled and owned by you).* PR professionals are embracing more brand journalism and storytelling by creating their own content. In a sense, they become their own media outlet. Branded websites, microsites, blogs, and trade and industry shows are just a few ways brands have done this. In one case, Gary Vaynerchuk, a *New York Times* best-selling author and entrepreneur who has built a media empire in VaynerMedia, has created his own brand and company with blog posts, videos, shows, and constant social media engagement. At the same time, Social Media Examiner, a company that hosts the annual social media conference Social Media Marketing World, has its own show called *The Journey.* While both of these companies interact with the media industry and with professionals in this space, they do not rely on it as much as they have in the past.

We Work With Advertising Professionals

It is important to understand the differences between advertising and public relations. Public relations focuses on building relationships with segments of the public through dialogue with media outlets to convey a story. **Advertising**, on the other hand, focuses on relationships that are built by paying for content to be placed at specific times in specific channels. Advertising and PR professionals have different views of what the other is doing, but acknowledge they need to be more integrated with each other (Supa, 2016). Advertisers have traditionally focused on measuring the impact of their messaging by using concrete metrics, whereas PR professionals have traditionally had a difficult time measuring their impact on their audiences. The differences are related to the measurement front, which is discussed in Chapter 12. However, as the lines between the two disciplines have blurred where the duties and responsibilities once separate or unique to one field are being added to the other, both have to acknowledge this and figure out how to work together to address this for their campaigns.

While integration is great, there are still some key differences between the two fields. Advertisers provide information directly to specific audiences through mass media. PR professionals, on the other hand, focus on key stakeholders, such as influencers, and match the right channel to their key target in a campaign. For example, Adobe wanted to reach marketing professionals who are using Adobe products in their work, so the company created an influencer group of Adobe Insiders who would be advocates and share their experiences with Adobe products in their work and at various industry-related conferences.

We can also see evidence of the differences in the budgets of advertising departments versus PR departments. The advertising budget is more focused on paid media, whereas the PR budget is more focused on staff. PR departments and firms have to invest in people to place content in media outlets because, unlike advertising departments and firms, they do not pay for this privilege. However, with the blending of the fields, we are seeing more paid media being added on to PR budgets as well.

Advertising is characterized by the use of "push," or one-way, message strategies to get messages across to audiences, while public relations uses a "push-pull," or two-way, dialogue designed to build mutually beneficial relationships. All advertising, like the campaign Spotify has done, is pushing a brand's messages out to the public with little feedback directly to the brand unless it is through sharing content and commenting on this work on social media.

One of the other challenges that PR professionals face, as mentioned previously, is getting a budget. Because advertising departments have more established measurement and evaluation tools than PR departments do—tools that allow them to know whether or not people have seen their content—they are more likely to get resources from management for media placements (where the content will appear in particular media channels). This is changing, however: PR professionals are adding more advertising and ad services to their repertoire while advertising professionals and agencies are adding public relations as a subcategory of the services that they offer to their clients.

Spotify ad
AdWeek

Public relations can support advertising by helping advertisers

- *understand the "why" behind advertising messages and taglines.* PR profession-als know how to promote and engage audiences through media with different platforms that focus on dialogue rather than broadcasting messages. Engaging audiences, rather than just broadcasting messages, can be helpful in establishing relationships. Case in point: Facebook used this strategy for the ads it sent out after the Cambridge Analytica crisis, in which Facebook was allowing data to be used by this research company during the 2016 presidential election to target various political ads to audiences and violating user privacy measures. PR efforts helped to clarify why Facebook went directly to advertising measures to try to restore trust with audiences.

- *strategize when audiences may be outraged by a brand's actions in a particular cam-paign.* PR professionals offer crisis and image response strategies. This was apparent in the Nike and Colin Kaepernick ad celebrating the 30th anniversary of the "Just Do It" campaign. This campaign was launched to address the con-nection and support of Kaepernick, who kneeled during the national anthem while playing for the 49ers professional football team.

We Work With Marketing Professionals

Marketing and PR professionals have worked together for many decades. In most cases, the PR department is part of the marketing department for major organizations, and it is a key part of the integrated marketing communication program. Yet public relations and marketing remain very different disciplines. **Marketing**, compared to public relations, focuses on the larger picture of how to persuade audiences through a range of different techniques to encourage the audience to make a purchase. Public relations, however, focuses on the relationship and communication factors needed to build a bridge between the publics and the organization.

Public relations offers a range of services that assist marketing departments and ben-efit organizations. We can support marketing by helping those professionals

- *understand influencers and nontraditional "media" platforms.* PR professionals can help marketing go beyond the transactional approach to understand the types of relation-ships needed by individual influencers (individuals who have a strong following and perceived area of expertise in a given area online). For example, influencers such as Ninja and The Rock want to partner with brands (as Samsung has done with Ninja and Under Armour has done with The Rock) that align with their own values and brands. Exploring these audience and relationship trends from a PR perspective can help marketing gain a better understanding of the relationship dynamic.

- *promote and understand the role the media plays in a campaign.* A marketing plan involves working with the media, and this is where public relations can help. With such a large range of media outlets, channels, and authors, it is critical to target the outlets that best align with the audiences at the focus of a campaign. PR professionals can help brainstorm ideas for how the media can best tell the compelling story of the campaign.

How Do We Use Storytelling?

Our field serves society, businesses, and individuals by advocating for stories to be heard, by managing relationships among audiences, by bringing forth new ideas, and by being the bridge that connects related disciplines. One element that makes public relations so effective is the power of stories. As PR professionals, we are natural storytellers and advocates for our clients' brands, campaigns, and initiatives.

That said, we know that consumers are the ones in power. Today, neither corporations nor the media are ultimately in charge of how messages are received, used, or interpreted. We have to take a step back and look at this from a communication perspective. That is, communication today is a receiver phenomenon thanks to the influence of social media on society and business. The receivers, or consumers, hold the power over the message and have become influential senders of messages as well.

In the past, newspapers and other media organizations were able to set their own agendas and publish the stories they felt were most relevant to their communities. Now, individual consumers go online to get the latest stories and information that is salient to them, all while bypassing traditional media outlets. Social media has revolutionized communication by creating platforms in which individual consumers control the stories and information they want *and* give feedback and voice to the organization or individual disseminating that message or story. This newfound influence allows receivers to establish meaningful and dynamic relationships with others while they transform themselves into individuals who also create and disseminate their own messages. The receiver has the power to discover connections with others who share similar interests and ideas regarding a given situation. In summary, social media has not created these conversations overnight (they were always there), but it has forced us in public relations to be proactive and responsive in a changing environment: We've never had control over the message. We must recognize that the power of communication belongs to the receivers of our stories: consumers.

Where Are We Headed?

Our field has been around for many years, as we will explore in future chapters in this textbook. We have embraced many different influences from fields including social psychology, journalism, marketing, and advertising. Today, we are at a crossroads for a variety of different reasons, including the following:

- Public relations will continue to have a strong presence in social media thought leadership but must do more to participate in major decision making. As discussed in a blog post by *PRsay* (Wright, 2018), PR professionals need to embrace social media practices to be able to create opportunities for dialogue with key stakeholders and publics. In addition, we need to have a seat at the decision-making table. In addition to implementing social media activities and strategies, PR professionals need to fully embrace and advocate for a more strategic management role in the industry. Some may think public relations should not venture too much into social media because it might not be "good" for the profession (Valentini, 2015). However, while social media presents challenges for PR professionals to address, it also offers great opportunities.

INTRODUCTION TO PUBLIC RELATIONS

What differentiates public relations from other related fields, such as journalism, advertising, and marketing? Public relations functions should have an integrated role along with marketing, advertising, journalism, and other related fields. Public relations can serve as the bridge that connects these disciplines together to make it a more collaborate and integrative team process for all of these disciplines to work and create together.

Here's how PR works with other related disciplines:

ADVERTISING

Understanding the why behind the advertising messages and taglines. Public relations professionals know how to promote and engage audiences through media with different platforms that focus on dialogue rather than broadcasting messages.

JOURNALISM

Embracing experiential media to tell stories. Journalists are all about using new ways to tell stories. Building a content marketing initiative through owned media.

MARKETING

Understanding influencers and nontraditional "media" platforms and understanding the role the media plays in a campaign.

Public relations is moving forward beyond just earned media coverage to paid media, working in sync with **ADVERTISING** professionals.

Public relations professionals are embracing more brand **JOURNALISM** and storytelling by creating their own content.

Public relations professionals can help **MARKETING** understand the relationship that is needed for individual influencers beyond the transactional approach.

PR

- *Public relations will continue to experience new ethical and legal challenges.* As technology and the social landscape change, so too do the issues that PR professionals face. New ways of lobbying (promoting certain efforts on behalf of others) are a key area for public relations to note (Myers, 2018), and cyberattacks and other crises, such as ethical conduct problems with brands (Wells Fargo, Uber, Michigan State University, USA Gymnastics, etc.), are additional factors for which we need to be prepared (as is discussed in detail in Chapter 3).

- *PR skills and insights will continue to be absorbed by other disciplines.* PR principles are being taught not only in PR courses, but in the courses of other disciplines, such as journalism. For example, brand storytelling (telling the story from the brand's perspective) is a PR staple that is now covered in journalism courses. English faculty, stating that they are the original storytellers, incorporate digital storytelling into their classes. Many types of academics and professionals are grabbing at new innovative channels, ideas, and perspectives that would normally be in the PR domain. Public relations needs to stake its claim and demonstrate its competence in these areas or risk becoming irrelevant.

- *PR educators and practitioners need to work together.* In the past, PR practitioners were not always aware of what PR instructors were teaching in PR courses at colleges and universities. Today, collaborative projects such as those addressed by the Commission on Public Relations Education (2018) help bridge the gap between the academic and professional worlds, but more work still needs to be done. One way to further build the bridge between theory and practice is to encourage PR educators and practitioners to attain Accreditation in Public Relations, or APR (Sha, 2011). The APR is the test to become accredited in public relations or licensed to practice in the field. It is not required to practice public relations, but it is a professional distinction that is respected in the field.

- *Public relations needs to embrace all related areas of specialization.* Innovation and creativity in messaging are not exclusively found in the field of public relations. For example, journalism creates innovative messages and embraces new media channels and tools including AR and VR.

- *Public relations needs to think outside of the field.* Public relations has taken ideas, theories, and perspectives from other fields to grow into a vibrant profession. Yet public relations for the most part stays within the boundaries of the discipline without venturing out too far. To evolve and take the field to the next level, public relations needs to expand and explore new perspectives, collaborations, insights, and trends that can be brought back to the field to help it evolve to the next level.

- *PR research needs to embrace more diversity in topics and perspectives.* Along with bringing in new viewpoints and ideas, public relations must incorporate diversity, including diversity of race, age, sexuality, and thought, into our practices and implementation of messages (Wright, 2018). (For more on this topic, see Chapter 4.)

- *Public relations needs to be aware of the implications of the sharing economy,* or the environment in which everyone is sharing rather than "owning" products

(Gregory & Halff, 2017). The sharing economy has disrupted the norm for many industries, such as transportation (Uber), hotels (Airbnb), shopping (Amazon), and photography (Instagram). Why is the sharing economy important in public relations? The sharing economy

- shows the power of key stakeholders and publics to change the behavior of others and go in new directions to satisfy needs and expectations;

- presents opportunities for new partnerships that PR professionals can leverage; and

- emphasizes the importance of being agile, responsive, and innovative in approaching new industries, challenges, opportunities, and relationships.

SUMMARY

Public relations is a field and discipline that is faced with a challenging decision to make. We can continue down the path that allows us to use the same perspectives, ideas, principles, and models to guide our practices. This is the safe route in many ways, and many gatekeepers who like the way things have always been will want to continue on this path.

An alternative path that public relations can take is one that requires our innovation, creativity, and understanding of the balance needed to bring the science and art of our field together. This path is unknown and unexplored, which allows public

relations to lead, through voice and vision, the other disciplines we work with. Public relations, like marketing and every other discipline, should have the opportunity to lead, grow, and foster a new way of approaching our professional activities. This is crucial to the progress of our field and profession.

As you will see, each chapter in this text will bridge traditional public relations and its core principles and models—but also expand these areas with new ideas, cases, stories, and takeaways to help the field move to the next level. Let's start exploring the future of public relations together.

APR EXAM

- Definition of public relations as a management function
- An understanding of the overall purpose of public relations

- Functions of public relations

KEY TERMS

Advertising 14

Engagement 5

Marketing 15

Public relations 3

Publics 5

Stakeholders 5

DISCUSSION QUESTIONS

1. What is your overall impression of the field of public relations?

2. Discuss the skills that a PR professional needs to have. Which two skill areas surprise you the most?

3. Public relations is about relationships. What are some of the benefits and challenges of this perspective?

GAME CHANGER
Stephen Waddington, PR Professional

Courtesy Stephen Waddington

How did you get your start in public relations?

Working as a tech journalist in the '90s, I reported on the explosion in electronics and the build-out of the internet. There was a shortage of people with skills to convey technical concepts in a way that the public could understand. I made the switch into public relations and doubled my salary. It seemed like a pragmatic move. I've since retrofitted a formal education.

What is your favorite part of working in public relations?

It is always changing, and it never stops. I thrive in that environment. I'm firmly a product of the modern media environment. I use my blog and Twitter as a personal form of media, networking, and learning and development.

What is the most challenging part of working in public relations?

The always-on dynamic is also a downside of working in public relations. It takes a deliberate and conscious effort to switch off. The conversation about mental health and well-being in public relations has begun to get louder in recent years. That's a good thing.

Who do you think are the biggest game changers for the PR industry?

The fragmentation of traditional media and the explosion of new forms of media. A series of massive technology platforms, namely Amazon, Apple, Facebook, and Google, have firmly established themselves as the new media ecosystem. Checks and balances remain a work in progress.

What are some things you wish you knew when you were starting out in PR?

How little the profession does to improve its own reputation; I firmly believe that we should have equal standing with other management professions, but only a fraction of practitioners adhere to the characteristics of a profession such as credentialing, qualifications, continuous learning, and a community between theory and practice. That's got to change.

Stephen Waddington is partner and chief engagement officer at Ketchum, helping clients and colleagues to do the best job possible engaging with the public. He is responsible for driving the integration of digital and social capabilities in client engagements across the agency's international network.

He is visiting professor in practice at the Newcastle University supporting the university and students through teaching and mentoring.

Stephen understands how the media landscape works online and offline and champions best practice as a writer, conference speaker, and award-winning blogger. He is co-author of #BrandVandals (Bloomsbury, November 2013) and Brand Anarchy (Bloomsbury, February 2012); editor of and contributor to Share This (Wiley, July 2012) and Share This Too (Wiley, September 2013); and editor of Chartered Public Relations: Lessons From Expert Practitioners (Kogan Page, February 2015).

In 2017, Stephen received the PRSA's award for outstanding contribution to digital public relations and was named a top 10 U.K. PR blogger by Vuelio. Stephen is a Chartered Public Relations Practitioner, an honorary Fellow of the Chartered Institute of Public Relations, and a Fellow of the PRSA.

CASE STUDY
Mayo, Florida, Renames Itself Miracle Whip, Florida

Miracle Whip ✔
@MiracleWhip

BREAKING NEWS: Mayo removed from a small town in Florida. Here's why. #NoMoreMayo

6:56 PM - Aug 25, 2018

♡ 2,115 ♡ 1,016 people are talking about this

Miracle Whip tweet
@MiracleWhip via Twitter

One way to generate buzz about a company and brand is to work with a town to change its name. That's what Mayo, Florida, did for a day. The city of Mayo changed its name to Miracle Whip as a grassroots effort to spark surprise and reactions from the residents of the city of Mayo (Associated Press, 2018). In addition to changing its name, the city changed its signs and also created content by showing residents throwing mayonnaise products that were not Miracle Whip out of their homes.

Why did this campaign generate buzz?

- This campaign showed a unique take on changing a town name. Past campaigns have done it to be part of a larger marketing or PR campaign, but this campaign focused on digital first in all of the content, stories, and reactions that were shared.

What were some of the ethical and legal issues?

- There were concerns about the parent company of the Miracle Whip brand, Kraft Heinz, meeting with the city council of Mayo, Florida, in secret to make sure no one in the city of 1,500 residents knew about this campaign.

- This could have resulted in a potential violation of Florida's open meeting laws, which would cause the city and the brand some legal problems.

What are some major takeaways to learn from this case?

- Understanding the role of entertaining and allowing people to experience your brand, and having a proactive approach in bringing forth audience members who could engage and interact with a brand to formulate relationships, is still key.

- Innovative ideas are great to have, but there needs to be sound execution of these ideas. It is important to follow the ethical and legal guidelines set forth before implementing an idea so there are no additional challenges and rising concerns about the campaign. In this case, the closed meeting circumstances could have been avoided.

CHAPTER 2

HISTORICAL CONTEXTS AND TODAY'S PRACTICES

LEARNING **OBJECTIVES**

- Understand the history of public relations and its major figures.

- Distinguish among the four traditional models of public relations.

- Analyze the main theoretical perspectives of public relations.

- Understand the current state of PR research, theory, and practice.

Introduction

The historical foundation of public relations is not just a collection of dates and theories. Our field's history is full of character, drama, and perspectives that span generations. In this chapter, these elements come together to form a neat package for you to enjoy and learn from.

Understanding the roots of public relations allows us to predict where our field is going and what we need to do to move it forward. As we look back in time, some ideas and incidents will raise a few eyebrows as we view them through the lens of today's ethical codes of conduct. However, our history has much to teach us. While we cannot undo past missteps, we can apply the lessons learned and shape the future.

Public relations is a relatively "new" field that came into being centuries ago. Since then, it has evolved significantly, especially in the last several decades, thanks to communication advances, inventions, and case studies that have shaped the field to what it is today. As we look at past stories, actions, and campaigns, the significant impact of public relations on society becomes clear. For starters, as a hub discipline, public relations connects with other disciplines for inspiration and collaboration. It is also, to an extent, based on family relations. For example, take Edward Bernays and Sigmund Freud. Bernays, who is considered the "father of modern-day public relations," is the nephew of Freud, the founder of psychoanalysis. Public relations has benefited from and aligned with fields including psychology, sociology, and anthropology.

In this chapter, you will also consider the influences of four traditional models of public relations. Key leaders, past and present, are discussed and highlighted based on their contributions. You will also become familiar with the emerging challenges of public relations in practice, theory development, and research, and look at the ways in which advances in technology, including social media, have affected the field's future foundations.

How Did the Field of Public Relations Begin?

To understand how public relations is practiced today, it helps to explore its four main models as described by Grunig and Hunt (1984). These models categorize the ways in which PR functions are organized and carried out:

1. Press agentry and publicity

2. Public information

3. Two-way asymmetrical communication

4. Two-way symmetrical communication

The Four Models: The Basis of Public Relations

Before discussing the characteristics of each model, let's look at what they have in common.

1. Press agentry and publicity focus on pushing the message across to get the most attention, with little opportunity for the audience to provide feedback.

2. Public information is more focused on putting audiences at the forefront, making sure they have the information they need to feel confident about a given situation.

3. Two-way asymmetrical communication focuses on providing a balanced conversation, but there is still one party that is overseeing the power within the conversation.

4. Two-way symmetrical communication is the ideal situation for collaboration, co-creation, and equal participation in the relationship-building phase for PR efforts.

The Four Models: Universal Themes and Messaging

Each of the four models shares the following universal themes:

- *Roles.* A specific role for the senders and receivers of messages is defined. In this aspect, PR models are similar to the traditional communication models discussed in most communication textbooks and classes.

- *Lines of communication.* There is always a line of communication—whether this is one-way communication (the sender sends a message to the receiver, but there is no opportunity for the receiver to respond) or two-way communication (there is an ongoing dialogue between the sender and the receiver).

- *Message strategy.* There is an overall goal to communicate a specific message to key audiences for a specific reason. Creators of messages often aim to persuade an audience to think differently about a brand or person. They craft messages in different ways to accomplish a goal.

- *Behavioral intention.* There is an ultimate goal to motivate audiences, through specific messages, to take some sort of action or to think in a different way, such as changing their attitudes. In many ways, behavioral intention is related to the established attitude and behavioral theories from psychology that can be applied to corporate reputation management. One is the Theory of Reasoned Action (TRA), which focuses on attitudes, subjective norms, and intention. This psychology model allows professionals (even PR professionals) to determine how much influence is given to a person's current attitudes and norms on a given situation. In order for PR professionals to persuade their audiences to take an action, we first have to understand what motivates them from a psychological level. Another theory from psychology that is useful for the study of public relations is the Theory of Planned Behavior (TPB). TPB adds perceived behavioral control—how much control the individual has in a given situation—to TRA's focus on attitudes, subjective norms, and intention. TPB can be used to predict the likelihood of a particular behavior (Ajzen, 1991). In the context of the TPB, an attitude "represents a summary evaluation of a psychological object captured in such attribute dimensions as good-bad, harmful-beneficial, pleasant-unpleasant, and likable-dislikable" (Ajzen, 2001, p. 28). Attitudes are a core aspect to better understand our key publics— attitudes give us a standing on how individuals feel or perceive our work, brand, company, and efforts. Attitudes are hard to change, but it can be done through strong relationship-building measures, strategies, and efforts.

How Do the Four Models Function?

As we explore the four main models that follow, compare and contrast how each addresses roles, lines of communication, message strategies, and behavioral intentions.

1. The Press Agentry and Publicity Model

Named after 19th-century press agents (also known as PR professionals at the time), this model is filled with pizzazz, extreme elaboration, manipulation, attention-getting strategies, and show business. A press agent focuses on generating awareness and publicity for a client or person, whereas a publicist is solely responsible for an individual person, brand, or client to generate interest across media and channels. The **press agentry and publicity model** is characterized by one-way communication from a sender to a receiver audience with the goal of getting that audience's attention, whether positive or negative. Practitioners of this model conduct no formal research to inform their message strategies. Of the four models discussed here, this one is generally considered to represent the lowest ethical standards, as the press agents did not restrict themselves to telling the truth to meet their goals. Compared to the practices today, this model focuses on generating news for the sake of news, as well as not always being transparent in providing all of the information everyone would want to have on hand to make a decision. When working as a publicist, there is a perception you are there only to "spin" the news for the positive for your client, but not to address the negatives if there are any.

The press agentry and publicity model was made famous (some may even say infamous) by legendary showman P. T. Barnum. Australian actor Hugh Jackman played P. T. Barnum in the 2017 movie *The Greatest Showman*, and it was clear that some within the PR field were not happy with the filmmakers' overall perspective and the treatment of Barnum as a hero (Wadsworth, 2018). Many of us in the field of public relations are sensitive to this model, as it contributes to negative views of PR efforts as "spin" or even propaganda. In the real Barnum's favor was the fact that although he saw nothing wrong with deceptive messages as long as the public got its money's worth from his shows, he went out of his way to attack "humbugs" who took advantage of the public, such as spiritual mediums who claimed to be able to contact the dead.

This model is not entirely historical, as it plays a role in our evaluation of current events. The popularity of tabloids and celebrity magazines today echoes the curiosity and skepticism of the public that was exploited by Barnum. The 2015 case of Martin Shkreli, who hiked the price of an antiparasitic drug called Daraprim by 5000 percent overnight, sparked outrage among his audiences because of the ethical issues and concerns that his actions were simply a publicity stunt (Arthur W. Page Center, n.d.-b). The action, while distasteful to the extreme, did ensure increased name recognition for Daraprim.

P. T. Barnum (1810–1891), the circus founder and master of hype and deception known as "the greatest showman on Earth," was a major practitioner of the press agentry and publicity model of public relations.
Harvard Library

2. The Public Information Model

The **public information model** (which focused on providing information to the public from the company's perspective) emerged in the 1920s, as journalists challenged press agents about the truthfulness of their messages. This model represents a one-way communication of messages from a sender to receiver audiences with the goal of providing truthful information to the audiences. This model shares its one-way line of communication and lack of formal research with the press agentry and publicity model but differs in its efforts to be truthful.

This model focuses on communicating relevant, meaningful information to key audiences from an organization's perspective. PR professionals use tools and tactics of journalists and other members of the media such as press releases, press conferences, and statements to the press from the organization's standpoint. In a sense, the PR practitioner serves as an "internal journalist." The public information model focuses on providing the media with information from the organization that would help journalists to write stories for their publications or media outlets. This approach is still commonly used today. Website content, newsletters, email marketing measures, feature stories, video news releases, and other aspects of owned media (media that the organization or individual controls) are consistent with this model.

The public information model also focuses on image and reputation. A reputation for a person, company, and PR professional is the most priceless possession to have. Reputation can be defined as "stakeholders' evaluation of their organization in terms of their 'affect, esteem, and knowledge'" (Deephouse, 2000, p. 1093). The overall goal is to present the organization as transparent by providing key audiences with accurate and timely information about any situation at hand. For reputation purposes, stories and testimonials make up a powerful element that compels people to either reinforce their overall perceptions of a brand or situation or be motivated to change them.

STATEMENT FROM THE ROAD

It Declares the Rails on the Bridge Must Have Fitted Exactly.

Special to The New York Times.

PHILADELPHIA, Oct. 29—This statement relative to the Atlantic City disaster was authorized by the Pennsylvania Railroad Company to-day:

On account of the difficulty of raising the trucks of the cars out of the water the railroad officials have not been able to discover the cause of the accident. They have ascertained, however, that there was no defect in either the drawbridge or its mechanism to cause the derailment. The bridge—both stationary and movable parts—is of the most approved modern type.

General Manager Atterbury is on the ground supervising the work of raising the trucks. Their great weight has so far defied the efforts of the wrecking apparatus, but attempts are still being made to get them to the surface. When they are examined, the railroad officials think, it will be shown that there was something about one of the trucks that caused the train to leap the track.

It is certain that the rails on the drawbridge and those on the solid section fitted exactly, for otherwise the signal could never have shown a clear track. By means of the interlocking system it is impossible for the motorman to get the "go ahead" signal until the rails are exactly in place.

The Pennsylvania Railroad Company is leaving nothing undone to get at the cause of the accident. The Coroner has already gathered a jury and is making a thorough investigation; the officials of the company are giving him every assistance in their power.

"MANNY BERNARD" KIILLED.

One of the victims of the railroad wreck at Atlantic City on Sunday was Emanuel Freed of this city, a vaudeville actor who was known on the stage as "Manny Bernard." He selected that stage name because he was a nephew of Sam Bernard, the comedian. Mr. Freed was a son of David Freed, President of a paint company at 458 Pearl Street, who lives at 1,227 Madison Avenue, and is the Foreman of the October Grand Jury. Mr. Freed, seeing the name of his son in the list of killed, got excused from jury duty yesterday and went to Atlantic City, where he identified the younger Freed's body. Judge Rosalsky appointed Henley Isaacs of 68 East Seventy-seventh Street as temporary Foreman of the Grand Jury in David Freed's place.

Emanuel Freed had started to Atlantic City to fill an engagement at Young's Pier.

Source: Lee, Ivy. "Statement from the Road. It Declares the Rails on the Bridge Must Have Fitted Exactly. Special to *The New York Times*." 1906.

One major takeaway from the public information model was the creation of a press release. A press release is a document formatted the same way as a traditional news release, but it is an official statement and story from the organization's perspective to be shared with the media outlets. The first press release, created by Ivy Lee, appeared in the *New York Times* on October 29, 1906. It is an example of the use of the public information model of public relations. In the release, Lee gives information about a tragic train crash—but his larger objective is to control the messaging from the point of view of his client, the Pennsylvania Railroad Company.

Lee helped establish the public information model for public relations and provided the field with case studies on the power of controlling the images of clients and transforming how they are perceived by key publics. Lee was famously hired by

John D. Rockefeller, who did not necessarily have the best of reputations based on his coal and railroad business transactions in the early 20th century.

Lee was able to bring more transparency when coal miners went on strike by allowing reporters to go underground and meet with the miners to listen to their complaints. He ensured that the information given to reporters was accurate and truthful (Museum of Public Relations, 2017). However, Lee had more difficulty when attempting to rebuild the image of Rockefeller after the 1914 Ludlow Massacre happened. Colorado National Guard troops and mine security forces attacked an encampment of striking miners and their families, killing 21, including women and children. This event was considered one of the most dramatic confrontations between labor and capital, and it happened at one of Rockefeller's mines (Public Broadcasting Service, n.d.). The event represented a huge personal and business crisis for Rockefeller. Lee provided detailed information about the situation as well as guidance for restoring Rockefeller's image as a person in the minds of key audiences, such as his employees, media, and other business partners. Lee, during this crisis, would send out informational bulletins to key opinion leaders to give them updates on what was happening from their side (Hallahan, 2002). If you were to look for a current example in which an organization required using the public information model to be the main source of information and stories, the National Aeronautics and Space Administration (NASA) and Elon Musk of SpaceX launches could tap the power of Lee's PR model in order to be the authority of information happening with this partnership, launches, and statements in a time of crisis. The NASA *Challenger* disaster on January 28, 1986, marked a tremendous tragedy for the world as the space shuttle exploded after liftoff. NASA and its communication staff had to communicate to the public and key audiences to provide the media and other stakeholders with the necessary information so they were aware of the situation and what NASA was going to be doing in response. SpaceX had its own disaster in 2016, and Musk controlled the narrative with his statements and updates on social media, but speculated on the reasons why the disaster happened (Davenport, 2018).

Ivy (Ledbetter) Lee (1877–1934) wrote the world's first press release in 1906. In it, he informed the public about a tragic accident, but did so with the interests of his client, rather than the public, in mind.

3. The Two-Way Asymmetrical Communication Model

Unlike the two previously discussed PR models, the **two-way asymmetrical communication model** focuses on two-way lines of communication, allowing both sender and receiver to participate in a conversation. The asymmetrical aspect refers to the fact that the receivers are not equal participants in the conversation, however. Instead, unlike the previous two models, practitioners using this model incorporate formal research into audience attitudes, which then constitutes the receiver's voice. Those who use this model apply the power of persuasion to craft messages that are based on audience feedback. These messages are meant to influence receivers to think or act the way the organization

Edward Bernays (1891–1995), known as the "father of modern-day public relations," used a two-way communications method to represent his clients and to persuade audiences to think or do something (whether ethical or not) that benefits the client.

Boston Globe/Getty Images

or other client wants them to do. PR professionals have raised concerns over this approach because it is perceived as manipulative for the benefit of a client, whose intentions might not necessarily be in the best interest of the audience members.

Edward Bernays, often considered to be the "father of modern-day public relations" for the 20th century, used the two-way asymmetrical approach extensively in his PR work. As noted earlier, Bernays was the nephew of famous psychologist Sigmund Freud, a detail that suggests the strong connection public relations has with psychology. Bernays sought to reach people at the unconscious level rather than at the rational level of reasoning.

Bernays brought public relations into the modern world by achieving a lot of firsts for the field. He was the first person to coin the term *public relations counsel*, which describes the role public relations plays in advising senior management in specific situations or campaigns. His approach to public relations can be seen at work in the following classic campaigns:

- **"Torches of Freedom" Campaign.** Bernays was hired by the American Tobacco Company in 1929 to help change the perception of women's smoking. Bernays suggested to the company that it needed to gather a group of women to walk in the women's marches in the 1920s while smoking Lucky Strike cigarettes as "Torches of Freedom."

- **"Light's Golden Jubilee" Event.** Bernays was hired by General Electric in 1929 to create an event to celebrate the 50th anniversary of the invention of the light bulb and the work of Thomas Edison (Museum of Public Relations, n.d.) on October 21, 1929. Bernays coordinated the event in style, showing the world the full potential of public relations as a means for producing positive experiences, great stories, and a true impact on society (Museum of Public Relations, n.d.).

- **Bacon and Eggs: The American Breakfast Campaign.** Yes, public relations can take credit for making bacon and eggs part of a true American lifestyle. Bernays was hired by the Beech-Nut Packing Company (which produced pork products) to increase pork consumption (Colleary, 2012). Bernays used research and insights from his "study of doctors" to persuade the American public that having a heavier breakfast of bacon and eggs was healthier for them than some of the breakfast items of that time (Colleary, 2012).

Bernays's influence on public relations continues today. Presently, there are many brands that have associated themselves with certain connections to reach and engage with audiences on a deeper level. Peloton disrupted the fitness market for its on-demand features and classes for customers to bypass paying for expensive fitness classes. Glossier embraces being a product that has a customer-focus initiative through engaging content about its culture as a brand along with producing high-quality products. Bernays's ideas reflect contemporary concepts such as brand association, which refers to the same less conscious, deep-seated connections people make with a brand. He was unabashedly engaged in what he called "the engineering of consent." In his early work, *Propaganda*, Bernays (1928) stated, "Those who manipulate this unseen mechanism of society constitute an invisible government which is the true ruling power of our country. We are governed, our minds are molded, our tastes formed, and our ideas suggested, largely by men we have never heard of. . . . It is they who pull the wires that control the public mind" (p. 37). The ethics of "unseen" manipulation of public attitudes is as big an issue today as it was in Bernays's time, and perhaps even more so.

4. The Two-Way Symmetrical Communication Model

The **two-way symmetrical communication model** is very similar to the previous model given its use of the two-way channel between sender and receiver. However, the two-way symmetrical communication model is more of a level playing field, making it the "ideal situation" for public relations. Instead of the manipulation inherent in the asymmetrical model, this model constitutes more of a negotiation with the audience with the goal of reaching a cooperative, win-win outcome. To achieve this goal, users of this model conduct essential formal research into audience attitudes. This information is then used to guide open, transparent conversations. In his later work, Bernays had advocated for this practice in public relations (the ideal way to communicate and function in public relations), which is a slight shift in what he had done in his earlier work.

While each of the four models for public relations is useful, we need a new approach to explain the nature of the role public relations plays in today's society. We need a new model that integrates the dynamics of how social media has changed the power of public relations, giving audiences—not organizations or other clients—the control in the situation. Such a model could perhaps explain how situations, crises, and circumstances are influenced when the audience is indeed "louder" than the brand (or organization or client) in question. The model could also help explain the rise of a kind of mob mentality (a group of people coming together for a particular issue) that exists on social media (Blevins, 2016), the outrage sparked by some campaigns (such as recent controversial Nike and Gillette commercials), and the view that consumers and influencers are trustworthy sources of information. Nike featured the controversial former football player Colin Kaepernick in its commercials (Kaepernick started the kneeling during the national anthem movement during National Football League games), and Gillette featured a commercial that created conversation on both sides of the aisle (pro/con) about addressing the issue of male toxicity in society.

Table 2.1 outlines the four models, the historical figures with whom they are associated, and the overall significance they have for the PR field.

Historical Models and Figures of Public Relations

Model	Key Figure and Campaign	Approach	Significance to PR
Press Agentry and Publicity	P. T. Barnum	One-way communication	Generating the buzz, excitement, and hype surrounding an event, person, or idea
Public Information	Ivy Lee	One-way communication	Becoming your own media outlet and passing along information and messaging in a transparent yet persuasive manner
Two-Way Asymmetrical Communication	Edward Bernays	Two-way communication with feedback that is not balanced	Utilizing persuasive messages
Two-Way Symmetrical Communication	Edward Bernays	Two-way communication with feedback that is balanced for both parties	Communicating with mutual understanding to create a win-win situation for both parties

Who Are the Notable Figures of Public Relations?

While PR history is filled with significant founders, it is also important to see where our field is being practiced today, who is leading the charge of new ideas, and who will be the future leaders and visionaries for our profession.

Historic Figures of Public Relations

In addition to Ivy Lee's and Edward Bernays's associations with the four models, others have made major contributions to where public relations is today.

Arthur W. Page and the Page Principles

In many ways, Arthur W. Page (1883–1960) earns the title of the father of "the modern-day practice of corporate public relations" (Arthur W. Page Center, n.d.-a). Page, who was the vice president of AT&T, was known for creating a sense of ethical and responsible corporate behavior, now known as the Page Principles (Arthur W. Page Center, n.d.-a). The Page Principles (Arthur W. Page Society, n.d.) include the following guidance for PR practitioners:

- **Tell the truth.** Let the public know what's happening with honest and good intention; provide an ethically accurate picture of the organization's character, values, ideals, and actions. For example, Taco Bell was transparent with its beef recall in 2019 and let the audience know the actions that the company was taking to address the circumstances. On the other hand, Boeing took additional time in disclosing its efforts in the 737 jet plane crisis that occurred in 2018. It was later reported that the company knew about the issues with this particular model of plane for two years at least.

- **Prove your claims with action.** Public perception of an enterprise is determined 90 percent by what it does and 10 percent by what it says. It is one thing for a brand to release a proper and ethical statement, but it is another to take action in response. When the issue of equal pay came into play in the news, companies like Adidas and Adobe responded with a promise they would make sure their female employees receive pay equal to their male counterparts.

- **Listen to stakeholders.** To serve the enterprise well, understand what your publics want and need and advocate for engagement with all stakeholders. Keep top decision makers and other employees informed about stakeholder reaction to the enterprise's products, policies, and practices. To listen effectively, engage a diverse range of stakeholders through inclusive dialogue. Adobe does this extremely well with its employees as well as its influencer group, Adobe Insiders, who are professionals in the marketing space and able to get the latest news and updates to share within their networks on- and offline.

- **Manage for tomorrow.** Anticipate public reaction and eliminate practices that create difficulties. In preparation for updates and potential concerns that may arise, brands such as Netflix make sure they are able to communicate with their audiences about any changes related to price increases or changes in their product offerings (e.g., taking the popular TV show *The Office* off Netflix).

- **Generate goodwill.** Conduct public relations as if the whole enterprise depends on it. Southwest Airlines, a brand that has been known for its communication and customer relations efforts, makes sure to do this with specific actions, particularly surprise and delight strategies. For example, the airline did this in October 2019 where it was able to provide food and drinks to a group of military servicemen and women as they were traveling to their base. Even though these professionals were not Southwest Airlines customers, the company felt it was the right thing to do.

- **Do not implement a strategy without first considering its impact on stakeholders.** As a management and policymaking function, public relations should encourage the enterprise's decision making, policies, and actions to consider its stakeholders' diverse range of views, values, experience, expectations, and aspirations. In 2019, Facebook Blueprint coordinated efforts to develop a new certification and program focused on engaging educators and students in social media. Before the official launch, Facebook coordinated a group of educators to be part of a pilot program to provide feedback, suggestions, and ideas for how to make the program better.

- **Treat employees well: They express the true character of the enterprise.** The strongest opinions—good or bad—about an enterprise are shaped by the words and deeds of an increasingly diverse workforce. As a result, every employee—active or retired—is involved with public relations. It is the responsibility of corporate communications to advocate for respect, diversity, and inclusion in the workforce and to support each employee's capability and desire to be an honest, knowledgeable ambassador to customers, friends, shareowners, and public officials. Many programs like Adobe, Intel, Dell, Humana, and General Motors have programs that highlight employees of the company to be able to share and articulate their stories to their networks.

- **Remain calm, patient, and good-humored.** Lay the groundwork for PR successes with consistent and reasoned attention to information and stakeholders. When a crisis arises, remember, cool heads communicate best. Ellen DeGeneres, the popular talk show host and comedian, had to address her audiences when a photo was released of her sitting with former president George W. Bush at a Dallas Cowboys football game. Ellen shared on her show that "'Here's the thing, . . . I'm friends with George Bush. In fact, I'm friends with a lot of people who don't share the same beliefs that I have. We're all different and I think that we've forgotten that that's OK'" (quoted in Henderson, 2019). This response received reactions from both sides of the political aisle, but most of the responses were positive toward Ellen and how she handled the situation.

Rex Harlow and the Public Relations Society of America (PRSA)

Rex Harlow (1892–1993) created the American Council on Public Relations in 1947, which later became the Public Relations Society of America (PRSA), the largest professional organization for the PR field. Members of the many different Public Relations Student Society of America (PRSSA) and PRSA chapters can look to Harlow as spearheading the establishment of the first PR professional organizations. As a result of his leadership, students, educators, and professionals can come together and explore current trends in public relations, discuss growing concerns and challenges facing the field, and gain valuable education and training to bring back to their profession and client work. Harlow was able to help make the PR field an established area where everyone can come together to discuss current issues and topics impacting the field. To this day, PRSA is the largest PR professional organization and hosts its annual international conference every year.

Betsy Plank and the Public Relations Student Society of America

As the first woman in public relations in a leadership position, Betsy Plank (1924–2010) opened the door for women interested in the field. Plank achieved many firsts, such being the first person ever to win PRSA's top three awards and to lead organizations including Illinois Bell and PRSA (Plank Center for Leadership in Public Relations, n.d.-a). In addition, Plank was a leading voice in the establishment of the student version of PRSA, the Public Relations Student Society of America. Because she was an alumna of the University of Alabama, the university created the Plank Center for Leadership in 2005 in her name to promote scholarship, research, and discussions surrounding leadership issues in public relations (Plank Center for Leadership in Public Relations, n.d.-a). Plank was a big supporter of bridging the gap between education and practice, and supported efforts to bring educators into PR workplaces so they could bring new insights back into the classroom. Plank actually has her own national day, created and launched by the Plank Center for Leadership at the University of Alabama, called #PlankDay, during which students and PRSSA chapters come together to celebrate the life of Betsy Plank and to share these insights with the community online (Plank Center for Leadership in Public Relations, n.d.-b).

Contemporary Figures of Public Relations

While we have reviewed some early pioneers of public relations, who are the individuals who currently shape the field? By exploring them, we can anticipate where our field is heading. Who knows—future leaders might be reading this textbook right now! Maybe you will be a significant figure in the practice of public relations.

Harold Burson

Among today's leaders is Harold Burson (1921–2020), who co-founded Burson-Marsteller, one of the largest PR agencies in the world. (After a February 2018 merger with Cohn & Wolfe, the agency is now known as Burson Cohn & Wolfe.) He has been described as one of the century's most influential figures in public relations (Burson Cohn & Wolfe, n.d.). Burson, who was a strong advocate for the integrated marketing perspective for public relations, which emphasizes that different disciplines need to work together, set a new standard for PR practices (Burson Cohn & Wolfe, n.d.). Public relations is viewed not as a silo field, but as a connecting arm to marketing, advertising, promotions, sales, and other related disciplines to work together.

Celebrate #BetsyDay!

Betsy Plank was the First Lady of public relations, a trailblazer for leadership in PR and the "Godmother of PRSSA."

Help us celebrate her renowned career in public relations!
Find out how you can participate at PlankCenter.ua.edu/BetsyDay

THE PLANK CENTER
FOR LEADERSHIP IN PUBLIC RELATIONS

@PlankCenterPR

University of Alabama Plank Center for Leadership in Public Relations promotions for Betsy Plank Day
The Plank Center

Richard Edelman

Richard Edelman (1954–) is another key figure in today's PR landscape. Edelman, who is the president and CEO of Edelman, has been recognized for his work in building the Edelman Trust Barometer, a longitudinal study looking at trust issues and trends in public relations, and working with some of the top brands in the industry to make Edelman one of the leading PR firms in the world according to prominent PR media outlets (Edelman, n.d.). Edelman has been a leader in identifying current trends and issues that have impacted the PR field globally and around the world.

Barri Rafferty

Barri Rafferty (1964–), the new CEO of Ketchum, became the first female PR professional to lead a top five PR firm (Ketchum, 2017).

Qualities of Today's Leaders

These are just a few of the prominent PR figures currently shaping the industry. You may be asking yourself: What unifying characteristics are consistent among all of these PR figures?

- **PR leaders are adaptive and responsive to change.** All are agile in responding to shifts in the industry. Public relations is a fast-paced field that thrives on change, and it is important for leaders and practitioners to be both responsive and adaptive. Today's leaders not only encourage their teams to maintain these characteristics, but embrace them personally as well.

- **PR leaders are open to varied perspectives in the field and in other disciplines.** These leaders look both inward and outside of the field to related fields including psychology and journalism for inspiration, ideas, and research to help them with their practices.

- **PR leaders are unafraid and exploratory.** Sometimes it is lonely to present new ideas, perspectives, and approaches that go against the norm. In order to make an impact, you may have to go against the common perspective or paradigm to make a difference. All PR leaders approach their work in new ways, differentiating themselves from others and solidifying themselves forever in PR history.

- **PR leaders know what is real and what is "shiny."** All of these professionals approach each of their efforts strategically with a long-term focus. It is very tempting to do something for the moment or for the short term, but real benefits and wins happen when you are able to look at the bigger picture. These professionals are not going to jump on a trending topic or platform just for the sake of it—they will be using their experience and insights to gather information whether or not it is on brand, on strategy, or even sustainable.

- **PR leaders contribute to new models and practices.** While knowing the foundation of PR history is crucial, doing something the way it has always been done will not make a memorable impression on the field. However, being able to add something that is new, exciting, and unique will do the trick.

The Four Models Today: What Can Recent Campaigns Teach Us?

Public relations has had its own evolution over the years, but is currently defined as "a strategic communication process that builds mutually beneficial relationships between organizations and their publics" (Public Relations Society of America, 2020). The themes, models, and leaders you have just read about do not live just in the past. They are strong and present in our practices today.

The one thing that we can almost guarantee about public relations is that we will always have case studies to turn to as lessons from the past and guidance for the future. Recent campaigns that have illustrated the creative aspects of public relations include Airbnb and its partnership with Mattel in making a Barbie-themed house for people to stay in, and the campaign through which Cheez-It® snack items merge with Pizza Hut® to tap into two existing fan bases. IHOP® has jumped on the train with reality show partnerships including A&E's *Tiny House Nation*. All of these campaigns are creative, collaborative, and innovative in that they tap into new strategies, audiences, and mediums.

These campaigns showcase the fact that traditional PR models are still relevant for current cases. So, let's take a moment to apply some of the principles discussed previously in this chapter to some contemporary cases.

1. The Press Agentry and Publicity Model: Today

While press agentry and publicity was the prominent model used by practitioners in the 20th century, this model continues to be practiced and integrated into current campaigns to this day. While some of these campaigns work or have worked to generate buzz and excitement regarding an event or other campaign (see the Red Bull® campaign, discussed a bit later in this section), others (see the Fyre Festival event, discussed next) have generated more negative publicity in response to their efforts. Regardless, we can gather and apply through case studies valuable knowledge on what to do, and what not to do, in PR efforts.

The Fyre Festival: An Audience Is Misled

This is a classic example that will also be discussed in Chapter 3 on ethics and the law, but it also shows the risks associated with using propaganda and illusion to mislead audiences. It is a big mistake to fool audiences into believing they will be gaining a positive experience when the experience will not and does not live up to the hype. This case of the Fyre Festival shows the risks associated with misleading audiences and withholding important information.

The Fyre Festival of 2018 was the culmination of influencer marketing (using individuals with large online communities to promote specific brands, products, or clients for compensation) going wrong. The festival was supposed to be the "Coachella of the Caribbean," but it turned out to be a festival that promoted fraud, misleading attendees with the notion they would be attending a luxury event. On the contrary, it was far from luxurious. Tents, cheese sandwiches, and turmoil were just a few things that characterized the Fyre Festival experience of attendees. This was not what they had been expecting. We can explore the Fyre Festival case through the lens of the press agentry and publicity model because of the organizers' one-way channel of communication with their receiver audience. However, because attendees took to social media, they were able to provide negative feedback and share their responses for the world to see, something that resulted in two documentaries highlighting the catastrophe-in-the-making by Netflix and Hulu. The marketing for the event was very effective, but the lack of preparation, issues pertaining to training and resources for those on the ground for the festival, and the ethical concerns for the investment to the event were all areas of concern that were highlighted in the documentaries.

The Red Bull Space Jump: An Extreme Event Pays Off

A space jump hosted by Red Bull in 2012 generated a huge amount of buzz, excitement, and brand awareness for the organization. The campaign was all about the hype of a jump—from 39,000 meters or 24 miles above Earth's atmosphere. It was something that had never been attempted, let alone livestreamed for the world to see. The campaign and planned event were a huge risk with a potentially big payoff for both the jumper and the sponsoring brand. A partnership with Red Bull allowed Austrian skydiver Felix Baumgartner to space dive from the stratosphere in record time, beating the previous skydiving record. The event was presented live on YouTube and resulted in 8 million views and more than 2.6 million mentions on the day of the launch alone (Boies, 2012). While this campaign was focused on creating hype and excitement around a risky event, the sponsor and skydiver pulled it off. Further, audiences were provided with the opportunity to engage, share, and comment about the event on a designated social media platform.

2. The Public Information Model: Today

The public information model is also still present and accounted for here in the 21st century. Being transparent and upfront with audiences from a brand's perspective can be very effective, or it can transform into a much bigger crisis for the brand.

Pepsi and Kendall Jenner: A Tone-Deaf Ad Sparks Outrage

This is a case in which a campaign's attempted goals turned into a crisis with a negative impact on a brand. Kendall Jenner, one of the Kardashian sisters and a model, was featured in 2018 in a Pepsi commercial designed to address current issues that had sparked protests. In it, Jenner appears as part of a generic protest while promoting Pepsi. What the campaign creators had hoped would be an in-touch commercial did not go over well with viewers. Pepsi felt it needed to respond, but instead of addressing the concerns of its key publics—that the commercial was cynical and hypocritical—Pepsi instead apologized to Jenner, something that sparked even more outrage toward the brand and campaign. In essence, how a brand or person publicly responds in a crisis is as important as how it handles the situation.

The Southwest Airlines Crisis: A Direct Response Works

On April 17, 2018, Southwest Airlines experienced a crisis when a passenger died following an accident that occurred in flight. Southwest Airlines Flight 1380, en route to Dallas, had to land in Philadelphia to address this tragedy (Arenstein, 2018).

The company could have approached this situation in several different ways, but the fact that all 144 passengers documented the event on social media as it happened makes a straightforward response ideal. Southwest Airlines wanted to be transparent, timely, and compassionate in regard to the death of a passenger and how that affected others on the plane. Southwest released several statements, including the one provided on the next page. CEO Gary Kelly recorded a video response to the situation ("Southwest Airlines Flight 1380 Statement #2," 2018). This showed the world what the organization would do to make sure this type of accident would not happen in the future, while giving the media, key stakeholders, and others the information they needed regarding this incident.

In a second press release from Southwest Airlines, dated April 17, 2018, the company confirmed the crash of Flight 1380, expressed sympathy to the loved ones of the deceased, and provided contact information for answering the questions of the media and public.

3. The Two-Way Asymmetrical Model: Today

These next few campaigns show that sometimes when we set the overall goal of engaging with key audiences, we tilt the balance of the conversation toward our source (that is, our organization or other client), rather than toward the audience. The purpose of messaging is to influence audiences to do something specific—whether it is to make a purchase (see "Gary Vee", later in this section) or to follow a specific Instagram account (see "The World Record Egg," at the end of this section). In the following examples, the communication between the parties and sources is not necessarily equal in footing, yet both sources seek to persuade audiences to take some sort of action based on the relationship they have created.

SOUTHWEST AIRLINES FLIGHT 1380 STATEMENT #2—ISSUED 3:00 P.M. CT

SOUTHWEST AIRLINES CONFIRMS ACCIDENT; OUR HEARTS ARE WITH THOSE AFFECTED

Apr 17, 2018

Southwest Airlines Co. (NYSE: LUV) confirms an accident involving Southwest Airlines Flight 1380. The flight made an emergency diversion to Philadelphia Airport (PHL) earlier today after the Crew reported issues with the number one engine which resulted in damage to the fuselage.

We are deeply saddened to confirm that there was one fatality resulting from this accident. The entire Southwest Airlines Family is devastated and extends its deepest, heartfelt sympathy to the Customers, employees, family members and loved ones affected by this tragic event. We have activated our emergency response team and are deploying every resource to support those affected by this tragedy. For a message from Gary Kelly, Southwest Chairman and Chief Executive Officer, please click here.

The aircraft involved today was a Boeing 737-700 (N772SW) and was enroute from New York LaGuardia (LGA) to Dallas Love Field (DAL). In total, the flight had 144 Customers and five Southwest Crewmembers onboard. We extend our heartfelt appreciation to the Southwest Pilots and Flight Attendants who acted professionally and swiftly to take care of our Customers during the emergency diversion and landing.

Finally, Southwest Airlines officials are in direct contact with the National Transportation Safety Board (NTSB) and the Federal Aviation Administration (FAA) to support an immediate, coordinated response to this accident. Southwest is in the process of gathering additional information regarding flight 1380 and will fully cooperate in an investigative process.

Please join the Southwest Family in keeping all of those affected by today's tragedy in your thoughts.

Source: Southwest Media. April 17, 2019. "Southwest Airlines Flight 1380 Statement #2 - Issued 3:00 p.m. CT: Southwest Airlines Confirms Accident; Our Hearts Are With Those Affected."

LeBron James and the NBA: An Unfortunate Blunder

In October 2019, Daryl Morey of the Houston Rockets sent out a tweet that read: "Fight for Freedom. Stand with Hong Kong." Morey was supporting the efforts of protesters in Hong Kong who were calling for democracy and basic human rights in China while facing authoritarian rule and police violence. Morey's tweet went viral, and as a result, the Chinese government withdrew a lot of support for the organization's games and teams. LeBron James, one of the biggest stars in basketball, was asked by the media (perhaps unfairly) to comment on the situation. He and the team were in China. Unfortunately, his response was confusing and, like the immediate reaction of many in the National Basketball Association (NBA), seemed pretty self-serving: Losing audiences in China was going to be a big problem. Without China's support and consumer base, NBA-related brands, organizations, and professionals stood to lose a lot of money. Unfortunately, instead of giving a neutral response, such as "I'm a basketball player focused on my game. I don't know the context yet, so I really can't answer," or a pro-democracy response, such as "I support human rights, democracy, and free speech," James responded as follows:

> "Yes, we all do have freedom of speech, but at times there are ramifications for the negative that can happen when you're not thinking about others, and you're only thinking about yourself. . . . I believe he [Morey] wasn't educated on the situation at hand and he spoke. And so many people could have been harmed, not only financially but physically, emotionally, spiritually." (quoted in Kennedy, 2019)

As a result, James's comments became the subject of controversy, something that he had to address as they quickly went viral. NBA teams and key leaders such as Commissioner Adam Silver also had to make statements about their attitudes toward China and how they will address that relationship going forward.

The Gary Vee and K-Swiss Campaign: A Successful Partnership

In 2017, Gary Vaynerchuk (aka Gary Vee), a global businessperson, wanted to change how people perceived entrepreneurs by raising them to the level of celebrities, such as athletes who benefit from endorsements. By partnering with the shoe brand K-Swiss, Vaynerchuk created a movement for other entrepreneurs to be able to sign exclusive deals for the shoe company, breaking the mold for what it means to "get a shoe deal." This showed you did not need to be a celebrity or athlete to get one. Vaynerchuk communicated these messages himself, by engaging with audiences with tons of content on his social media channel, but used the community and audience members he engaged with to amplify the messages as well. Gary shared updates on his accounts and with his team, but also made sure to communicate with people online and in person during meet-ups.

The World Record Egg Instagram Campaign: A Simple Idea Raises Awareness

In 2019, Kylie Jenner lost the title of having the most liked photo on Instagram to an egg. Yes, an egg. This account, called @world_record_egg, generated 52 million likes (Bromwich & Maheshwari, 2019). However, ahead of the 2019 Super Bowl, the account displayed a change in the egg, showcasing it as a football and asking its audience members to stay tuned for the event and watch for Hulu. This approach generated a huge global reaction and discussion, building the hype and excitement for where the account was going. When audiences pushed the button to post, an account that generated millions of likes became as valuable (some say more so) as a Super Bowl ad. Some have estimated the account is worth about $10 million based on analytics and reach calculations. When it was uncovered that the person behind the popular, iconic account worked in advertising, he partnered with Hulu to create more awareness about mental health after the 2019 Super Bowl (Bromwich & Maheshwari, 2019).

4. The Two-Way Symmetrical Model: Today

The 2008 and 2016 Presidential Elections: A Win for Social Media

World record egg and mental health campaign with Hulu

Source: @world_record_egg via Instagram

FOR MORE INFO VISIT:
TALKING eGG.iNFO

#TALKINGeGG
eGG GANG

Both of the campaigns in the 2008 and 2016 U.S. presidential elections were based on the two-way asymmetrical model. In both cases, two presidential candidates (Barack Obama and Donald Trump) persuaded voters they were "outsiders" relative to Washington, DC, politics. Both candidates in their respective elections also communicated using social media as a way to persuade audiences to join their cause and campaign. Both presidential candidates in their respective elections engaged in conversation, but ultimately, it was the different groups having conversations with other groups that coordinated these particular campaigns together according to the two-way symmetrical model for public relations.

For many great minds in public relations, politics has been at the forefront of their thinking when it comes to the use of social media for campaign messaging. However, it is important to note that social media played a role in two separate elections that resulted in two different results. The first, 2008, has been listed as the first "social" election, where Obama was one of the first presidential candidates to tap the power of social media for his campaign. Fast-forward a few years later, and we see that Trump not only used social media for his campaign but focused specifically on Twitter to get his messages and statements to the public. Whether you are on one side of the aisle or another, many different social media lessons and takeaways from both of these elections will impact future PR efforts in the political arena. More focus on this specialization will occur in Chapter 14.

Why Study PR Practices, Research, and Theories?

Because public relations is an established area of research, a field founded in theory, and a dominant profession, it's important to study it. We need to look at what has been done before, but also at where our field is going so that we can identify and get ahead of future issues and challenges and make the most of opportunities that will impact what we do. Looking at the concrete practices of public relations also helps us define our work and our roles as practitioners—and allows us to make public relations as effective and relevant as possible.

Our Practices

There is a common phrase in the industry: "Stay in your lane." This is all fine and good if you want to get on the fast track to insignificance. As more disciplines, including English and journalism, embrace content and training similar to that taught in PR courses, public relations will need to adapt to continue thriving.

Our positions as PR professionals within organizations are shifting rapidly. That doesn't mean that PR functions are not happening; rather, organizational structures have sometimes blended what used to be the PR department with other departments, such as marketing. Outside of such organizations, what were once free-standing PR firms are now agencies that label themselves as expert in "integrated marketing communication," "communication marketing," or "strategic communication." For example, Edelman, one of the largest global PR agencies in the world, now lists itself as a marketing agency. In addition, the public may struggle with its perception of public relations, of what it does, especially in relation to marketing. Even among those who are familiar with PR functions, there are misconceptions. Some assume we just do press releases, publicity, and other earned traditional media work (e.g., networking and media relations work with media professionals). However, this is not the case. Public relations has a strong stake in the areas of new emerging technologies and tools. For example, social media, a core set of platforms based on relationships, is a perfect area of specialization and focus for PR practitioners. To continue our success, we need to embrace and take ownership of these new areas wholeheartedly. We must—and should—advocate for what we can do, what we have to offer, and why our positions are crucial to the success of an organization or other client.

How does public relations do this exactly? Embracing new perspectives and ideas is key. Self-appointed gatekeepers on the practice side might also hinder new ideas and

HISTORICAL CONTEXTS AND FUTURE OF PR

There are several perspectives and historical models public relations professionals can look to as a guide for how the field has been practiced and embraced over the years. The four that are listed here are press agentry/publicity, public information, two-way asymmetrical, and two-way symmetrical. All four of these models have strong characteristics that have both made the field of public relations into what it is today and provide key lessons and case studies to note for the future. Like all other aspects of society, it is important to know our field's history so we do not make the same mistakes that were made in the past, and know where the field needs to go.

PRESS AGENTRY

The press agentry and publicity model focuses on the party, individual, or organization in question communicating in a one-way fashion where the information is focused on the intended receiver.

PUBLIC INFORMATION

This model is focused on getting relevant and meaningful information to key audiences from the organization's perspective by utilizing key tactics used by members of the media and journalists.

TWO-WAY ASYMMETRICAL COMMUNICATION

The two-way asymmetrical communication model is focused on two-way communication, allowing both parties to have a chance to have a conversation, though one has more power than the other.

TWO-WAY SYMMETRICAL MODEL OF COMMUNICATION

This model is very similar to the previous model, except that the symmetrical model focuses on equal power between the parties in conversation.

perspectives in the field that do not emerge from the "right" sources. The field cannot afford holding ideas or people back just because they did not come from a particular program, school, or PR professional organization. Everyone needs to be on board and work together to move the field forward, rather than circling around the same spot like a plane trying to land at Chicago O'Hare airport.

Our Research

The importance of understanding the impact of new areas of specialization, such as influencer marketing, advocacy, and even social media, on the field of public relations is crucial (Museum of Public Relations, n.d.). Researchers are working together to explore emerging challenges and opportunities.

One of the significant challenges facing researchers today is the need to question "traditional models." Certain dominant perspectives—such as the four models covered earlier in this chapter—have shaped the PR field to date, yet the only way for the field to grow and evolve is if these perspectives are continuously challenged, examined, and tested against new approaches such as big data analysis, network analysis, and others.

PR research has not pushed its boundaries very far due to fear of change and, in some cases, an inability to get past gatekeepers and cliques within the PR research field. In some ways, academic and even professional agency dynasties can be like the houses in television's *Game of Thrones*. For example, "academic families" representing certain theoretical perspectives and schools are not always welcoming toward competing individuals and ideas. What? A new approach from an outsider? Dracarys! Where is Drogon when you need him?

In all seriousness and dragons aside, for a field's research to thrive, we need to encourage fresh ideas, perspectives, and theories regardless of the pedigree of the sources. Without new ideas and perspectives, PR research will not keep pace with the times and will risk becoming stale and irrelevant.

Along with having new fresh ideas and perspectives, PR researchers need to diversify the different tools used to measure and evaluate questions and concepts. New method and measurement approaches (or rather their lack) are another growing concern about PR research. PR researchers should expand their horizons by experimenting with new ways to evaluate behaviors, attitudes, and other relevant constructs. Being aware of advances in related fields, such as psychology and marketing, as well as engaging with transdisciplinary research teams, can stimulate breakthroughs in research. What is cliché in one field is often just the perfect thing that is needed to advance another.

Our Theories

Theories are sets of facts—and relationships between facts—that help us explain and predict phenomena of interest. They help us understand how or why something works the way it does. Why are some Instagram accounts more influential than others? How do brands identify best practices for their social media activities? Some people confuse evidence-based, scientific theories with the alternate uses of the word *theory* to describe a guess or a hunch, such as "I have a theory that the New England Patriots might win the Super Bowl." Unlike guesses or hunches, evidence-based, scientific theories not only focus on the why and how aspects of a phenomenon, but they are also built up through extensive and systematic observation and experimentation.

PR theory building has resulted in a rich repertoire of systems that help explain and predict many of the phenomena described in this textbook. Some of these theories originated in public relations itself, while others have been adapted from fields including psychology. For example, the Theory of Planned Behavior (TPB) and the Theory of Reasoned Action (TRA) helped psychologists predict how people's existing attitudes and social influences might lead to particular behaviors, such as quitting smoking (Fishbein & Ajzen, 2010). Because shaping attitudes is an integral part of public relations, these types of theoretical models have been invaluable.

Table 2.2 provides a brief introduction to many of the theories used in public relations that you will meet throughout your course and in later parts of this textbook. Note the rich variety of disciplines that contribute to our understanding.

▼ TABLE 2.2

Outline of Key Theories in Public Relations

Theory	Summary	Origin of Theory
Two-Step Flow	Focuses on how information from the media proceeds in two different steps: first to opinion leaders, and then to the other audiences for a message. Traditionally has focused on mass media implementation but has since been applied to new media channels.	Communication
Framing	Focuses on the essence of certain issues and topics rather than a particular topic at hand. Very closely aligned with agenda-setting theory.	Communication
Agenda Setting	Powerful influence of the media to designate issues and topics the audience needs to know.	Communication
Situational Theory of Publics	Audiences are identified and classified into groups based on how aware (or unaware) they are about a situation, issue, or problem in question.	Public Relations
Diffusion of Innovation	Explains how innovation for a product, topic, or issue diffuses over time based on level and timing of adoption.	Communication
Uses and Gratifications	Audience-centered approach looking at what audience members do with media (their use and the reasons behind it).	Communication
Attribution	Understanding how audiences assign certain characteristics, feelings, and intentions to people to better understand them.	Psychology
Reasoned Action/ Planned Behavior	Links behavior with one's beliefs, attitudes, and perceived behavioral control. TRA is the earlier model, and TPB addresses the concept of behavioral control.	Psychology
Rhetoric	The original persuasion method of communication.	Philosophy
Critical	A fundamental approach in the social sciences. This approach looks at social phenomena happening in society and in our environment and critiques how it impacts our human interactions and practices. With social media, it is used to discuss how having access to the tools of communication has been beneficial (or not) to our relationships, identity, and how we practice in our field.	Philosophy
Convergence	Focuses on the intersection between traditional and social media.	Communication
Excellence	How public relations makes organizations more effective and organized based on how they are managed and organized.	Public Relations
Dialogic	The main focus is that dialogue is about the exchange of ideas and perspectives, and there needs to be channels in which these conversations can be used for organizations with their publics.	Rhetoric
Organization–Public Relationships (OPR)	One of the fundamental perspectives in the PR field. The primary focus is on the management of mutually beneficial relationships between the key publics and the organization in question.	Public Relations

Social Media: What Is Its Impact on Public Relations?

Many factors have influenced the field of public relations over the years, but few have the potential impact that social media has. Social media can be defined as

> the ultimate personalized online networked hub of information, dialogue, and relationship management. Essentially, social media combines the use of innovative strategies with digital communication technology platforms, enabling the user to share knowledge, engage in digital storytelling through conversations and visual components, collaborate with others, engage in crowdsourcing tasks and contribute ideas to solve problems, conduct strategic monitoring and analytic analysis online, and build relationships within a community sharing common interests, investments, and needs. (Freberg, 2016)

Social media has transformed PR efforts in practice, research, and theory development. With each advance that occurs in the social media industry, PR research adapts and explores the changes and discusses the implications for the field and for society. Compared to other fields claiming to "own" social media, public relations has a strong argument for being the field that should be most closely linked to social media. Why is this the case? Our claims are based on the how and why of our use of these tools to communicate and spark conversations to formulate relationships. As Taylor and Kent (2010) noted, public relations focuses on building relationships and understanding between organizations and their key publics.

How has social media changed the PR field? Social media has been at the forefront of bringing both pain and delight for brands, organizations, and PR professionals over the past several decades. It has been the means of some of the more recognizable campaigns as well as crises in the PR profession. Several iconic PR campaigns can look to social media as a driving impact factor for their campaigns, like the @world_record_egg account campaign described earlier. This campaign sparked an interest and active presence on the platform for one common reason: to support an account's mission to get the most likes on the platform. However, this was just the beginning, and the account partnered with Hulu to bring awareness to mental health. This was a global, real-time, and unexpected partnership people all over the world were able to witness and see for themselves. Yet it changed the way in which brands and accounts interact with each other, and helped bring forth this relationship in a new way.

SUMMARY

Public relations, as a profession, has an established history filled with specific models, key figures, and significant contributions that have brought the field to where it is today. Ours is a field and profession that is still relatively young in nature but mature enough to stand on its own two feet. With that being said, we need to consider long and hard where we want to be in the future. Moving forward, PR professionals have to drive the direction of the field. There are two paths public relations can take: one to continue the way in which the field has always operated and practiced, and another that shows room for growth by adding in new perspectives and elements. To evolve, public relations has to embrace both its past and its present but look toward the impact it wants to continue to make in the future.

GAME CHANGER
Matt Kelly, PR Professional

How did you get your start in public relations?

I started in public relations in the same way almost anyone does: a crippling realization that I was monetizing a journalism career. Kidding (but, seriously). I majored in journalism in undergrad at Eastern Illinois University, which in my opinion is one of the best programs in the country. Coupled with my creative writing minor, I was certain I had chosen a lucrative education mix that would guarantee endless career prospects and wealth. The bottom dropped out of the newspaper industry, and I decided to use writing and communication skills in another way. That way was public relations.

After undergrad, I attended Ball State University to pursue my master's in public relations with a concentration in business. Between my first and second years, I interned at State Farm's corporate headquarters in Bloomington, Illinois. While I was there, brands were just starting to get into using social media to support business objectives. I decided to stay at State Farm while writing my thesis in the evenings. It was one of the busiest times of my life. With the support of some great colleagues at the company, I started the company's first social media team within public affairs with two brilliant colleagues, Griffin Hammond and Matt Edwards. Mike Fernandez, the former vice president of communications at State Farm and a global PR leader, gave us all the resources we needed to make that happen. Agency life isn't easy, but it's the most interesting and dynamic sort of work you can experience in the field. I firmly believe that.

From there, I've become sort of a journeyman in the agency world. Normally, you would go from the agency to the client side. I did the opposite. I've now worked at Weber Shandwick, Ogilvy, and Golin. I'm now at Burson Cohn & Wolfe, working with some of the brightest minds in communications to grow our digital offering in North America.

What is your favorite part of working in public relations?

This is an interesting question because it's changed with my age. When I was younger in the agency world, I'm not sure I would've had a favorite part. I worked so much that my favorite part of public

relations may have been the sleep I was able to squeeze in before the daily 4 a.m. social listening reports I had to send. Even on the weekends.

Now that I'm more senior in the field, I do have favorite parts. I love thinking about the best way to reach audiences/publics who matter to brands in interesting ways. Public relations, marketing, advertising, and other fields have blended so much over the past five years as a result of digital integration. Now, we all have to think like integrated marketers, and it's more fun. For example: I used to think about the best way to pitch media to get consumers to think about a product. Now, I think about things like the best way to geo-fence retail locations and use programmatic messages to drive consumers down the funnel. See? Much more interesting and more impactful for the business.

I also love the variety. One day, you'll work on corporate reputation. Another, you'll be in a brainstorm trying to figure out how to sell more dog food. Today, I'm writing this from a social media conference in San Francisco. I arrived late last night after giving a workshop about executive social media in New York. Tonight, I take the red eye flight back to Chicago. I have two presentations I need to create on the plane. So it goes. It's not for everyone, but I love it.

What is the most challenging part of working in public relations?

Work-life balance.

Who do you think are the biggest game changers for the PR industry?

To me, all of the best thinking around influencing audiences happened in the past. There aren't enough practitioners within agencies and corporations who understand the history of public relations, so we tend to reinvent the wheel when it comes to engaging people. For example: When Edward Bernays was approached by a group of publishers to help sell more books, he said, "Where there are bookshelves, there will be books." He worked with interior designers and architects to build bookshelves into the homes of what we'd call opinion elites now. He knew their homes would be photographed for magazines, and people would clamor to have bookshelves built into their own homes. It worked.

When PR practitioners are approached by clients today, we often don't respond with an ounce of the creativity Bernays employed. In that situation, most PR people would enlist an expert to talk about the value of books. They'd hire bookish Instagram influencers to share about their favorite books. They might even hold an event in Times Square to get people to read more. But they probably wouldn't sell more books.

The biggest game changers in the PR industry know the difference between making a real business impact and making things shiny. And the best of those understand the history of public relations/marketing/ advertising, have a foot in the academic side, and aren't afraid to lead with ideas instead of messaging.

What are some things you wish you knew when you were starting out in public relations?

When you have a degree in public relations, it's not a guarantee that you know anything about how to do your job. This seems counterintuitive, sure, but it's true in my experience. When I graduated, I had worked on real accounts within a student-run agency. I knew the ins and outs of all the PR theories. I was a well-oiled machine, ready to conquer the world of public relations. Turns out, frantically busy executives at agencies don't always want to hear a 20-something pontificate about framing theory. If you have a background in the academic side of public relations and want to make an impact at an agency, figure out a way to package your knowledge into an approach that capitalizes on a trend. Then, go make the firm money with it.

Five other things you wish you'd known in the beginning:

- Nobody cares about your background; you need to prove your value every day.

- If you don't know whose job it is, it's yours.

- Wherever you are, be there. Being present is extremely challenging, but critical.

- Don't ask questions—make statements. You'll eliminate email, and leaders will thank you.

- Crying is completely natural, but unbillable— so, stop it (kidding).

Matt Kelly has worked with top brands like State Farm (client side), McDonald's, Discover Card, BP, Dow Chemical, SC Johnson, Conagra Brands, and others to improve their reputation and advance business objectives through smart strategy and creativity. A trusted digital crisis expert, he worked on the PR response after Hurricane Katrina while at State Farm and took those learnings to Ogilvy to lead the social engagement team for BP after the 2010 incident.

He loves to "yes, and" and use a high reference level to come up with the next, not-so-obvious idea—like creating a 24-hour marathon for McDonald's where the brand complimented more than 1,300 strangers. He's also a research nerd, coming up with new ways to assess influencers. He also rode a motorcycle through the Himalayas.

He wrote his thesis, "Fortune 500 Foray: How the Nation's Largest Insurer Leverages Social Media," while starting State Farm's first social media team in public affairs (published in PR Journal*). He has since been a presenter at the International Public Relations Research Conference and at events from the International Association of Business Communicators, Word of Mouth Marketing Association, and Public Relations Society of America. He has also served as faculty for the Arthur W. Page Society. Most importantly, he's cat dad to Biggie, Marshall, and Eve.*

APR EXAM

- PR models
- PR theories

- Current landscape and modern thought leaders

KEY TERMS

Press agentry and publicity model 24

Public information model 25

Two-way asymmetrical communication model 27

Two-way symmetrical communication model 29

CASE STUDY

Toxic Masculinity and the Gillette Commercial for #TheBestMenCanBe

 Gillette ✔
@Gillette

(Follow)

Gillette is donating $1M each year, for the next 3 years, to nonprofit orgs helping boys & men achieve their best. We welcome grant applications from nonprofits standing up to bullying, championing inclusion, building confidence & more. Apply at TheBestMenCanBe.org.

Gillette 'THE BEST MEN CAN BE' GRANT

For eligible nonprofits helping men of all ages achieve their personal best.

Apply now at
TheBestMenCanBe.org

`0:02` `26.8K views`

5:00 PM - 30 Jan 2019

Source: @Gillette via Twitter

Gillette, the popular razor company, released a 2019 commercial titled "The Best Men Can Be," which sparked both outrage and praise from communities on- and offline. The ad was first shared on Gillette's social media accounts (YouTube and Twitter), asking audiences to watch the 48-second spot that addresses societal issues like bullying, sexual harassment, and the #MeToo movement (McCluskey, 2019). This commercial, which addressed the issue of toxic masculinity, sparked outrage, leading many to the brand's social media accounts to voice their concerns publicly (Cain, 2019). On the other hand, others praised the commercial for bringing a powerful message to younger generations of consumers and for generating a high level of attention: "Everybody's talking about it" (Kerpen, 2019).

Why did this campaign generate buzz?

- This campaign generated strong feelings on both sides of the issue. Some people saw the ad as a very powerful message needed to highlight an important social issue, while others were outraged due to a perceived negativity toward males in general.

- Views of this campaign ranged from an empowering message against toxic behavior to an insulting message that grouped all males together as toxic. Both perspectives are opposite ends of the continuum for the brand, leaving no middle ground for the view of the brand and commercial on this account.

What were some of the ethical and legal issues?

- Both Gillette and the audiences voicing their views about the commercial are able to communicate and share these perspectives.

- From an ethical standpoint, Gillette should consider integrating social issues that are part of its brand into the mix. This could produce a short-term gain or have longer-term effects on brand standing within the industry.

- This is another case that highlights the trend for brands to integrate causes, social issues, and topics that may be controversial for some audiences. Considering whether this is legal or ethical is a topic of conversation that merits further discussion.

How did social media play a part in this campaign?

- Social media played a huge part in this case because the commercials were initially shown not through traditional media channels, but rather through specific platforms like YouTube and Twitter.

- This case also shows the power of the brand owning the narrative. This was not an agency or an individual sharing this content for the world to see—it was coming from the source itself.

- The response has been mixed on this case, with both positive and negative sentiment toward the brand. Time will tell how this will impact the brand in the long term.

What are some major takeaways from this case?

- PR models can be viewed and applied in this particular campaign to this day.

- It was not discussed in the advertisement or commercial if the company had done any research to see how this would affect audiences using its products.

- Gillette was transparent in providing its message to audiences and owned the narrative of what it was talking about. The company was selectively engaging with audiences on social media, mostly with those who were praising its efforts. The brand was not talking to all sides on this issue.

- Taking on issues and addressing them head-on for a brand may bring forth both praise and controversy—and it is important to know all of the pieces of the puzzle.

- The rise of new models and perspectives for public relations may be adopted and discussed from this case study. For example, several marketers and professionals in the field have called this campaign the rise of "woke advertising," which focuses on addressing issues and generating awareness of important facts about social issues and tying this into their communication and marketing strategies (Hearn, 2019).

DISCUSSION QUESTIONS

1. Identify the four models of public relations. What are the main characteristics that are unique to each of the theories? What features do they share in common?

2. Imagine if P. T. Barnum, Ivy Lee, and Edward Bernays were present in today's PR world. How would they view the field? Discuss your rationale and provide a current campaign or case study that utilizes their perspectives today.

3. Review the case studies (Gillette, Fyre Festival, the 2008 and 2016 U.S. presidential campaigns, @world_record_egg, and Red Bull) through the lens of the PR models. What are some of the consistent characteristics for each of these cases? What do they bring to the table that is new for PR professionals to note?

4. Of the PR theories and perspectives being used today in research and practice, which one do you think is the dominant perspective? Provide your reasoning.

CHAPTER 3

ETHICS AND THE LAW

....

LEARNING OBJECTIVES

- Define ethics and core ethical areas of public relations.

- Explain the key ethical challenges facing PR professionals.

- Define the legal implications of public relations.

- Outline the areas of law that PR professionals need to know.

Introduction

Before we begin to practice public relations, implement strategies, or even discuss ideas for how to create effective messages, as PR professionals we must first identify a solid ethical and legal framework for how to conduct ourselves professionally.

To be successful, we must each have a sound foundation for handling difficult situations should they arise. For example, fake news, cyberbullying situations, new ethical dilemmas, privacy concerns, and more impact different areas of our industry on a global scale. In addition, while new technologies have brought forth improvements, they've also brought plenty of new challenges—in the areas of influencer relations (including those who amplify their presence based on fake followers and likes), fake news (presenting to the public information that is false, but looks like it is real news), misleading information for personal or agency gain, transparency and privacy considerations, and much more. As PR professionals, we must be aware of and ready to manage such problems.

To prepare ourselves to make the most ethical choices, we must ask ourselves these questions:

- Am I really being transparent to my audiences through my messages and actions?

- Am I representing and being inclusive to all audiences and their perspectives?

- Am I doing all that is necessary to protect the privacy of my audiences through my information and actions?

- Am I successful and powerful enough that I can assume I'll "survive" an ethical crisis?

- Am I being fair to all parties involved?

- What challenges could arise through this campaign or other activity?

- Will what I am doing violate the trust or fail to meet the expectations of my audiences?

- Am I being truthful about my actions and intentions?

Many professionals have faced these questions in a variety of different situations in their professional and personal circles. Further, these are questions you may be asked by others at any time, so you want to make sure you are prepared and know how you will answer.

In the classic movie *Liar Liar*, Jim Carrey plays a lawyer who always tells the truth. In one classic moment, the lawyer tells a character who has done wrong: "You got to stop breaking the law!" (He adds in a few colorful words that I won't include here, so your homework assignment is to see this movie!) Another way of saying this is: You've got to be your best self. In public relations, our ethical and moral behaviors should reflect the best of who we are—and model for others what we expect from our clients and business partners. Too many times we have seen PR professionals get into hot water or damage control over even the simplest of ethical mishaps. Such behavior is not only detrimental to our individual careers and our clients; it's detrimental to our profession as a whole. When PR professionals state that "we are transparent, we are following ethical guidelines, and we have a strong code of ethics that we follow as a profession" and then do not adhere to this on the job, they violate a basic trust. Such violations of confidence and expectations hurt everyone.

Ethics, for the most part, is a topic that is frequently missing from PR curricula. Unless we address this omission, it will likely become a problem for our field and for future professionals. So, as practitioners, educators, and students, we need to emphasize that at the core of who we are as a profession is a strong ethical foundation.

With such a foundation, we can address ethical crises such as those of recent years. Some examples include the crisis of Facebook's use of customer data and its dishonesty about privacy practices, the crisis of Wells Fargo opening banking accounts without customer permission, and the crisis at Michigan State University regarding Larry Nassar. We can do better, going forward, by adhering to ethical behaviors and practices.

To fully practice what it is to be an ethical and responsible PR professional, it's crucial to identify, implement, and sustain ethical principles on a regular basis. Ethical behavior is not adequate if it is just a slogan or "mission" or "vision statement" that professionals add to their keynote presentations or Twitter bios. It is an ongoing and sustainable practice that needs to be embraced in the professional circles of public relations, as well as when the cameras and spotlight are not there.

What Are Ethics and Ethical Conduct?

Based on current research in public relations, ethics is one of the growing areas within our profession. Yet there is a disagreement among scholars on what ethics really is (Bowen, 2016).

Ethics can be defined simply as a code for how one should behave, a code that is based on values, and an understanding of what is right or wrong. As professionals, we must each have a foundational, personal code of conduct that will guide our actions and interactions with colleagues and clients. We must be aware of the standards that our organizations expect us to uphold, and also the standards that others, including clients and employers, must be held to. As Professor Shannon Bowen (2007) of the University of South Carolina states, ethics for public relations focuses on "values such as honesty, openness, loyalty, fair-mindedness, respect, integrity, and forthright communication. This definition of public relations ethics goes far beyond the olden days of 'flacking for space' or spinning some persuasive message, but this view is not shared by everyone."

One of the biggest responsibilities that we have as PR professionals is that we are viewed as the "consciousness" of our brands and organizations, meaning we have to have strong ethical practices ourselves. In this same light, we are often tasked with providing ethical counsel for our clients and senior management (Neill, 2016), making ethical conduct essential.

Behaving Ethically, Avoiding Misconduct

Is being ethical simply knowing what is right or wrong? Should our conduct be based on what our employers or clients say is right or wrong? These are areas in which we may struggle daily in our personal lives and as PR professionals. What qualifies as misconduct? Some types of ethical misconduct include accepting gifts from clients and adapting research to present only one angle of a story rather than reporting information factually. Ethical behavior is about more than adhering to a set of guidelines posted in business and office quarters—it is a mindset and framework that informs every action, decision, and process that we face.

One of the biggest problems we may face in public relations is the possibility that we or others may somehow fail to meet ethical expectations. If we do not conduct ourselves ethically, we create conflict and violate trust. Ethical misconduct characterizes some of the biggest crises in PR history and offers us case studies from which to learn. For example, Wells Fargo has been around for years, yet the company tested its ethical code when it opened new banking accounts without telling its customers. Not being honest and trustworthy about this resulted in a huge scandal from which the company, despite its rebranding campaign, is still trying to recover. Such ethical misconduct can be prevented when professionals understand how their actions will be perceived and interpreted by their key audiences. In the Wells Fargo case, the brand's unethical actions speak louder than its positive messaging and rebranding attempt. Companies are also not immune to these situations—PR agencies can be guilty of this as well. In February 2020, 5W Public Relations, a PR agency in New York, published a survey in a press release that stated 33 percent of beer-drinking Americans would not buy Corona beer due to the fears of coronavirus, which causes COVID-19 (5W Public Relations, 2020). This survey went viral, and as a result, Corona's sales and reputation were impacted. However, the issue with this survey, and interpretation of the findings, is manufactured according to *The Atlantic*, and this was a move to mislead the public in a shameless way to gain exposure for the agency in the popular press (Mounk, 2020).

One incident can change someone's opinion of who we are as people. While ethics is a focus within our profession and integral to how public relations and related disciplines are taught, it can still be a challenge to teach someone how to be ethical—how to be a proactive and positive member of society and the world of business. However, adopting some basic rules can help us maintain some checks and balances. According to the Arthur W. Page Center (n.d.-b), there are certain pillars of truth that we need to adhere to, such as veracity (to tell the truth), non-maleficence (to do no harm), beneficence (to do good), confidentiality (to respect privacy), and fairness (to be fair and socially responsible).

Challenges to Ethical Practices

As mentioned in the introduction to this chapter, Ethics is one of the most important courses for students of public relations to take, but it is usually the one class missing from most PR curricula (Commission on Public Relations Education, 2018). In addition, research on undergraduate students shows that most are not aware of the growing emphasis on ethical training, management focus, and strategic planning that is involved in PR practices (Bowen, 2003); shocked by the level of strategic decision making required of practitioners; and surprised by the amount of research knowledge and activity necessary in the field. Data were collected at two universities over a two-year period. Two separate phases of qualitative questionnaires of students in four principles courses were conducted, and three focus groups with these students gave additional explanation. In conclusion, the public relations profession is doing a lax job of communicating its core responsibilities and activities to new and potential university majors. This is also an issue in professional settings. Neill and Weaver (2017), in their study of more than 200 young professionals, found that there were differences between their readiness to offer ethics counsel and the availability of ethics training at work. They were willing to give advice on ethics, but lacked the educational background needed to do so responsibly.

There are some ways to address these challenges, such as taking advantage of ethics-focused webinars and training sessions offered by professional organizations such as the Public Relations Society of America, or attending workshops and presentations given by local PRSA chapters to further our educations. Another solution, especially for young professionals, is to find and work with professionals who practice ethically and ask them to be a mentor. The point is to educate ourselves and explore tools for grounding ourselves, ethically speaking. For example, the Commission on Public Relations Education (CPRE) has studied and reported on the current state of PR education and identified some much-needed changes to university curricula. Following are some of the organization's findings:

- *Even when ethics courses are taught in college, PR departments and firms consider graduates to be unprepared.* In the 2018 CPRE report, researchers found that while educators felt that they were teaching students to be ready to use ethical practices and handle situations, the industry disagreed (p. 66).

- *A lack of legal knowledge places both the PR practitioner and the organization or client at risk of increased legal liability.* This has been raised as a "must need" in the latest report from the CPRE (2018). In fact, the 2018 report discussed how other courses, including Law, need to be added to the PR curriculum as required courses (p. 8), especially because of the rise of fake news, disinformation, and false rumors and information circulating in the media. Having a course that covers the type of legal decisions that have ethical implications is not only the recommendation made by the CPRE, but also how ethics needs to be incorporated into every course and area covered within the curriculum.

- *There are high expectations for PR professionals to be sensible, resourceful, accountable, and principled.* As noted in the findings in the report, PR professionals entering the workplace are expected to have certain "desirable skills," most of which are related to integrity and ethical behaviors (CPRE, 2018). Yet we professionals and students have these expectations already laid out and incorporated into our curricula, so why are ethical crises still emerging in the field?

- *The field is under scrutiny by the general public, by nonprofit organizations, and by the government.* We don't necessarily enjoy the best reputation among colleagues and associates. Many people think PR professionals are "spin doctors," or even "flacks," due to a negative experience they may have had. If we are aware of these perceptions, we can embrace them as challenges to address and reverse. We can only control our own actions, so the best step forward is to lead with ethical and sound practices, thereby showing others that negative stereotypes do not apply to all of us. We cannot let the unethical professionals among us control the narrative and influence the perception of our field—they are not the ones who should be shaping the reputation of our field.

- *People want to do business with companies and professionals who are socially responsible and practice ethical behavior.* This has become a standard practice and approach for many professionals in the industry. Case in point: If you had to choose between doing business with USAA® Bank and Wells Fargo, which would you choose? Wells Fargo was responsible for creating fake accounts for its customers without their knowledge, while USAA has not done this. Instead, USAA has done more to make sure it is transparent with its actions as a bank, to invest in customer services for its clients, and to go the extra mile in making sure it is honest about its role and what it does for its customers in its banking services. The choice is pretty easy in this case.

What Codes of Ethics Do We Follow?

As they say in *Pirates of the Caribbean*, stick to the code!

Well, this does not mean that PR professionals should band together, jump on a ship, and set sail with Captain Jack Sparrow around the Caribbean on the *Black Pearl*. But the code of conduct that pirates follow is somewhat aligned with what we in public relations set forth: a list of behaviors and expectations for everyone to follow, behaviors that are based on shared values.

Most organizations define what they are, what they do, and how they do it. The purpose of such a code is to apply ethical values within an organization, to the people whose work makes them part of the brand. A code also shows audiences that the brand is ethically sound—that ethics is a part of its mission and overall culture. So, like pirates, let's stick to the code!

ETHICAL CHALLENGES

Ethics in many ways is simply defined as the conduct that governs one's behavior based on values and determination of what is right or wrong. Public relations professionals face a lot of ethical challenges, both personally as well as professionally. The 2018 Commission for Public Relations Education report outlined some of the main ethical challenges facing public relations professionals today.

NOT ENOUGH COURSES

Even when ethics courses are taught in college, public relations departments and firms consider the graduates to be unprepared. Ethics courses continue to be one of the least offered courses, but recommendations in the CPRE 2018 report that this needs to change.

LACK OF KNOWLEDGE

A lack of legal knowledge places both the PR practitioner and organization or client at risk of increased legal liability. Having an ethics course was not the only recommendation made by the CPRE, but it also suggested that ethics needs to be incorporated into every course and area covered within the curriculum.

HIGH EXPECTATIONS

There are high expectations for public relations professionals to be sensible, resourceful, accountable, and principled. Along with the findings in the report, PR professionals entering the workplace are expected to have certain "desirable skills," most of which are related to integrity and ethical behaviors.

SOCIAL RESPONSIBILITY

People want to do business with companies and professionals who are socially responsible and practice ethical behavior. This has become a standard practice and approach for many professionals in the industry.

Reference: Commission on Public Relations Education. (n.d.). Retrieved January 14, 2019, from http://www.commissionpred.org/

The Code of the Public Relations Society of America (PRSA)

What exactly is a **code of ethics**? And why should you want to have one? Simply put, a code of ethics is a list of values and principles that you believe in and that will help you to respond and react to specific situations. These values and principles set forth expectations on what specific actions to take (or not take).

For PR professionals, PRSA has its own code of ethics that is shared with the professional PR community. PRSA is the largest governing body for PR professionals and has set forth certain guidelines for ethical conduct in practice. The PRSA Code of Ethics (found at www.prsa.org/ethics) focuses on six areas:

- *Advocacy.* We serve the public interest by acting as responsible advocates for those we represent. We provide a voice in the marketplace of ideas, facts, and viewpoints to aid informed public debate.

- *Honesty.* We adhere to the highest standards of accuracy and truth in advancing the interests of those we represent and in communicating with the public.

- *Expertise.* We acquire and responsibly use specialized knowledge and experience. We advance the profession through continued professional development, research, and education. We build mutual understanding, credibility, and relationships among a wide array of institutions and audiences.

- *Independence.* We provide objective counsel to those we represent. We are accountable for our actions.

- *Loyalty.* We are faithful to those we represent, while honoring our obligation to serve the public interest.

- *Fairness.* We deal fairly with clients, employers, competitors, peers, vendors, the media, and the general public. We respect all opinions and support the right of free expression.

These guiding principles are used to foster a strong sense of understanding of ethical practices in public relations. Each of these areas is covered in most PR courses and encouraged in practice.

The Codes of Other Organizations

There are, in fact, organizations besides PRSA that provide not only ethical resources, but also opportunities for researchers to explore and obtain funding to conduct ethical research. One such organization is the Arthur W. Page Center for Integrity in Public Communication at Pennsylvania State University.

The Arthur W. Page Center: The Page Principles

As explained on its website (bellisario.psu.edu/page-center/about/arthur-w-page/the-page-principles), the Arthur W. Page Center (n.d.-a) is a research hub at the Donald P. Bellisario College of Communications at Penn State dedicated to the study and advancement of ethics and responsibility in corporate communication and other forms of public communication. The organization's code of ethics is similar to the focus of the

Codes of Ethics for IABC, CIPR, and Global Alliance

Name	Link	Key Concepts in Code of Ethics
International Association of Business Communicators (IABC)	www.iabc.com/about-us/governance/code-of-ethics/	Business ethical practices for communication
Chartered Institute of Public Relations (CIPR)	https://newsroom.cipr.co.uk/cipr-supports-global-principles-of-ethical-practice/	PR practices on a global scale
Global Alliance	www.globalalliancepr.org/code-of-ethics/	PR practices on a global scale

PRSA code of ethics, but the Page Center identifies and focuses on these efforts as they pertain to corporate and leadership practices in the PR field.

IABC, CIPR, and Global Alliance

Of course, still other organizations have their own codes of ethics for public relations, which is important to note. Table 3.1 lists these professional organizations and links to their codes of ethics.

One thing to keep in mind when it comes to codes of ethics is this: They are only broad statements and do not explain how to handle every situation. We must each develop a strong personal and professional sense of right and wrong, and of how to handle gray areas. It takes time and experience to determine what core values are nonnegotiable. This is important not only for our careers, but for determining where we want to work—for example, a department, an agency, a boutique firm, or a major organization—and whom we want as colleagues. Understanding the ethical culture of a brand or organization, and the attitudes of team members, tells us a lot about how the brand or organization practices public relations. If you ever find yourself in a work culture that does not promote ethical behavior, run! Even if you have a strong sense of ethics and behave accordingly, working for a brand, agency, or organization that does not practice ethically can impact your reputation and future in the profession.

Ethical Dilemmas: What Can Recent Campaigns Teach Us?

As PR professionals, we need to be alert to the types of challenging ethical situations we face when working for a brand or other client. While most professions can identify and predict various scenarios that they may face, in public relations there are always some surprises in the mix. Given the constant change in the media and technology spaces, there will always be new learning experiences on how to apply ethical practices.

Potential Situations

You may be asking yourself: What are the chances that I'll find myself facing an ethical dilemma? The answer is simple: Ethical challenges do not discriminate. They will find you. They find all of us. There will be times when you face situations that cause you to pause, evaluate, and respond. In some situations, it will be very clear how to best respond, whereas in others, it will not be so clear. In particular, social media has brought forth new challenges for us to prepare for and address. Remember, too, that you can have the best code of ethics for your brand, but if you do not follow those principles—if you don't "walk the walk"—your code is meaningless. For example, TikTok has promoted its platform as one that is for entertainment and creative purposes, but the networking service has been reported to censor stories and content on a variety of topics including political speech; lesbian, gay, bisexual, transgender, and queer/questioning (LGBTQ) issues; and coverage of the Hong Kong protests (Hern, 2019).

When it comes to ethics, we must be holistic and consistent. For example, if a professional organization is on a mission to support women's empowerment in the industry, it is unwise for that organization to host a reception that promotes the opposite of that message. This is what happened at the 2019 Advertising Week industry event, at which there were many panels and sessions promoting equal pay, diversity, and other issues affecting women in the industry. Yet the closing of the event featured the rapper Pitbull and his female dancers. An organization may say that it supports ethics and professional standards, but its actions are what audiences remember.

Here are some situations you may find yourself in as a PR professional, along with advice on what to do:

- *Making comments to the media.* When a journalist, reporter, or media professional says, "This is off the record," consider that as a giant red flag. Nothing is ever "off the record." It's important to remember that, like PR professionals, journalists have a job to do, and that job is writing a story for their publication or other media outlet.

- *Disclosing your associations.* When doing business or working with clients for PR accounts or presenting yourself to the media, make sure to fully represent yourself in a transparent manner. This means in all situations, whether online or offline, on the phone or in person. This means you must identify yourself, your role, the sources of the information you've gotten from your client, and the research you've gathered for your campaign.

- *Disclosing your partnership, relationship, and affiliation during news programs or at events.* This is a big one, and it is somewhat tied to influencer relations. If you represent a celebrity who appears on a newscast or talk show, and who discusses a product but does not disclose he or she is getting paid by the company for promoting it, that's a violation of trust. It is key to be clear and upfront with the media and your audiences on what you are doing and whom you represent. When you mislead your audiences, you begin to travel down the path toward a damaged reputation.

- *Giving or receiving gifts.* We all love gifts, but PR professionals should not give gifts or try in any way to materially reward journalists, bloggers, or influencers. Even offering modest "swag" or other potential incentives to persuade them to create positive buzz, press, or acknowledgment of your client or product is off-limits.

Types of Ethical Situations That Could Arise for PR Professionals

Ethical Situation	Areas of Focus
• Gifts or bribery • Spam and cookies • Attacking competitors with false information • Setting up "front groups" and stealth marketing • Fake data from influencers • Not representing true self (e.g., fake reviews) • Issue of overcharging clients • Conflict of interest	• Journalists, news media, influencers • Social and digital companies (TikTok, Facebook, etc.) • Consumer brands • Government or public affairs • Online reviews (Yelp, TripAdvisor®, Google, Apple, etc.) • PR firms and agencies

- *Being honest about influencer relations.* Influencer relations, mentioned earlier in this chapter and discussed in detail in Chapter 9, has brought forth new challenges and obstacles for PR professionals. From the ethical standpoint, if you represent someone who gets paid to create content about a specific product, the big challenge is making sure to disclose that a payment has been made—and that the content (whether a blog post, social media post or update, video, story, or otherwise) is paid for. Many influencers, including DJ Khaled and Kim Kardashian, have gotten into trouble with the Federal Trade Commission (FTC) for not disclosing that they received payment for their product- or event-related posts.

- *Being aware of the trademark, copyright, and ownership of creative works.* You must be aware of the copyright laws and regulations for any content or other material that you want to use. Some of it is okay; most is not unless you work out an agreement or licensing deal. For example, most brands have strict guidelines on what logos and colors can and can't be used for marketing and promotional items, and being aware of the risks associated with using photos or videos without permission is crucial.

- *Being careful of what you say and do online.* Social media allows us to communicate online in real time, but as we know, its platforms are not private. Think critically and make thoughtful decisions about what you do, say, and share online. For someone who makes an error or crosses a line of appropriateness, the internet does not forget. Keep in mind the power of the screenshot. Once someone makes a copy of what you tweeted, shared, snapped, or posted online, even if you've deleted your post, it is still there, forever.

There are many different situations that PR professionals may face that are not always covered in class or in a textbook. Yet, with the changes happening in the industry, we have to be able to identify them and know where they come from. There are going to be some cases where they happen across all fields, but some are more specifically related to a particular area within the PR industry (see Table 3.2).

Recent Case Studies

One of the things that is not lacking in the field of public relations is cases in which professionals, brands, and even PR firms do things that they should not be doing. Even with today's emphasis on ethics, there are still individuals who feel they are "above everyone else and the law" and believe they can get away with dishonest behavior. The case studies that follow are fairly current and show how we, as a profession, still have much to do in order to practice and act in ways that are right, fair, and equitable.

Carlos Ghosn (1954–) was the chairman of Nissan in Japan. He has been charged by the Japanese government with financial crimes including the underreporting of earnings and misuse of company funds.

The Asahi Shimbun / Getty Images

Nissan: A Case Study in Greedy Leadership

Sometimes when there is an ethical crisis, it is blamed on PR professionals even though they are not the ones involved. This is what happened in the case of Nissan. One of the largest global brands in the automotive industry has been in an ethical battle for its reputation based on the actions of one of its senior executives. Auto executive Carlos Ghosn, the former chairman of Nissan and Mitsubishi Motors, improperly received an estimated $9 million in compensation and other payments from the joint brands without the other board members' awareness or approval (Shane, 2019). In the same case, Nissan was also indicted for the same violation of the Japan Financial Instruments and Exchange Act, which focuses on making sure there are no false disclosures in annual security reports (Nissan Motor Corporation, 2018). Nissan released a statement about the misdeed:

> Nissan takes this situation extremely seriously. Making false disclosures in annual securities reports greatly harms the integrity of Nissan's public disclosures in the securities markets, and the company expresses its deepest regret.

> Nissan will continue its efforts to strengthen its governance and compliance, including making accurate disclosures of corporate information. (Nissan Motor Corporation, 2018)

As presented within the investigation, some direct comments were made about how the ethical leadership (or lack thereof) from Nissan is what got the company into trouble in the first place. The investigation quoted committee co-chair Seiichiro Nishioka as follows: "Having read the report on the internal investigation, my initial impression was that the head of the company may have had questionable ethical standards" (Shiraki & Tajitsu, 2019). Ghosn had been credited with bringing forth new financial gains and support for Nissan; however, he clearly did so at a significant cost (Leggett & Palumbo, 2019). Ghosn, who was also doing the same leadership practices with the European brand Renault, was ruthless in closing Nissan factories, cutting jobs, and creating new initiatives to make the brand gain a profit (Leggett & Palumbo, 2019). This is a case in which leadership—for the sake of gaining a short-term profit for a brand—caused an ethics scandal at the cost of a brand's global reputation.

Facebook: A Case Study in Audience Deception

The largest social media company in the world has had more ethical challenges than any other of today's social platforms. Most of these issues have to do with privacy and data collection. When it comes to the terms of service agreements, most platforms state your data and privacy are protected. Yet this issue was brought up front and center during the 2016 presidential election in the United States. The company has not chosen the best communication tactics when it comes to the public's rising concerns over the past few years. In a *New York Times* article, Facebook is portrayed as using the denial, delay, and deflection strategy for all of its communication efforts; the company feels it has been portrayed "unfairly" in the news (Frankel, Confessore, Kang, Rosenberg, & Nicas, 2018). Facebook has struggled with handling the revelation of its actions in regard to Cambridge Analytica; Facebook collected data from users without their permission, and conducted an "experiment" to see how people would respond when presented with positive or negative content on their timelines (Booth, 2014). These factors have led people to lose trust in the company. Facebook users are looking to the organization to take responsibility and to change its actions and behaviors. The only way that Facebook can achieve this is if the company puts ethics at the top of its list of priorities (Balkin, 2018).

Mark Zuckerberg, CEO and founder of Facebook, has made several trips to Congress to address rising concerns involving fake news, data collection, and privacy. The PR team could only do so much in this case, but there are some things the company could have encouraged and promoted in response to what happened—for example, integrating more transparency in its messaging, as well as discussing the steps it would take to make sure this does not happen again. Since this case happened, Facebook is doing more to address these concerns. Yet these are some new ethics violations that PR professionals need to be aware of and ready to address. Will Facebook change its behaviors and actions to embrace a more ethical and legal stance for its business practices? Time will tell.

Papa John's: A Case Study in Racism and Brand Rehabilitation

"Better Ingredients. Better Pizza." How about "Better Ethics"? Perhaps not, Papa John's. The face of the brand, founder John Schnatter, had been a staple of the marketing and promotions efforts for the global pizza franchise for years. Papa John's had been a staple presence in many places, most notably being the official pizza sponsor for the National Football League (NFL). However, this all changed over the past few years because of the actions of the brand's leadership. In November 2017, Papa John's made the call to withdraw as an NFL sponsor because of the CEO's objection to the national anthem protests in which some NFL players, instead of standing, took a knee during the anthem to protest police brutality being carried out in the United States against African Americans and other people of color. Schnatter said that the protests that were happening during the NFL games were impacting the company's overall sales, since it was one of the major sponsors of the NFL, which was one of the other factors in the decision to pull out (Moore, 2018).

Yet this was just the beginning of the pizza brand's troubles, and 2018 would mark the year that Schnatter took things to another level. Papa John's ended its NFL sponsorship in February 2018, and on July 11, 2018, *Forbes* reported that Schnatter used

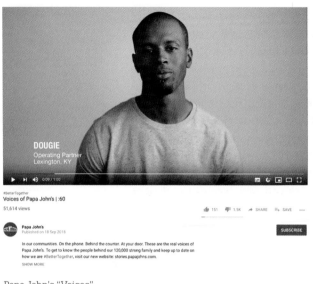

Papa John's "Voices" campaign

the *N*-word on a conference call with his creative agency, Laundry Service (Moore, 2018). Ultimately, Schnatter resigned as chairman, and the PR professionals at Papa John's made efforts to rebrand the company, creating new marketing efforts to separate the brand from its founder (Moore, 2018).

Instead of focusing on using leadership as the brand voice of a company, Papa John's created a new campaign titled "Voices," which showcased actual employees who are behind the brand, including franchise owners, pizza makers, and drivers (Richards, 2018). Since then, Papa John's has engaged in more proactive and sustainable efforts both in its leadership practices and in the brand presence as a whole. The company's latest spokesperson, Shaquille O'Neal, has been successful in reaching new audiences as well as tapping into new sports fans, including basketball fans, for the pizza brand.

The case is still ongoing with Schnatter and the Papa John's brand. Both parties are still in legal discussions over the control of the name and access to communication materials from the period when Schnatter was still with the company.

Bell Pottinger: A Case Study in Inciting Social Unrest

One of the biggest recent scandals in the world of public relations happened in 2017 when Bell Pottinger, a London PR firm, was banned from the United Kingdom's Public Relations and Communications Association (PRCA). This happened as a result of PRCA's investigation into Bell Pottinger during which the organization discovered Bell Pottinger's "secret campaign to stir up racial tension in South Africa on behalf of Oakbay Capital" (Conner, 2017).

This was not even the firm's first crisis. In fact, Bell Pottinger was also the agency responsible for representing some controversial figures and political leaders (Segal, 2018). One of the more recent clients the firm represented was Oscar Pistorius, the Olympian from South Africa who gained worldwide fame in the 2012 London Olympics—and who was later convicted of the murder of his girlfriend (Segal, 2018). Pistorius hired Bell Pottinger after he was charged with murder to help restore his image in South Africa and around the world. But the situation that ultimately brought down Bell Pottinger occurred when the firm chose to represent the Guptas, a powerful and influential family in Africa who had a multibillion-dollar empire in South Africa (Segal, 2018). When the media began to focus on some of the company's activities, Bell Pottinger was brought in to build a PR campaign to create "a distraction that would draw attention away from them and onto their many enemies" (Segal, 2018, para. 3).

Bell Pottinger's work for the Guptas began with a 2016 PR campaign to help them gain influence in the country. The firm's strategies included creating fake Twitter accounts, building an attack website, and inviting influential people to give speeches arguing against the wealthy white leaders in South Africa (Segal, 2018). Bell Pottinger's actions were coordinated with proper media training, funds, and support from Oakbay Capital, which was owned by the Gupta brothers (Segal, 2018). Once these unethical practices were discovered and revealed by PRCA, Bell Pottinger's actions caused outrage both in and outside of South Africa. This sparked an outcry in the PR industry—how this had been occurring for such a long time and how these practices go against the ethical principles PR professionals adhere to. As a result, Bell Pottinger was forced to declare bankruptcy (Segal, 2018). The courts in South Africa found the firm had "exploited racial divisions on behalf of the Gupta family" (PRCA, n.d.). As a result of this case, PRCA terminated Bell Pottinger's membership in the professional organization because the firm failed to protect its reputation and the standing of the PR profession (PRCA, n.d.).

What Legal Matters Do We Need to Know About?

PR professionals deal with many different legal matters, including libel, slander, and defamation, to name a few. Like ethics, law is an area that needs more emphasis within PR curricula. While the purpose of this textbook is to introduce you to the field of public relations, part of your introduction needs to include a few of the major aspects of the law that PR professionals deal with.

Libel

One of the most common elements that comes into play is the difference between libel and slander. They are essentially the same, but one involves printed falsehoods, and the other is spoken. **Libel** is printed falsehood, and in order to prove libel, you have to show that harm was caused by a published story or broadcast (such as in a news article or advertisement) in which a person or company is named, that the media was at fault or made an error, and that the "facts" presented by the media were false.

Slander

Slander is a false oral statement, one that may come up at a press conference, at a public event, or even during an interview. However, **defamation** is considered to be any false statement about a person or organization that creates public hatred, contempt, or ridicule, or that inflicts injury on a reputation. For example, celebrities are known to sue media outlets (most of the time tabloids) for defamation. Most recently, actress Rebel Wilson won a $3.66 million defamation suit against Bauer Media after the company wrote damaging stories about her, saying she was a "serial liar who had fabricated almost every aspect of her life" (Izadi, 2017). This case gained a lot of attention in the media since it was picked up by many other media outlets, and it did occur during a prime time in Wilson's career, which was impacted by these stories.

Deception

Another legal matter that PR professionals need to understand is the difference between puffery and deception. These are two similar, yet different, concepts that you should

KIND

December 1, 2015

Dockets Management Branch
Food and Drug Administration
5630 Fishers Lane, Room 1061
Rockville, MD 20852

CITIZEN PETITION

Dear Sir/Madam:

When the Scientific Report from the 2015 Dietary Guidelines Advisory Committee (DGAC) was released early this year, it reiterated an important shift in U.S. dietary guidance that was the basis of the 2010 *Dietary Guidelines for Americans*. These documents shined attention on the importance of eating certain *foods*, including vegetables, fruits, whole grains, low- or non-fat dairy, seafood, lean meats and poultry, eggs, legumes, and nuts and seeds, in achieving better health and wellness. This is in contrast to prior federal dietary guidance, which placed greater emphasis on the specific *nutrient levels* in the diet rather than the overall contribution of recommended foods to a healthy diet. Many current federal labeling regulations are based upon this past thinking, preventing foods that contain beneficial whole ingredients and are recommended for consumption—like nuts, avocados, olives, and salmon—from bearing the word "healthy" in their labeling.

KIND respectfully submits this citizen petition requesting the Commissioner of Food and Drugs to update the Food and Drug Administration's (FDA's) existing requirements related to food labeling to become consistent with current federal dietary guidance as set forth in the 2010 *Dietary Guidelines for Americans* and with the latest scientific evidence discussed in the *Scientific Report of the 2015 Dietary Guidelines Advisory Committee* (2015 *DGAC Report*). The requested changes outlined in this petition are also in line with the DGAC's decision against recommending a limit on total fat intake as well as its decision to emphasize *whole foods* and dietary patterns rather than *specific nutrients* like fat. The 2015 *DGAC Report* will form the scientific basis for the 2015 *Dietary Guidelines for Americans*, which is anticipated later this year.

Under FDA's current application of food labeling regulations, whether or not a food can be labeled "healthy" is based on specific nutrient levels in the food rather than its overall nutrition quality. FDA formulated those regulations more than 20 years ago, when available science *and* federal dietary recommendations focused on limiting total fat intake. Today, these regulations still require that the majority of foods featuring a "healthy" nutrient content claim meet "low fat" and "low saturated fat" standards regardless of their nutrient density. This is despite the fact that current science no longer supports those standards.

KIND Snacks citizen petition note

keep in mind when creating a message strategy. **Deception**, the more serious legal violation, occurs when someone makes a false or misleading statement in order to persuade audiences. For example, the Lucky Strike campaign of 1929 focused on tying women's liberation to smoking during the women's suffrage movement. While this campaign was successful for the tobacco company in getting women to view smoking differently, its messaging was deceptive in nature. Persuasive, yes. Ethical, no. Another area that PR professionals need to be aware of involves food labeling. Most brands, especially consumer products, have to list all of the ingredients that go into their products in order to meet the requirements of the Food and Drug Administration (FDA). However, there have been cases—such as one involving Tyson Foods and another involving Vitaminwater—in which companies have not done this. In these situations, both companies had to address the deception and admit their products were not what they appeared or presented to be, which provided their PR teams a challenge in addressing these concerns among their key publics.

In these deception cases, the common theme is that brand strategists have made statements that are not true, as in the case of the Lucky Strike campaign, or they have left out significant information, as in the case of Tyson Foods and Vitaminwater. Tyson Foods got into further trouble when it did a promotion campaign focused on its products being "raised without antibiotics." When it was discovered that this was not true, the company had to settle a $5 million suit (Truth in Advertising, 2012). Vitaminwater, a brand that promotes itself as a healthy drink, actually contains more sugar than Coke (Addady, 2016). On the other hand, a different brand that promoted itself as a healthy product won a battle with the FDA. In 2015, the FDA sent a note to KIND Snacks, telling the company that it couldn't use the word *healthy* on its packaging (Kowitt, 2016). To respond to this request, KIND actually created a citizen petition campaign regarding the situation. As a result, the company was able to keep its branding of being a healthy snack product.

KIND addressed the situation head-on, concerned that the FDA's removal of the word *healthy* from its packaging would damage the brand. At best, the company would have to rebrand its entire product line; at worst, the company would have to shut down completely. However, with the help of its key audiences, KIND gathered evidence to support its claim about the product, and won the case. *Healthy* still appears on KIND's packaging and remains central to the company's branding.

Puffery

When compared to deception, **puffery** is more of an exaggerated statement in which a firm may say something like "This is the best brand ever" or "This is the greatest and best event you could ever go to." Can a PR professional prove this? No. Does it make it right to still do? No. The best course of action is to be honest and truthful on what your brand, campaign, and organization represent. Never mislead your audiences to take action based on what you think people will want; rather, provide all of the facts and information and let them make the decision for themselves. Being honest and transparent will always win in the long run.

What Are Best Practices for Functioning Ethically and Legally?

As a *PRWeek* article (Raab, 2018) discussed, there are certain things that PR practitioners need to do, from a professional standpoint:

- *Be aware that, when you take on controversial clients, organizations, or brands, public perception and your reputation will be affected.* Association—whether it

GAME CHANGER
Jason Falls, PR Professional

Courtesy Jason Falls

How did you get your start in public relations?

My high school days were mostly spent on the radio calling play-by-play for my high school football and basketball teams. When I got to college, I wrote for the campus newspaper until one day the sports information director said, "How would you like to do that but get paid for it?" I was scraping by, so I said, "Hell yeah!" And the next semester I was a student assistant in the sports information department, which is the PR department for athletics. Because I had a lot of experience covering games as a broadcaster, I immediately took over running the stat crews, computer systems, and so on, and was pretty senior despite being a student. After grad school and a two-year jaunt back into broadcasting, I walked right back into sports information as a full-time assistant, then director, and did that job for eight more years. When my son was born, I transitioned out to an agency where I was hired primarily to do PR for Louisville Slugger based on my sports background, but quickly was assigned and learned public affairs, consumer goods, and other areas. The skills are the same. It's just having the ability to adapt to the different types of audiences and environments to connect your messages.

What is your favorite part of working in public relations?

Having an inside look at how the media is made has always been my fascination. Whether it's being a hands-on part of it, coordinating the announcement of the Silver Slugger Award winners live on ESPNews, or just being the liaison between a beat writer and a player or coach whose story gets told because I helped amplify it the right way behind the scenes, seeing and being a part of the mechanism that gets the paper to press, the TV show to air, the talk show on live, or the website content pushed has always been fun for

me. I think it's why I became so quick to adapt to social media—I love being able to hit "Publish" or "Submit" and see my words and pictures live for the world to see. It's probably some weird psychological ego trip thing, but it works, so I just roll with it.

What is the most challenging part of working in public relations?

By far the most difficult part for me has been fighting the stigma left behind by the hacks and the wannabes who aren't in it genuinely. When you have to fight reporters' preconceived notion that PR flacks are just in it for a story and don't care about them or their audience, plus you have to convince them the story is good enough to cover, that just makes it twice as hard. I've always had a genuine interest in knowing the reporters and—I guess it's fair to use this now—influencers I've worked with over the years, and well beyond any story or pitch I've thrown at them. My intent as a PR pro was to always be useful to the media I worked with, no matter what, when, or where. That's my mentality for audience members of my clients and brands I work with in social media, too. But too many self-absorbed or task-focused media relations hacks over the years have used media members too flippantly, tossing them aside or ignoring them when they've gotten what they wanted out of them, so for guys like me, the road was harder to navigate along the way.

Who do you think are the biggest game changers for the PR industry?

Social media has completely flipped the lid on public relations. Everyone is now a publisher. We're no longer in the business of media relations. We're now in the business of influencer relations. And many influencers are individual Instagram users, not multimillion-dollar broadcast entities. It's sick when you think about it. And the fact that single individuals are trumping big companies for eyeballs and attention means PR folks are having to deal with egos they never imagined were possible. It's one thing to have to navigate prepping a client to be interviewed for

Crossfire. It's a completely different animal to have to convince a 22-year-old selfie-addicted gum-popper she has to report back analytics if your client is going to cut her a $15,000 check. Public relations has changed. Trained journalists were a pain in the ass sometimes, but they weren't DFNRs (divas for no reason).

What are some things you wish you knew when you were starting out in public relations?

Well, I certainly wish I knew that individuals would one day rule the day. I could have carved out my own mint far before others did. Ha! But the one thing I really wish I had known in the late 1980s when I got into the professional world was that the world of public relations was so vast and variable. I lived for 15 years in the niche world of sports public relations. And that is a hardworking, long-hours, no-pay grind of a world. If I had known then that I could work at an agency and make twice the money for half the hours, my 20s and 30s would have been a bit saner, and I might not be in nearly as much debt. But I did get paid to watch ballgames for a living for 15 years, so there's a yin and a yang to it all.

is intentional or not—can be the deciding factor between a strong reputation and one that is not as strong or positive. Clients come in all shapes, sizes, and backgrounds, and as PR professionals we need to know our core values, professional practices, and nonnegotiables when it comes to working within certain industries and situations. For example, taking on a client such as O. J. Simpson or Harvey Weinstein may be quite the challenge in light of the crises he has been in over the years and how his reputation is not pristine in the eyes of the general public.

- *Know that ethical practices are different from country to country.* This is a key element to remember as the world becomes more globalized. Each country has its own ethical and legal practices, and it is important to be aware of the similarities and differences in these practices. For example, paying journalists for media coverage or accepting gifts from clients may be acceptable in some parts of the world, or even expected. It's important to know the ethical practices of the different countries you do business with. For example, paying reporters or media professionals for stories is not acceptable in the United States as a practice, but in other countries (e.g., Russia), it may be.

- *Set clear expectations and take specific actions when responding to an ethical challenge or crisis.* The risks associated with ethical challenges increase exponentially when PR professionals do not take direct and immediate action. We need to move quickly and be very clear in both our communications and our actions when an ethical challenge or crisis arises. We need to state what next steps to take in order to manage relationships. Whether you are fixing a relationship or ending one, there should be no gray area in your communications.

- *Act in the public interest by setting a strong ethical example.* Be aware of what is good for the majority of the people while making sure you are honest with your audiences and truthful in your information and your standing or role, and be fair to all of your audiences (both internally and externally).

LetItBreeze.com; Crystal Bleecher

If there was a cautionary tale for PR professionals, especially those who want to go into event planning, the Fyre Festival case study would be the poster child for what not to do in the event. In 2017, Fyre Media founder Billy McFarland and rapper Ja Rule decided to create a music festival on Great Exuma island in the Bahamas. The festival was going to be one for the books, but unfortunately, it will go down as one of the worst festivals that ever happened due to greed, fraud, misleading information, and unethical lack of transparency with marketing and influencer relations efforts.

Why did this campaign generate buzz?

- This campaign generated a lot of buzz for the event, especially on social media. The festival did a great job in tapping into influencers (nearly 400 of them) to help market the event.

- The event showcased beautiful pictures on Instagram and became one of the events "not to miss" in 2017 (Lee, 2017). Influencers and celebrities like Bella Hadid, Kendall Jenner, and Hailey Baldwin Bieber were just some of the people promoting the event on Instagram.

- The promoters, Ja Rule and Billy McFarland, were the ones who created and launched the Fyre Festival.

What were the ethical and legal issues?

- While social media was the festival's best friend in marketing, it was also its worst enemy in ethics since it emphasized the festival being put on the global stage for everyone to see, follow, and discuss what was going on before, during, and after the event. The festival's image crumbled with each social media update that showed what was promised to the attendees was quite the opposite. This disconnect between what was expected and the reality of the situation caused the viral outrage for the festival.

- When festival attendees came to the event, they came to the immediate realization that what was promoted on social media was not what was happening in real life. The tents were homemade, no gourmet food (as promoted and showcased) was served, and the big promise of glamour was instead looking more like a disaster relief situation.

- There are currently eight lawsuits going on for damages, including one for $100 million (Petit, 2017).

- McFarland is currently serving a six-year prison sentence for fraud, and Ja Rule is still out and states that the festival was not a "scam" (Bucksbaum, 2019). In addition, Ja Rule has been making waves in presenting at various social media and marketing conferences to help restore his brand image.

- There were two documentaries based on this crisis that were produced by Hulu and Netflix. However, Netflix has had to deal with its own ethical challenges since it worked with Jerry Media, a social media agency that did the marketing for the Fyre Festival (Baysinger, 2019).

- Everyone associated with the festival was not honest or transparent about the situation or what to expect. Yet, with social media, many of the attendees went to their accounts and shared their experiences, frustrations, and experiences for the world to see. As a result, the news media around the world picked up on this and ran with it. Many of these photos, like this one, went viral.

Viral cheese sandwich picture from the Fyre Festival

Twitter/@trev4president

What are some major takeaways from this case?

- Honesty, transparency, and fairness for all parties were seriously lacking. No ethics whatsoever were shown or considered in this campaign. This case showed how greed influenced the leadership and direction of the festival and as a result caused a lot of people frustration and anxiety, and ultimately the Fyre Festival is a case study that will be one for the books for years to come.

- Influencer marketing is very effective—as shown in this case. People were able to listen and take action based on the word-of-mouth marketing efforts by individuals associated with the festival. Yet, while this festival had a major crisis, the influencers who promoted it had to do damage control as well since they were also linked and associated with the event.

- Apologies in some cases are not enough. Significant damage in trust, natural resources, and influencer marketing was done through this case. Even though McFarland made this statement from prison, there will not be any changes in public perception of him and what he did with the Fyre Festival:

I am incredibly sorry for my collective actions and will right the wrongs I have delivered to my family, friends, partners, associates and, you, the general public. I've always sought—and dreamed—to accomplish incredible things by pushing the envelope to deliver for a common good, but I made many wrong and immature decisions along the way and I caused agony. As a result, I've lived every day in prison with pain, and I will continue to do so until I am able to make up for some of this harm through work and actions that society finds respectable. (Keating, 2018)

SUMMARY

As the famous saying goes, it is not only who you know, but *who knows you*. In the present PR field, it's who knows you and what you stand for that counts. Being an ethical PR professional is not about memorizing a code of ethics or sharing it on social media. It is about embracing these values wholeheartedly and truthfully. In other words, don't tell me you are an ethical PR professional; show me. Actions, especially when dealing with ethical and legal situations, mean more than words and prepared statements. PR professionals need to take action to address ethical and legal concerns. Doing so will positively impact not only the current perception of our profession, but our future as well.

In order to have a strong reputation and presence in the industry, PR professionals need to study ethics and be able to show others that we have what it takes to do things professionally and ethically on a consistent and sustainable basis. As PR professionals, we need to tap core principles and values, including honesty and integrity, as a guide for our actions, especially in challenging situations.

Rome was not built in a day, and the same can be said for having a consistent and universal approach for ethical and legal behavior for PR professionals. Yet we can all get there one step at a time by doing our part every day.

APR EXAM

- Ethics is critical to the field of public relations.
- Values, which are listed in the PRSA Code of Ethics, need to be considered and applied in various situations facing PR professionals.

- Situations will arise, and you have to be able to apply which ethical principles will help your decision-making process.

KEY TERMS

Code of ethics 54

Deception 62

Defamation 61

Ethics 50

Libel 61

Puffery 63

Slander 61

DISCUSSION QUESTIONS

1. How would you define ethics? What are three values you would consider to be the most important ones for your future in public relations?

2. Review the PRSA Code of Ethics. What are the core principles you feel most strongly about? List a case study you have seen that addresses each of these components.

3. What are the biggest ethical and legal issues you see presently happening in society? Explain your answer.

4. What are three steps you will want to take to make sure you are practicing ethical and legal public relations?

DIVERSITY AND INCLUSION

CHAPTER 4

LEARNING OBJECTIVES

- Define diversity and inclusion.

- Understand diversity and inclusion in the context of public relations.

- Explore how organizations and brands integrate diversity.

- Identify ways to integrate more diversity into PR efforts.

Introduction

In public relations, there are many opportunities that the field brings forward to society from creative ideas, innovative perspectives, and new approaches. However, one of the areas that have been a focal point for many professionals, brands, and audiences is the lack of diversity in the PR industry.

When we talk about diversity, we mean a situation that includes people of different races, ethnicities, genders, sexualities, cultures, and thought processes. Yet many professional fields, including public relations, need to do better to become more diverse. For example, gender pay inequality is a problem and a growing area of concern among PR professionals. Another concern is that the leaders of most organizations do not represent or reflect the diversity, especially in terms of race and gender, of the audiences they serve. And while PR strategists may tap diverse audiences in their campaigns, their real purpose is to make money. The goal is to help the firm's bottom line—not to integrate principles of diversity into its culture or make changes around who gets hired and who gets promoted. In many industries, differing political ideas are either ignored, discouraged, or actively opposed. To make our field and careers as bright as possible, we must continue to work at changing existing attitudes and practices.

In this chapter, you will learn what diversity and inclusion are, and how these concepts are being integrated into specific campaigns and messaging strategies. You will also discover the next steps that PR agencies and brands need to take to become more inclusive and fairer in hiring, practicing, and bringing forth different perspectives.

What Do Diversity and Inclusion Mean?

Before discussing how diversity and inclusion can become more integral to PR efforts, it is important to understand what each term means and how it is used in the general context.

Diversity

Several components contribute to **diversity**, such as embracing people who may differ in race, ethnicity, gender, sexuality, culture, and political thought. Interestingly, the significance of diverse political thought is an area that is least explored in discussions about diversity (Duarte et al., 2015). Many brands, such as Airbnb, make sure they have equal representation in all of their promotions, campaigns, and initiatives. But that's not always enough. Diversity is not only about creating messages that represent and draw in people of various backgrounds. It's about engaging with colleagues and audiences who have different backgrounds. This is especially important to those in the PR industry who produce creative content. We all benefit when we and our colleagues can bring different perspectives to the table (King, 2019).

Inclusion

Inclusion is the bringing together of people with different experiences, backgrounds, and ideas to make sure each group is representative of its audiences and the public at large. Inclusion also means educating each other not only on the messaging and ideas that work but on those that do not work or may even offend. Inclusion is all about understanding each other and moving forward together (King, 2019). For example, Everlast, the popular boxing brand, launched a new "trailblazers" campaign featuring new boxers from various audiences, including transgender and amputee boxers. Everlast was able to share real stories and connect with new audiences.

The Differences Between Diversity and Inclusion

There are clear differences between diversity and inclusion. First, diversity refers to the differences within a group, whereas inclusion focuses on how members are treated and how they feel about their work (Puritty et al., 2017). Embracing differences in background, experience, culture, and thought process is part of what diversity means, all of which requires people to understand, appreciate, and respect these differences in the professional setting. Second, it's important to remember that without inclusion, diversity initiatives do not work. Inclusion requires the full integration of resources that will educate a community or organization (Puritty et al., 2017). Third, focusing on differences does not prevent prejudice or stereotyping in society or the workplace. Creating a diversity and inclusion program is a start, but it has to be sustainable and integrated to address, truly and authentically, all perspectives and backgrounds.

How Diverse and Inclusive Is Public Relations?

One of our growing areas of focus in the industry is the issue of diversity as people of color continue to face challenges such as retention (Commission on Public Relations Education, 2018). In her book, Lee Edwards (2015) outlines why public relations, despite its diversity initiatives and programs, has failed to increase diversity and inclusion in the field. In other words, while PR practitioners are "talking" about diversity and inclusion, they are not "walking" the line by fully adopting and implementing these concepts.

The Concerns of Professional Organizations and Educators

Not only are practitioners and scholars raising these concerns, but organizations such as the Public Relations Society of America (PRSA) and even the Commission on Public Relations Education (CPRE) are, too. PRSA (2020) states:

> While the practice of public relations in the United States has undergone dramatic changes, a lack of diversity in the communications profession persists. Many studies indicate that the industry still struggles to attract young black, Asian and Hispanic professionals to pursue public relations as their career of choice.

Overall, public relations is facing major diversity challenges, as Chitkara (2018) explains:

- Racial and gender representation in the industry remains skewed.
- The ethnic makeup in public relations is majority white in the United States (87.9 percent white, 8.3 percent African American, 2.6 percent Asian American, and 5.7 percent Hispanic American).
- Women make up 70 percent of the industry, but only 30 percent are in CEO or other leadership roles.
- Women make on average $6,000 less than their male counterparts.
- Women of color make less money than their white female colleagues.

The CPRE (2018) has discussed how diversity is a concern not only for the industry, but for the academy as well. Given the challenges facing people of color who enter the field, we need much more representation in leadership roles. While there are organizations that claim diversity and inclusion as part of their missions and core business practices, academic researchers and PR professionals say that simply making the "business case" for diversity and inclusion is not enough anymore (CPRE, 2018). This means organizations must do a lot more to implement and integrate these concepts throughout their cultures, processes, and communication initiatives, both in-house and with audiences.

Directives for Change

The biggest thing that agencies, organizations, and professionals need to understand when it comes to diversity is that it must be integrated internally (within the organization itself) as well as externally (in all audience-facing campaigns and events).

Leadership must be diverse.

Making sure that those at the head of organizations are themselves diverse in terms of race, gender, culture, and other factors has been one of the greatest challenges (CPRE, 2018). Many brands and agencies have considered bringing on board a **chief diversity and inclusion officer**, but most have not actually followed through and done so. However, there are leaders from diverse backgrounds at some of today's largest corporations, such as Microsoft (Satya Nadella), Adobe (Shantanu Narayen), Hershey (Michele Buck), and

DIVERSITY AND INCLUSION STATEMENT

This is a sample brand diversity and inclusion statement from Kellogg's, which has had a strong culture and promotion of diversity issues internally and externally as a company. This statement along with more background information on their efforts can be found at https://www.kelloggcompany.com/en_US/about-diversity.html.

Kellogg Company's commitment to diversity can be traced back to our founder, W.K. Kellogg, who was a pioneer in employing women in the workplace and reaching across cultural boundaries. The company continues his legacy more than 100 years later by making diversity and inclusion top priorities.

Throughout our rich and proud history, we have made significant strides toward the more equitable inclusion of women, people of color, lesbians, gays, bisexuals, transgender individuals, people with disabilities, veterans and other demographic groups. Our goal is to reflect the diversity of our consumers throughout our company. We have done much to achieve this objective, and we are firmly committed to making continued progress.

Our focus on diversity enables us to build a culture where all employees are inspired to share their passion, talents and ideas. They become part of a team that works to better serve the needs of our diverse consumers by delivering fresh thinking, product innovations and quality brands.

In addition, thanks to technology, demographic shifts and worldwide connectivity, we live in a world where change occurs at a rapid clip. For Kellogg to be part of, and ahead of, that change, we know we must continue our progress in diversity and inclusion—allowing us to bring our best to people all around the world every day.

This shows that the diversity and inclusion efforts by Kellogg's has history and a long tradition as a core pillar for the company.

It is key to communicate this is not just a new thing for a company or client to integrate into their PR efforts – but more of bringing forth awareness of their history and values as a company on this topic for all of their audiences.

These are some of the groups that are usually classified and focused on diversity and inclusion efforts. It is important to note and adapt if any new groups emerge and need to be added to this section.

This is good to have as an internal commitment as a brand, but it may be also important to note this for their external audiences (e.g., customers, vendors, partners., etc) as well.

Good focus on diversity, but also needs to have some action statements on some of the specific initiatives and efforts that are being made toward inclusion. Many times, there is a strong focus in these efforts on representing diversity, but there needs to be more emphasis on inclusion in these programs as well.

Good list of efforts that shows evidence and commitment toward diversity. It is one thing to state you are supporting diversity, but it is another to walk the walk. In any diversity and inclusion statements, evidence and commitment need to be present.

Diversity and Inclusion Programs

- D&I Champions: We live our founder's values by operating ethically, protecting human rights and embracing diversity and inclusion.
- Marketplace: At Kellogg, consumers are at the heart of what we do.
- Workplace: To serve the needs of our diverse customers, we nurture the talents of our diverse workforce.
- Community: We champion diversity and inclusion in the communities where we live, operate, and serve.
- Business Employee Resource Groups (B/ERGs): Our B/ERGs help us gain critical insight, drive results and positively impact business strategies.
- Awards and Recognition: We continually strive to create an inclusive workplace and are proud to be recognized for our efforts.
- Careers: At Kellogg Company, we're always looking for fresh-thinking achievers to join our diverse team.

General Motors (Mary Barra). More initiatives are being made for changes in leadership roles in the PR agency sector as well (Ketchum, 2017).

However, the common practice for most brands is to hire a **diversity head**, a person who oversees the diversity and inclusion programming, training, and mentoring efforts for the company internally (PR Council, 2018). In addition, diversity heads are in charge of integrating audience research and messaging into PR campaigns to reach diverse audiences. However, for diversity heads to be successful at an agency or with a brand, they must have direct access to the agency head or brand CEO (PR Council, 2018).

Agencies and brands must represent the diversity of their audiences.

For PR professionals, striving for diversity and inclusion means doing so outside of our employers and organizations as well. We must think of our audiences as we prepare messaging, choose channels, and address our audiences' needs and expectations. Doing so will make us most effective in creating a win-win situation.

Hiring practices must embrace diversity and inclusion.

Not only do we need to embed diversity and inclusion values into all of our agencies' internal practices, but we need to particularly emphasize these values when it comes to recruiting and hiring employees, creating internships, and conducting trainings and mentorship programs (CPRE, 2018).

We need to go beyond the "business case" for diversity.

The CPRE (2018) report states that we need to address the "growing call to move beyond focusing only on the business case for diversity, which argues that a diverse organization leads to diverse and creative thinking, which in turn makes an organization nimbler and more competitive and ultimately helps the bottom line" (p. 140). While diversity benefits an organization's bottom line and diversity programs are valuable reputational assets, we need to argue for major benefits to the people in the industry and members of the greater society. Currently, diversity programs do not benefit their intended audiences as much as they benefit the brands themselves (Logan, 2017).

As a 2018 McKinsey report titled "Delivering Through Diversity" points out, there is a positive link between a firm's financial performance and its diversity, which strengthens the financial argument for integrating diversity into leadership (Hunt, Yee, Prince, & Dixon-Fyle, 2018; see also "Science Benefits From Diversity," 2018). However, it is a big problem if audiences believe that a firm's only motive for increasing diversity is to make money. Agencies must recruit and hire diverse employees and establish a sustainable culture of inclusion.

Agencies and brands must implement their diversity programs.

It's one thing to say you are integrating diversity into your brand and hiring practices, but it's another to actually implement practices that will establish diversity and inclusion. We must look at our agencies' internal workings to make sure we are practicing what we preach to (and for) our clients and audiences.

Surprisingly, while many PR agencies state that they're working at becoming more diverse, few have accomplished this. Burson Cohn & Wolfe is noted for the diversity of its leadership team, as are other firms including Weber Shandwick and Ogilvy. These agencies also have employee resource groups (otherwise known as ERGs), which allow employees to come together to ask questions, connect with mentorship opportunities, and host training sessions on diversity and inclusion topics (Shah, 2018). Porter Novelli created the "Porter Novelli Perspectives," which are tools for fostering empathy and connection—and for sharing topics on various subjects related to diversity and inclusion (Shah, 2018).

Some agencies have argued that the activities of ERGs should not be separated from employees' other daily tasks, but instead should be integrated as part of the brand or agency's cultural and business philosophy. Porter Novelli's former CEO, Brad MacAfee, has said:

> For many organizations, diversity and inclusion programs provide initiatives for affinity groups, training, onboarding, and more. The concern I see is that these programs can run separately or parallel to the overall business rather than integrated into daily business strategy. The most senior ranks within an organization must embrace diversity and inclusion as a philosophy for day-to-day operations across the organization, not just outsourced to HR as a program. (Shah, 2018)

Table 4.1 shows a sample of different diversity and inclusion statements. It should be noted that most PR agencies do *not* have a public statement or section of their website dedicated to diversity and inclusion, which shows the need for more education and awareness on this issue in the field.

▼ TABLE 4.1

Sample Diversity and Inclusion Statements

Brand/Agency/Corporation	Statement	Source
Edelman	"At Edelman, we know that diversity of all types—gender, race, ethnicity, age, sexual orientation, religion, veteran's status, disability and more—and inclusion enhance our vibrant work culture and help deliver stronger business results. We also believe that a workforce, comprised of employees from all demographics and with diversity in backgrounds and experiences, provides our clients with diverse perspectives that reflect our changing world and enhances our vibrant work culture. Through maximizing and leveraging this talent we are able to provide innovative and creative solutions for our clients which is central to who we are and what we do at Edelman."	www.edelman.com/careers/diversity-and-inclusion
Ketchum	"Enhancing idea generation, bringing forth differentiated perspectives, and improving business outcomes are all reasons businesses focus on their commitment to diversity, equity and inclusion. As a communications consultancy, and on behalf of our clients, these motivating factors play a role, but the most important consideration is our commitment to the employees who work here."	www.ketchum.com/diversity-equity-inclusion-assembling-a-symphony-of-leaders-as-we-push-for-progress/

Kellogg's	"About 10 years ago, Kellogg made diversity and inclusion a key corporate initiative. And in 2005, Kellogg established an Office of Diversity and Inclusion. Since that time, this office has been singularly focused on recruiting and retaining diverse employees, creating awareness of diversity issues, fostering a supportive, positive environment where inclusive behaviors are the norm, and embedding accountability for diversity throughout the organization. Through these efforts we place value in our people and nurture their development while ensuring that all employees go through a consistent process and have equal opportunity for success. We are committed to creating an environment where all employees are included, are treated with dignity and respect and are in a position to contribute to our future success. Fostering all employees' passion for our business will help us win in the marketplace. Kellogg Company is making great progress in the area of diversity and inclusion. But we still have work to do and much to learn."	www.kelloggcompany.com/en_US/about-diversity.html
Adidas	"At adidas, diversity isn't a box to check, it's our secret formula for inventing the future of sport. Adi Dassler built his business with an insight that is still true today: Every innovation starts with seeing a problem through fresh eyes. To invent new solutions, you need to see a problem in as many different ways as possible. The more unique identities, backgrounds and perspectives we can assemble at adidas, the easier it is to find our way around roadblocks and change lives through the sports we love. To attract and retain a diverse team, we place a premium on creating and living an inclusive, respectful company culture. It's why our world headquarters boasts employees of 100 nationalities, why we've been ranked one of the most LGBT-friendly companies around, and why we are cultivating a gender-balanced leadership. It's why we stay at the cutting edge of sport culture."	https://careers.adidas-group.com/life-here/diversity?locale=en
Coca-Cola	"As both a global and local business, diversity and inclusion are at the heart of our values and is an important part of Coca-Cola's success. For us, creating a diverse workforce and inclusive workplace is not only the right thing to do—it is a strategic business priority that fosters greater creativity, innovation and connection to the communities we serve. The Global Office of Diversity and Inclusion is responsible for driving strategy, ownership, and results of diversity and inclusion across the company. Serving as an internal consultant, the Diversity and Inclusion Office works cross-functionally with senior leaders, Human Resources, Business Resource Groups and Councils to help create an inclusive environment. We focus on four strategic imperatives under the CARE acronym: create, articulate, regulate and evaluate. 1. **Create** an inclusive environment by engaging diverse talent and influencing recruitment, development, advancement and retention. 2. **Articulate** our Diversity & Inclusion progress through proactive communications. 3. **Regulate** and manage workplace equality, fairness and 4. **Evaluate** by creating and updating a systematic set of tools and resources."	www.coca-colacompany.com/policies-and-practices/global-diversity-and-inclusion-mission

(Continued)

Twitter	"All voices welcome. All voices needed. Our goal is for the team that makes Twitter to be as diverse as the people who use it."	https://careers.twitter.com/en/tweep-life.html
Airbnb	"Airbnb is truly powered by people—both our hosts and guests around the world and internal community of employees and business partners shape the ways we work and grow. We believe that diversity is essential to building a world where everyone can feel they belong, and we're taking action to end discrimination and build a more inclusive company. We're committed to transparency as we work to make Airbnb a workplace where everyone feels welcome and all voices are heard."	www.airbnb.com/diversity

What Benefits Do Diversity and Inclusion Bring to Public Relations?

As we work to make public relations more diverse and inclusive, we find that many opportunities arise when we bring on board people with different perspectives and backgrounds. The field has been somewhat at a standstill when it comes to bringing forth new talent and ideas, and what better way to bring public relations into the 21st century than to embrace a new global and inclusive community in the workplace?

The Benefits of Diversity and Inclusion: In the Workplace

A major benefit of integrating diversity and inclusion in the workplace—of working with colleagues of different backgrounds—is being able to draw on new creativity and strategies (Phillips, 2014).

A More Dynamic Work Environment

Being able to bounce around ideas among colleagues from all backgrounds and perspectives can bring forth new and innovative ideas.

Greater Creativity and Improved Messaging

A major benefit of integrating diversity and inclusion is being able to draw on new creativity and strategies (Phillips, 2014). By gaining insight and feedback from different groups, PR teams can better work together to create interesting content.

Better Collaboration, Problem Solving, and Response to Challenges

If we want to be effective in reaching key audiences in a certain group, we have to make sure we work with colleagues who are part of these communities. Doing so will help us align with our messages, ensure that we're respecting the perspectives and values of others, and allow us to be as successful as possible in making decisions and creating campaigns. Further, when practitioners have different viewpoints, we can actually help solve problems faster (Phillips, 2014).

The Benefits of Diversity and Inclusion: In Audience-Facing Communications

Another major benefit of integrating diversity and inclusion is the potential to engage with new audiences, including growing global audiences (Phillips, 2014).

Audiences are more engaged by inclusive strategies.

If audiences see, feel, and experience stories that they receive from people like themselves, they will be more likely to engage with the brand or company involved.

Audiences respond to diverse campaigns.

Representation matters, and it's important that everyone in the audience finds someone or something to identify with in a PR campaign.

A major benefit of integrating diversity and inclusion is fresh engagement with audiences, including growing global audiences (Phillips, 2014).

The Benefits of Diversity and Inclusion: For the General Public

New efforts toward collaboration, idea creation, and idea execution are just some of what brands and PR professionals gain when diversity and inclusion are central to our missions (Phillips, 2014). These gains, in turn, are viewed positively by the public, and can spark the following.

A More Positive View of Public Relations, Greater Goodwill

We all come into the field from different perspectives, so it is good to see different backgrounds, stories, and people represented.

Potentially, an Influx of New Talent

Inclusive campaigns raise the profile of public relations and attract audiences that include potential colleagues. To grow as a field, we have to open our minds to new possibilities and talent that can help shape public relations for the future.

Fairer Workplaces and a Better Environment, for All

Integrating diversity and inclusion into public relations can foster the growth of new ideas for addressing challenges and opportunities on a large scale. Following are some of the issues that PR agencies and companies are addressing, thanks to efforts to become more diverse and inclusive.

- *A greater focus on gender pay issues.* Many companies and brands would like to do better in this area, but LUNA®, which is part of the health food company Clif Bar, partnered with celebrity actress and sports figure Gina Rodriguez to create a campaign to support pay equality on Equal Pay Day (Clif Bar & Company, 2017). For this campaign, LUNA created a plan that worked with LeanIn.org to launch #20PercentCounts, and the company offered 20 percent off any bars sold during the week of Equal Pay Day. Rodriguez said she wanted to partner with LUNA because of the issue women face with the pay gap (Clif Bar & Company, 2017). Along with this partnership, LUNA was able to support the U.S. women's national soccer team in a big way by donating $718,750 to the players' bonuses for the 2019 World Cup (Guzior, 2019). This made the bonuses the female players received equal to what the U.S. men's national soccer team players received.

  Working with LUNA was Golin (2020), a leading PR agency, and as a result of this campaign, LUNA gained a 30 percent increase in bar sales, a 283 percent

LUNA Bar ✓
@LUNAbar

We love when badass ladies stand up for what they deserve. And we're in awe of U.S. Women's National Soccer Team (@USWNTPlayers). Learn how we're helping them level the playing field. Because equality can't wait for someday. #somedayisnow #Equalpayday

♡ 1,379   12:30 PM - Apr 2, 2019

💬 453 people are talking about this   ❯

LUNA supports equal pay
Twitter/@LUNAbar

increase in traffic to its website, and a nine-point Brand Love Score increase. This is significant since it shows this is a powerful issue many audience members want to support, and PR professionals need to evaluate how they can align brands and their clients strategically with such issues and topics in a natural way that resonates with audiences.

- *A greater representation of women, people of color, and more.* Another area of focus for diversity and inclusion campaigns is representation—of races, ethnicities, genders, sexual orientations, and disabilities, for example.

1. *IBM.* The popular global technology company IBM wanted to focus on identifying unknown figures who had made a significant impact on the field of science, technology, engineering, and mathematics (STEM). To raise awareness of their contributions, IBM used augmented reality (AR) technology to spotlight and highlight 10 "hidden figures" from history in different parts of the United States (Webby Awards, 2018). The overall purpose of this campaign was to inspire future hopefuls with the accomplishments of these historic figures in the industry (Webby Awards, 2018). IBM has been a supporter of diversity and inclusion initiatives for decades, and felt this campaign raised awareness of the diverse workplaces that have existed in history and gave praise to those who have made an impact on the profession.

2. *MGM.* Campaigns focused on engaging with the lesbian, gay, bisexual, transgender, and queer/questioning (LGBTQ) community have continued to grow over the past few decades, and some brands and campaigns have been strategic and innovative in the PR space. The Human Rights Campaign's Corporate Equality Index discusses the rise in the numbers of companies investing in sexual orientation and gender identity training and protection measures (Kozuch, 2019). Some of the findings shown in the latest report are that

- 16.8 million employees now work in a place where there is a policy prohibiting discrimination based on sexual orientation and gender identity;

- gender identity is now part of the nondiscrimination policy at 85 percent of Fortune 500 companies, an increase from just 3 percent in 2002; and

- more than 500 employers have adopted inclusion guidelines for transgender workers (Kozuch, 2019).

For example, MGM Resorts launched a campaign to tie into the LGBT community its investment in the music industry. MGM Resorts partnered with established musicians and launched *Universal Love*, a music album that reimagined traditional love songs and rephrased them from an LGBTQ point of view (Shorty Awards, n.d.b). As a result of the campaign, *Universal Love* made it to number 9 on iTunes with 440,000 streams within the first month after launch (Shorty Awards, n.d.-b).

3. *Uno.* Uno, the popular card game with four colors, partnered with Weber Shandwick (2020) to create a campaign to allow individuals who are color blind to play the game. The overall goal of this campaign was to focus on inclusion—that anyone should be able to play the game. Uno, which is owned by Mattel, not only generated a lot of media coverage for this campaign, but was able to make a difference in an untapped market for the brand and foster a relationship with a new audience (Weber Shandwick, 2020). By including new audiences in this campaign, Uno was able to extend its reach as a brand and community.

4. *Warrior Games.* Other PR agencies have launched specific campaigns to target other underrepresented groups in society. In 2017, Edelman partnered with the Warrior Games (2020), an event in which about 300 wounded, ill, and injured service members and veterans compete each year. During this campaign, Edelman (2020) created research, message strategies, and target outreach for this event in 2017, the first year the competition would not be held on a military base and would be open to the public. By doing this, Edelman helped educate and invite the community to be part of an overall experience and see athletes and armed forces veterans come together to compete. In addition, this event helped raise awareness about the injuries and illnesses that affect our veterans from all over the world. The athletes represent not only U.S.-based military armed forces, but also those from Canada, the United Kingdom, the Netherlands, and Australia (Warrior Games, 2020). The overall focus of the initiative was not only to generate awareness about the event, but to educate the public on why it is so important to have such events (Edelman, 2020).

Warrior Games competition
Aclosund Historic / Alamy Stock Photo

5. *Microsoft.* In another campaign, Microsoft brought forth the message of accessibility and representation in its 2019 Super Bowl campaign featuring children with disabilities (Warren, 2019).

In the company's commercial titled "We All In," Microsoft was able to showcase how all children—no matter their standing in life and despite their disability—can play one of its games with the Xbox Adaptive Controller (Holt, 2019). Microsoft's commercial was one of the best reviewed for the 2019 event for its strong message of inclusivity (Fitzpatrick & Law, 2019).

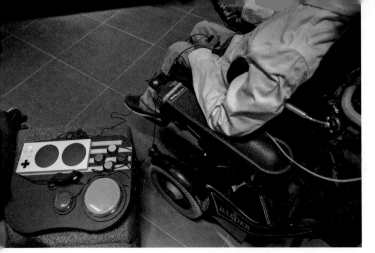

Microsoft Xbox Adaptive Controller

Bloomberg / Getty Images

Both the Warrior Games/Edelman and Microsoft campaigns, which focused on representation, brought together two groups that may not have been represented traditionally before, and included them as part of a brand identity and community. These campaigns embraced the full essence of what it means to be inclusive in our work, our communication practices, and our PR initiatives.

- *More successful community initiatives.* Another way to engage with the community that a brand, agency, or PR professional represents is to work on community initiatives. Community initiatives are cause-related or audience-driven projects to build forth a stronger line of communication and enhance relationship building.

1. *Atlanta Hawks.* The Hawks, a professional basketball team headquartered in Atlanta, Georgia, realized their audience and their city were diverse in nature, and wanted to make sure they were able to create an environment committed to diversity and inclusion not just at work but also in playing basketball (Shorty Awards, n.d.-a).

This integrated campaign with the Atlanta Hawks focused on

- engaging audiences that are underrepresented in the Atlanta community, which the team invited to a conference titled Mosaic, which featured speakers including sports commentator Jemele Hill and transgender businesswoman Gabrielle Claiborne;

- creating business resources for specific groups focused primarily on women and the LGBTQ community, including Love Wins Pride Night (NBA Media Ventures, 2020);

- having conversations among employees called Courageous Conversations to discuss external events and issues, which brought forth more awareness of these issues internally; and

- making sure no one suffers from discrimination as a result of race, ethnicity, gender, sexual orientation, or any other reason.

What Best Practices Can Make Public Relations More Diverse and Inclusive?

As PR professionals, to bring diversity and inclusion into our environments, we need to consider some specific principles and concrete practices.

We Need to Implement Principles

Public relations as a field needs to be more diverse and inclusive in its efforts across the board. From talent management to campaign representation, much work still needs to be done to foster this movement in the field. However, there are ways in which public relations can move forward in addressing these efforts in a proactive manner, as discussed in this section.

Support

Support can come in different forms, including emotional, financial, time, and sustainable commitment. As stated earlier in this chapter, diversity and inclusion initiatives are somewhat implemented, but do not always have the complete internal support needed to make them sustainable. Investing in diversity and inclusion efforts does not happen overnight; it must be a purposeful and long-term investment for the organization, agency, or corporation. This support has to come not only from an emotional or business perspective, but also from a financial one. These programs are not free, and to fully commit to implementing diversity and inclusion, they must have some financial backing to make sure the right leadership, employees, programs, and trainings are implemented. On-board training of employees, mentoring programs, and sponsorship of diverse employees are all areas that need to be supported and invested in internally (Chitkara, 2018).

Leadership

Leadership is not only present and invested in diversity and inclusion efforts, but leaders also represent the diversity of candidates and audiences they represent. Leadership has to bring forth to the table a wide range of candidates with different backgrounds, perspectives, and experiences. If all leaders come from the same background, no new ideas will emerge.

Hiring Practices

We often hear of hiring practices in which all backgrounds of candidates are considered, but are they really? A look at the job market and who is actually hired suggests this may be something public relations needs to work on, and that goes for the traditional areas of gender, ethnicity and experience, and even education. Yes, including individuals with different educational backgrounds is key to having a diverse PR group. Certain programs have the same perspective, or school of thought, of how and why public relations operates. While it is key to understand these various perspectives and curriculums, this fosters the same mentality among the young professionals entering the industry. Companies, across the board, are faced with the daunting task of exploring the challenges and opportunities the future will bring to our work in the PR field. Some say it is more challenging than ever to find "the right talent." However, that may be due to the fact that companies and agencies are only looking in certain areas, and not seeing the complete picture. Chitkara (2018) made this very point in a discussion of how companies and agencies need to open up recruitment by fostering more diverse relationships with colleges to build a pipeline for talent. It is important to expand our options beyond the established PR programs and branch out to the emerging ones.

Experiences

Experience and background are two important elements to consider in public relations when it comes to candidates. Not all applicants to work in public relations come in from a traditional PR background in school. Some come in from journalism, which is quite common, but others come in from English, computer science, graphic design, and even history. These different experiences emphasize for public relations the fact that everyone has different levels of experience and background, and this should be considered and encouraged.

Perspectives

Perspective refers to the ideology a PR professional brings to the table. This is one area that has not been discussed as much in public relations, but considering different perspectives can help us better understand our audiences in a more comprehensive way. Having a mixture of political thought on a team can bring forth a better understanding of how certain audiences think, feel, and react to certain messages or initiatives. If we go forward with only one perspective in mind, we will have only one piece of the puzzle. Ignoring all political, religious, and lifestyle perspectives is like driving while wearing a blindfold. To gain all perspectives, diversity of thought needs to be taken into consideration internally by companies and agencies.

We Need to Implement Practices

PR education, research, and practice are moving forward to integrate more diversity and inclusion measures every year, but still there is room to grow as a field. To foster growth and incorporate these principles into our profession, there are some recommendations and best practices we can integrate into our daily activities in our work.

Focus on Respect

As PR professionals, we may not always agree with each other on certain topics and areas, but it is important that we respect each other and acknowledge these disagreements in a professional manner. This has actually been a focus for several brand campaigns, including one with *Sesame Street*, the popular children's show, whose "Respect Brings Us Together" campaign focuses on how people can get along (Sesame Workshop, 2019). The campaign features pop culture icons discussing the topic of respect with popular *Sesame Street* characters, such as when Cersei and Tyrion Lannister from the hit show *Game of Thrones* meet Elmo.

Game of Thrones siblings Cersei and Tyrion Lannister, with the Muppet character Elmo as negotiator

tvweb.com

For this campaign, characters Cersei and Tyrion, who do not have the best relationship, sit down with Elmo to discuss the importance of treating each other fairly, respectfully, and professionally. This was the first partnership between *Game of Thrones* and *Sesame Street*, and it focused on the messages of civility and the importance of understanding different points of view.

The president and CEO of Sesame Workshop, Jeffrey D. Dunn, stated in the campaign announcement:

> Our society is increasingly divided on many issues, and we know that kids pick up on this tension. We have always shown preschoolers that everyone is welcome on *Sesame Street*. Our hope with this campaign is that a lighthearted look at a very serious subject can help us all pause for a moment to remember the value in respecting the viewpoints of others, even when they differ greatly from our own. (Sesame Workshop, 2019)

To move forward with diversity and inclusion programs and initiatives, PR professionals first and foremost have to respect each other based on what makes us different and unique. Bringing forth different perspectives, whether we agree with them or not, helps generate further conversations and can help the field and society move forward.

Teach Diverse and Multicultural Perspectives

Diversity and inclusion topics are necessary to cover not only in the United States, but also in other parts of the world. In PR courses, we have to integrate both national and global perspectives of diversity and inclusion in our classes, assignments, and exercises. We are a global society, and we have to understand the ways in which diversity and inclusion practices are implemented around the world in public relations, as well as identify some of the global opportunities and challenges that need to be addressed.

Support Research in Diversity and Inclusion

PR scholars Natalie Tindall (Lamar University), Dean Mundy (University of Oregon), and Erica Ciszek (University of Texas at Austin) are some of the scholars who are researching various aspects of diversity and inclusion in PR practices. Not only do we need to better understand the underlying issues and challenges facing public relations, but we need to determine best practices and strategic applications for how the industry can address them. More collaboration and partnerships with researchers and industry need to happen in this area.

Support Empathy in Leadership

For real change to happen internally within a company or agency in terms of diversity initiatives, the leaders need to feel that they belong (Florentine, 2019). Implementing a top-down approach or one separate diversity and inclusion program is not enough. A leader has to listen, evaluate, and invest in trainings throughout the organization while adopting new measures to address the current issues and challenges in society with all employees.

Be Agile, Proactive, and Responsive to Change

Like technology and other forms of media, diversity and inclusion issues and challenges are evolving. PR professionals need to audit and review what they are doing presently with their diversity and inclusion efforts, what is missing, what is working, and what steps need to be taken to move forward. These efforts need to be evaluated on a consistent basis internally, and findings should be shared internally for everyone to see.

GAME CHANGER

Kara DeLost, Marking Professional at KFC Yum! Brands

@iwantbdphotography

How did you get your start in the industry?

Networking and as a mentor. Definitely not grades or a graduate degree. I got started because I was willing to get a job in the meantime, and really looked into what I wanted to do. And then, I finally got what I wanted.

Here's how it went: the worst way ever. I was working part-time making cold calls, while interviewing at an agency. I didn't get the job. Then a few weeks later, the company I was working for got bought out by the agency I was rejected from. And then, I had to see everyone who rejected me . . . every day. No one has to see those people ever, usually. I had to see them every day. I kept putting myself out there, and eventually, I was hired on at the agency full-time.

I wrote a blog; it was picked up by *Forbes*. I was only 22 at the time. It doesn't feel big now, but it did then. I won some local awards and moved up in the agency world. I took a director position on my 26th birthday. It was one of the best experiences of my life, but it was time for a change.

Now I'm at KFC headquarters making drinks with Pepsi.

What is your favorite part of working in the industry?

Being a part of culture. Having a job that I can talk to anyone about, and they can relate. Being in brand is something I genuinely enjoy about my life.

What is the most challenging part of working in your industry?

It's all subjective. Learning to have an opinion is hard. Having to fight for your opinion to matter is hard. Learning to articulate and defend your opinion is hard. But a lot of what we do as marketers is subjective,

and there is some nuttiness about that, and the lack of diversity. Both in advertising and in corporate, I've had to lead and educate on diversity. It's a burden at times. And most of the time that burden is never understood or compensated for—you always have to do it as volunteer work. I know things are getting better, but until we have a real understanding of representation and institutional barriers, it's always going to be a battle. We need to do better, y'all.

Who do you think are the biggest game changers for your industry?

I don't know—this is a really hard question. It's hard to name a company or a person or a generation or a "who" that feels like a good answer.

But really, I like brands like Lululemon. I think Netflix rules our world just as much as Apple and Google and Amazon. I think people will always love shopping at Target and eating McDonald's. I think everyone loves ice cream, and more people hate dairy. I think Gen Z is scared; I think women will lead the way. I think multi-ethnic people will change the game. I think we're all a part of being the game changers.

What are some things you wish you knew when you were starting out in the industry?

Politics are a real thing—may the odds ever be in your favor. Burnout is real—keep an active relationship with your mental and emotional health. You gotta move—staying in one place for too long will not benefit you or the company. You're not going to get paid that much in advertising, hence the move to corporate. The only person responsible for your career is you—never be afraid to speak up for what you want. It's a tough industry to be in, no matter what your function is.

Have fun—enjoy the ride and tell the story; that's all a part of it.

Kara DeLost is an agency girl turned fried chicken saleswoman, living in Louisville, Kentucky. After six years of working in the agency world, she took the jump many of those battered souls make (only kidding, kind of) and turned "client side" when she joined KFC US working in brand. From the "social media girl" to the "beverage girl," Kara is currently in the newest chapter of her career as she navigates the experience of corporate America. She's a typical millennial with an old-school heart. She loves the work she does but understands the importance of work-life balance and trying to maintain relevant, healthy, and happy.

At work she's launching KFC's first exclusive soft drink with PepsiCo, and at home she's teaching yoga, sharing her experience as a Korean American adoptee, and taking pictures of her dog, Noodle.

She's passionate about culture, her sister is a pastry chef in Chicago (featured on Food Network twice), and she lives a fairly normal life—or so she says. The rest of her résumé is on LinkedIn.

Connect professionally: LinkedIn (www.linkedin.com/ in/karadelost)

Connect personally: Instagram (www.instagram.com/ kdelost)

SUMMARY

While public relations has embraced diversity and inclusion initiatives of late, the field has a long way to go to really accomplish this across the board. Presently, only a few agencies and companies have launched diversity and inclusion programs, and those who have are only focusing on certain types of diversity and inclusion. If public relations is going to be a leader in this area, it has to invest, support, and sustain complete diversity and inclusion measures across the board. In addition, more education and training are necessary to discuss the importance of and best practices for how to accomplish this both in practice and in education.

The Commission on Public Relations Education in its 2018 report has set forth a good foundation for what needs to be emphasized in PR curriculum, yet it still is missing different aspects of diversity and inclusion, such as education, political, religious, and lifestyle perspectives.

With that being said, there is room to grow and expand this effort in the PR field. More discussion and work need to be done, but this is an area of opportunity to come together as a field to make sure we are not only talking about diversity and inclusion, but also walking the walk and leading the other disciplines (communication, marketing, journalism, etc.) in this way.

APR EXAM

- Diversity and inclusion in public relations
- Definition of diversity
- Diversity in public relations
- Commission on Public Relations Education

KEY TERMS

Chief diversity and inclusion officer 71

Diversity 70

Diversity head 73

Inclusion 70

DISCUSSION QUESTIONS

1. What is the difference between diversity and inclusion?
2. What are three ways diversity and inclusion help PR efforts?
3. Explain what a diversity and inclusion statement is.
4. What areas of diversity and inclusion are represented in PR efforts? Identify one category and discuss a case study that represents this.

ACTIVITIES

Building Your Portfolio

Writing a diversity and inclusion statement and policy. You have been asked to do research and create a diversity and inclusion policy for your internship project. For this activity, you will have to do each of the following:

- Research how PR agencies, brands, and organizations address diversity and inclusion.
- Outline what they are doing as far as activities and programs for their employees (e.g., chief diversity and inclusion officer).

CASE STUDY

The Beyoncé and Adidas Partnership: Diversity and Leadership

BEYONCÉ

Beyoncé × Adidas logo
Adidas.com

Beyoncé is one of the biggest stars in the entertainment business. Her brand has flourished over the years from her music with Destiny's Child to her solo career. Beyoncé of course has been selective in her partnership and endorsement deals with her personal brand. Yet, in 2019, she announced she would partner with Adidas to create a new shoe and clothing line with the athletic apparel company (Bromwich & Friedman, 2019). As Eric Liedtke, executive board member for global brands at Adidas, mentioned:

> As the creator sports brand, Adidas challenges the status quo and pushes the limits of creativity through its open source approach. Beyoncé is an iconic creator but also a proven business leader, and together, we have the ability to inspire change and empower the next generation of creators. ("Adidas and Beyoncé Announce Iconic Partnership," 2019)

When the partnership was announced, it was reported that Beyoncé actually declined a partnership deal with Reebok by stating to Reebok staff members: "Nobody in this room reflects my background, my skin color, and where I'm from and what I want to do" (Gassam, 2019). However, Reebok released a statement denying this was the case (Amatulli, 2019).

Beyoncé is known in business for requiring black representation in her partnerships. To work with Adidas, she needed to first make sure that the brand was truly diverse and inclusive of people of color in attitude, culture, and work environment. She made this point when she announced her partnership with Adidas, sparking a discussion among brands, businesses, organizations, and agencies that diversity and inclusion are now part of what is expected of them.

Why did this generate buzz?

- This generated a lot of discussion and press due to the fact Beyoncé is a global superstar who has had a strong voice and opinion regarding the issue of diversity in the industry and for her brand.

- Many have attributed her observation of the lack of diversity in leadership roles in this case as jump-starting a bigger conversation on the issue across different sectors and businesses in society.

What are the ethical and legal issues?

- There are some legal considerations to be had here. While it is important to have diverse representation in leadership roles, focusing on one aspect of diversity above others has to be taken with consideration.

- While diversity brings forth new perspectives and helps represent our global society, the issue and question for this case moving forward is inclusivity. By focusing on our differences, we lose light to what can bring us together for a common purpose.

- Employee hiring and human resource practices have to be reviewed to determine if all diversity areas are considered along with the necessary expertise, experience, and skills.

What are some of the major takeaways from this case?

- More audiences are looking for brands, agencies, and companies who are able to integrate diversity and inclusion not just on their website, but also throughout the different levels of their organization from top to bottom.

- There is a growing focus on diversity, but inclusion is still an afterthought even with this case. To address this area of public relations, we have to make sure we are accounting for all audiences and working together, not creating more divisions between groups and audiences.

- Collect and analyze their definitions of what it means to embrace diversity and inclusion.
- Identify what is missing, and some proactive initiatives for embracing diversity and inclusion.
- Outline best practices and policies you would recommend that embrace both diversity and inclusion.

Building Your Brand

- Every brand, agency, and organization should have a diversity and inclusion statement as part of its mission and vision statement. As PR professionals today, and as we will learn in Chapter 6 on personal branding, we all have a brand as well, and so will need to include our own diversity and inclusion statement.
- Write what your diversity and inclusion statement will be as a PR professional. Make sure this statement is two to three sentences in length. Provide your rationale for why this will be your statement as a PR professional and how you will integrate it as part of your brand and in professional documents (résumé, cover letters, website and social media platforms, etc.).

CHAPTER 5

RESEARCH AND EVIDENCE-BASED PRACTICES

- Define research and understand its role in public relations.

- Understand evidence-based practices for research.

- Understand research methods—how to conduct, evaluate, and apply research.

- Determine best practices for conducting research.

Introduction

How do PR professionals know whether something is a good idea? What materials do we need to plan, create, implement, and support a compelling campaign? How do we build and manage solidly grounded relationships? The answer is, we have tools—and some of them may surprise you.

Now is a good time to ask yourself why you are interested in the field of public relations. Some common responses include these:

- "Because I am a people person."

- "Because I am creative."

- "Because I don't want to deal with numbers or technical stuff."

These statements reflect some misconceptions. Yes, ours is a people-focused industry, but it is more than that. It is a systematic and strategic field in which data and numbers are part of every campaign, action, and communication with clients and the public. In the 21st century, public relations is both a creative and a scientific field, and research encompasses both areas naturally. If you have a curious mind, an affinity

Research: PR people work with facts, figures, and spreadsheets.

iStock.com/fizkes

for facts and numbers, and an enthusiasm for blending your creative and scientific talents, let's get you started. If not, this may be the time to reconsider public relations as a possible career choice.

What Is Research? How Does It Function in Public Relations?

In the PR industry, we research information and use it strategically in our campaigns and in all of the work we do for our clients and organizations. **Research** provides us with data and insights that will boost our credibility, help us make positive first impressions, and allow us to do our best work. Public relations embraces research in a variety of ways. Sometimes agencies conduct their own research in-house, while in other situations a research or marketing firm is brought in from the outside. Given the state of the economy, many agencies that used to outsource research are bringing it back inside, raising the expectation that new hires will have strong research skills. In fact, research is one of the top skills (along with writing, covered in Chapter 7) expected of today's PR professionals.

To succeed in public relations, you will need knowledge of what research entails—why and how it is done, and how findings are evaluated and applied in the workplace and industry. As you learn to conduct research using various methods, you will also learn how to analyze your data and put it to use, activities that require a sense of balance. Gathering big data (collecting a vast amount of digital data to analyze, interpret, and report the findings based on the information collected) is quite the rage for PR agencies, but if we do not know how to apply the insights we gain in a meaningful way, we just end up with a lot of data floating around. On the flip side, focusing on the creative application of insights without knowledge of where the ideas came from is also limiting. We need to give research and application equal consideration.

Research Defined

Research is the *systematic gathering of information conducted in a scientific and objective manner* to help answer questions. It is one of the primary duties we have as PR professionals. PR research can come in various forms:

- Conducting focus groups to determine the right copy and messaging that needs to be incorporated into content for audiences

- Interviews on the perception of a brand after a crisis situation (see Chapter 6 for more on branding)

- Social media analysis to determine the history, previous campaigns, and health of the community of potential influencers to collaborate with

- Experiments to determine which message frame to use for a new campaign among targeted audiences

RESEARCH AND EVIDENCE-BASED PRACTICES

Research is one of the most important tasks a public relations professional needs to have in their toolkit. There are many approaches and methods that are used in research—from traditional to evolving. Research is not black and white. It is a mixture of grays following a long continuum of different attributes that make it hard to determine which method, service, platform, or metrics to use. Here are some that are commonly used by public relations professionals.

QUALITATIVE RESEARCH METHODS

Qualitative research methods address questions of quality and characteristics that emerge for researchers and professionals. Qualitative research is more about exploring what is happening in detail on a one-to-one basis, or one-to-many.

- Interviews, focus groups, and ethnographic methods fall into this category.

QUANTITATIVE RESEARCH

Quantitative research addresses questions of "what" or "how many," and is usually evaluated using formal statistical methods. This type of research focuses on more objective measures and aims to predict how certain concepts and variables will act in a controlled setting.

- Experiments, surveys, and questionnaires are examples of this type of research.

SOCIAL MEDIA ANALYSIS

Social media analysis is not new, per se, but as social media channels evolve, so do the metrics and third-party tools associated with each platform.

- Examples of channel (or platform) analytics include Facebook Insights and Twitter Analytics.
- Third-party tools include Salesforce, Zoomph, Talkwalker, Brandwatch, and Crimson Hexagon.

SOCIAL NETWORK ANALYSIS

This approach is otherwise known as SNA, which looks at the social relations and structures that emerge in a community through networks and graphs. Social media is a collection of accounts and profiles that are interlinked and connected to each other. By using social network analysis, public relations professionals are able to see the ties, links (relationships), and size of a community that is part of a particular account.

- Other tools like NodeXL, Mentionmapp, Audiense, and SocNetv also help visualize communities online.

NEUROMARKETING

The tie between Edward Bernays and Sigmund Freud in psychology is not the only connection that is emerging for public relations professionals. Participants' brain activity can be assessed using brain imaging technologies as they respond to images and messages and make decisions.

- Network analysis to determine unique connections and relationships among influencers and advocates online for a potential influencer collaboration project

- Media monitoring and content analysis projects to determine overall tone and impact of a brand in the media

These are just a few of the ways in which PR professionals can conduct research in their practices. However, it all comes down to the research tools and methods that are at our disposal, and some are used more frequently than others. Some methods are traditional in nature, whereas others have been created to fit the growing digital trends facing the industry. The important factor to note here is to be skilled and experienced in each of these methods to build upon your research tool kit as a PR professional. The more tools you have, the more effective and marketable you will be as a PR professional in helping to answer significant questions facing the industry, community, and society.

The Role of Research in Public Relations

Research can provide direction for understanding our key audiences. For example, Popeyes® Louisiana Kitchen, which has a strong fan base, likely conducted focus groups or other research in 2018–2019 to determine that launching a new chicken sandwich would make its fan base happy, improve its brand relationships, and even reach new customers.

Research can also help us identify any gaps and opportunities relative to our competitors, as can be seen in the work of Tesla and Ford. After Tesla released its Cybertruck in 2019, Ford immediately responded with how it could be competitive with the Tesla brand. Yet Tesla had noted this competition ahead of the Cybertruck release and was prepared for its competitors to respond. Further, research helps us describe current environmental landscapes such as the growing changes in influencer marketing for public relations. Brands such as Kellogg's, Pacific Gas & Electric, and Adidas have all done research exploring the benefits of tapping influencers, and how to do so, which has helped them in their own practices. In addition, Starbucks, in the context of its recent crises and problems with addressing diversity and inclusion, has likely been conducting research in an effort to retrain staff and improve the brand's reputation. Lastly, research can pinpoint motivational factors and user attitudes toward various trends and brands, as is the case for Toys "R" Us. The company went bankrupt in 2019, but is being brought back thanks to the overall nostalgia that people have for the brand. No doubt its research efforts are aimed at helping the company connect with customers and reemerge successfully.

Research in public relations is universally important for the following reasons.

Research informs our campaigns and strategies

Research is crucial to building a foundation for creating effective strategies. Media monitoring and social listening methods allow us to understand which stories, messages, and approaches will be most effective for a company or brand. For example, Disney was relatively late to the game when it came to streaming services like Netflix, Hulu, and HBO. But Disney took the time to use modern research methods, such as social listening, to determine whether the company should get into the mix of streaming services and compete with the big brands for the slice of the pie. As a result of this research, Disney+ was born. Upon launch, Disney+ quickly realized it had a hit on its hands given the amount of audience engagement with new show *The Mandalorian* featuring new character Baby Yoda. However, once audiences began to share GIFs and other images of Baby Yoda on social media, Disney reacted by telling audiences to stop using Baby Yoda's image, which is copyrighted. Based on the media coverage, outrage, and discussions that followed on social media, Disney reevaluated its stance on the Baby Yoda issue. This example shows that research and competitive analysis can not only help a company such as Disney to enter a new space with a brand, but also help those behind the brand to better understand the passions and wishes of their fans.

Research helps us determine the following.

- What is the best type of campaign and content for this situation? If a client's company or brand is in crisis, what concerns do we need to address?

- What are our audiences experiencing? How or why are audiences engaging—or not—with the content (video, images, memes, text, etc.) whether on- or offline?

- Which key messages will be most effective? Where and how should we communicate these messages?

Research is the basis for innovation

Research can serve as the foundation for new ideas and innovations. Creativity is at the heart of public relations, and research can indeed be creative as well. This is what was illustrated in the Disney+ example. Creativity has a place in research, and evaluating what insights are gathered through various methods can help PR professionals come up with new applications for addressing new expectations and challenges. Exploring new insights is a perfect jumping-off point for a PR professional to start something new. For example, two brands you may not see collaborating on an everyday basis are the mint company Tic Tac and the music streaming service Spotify. However, based on competitive analysis, the two brands joined together to create a mutually beneficial experience called Hear for It, a new interactive event. Spotify will help target listeners to promote the personality of Tic Tac for its audiences.

While research in public relations provides many benefits, it is not limited to exploring what happens in a campaign. Research can help professionals accomplish great things and can bring forth new ideas as illustrated by Spotify and Tic Tac.

Lindenmann (2006) highlights how research should be integrated into PR practices in a variety of different ways. Research allows PR professionals to do each of the following:

- *Collect information for job-related tasks.* PR professionals must be aware of the kinds of information they need to make informed recommendations for their clients and organizations. In addition, professionals must explore any data that help support (or even question the merits of) what they are trying to accomplish. Evidence gathered through research is critical in getting investment for a campaign, client, and proposed messaging.

- *Analyze audience data.* Without client data, PR professionals would be practicing in the dark. The more information we are able to gather about the audiences we are trying to reach, the more effective we will be in understanding their needs, expectations, motivations, and wants.

- *Sustain a solid campaign and measure success.* As mentioned previously, research happens before, during, and after any PR campaign so that professionals can succeed in their goals and evaluate their methods.

Research is central to the PR models that guide our work

Research is the universal feature at the heart of every model in public relations. Whether you are going forward with the ROPE or RACE model in public relations, it starts with *R* for research. More explanation and application of these models will be highlighted and discussed in Chapter 8.

What Are Evidence-Based Practices for Research?

For all of its benefits, conducting and using research is not straightforward or black and white. Instead, it is a mixture of grays, or features that can make it a challenge to determine the best methods and assessment tools (metrics) to use. The good news is that we have an industry-wide standard for conducting research. To be of value, research must be based on sound evidence that is applicable and relevant. Using **evidence-based practices (EBPs)** for research gives us a comprehensive view of what is happening in a campaign and a road map for how to address challenges. Conducting research requires us to blend art with plenty of science, and EBPs are key for bringing these perspectives together.

Environment and Organizational Contexts

Before we can explore the nature of what is happening internally in an organization, it is important to explore outside of the arena to see what is happening in society (external environment) and in the industry in general (organizational context). Looking at both of these areas allows us to understand the larger issues, trends, challenges, and opportunities that we need to address, and know what questions to ask going forward.

Evidence-based research is "bottom-up and begins and ends with the client, moving well beyond a one-size-fits-all model [to] encompass clients' unique experience with their presenting problems" (Shlonsky & Gibbs, 2004, p. 138). We must understand the professional and scientific research related to our field while acknowledging and applying principles and best practices that come from our experiences. Figure 5.1 shows the key things we need to take into account when applying effective EBPs. First, we must understand our clients' background and overall standing based on their values, history, and preferences. This gives us a better historical view of what they have been dealing with as a brand and as a company. Next, we need to identify what resources, experiences, and expertise we can bring to the table. Based on previous successes, we can provide our clients with advice and insights about which practices have worked and which have not. The final component of EBPs is to research the industry for any relevant information that may apply to a given situation. The overall benefit of using the EBP model is to tie in together all of the parties—clients and PR practitioners—with the necessary research and evidence. This practice allows us to make a collaborative and effective case for applying research practices in a PR campaign.

Audience Segmentation

To help us understand the audiences who receive our messaging, we use **audience segmentation**, a process of categorizing people into certain groups based on specific criteria. These criteria can be (1) broad in nature, such as those based on demographics and population data, or (2) niche—that is, very specific and focused on characteristics such as experience, how visually driven an audience is, or other industry or special interest requirements. Through the use of audience segmentation, we collect information so we

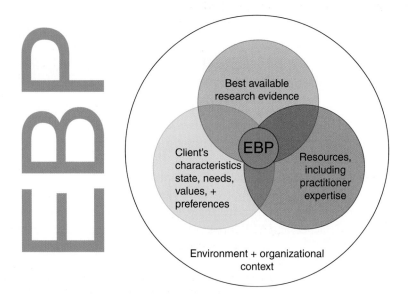

▼ FIGURE 5.1

Evidence-Based Practices for Research

can create profiles of audiences with whom our organizations and brands should engage. By gathering and analyzing this information, we can broadly target audiences—for example, prioritizing which ones to reach first. On the other hand, we can also be specific, identifying individual audience members who should receive our messages and content. To formulate the most effective message strategies, we must understand completely the audiences we are trying to reach. We do so by looking at two key concepts that help us describe audience characteristics: demographics and psychographics. Based on these concepts, we then create personas (which are covered in the next section).

As we apply EBPs for research, we must be able to personalize and apply strategic messages—the messages that we create based on insights gathered through research methods—and best practices in our scientific research and campaigns. Drawing on the perspectives of clients and all stakeholders, while thoroughly examining environmental issues, trends, and attitudes in our audiences, is key to our success.

Demographics help us identify and understand audiences

Demographics are the characteristics of populations that are based on data and used to identify audiences. Applying demographics allows us to group audiences together based on general characteristics such as age, gender, language, education, ethnicity, income, location, and job. These characteristics are universal in nature since they are population data characteristics each individual has. (See Table 5.1 for an example.)

Psychographics help us understand audiences in more depth

More complex than demographics, **psychographics**, as the name suggests, are characteristics of populations and individuals that are based on psychological attributes, including attitudes, behaviors, values, and opinions. We also determine psychographic characteristics according to an individual's interests, hobbies, and social needs. (See Table 5.1 for an example.)

Dog Lovers: Creating a Persona by Using Demographic and Psychographic Characteristics

Persona	Australian Shepherd Owner (Female)
Photo	 Courtesy of Laura Freberg
Name	Laura
Demographics	• 68 years old • Married • Mother of three children • Grandmother of one child • Lives in California • Has a PhD in psychology • Professor
Psychographics	Loves spending time with family and friends. Avid walker and outdoors fan. Connected online within various social media groups for Australian Shepherds. Focused on buying products with natural ingredients and shops online. Plays video games like *Legend of Zelda* in her free time.
Sources and Influence	Family, friends, trusted sources for natural dog food companies.
Quote	"My puppy is a beloved member of our family."
Persona	Australian Shepherd Owner (Male)
Photo	 Courtesy of Roger Freberg
Name	Roger
Demographics	• 68 years old • Retired • Father of three children • Grandfather of one child • Lives in California • MBA and MSBA at the University of Southern California
Psychographics	Loves spending time with family. Avid walker, but more toward destination. Highly engaged user for social media platforms and loves taking photos of Australian Shepherds. Foodie—very careful at looking at ingredients for products and where brands stand on various issues in society. Loves researching history of recipes to make at family gatherings. Avid walker and community member.
Sources and Influence	Family, friends, online communities.
Quote	"Our puppy is our world. We want to give her the very best life and get her the very best products out there!"

Personas give us representative sketches of audiences

Once we have gathered information based on demographics and psychographics, we can create a kind of model customer, or **persona**, to further define our audiences. A persona reflects a customer who typifies the audience we are trying to reach. Creating a persona allows us to illustrate the unique characteristics that separate one audience from another and help us better understand the motivating factors and influences that drive a particular audience to engage with, act upon, or respond to certain messages and campaigns. (See Table 5.1 for an example.)

Let's consider how personas might be used. Say that Purina is looking to engage more with baby boomer pet owners, specifically with those who own Australian Shepherds. The brand wants to reach the members of that audience in order to sell them its products. Based on the demographic and psychographic research it has conducted, Purina comes up with representations of the types of customer it wants to appeal to. Table 5.1 shows two of them.

Purina would want to implement these personas into its PR campaign because they help the people behind the brand to understand their key publics a bit more. If the brand went forward just targeting dog owners with Australian Shepherds, the messaging might not be as effective as it could be. However, by taking the steps to better understand their audiences through a psychological lens that looks at individuals' motivational factors, attitudes, and opinions, brands can be more effective in reaching these audiences. The more we understand our audiences, the better off we will be, and this can be accomplished through research.

Outputs and Outcomes

When using EBPs for research, it's important to be able to measure our effectiveness. Two results that we look for are outputs and outcomes. **Outputs** are the more immediate and direct results of a particular PR or communication program (Lindenmann, 2006). These are pieces of content that we send to audiences as part of a PR effort, such as our press releases, articles, social media posts, or other communications. **Outcomes**, on the other hand, are more important results because they reflect the behavioral actions of our audiences: They indicate how individuals responded to the specific messages and stories that we sent them as part of a campaign. These behavioral, attitudinal, and opinion-based results are a bit harder to measure, but they are worth the investment and time because they help determine whether or not the actions from the campaign were successful (Lindenmann, 2006). Outputs and outcomes are measured in different ways—outputs by focusing on the number of items produced (e.g., number of stories and sales made due to the efforts in the campaign) and outcomes by various methods to evaluate the impact of these efforts (e.g., change in attitude or behavior), including traditional methods such as surveys, questionnaires, and focus groups, to name a few. In essence, outcomes take more time and effort to measure than outputs, which is a key distinction to note.

One campaign that demonstrates the difference between outputs and outcomes is Burger King's "Unhappy Meals" for promoting mental health. The people behind the Burger King brand created a campaign focusing on the fact that not every day is happy, and on the need for more awareness of mental health issues that challenge society (Daniels, 2019). Let's examine the output and outcome measures for this campaign.

The press releases, media coverage, and social media posts that Burger King created for this campaign can be classified as outputs, because these pieces of content were generated to create awareness of the campaign. However, the outcomes are a bit more complicated because they deal with the audience's response to the brand's campaign—that is, people's attitudes and opinions about the messaging in relation to the brand. Burger King was able to measure the output based on the number of stories produced in response to the press release announcing the campaign. But to measure the overall outcome, Burger King had to conduct surveys or focus groups to determine whether the campaign changed the behaviors of its key publics. Based on the reactions that audiences had to Burger King's mental health awareness campaign, the outcome was mixed: Some people liked it, and some did not. Some praised Burger King for taking on this key issue, but the brand also received some backlash (Lee, 2019). Time will tell if the company saw an increase in sales and brand awareness or if the campaign boosted the brand's reputation.

The Burger King campaign focused on output and outcome measures in a unique way. If we focus only on output measures, then this campaign was a success because it generated a lot of media coverage and stories for the brand. However, given the mixed reactions to the campaign's overall theme, the outcome measure presents a different result for Burger King to consider when evaluating the campaign's success. What this shows is the importance of implementing and reporting both output and outcome results through the research and evaluation phases of a campaign. This is discussed in more detail in Chapter 12 on measurement and evaluation.

Social and Digital Communications

Another aspect of using EBPs for research is addressing an audience's use of digital and social media platforms. Two different types of research and measurement happen in these spaces. While these are two areas of focus for social and digital communications specialists, they also align with our research duties.

Monitoring allows us to report on our success

In achieving our business and communication goals, monitoring is the systematic process of understanding, analyzing, and reporting insights on a brand's position and reputation, the health of its audiences and communities, and the opinions of key audience members. It takes place in digital and social media spaces. For example, the annual Macy's Thanksgiving Day Parade is broadcast on TV and on social media, and the brand must report to its sponsors the impact of the event and the extent to which it offers a return on investment. To do this, Macy's must monitor certain metrics such as engagement, reach, and influence (e.g., influencers who are talking about the event).

Listening allows us to explore new opportunities

Allowing us to discover new brand partnerships, identify emerging trends, and engage with new audiences, listening is about learning and uncovering the latest issues and events that may impact our clients either positively or negatively. Although monitoring and listening are different approaches, they are essential to the research we do as modern-day PR practitioners. For example, as noted earlier in this chapter, after Tesla released its new Cybertruck, many competing brands responded to Tesla on social media. By listening to the conversations emerging online, we can help brands to strategize whether it is worthwhile to take advantage of such an opportunity. One brand did so in a big way, and that brand is LEGO®. Based on research and understanding of its audiences, LEGO did what the company had not done before: engage in the conversation with Tesla, which sparked more discussion of the LEGO brand. LEGO succeeded by increasing the number of stories and social media mentions, which resulted in a boost of brand awareness among audiences.

What Research Methods Do We Use in Public Relations?

Research skills, which are essential to our work, include the ability to be proactive and to choose the right method for evaluating, analyzing, and reporting our findings to our teams and clients. To do this, we need to work with traditional, new, and emerging methods. The following sections explore these methods and discuss their role in our efforts.

The Concepts of Reliability and Validity

Before getting into the various research methods available to us, we need to first understand the concepts of reliability and validity. **Reliability** refers to the ability to replicate the results of our research. If a scale or result of our research cannot be duplicated in another situation, then it is not reliable. For example, if your bathroom scale gives you very different numbers when you step on and off a few times, it is not reliable. Nor is it reliable if it gives you very different numbers than the scale at your physician's office. **Validity** refers to whether a measure does what it is advertised to do. If you invent your own "Creativity Scale," it should correlate with other established measures of creativity, and it should be able to predict people's creative output. Otherwise, we would not consider this scale to be valid.

PR research has been criticized on the basis of reliability and validity because of the often-intangible attributes we measure, such as impressions, attitudes, opinions, and values. We know they are present, but we cannot see or touch them. In all cases, we must take extra care to demonstrate that results can be replicated and that what we are measuring is what we want to measure. Getting to this stage in research takes time, effort, expertise, and resources.

Questions to Explore

Our choice of research method is based on the questions that we want to explore and the causes and effects of the variables that we want to examine. Our choice of research method may also be based on our wish to explain how and why something is happening. Some questions that address a cause-and-effect situation include the following:

- What factors contribute to an influencer's success?
- What contributes to a brand's success in handling a crisis?
- What impact does a CEO have on a brand's reputation?
- What is the relationship between students and coffee?

However, if you want to explore how and why things are happening, you would ask questions such as these:

- Why do Generation Z members prefer to engage in business online?
- How do professors decide which coffee brand to purchase?
- Why are direct-to-consumer (DTC) brands effective in reaching millennials?
- How can we incorporate more diversity and inclusion efforts in our work?

To determine what research method to implement, we must finalize and get any necessary approval for our research questions beforehand.

Formal and Informal Research

In public relations, we conduct both formal and informal research. When we conduct **formal research**, we use the **scientific method**. The scientific method is a method of research in which we identify a problem, gather relevant data, form a hypothesis, and then test that hypothesis empirically. In public relations, we follow certain rules for recruiting participants and selecting samples, such as random sampling, or giving each person an equal chance to participate. We also establish specific procedures for communicating our study and results so that they can be replicated by others.

Academic research (research that is published in specific research journals and publications for academia) falls into the category of formal research. When we conduct academic research, we use the scientific method, but in our campaigns, we also follow ethical guidelines for the use of human subjects such as members of key audiences. Further, we seek the approval of an institutional review board (IRB). The IRB exists to make sure researchers are ethical and professional, and that we follow standard protocols when working with human subjects. Most of the research in public relations and other social sciences involves human subjects and needs to go through an IRB for approval.

On the other hand, when we conduct **informal research**, we look for potential ideas to test or implement in a campaign. In such cases, we do not go through the process of getting our research method or questions approved ahead of time. We do not seek approval from IRBs, for example. Informal research, such as the observation of activities and messaging at local shops or other popular locations, allows us to generate and explore new ideas. Further, it helps us determine whether to go forward with formal research. While formal research is likely to be published in a peer-reviewed outlet, informal research, which lacks a formal approval process, is generally not published.

Primary and Secondary Research

In addition to conducting formal and informal research, as PR professionals we also carry out primary and secondary research. **Primary research** is original research, conducted by an individual or team, that has not been published or presented previously.

Secondary research is the collection and summary of already-published materials such as reports, articles, communication audits, news reports, and academic articles. These materials have been reviewed by experts—the authors' professional peers—to evaluate quality and identify new insights that the work presents (Lindenmann, 2006).

Our goal in conducting secondary research is to uncover gaps in professional literature that have not yet been explored and to make sure we're not reinventing the wheel (Lindenmann, 2006). For example, looking at published articles, campaign summaries, case studies, and other documents that explore our area of interest shows us what has been said and done already, and what represents potential gaps in the literature. Such research also serves as helpful evidence for your team; they need to know whether the topic you're interested in has been researched and written about already. This type of research is an important part of EBPs.

Contrary to the implications of its name, secondary research is usually conducted first: We need to know if anyone else has conducted research in our area of interest. We do not want to make an incorrect claim that something is innovative or revolutionary if someone else has done it before. Doing this research ahead of time will save money and potential reputational issues down the line.

Primary Research: Qualitative, Quantitative, and Mixed Methods

Three types of primary research approaches are commonly used: qualitative, quantitative, and mixed-methods research.

Qualitative research allows us to discover how and why things happen

Qualitative research methods address our questions about the quality of something. This type of research allows us to explore an event or phenomenon in detail, on a one-to-one basis or a one-to-many basis. It is less about seeing the overall cause and effect of a situation.

The data that we collect from qualitative research—such as field notes, sound bites, and other recordings—are usually narrative in form, consisting of quotes, themes, observations, and collections of documents that explain how and why something is taking place. For example, we might choose to conduct qualitiative research if we want answers to the following types of questions:

- Why do Gen Z audiences behave differently online than other generations?

- What motivates fans to follow the Korean pop band BTS all over the world?

- What are some common concerns that customers have about flying Spirit Airlines?

- How do audiences decide which causes to support on the National Day of Giving?

Popular methods for conducting qualitative research include interviews, which are a great way to exlpore the how and why behind an event or action. To conduct an interview, we ask specific questions of select audience members, working from an interview guide or list of standardized queries. These questions must be flexible enough to allow participants to ask new or follow-up questions. Interviews are especially valuable tools because they reveal information such as particular attitudes or opinions about a given topic, issue, or brand. We can then take this information and apply it to our campaign strategies and messages, allowing us to better engage with key publics.

Focus groups are another popular tool for conducting qualitative research. Running a focus group allows us to work with an audience to generate ideas and insights about a specific plan or product—or to gather perspectives on a specific question. The value of the information we gather from focus groups is that it is rich in data that help us better understand the depth and meaning of our audience's thinking. When planning a focus group, enlisting five to seven individuals is a good practice. Inviting more than that to gain a range of insights may be tempting, but including too many people can lead to one person dominating the conversation or too few people speaking up. We use an interview guide (our list of questions for focus group members) to help guide the conversation. Once the data are collected (by audio, video, or both), we analyze and share the data with our team. We then use the data as evidence and a launchpad for brainstorming creative and strategic ideas for a campaign.

Fieldwork, which is work that we do in the real world, includes observation and enthography studies. Fieldwork happens in the natural environment and in various settings such as communities and corporations, and takes a lot of time. As we conduct this research, we must make notes on what we see, feel, and understand about what is taking place in the chosen setting. Once we've collected these notes and observations, we analyze them to explore any consistent emerging themes. We must keep careful and detailed notes that will allow for the thorough analysis of our data.

Quantitative research allows us to explore cause and effect

Quantitative research addresses questions of "what" or "how many," and is usually evaluated using formal statistical methods. Using this type of research, we can focus on objective measures to predict how certain concepts and variables will act in a controlled setting (a setting, such as a lab, that is controlled by the researcher). Unlike the questions that we ask in qualitative studies, quantitative research questions are closed in nature, meaning that respondents must pick one answer and cannot write in their own response. Closed questions force the participants to answer questions based on the options presented to them. Open-ended questions allow the participants to provide their own insights and perspectives, which are more aligned with qualitative research.

Quantitative research questions often feature scales (e.g., Likert questions) that have been tested over time to measure attributes such as attitude formations, relationship management, and trust, to name a few. These scales reflect concepts that can be evaluated through numerical measures and values.

Some common quantitative methods that we use include experiments. Experiments test hypotheses and predictions in a controlled setting. For example, if we wanted to test the impact of messaging for a food safety campaign for the Centers for Disease Control and Prevention, we could conduct an experiment to test audience response. We might carry this out by testing certain variables—for example, testing the credibility of a message for the CDC in the context of a food crisis scenario. Each scenario would include a version of the variable in question (e.g., message credibiltiy vs. no message credibility), and the participants in each scenario of the experiment would respond to the same questions. This experiment would show the impact of the variable based on how the audience responds to the scenario and messages.

Another quantitaive tool for PR professionals is the survey. Surveys consist of a group of questions presented in various forms (mail, telephone, online, and mobile) that can be evaluated in a quantitative way. Surveys range in length and complexity (some are only a few questions, and others are longer and more elaborate). In addition to the length and complexity of our surveys, the distribution we choose affects our response rate and cost.

- Survey by mail: These are the most expensive type of surveys, and the response rate for mail-in surveys is extremely low.

- Survey by phone: This is another expensive type of survey that works well in certain circumstances, such as conducting political polling. However, due to the existence of the "no call" list and use of cell phones with numbers that are not typically listed, surveying by phone is not as effective as other survey methods in reaching representative samples. Most PR firms and professionals hire outside companies to conduct telephone interviews, which takes a lot of time and money.

- Survey by digital media: Online surveys are the most popular tool among researchers. Email, social, and mobile surveys represent an affordable way to gather data. Programs such as SurveyMonkey, Google Forms, and Qualtrics allow us to gather information quickly and inexpensively. However, we never know who is completing the form, which affects the quality of our resulting data.

Mixed-methods research gives us a complete picture of a topic or situation

The combination of qualitative and quantitative methods is called **mixed-methods research**. This is a popular approach in public relations because we begin most campaigns with either focus groups or interviews, and then we use the findings to construct surveys and experiments. Table 5.2 shows the breakdown of the research methods, their overall focus, and how we apply them.

Social Media Research and Analysis

Social media research is on the rise in public relations. Because social media exists through channels (platforms) that constantly evolve, we must adapt our methods of conducting research and analysis in an ongoing way. Changes to platforms, such as the

▼ TABLE 5.2

Differences Between Qualitative, Quantitative, and Mixed-Methods Research

Research Method	Focus	Applications
Qualitative	• Explores how and why questions • Subjective in nature • Data involve quotes, observations, collection of information • Not generalizable in results (can't state these results would be the same for a larger population of people) • Open-ended questions	• Focus groups • Interviews • Field studies • Observations • Ethnography • Case studies
Quantitative	• Addresses cause-and-effect questions • Follows the scientific method with research questions and hypotheses • Objective • Focuses on statistics and assigning values to information • Generalizable in results • Closed-ended questions	• Experiments • Questionnaires • Surveys (mail, telephone, and online) • Polls • Content analysis (exploring themes and trends in text)
Mixed-Methods	• Combination of qualitative and quantitative methods for research • Allows for exploring certain concepts in detail (qualitative) and then testing them to see if they are true (quantitative)	• Campaign message testing • Reputation management • Trends and analysis

revision of algorithms, affect the associated metrics (e.g., video views on Facebook) and third-party tools that have gained access to the platforms via their application program interface, or API (e.g., Salesforce, Zoomph, Meltwater, Sprinklr, Hootsuite, or Brandwatch). Examples of channel or platform analytics include Facebook Insights and Twitter Analytics. Third-party tools include Salesforce, Zoomph, Talkwalker, Brandwatch, and Crimson Hexagon. In social media analysis, the overall point is to be able to listen, monitor, evaluate, and respond to the conversations emerging in real time around the world. It's important that we choose social media tools that provide access to the platform's API so that we can obtain quality data. In most cases, PR agencies have access to such tools because we must have these for our clients. Some of these tools are more expensive than others, so it is important to conduct a thorough audit (analysis of the tools based on certain criteria and features you want) to determine whether the tool is the right choice. Keep in mind there is not a perfect tool (or unicorn) out there to do this. If there were, we'd be hearing about it from everyone. Based on budget, feature requirements, and expertise, we can choose the best option for our clients.

Social Network Analysis (SNA)

The social network analysis approach, known as SNA, looks at the social relations and structures that emerge in a community. This approach has value because SNA tools can collect a vast amount of online data and present it clearly as networks and graphs. Social media is a collection of accounts and profiles that are interlinked. By using SNA, we can see the ties, links (relationships), and size of a community that is part of a particular account. Most brands and PR agencies use this method when exploring a specific hashtag trending on social media. Other tools like NodeXL, Mentionmapp, Audiense, and SocNetV also help visualize communities online.

Many brands have used this to see the impact influencers have on driving conversation among their communities online. For example, Adobe used Trust Insights to help visualize the impact of influencers who attended its Adobe Summit conference. Adobe can see that, based on the results from the SNA analysis, it is one of the dominant accounts that Adobe Summit attendees are engaged with. However, Adobe can also see which accounts are helping to drive conversations for the brand, such as the accounts of marketing influencers Jay Baer, Scott Monty, Peter Shankman, and Cathy Hackl. These insights can help Adobe engage with these influencers on a more formal basis for potential brand collaborations. In essence, SNA helps us identify communities, influencers, and current or emerging relationships that are happening online.

Neuromarketing Research and Analysis

As mentioned in Chapter 2, psychology and public relations have a natural connection. This is also true in the realm of research: A method used in psychology is being integrated into PR practices. The method, which involves neuroscience, has activated the rise of neuromarketing, which plays a big part in PR campaigns.

As participants are asked to respond to images and messages to make a decision, their brain activity can be assessed through brain imaging technology. Hollywood trailers and political speeches have been evaluated using brain imaging technologies, but the steep cost (approximately $1,000 per hour) and the expertise required for evaluation are high barriers to common use among PR professionals.

Take-away: Brain activity (b) was better at predicting behavior (c) than subjective ratings of the three campaigns (a).

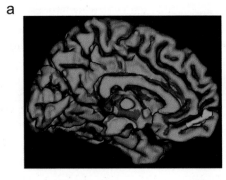

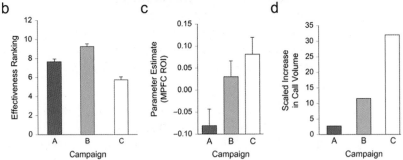

Source: Falk, E. B., Berkman, E. T., & Lieberman, M. D. (2012). From neural responses to population behavior: neural focus group predicts population-level media effects. *Psychological science, 23*(5), 439 -445. https://doi.org/10.1177/0956797611434964

What Are Best Practices for Conducting, Evaluating, and Applying Research?

In this chapter, we have discussed how we gather, analyze, and use data to carry out the work we do as PR professionals. Recommendations for best practices in public relations, as well as help with finding sources and obtaining data, appear in the following sections.

Best Practices

To do our best work as researchers, we must do the following.

- *Understand the ethical expectations for research.* Ethics is a key part of doing professional research, and there are certain associated risks that we need to address. Providing supporting documentation and full transparency of the work done for our clients is a big part of doing ethical research (Michaelson & Stacks, 2014). Unethical situations can arise in PR research, such as sharing misleading results, not reporting all of the results, using research for unethical message strategies, not disclosing the process of collecting data, or misrepresenting data for clients and audiences. Obviously, systems should be in place that reduce the likelihood of these unethical practices.

- *Align theory, method, and practice together.* Because these areas are interconnected, if we focus on only one aspect of the evidence-based model, our work will be incomplete. To fully integrate these elements, it is important to understand how and why things are happening (theory), how to best explore what is going on (research), and how to integrate these insights into actionable strategies (practice).

- *Determine the roles and team members in charge of investing, leading, and coordinating research efforts.* It's critical to identify the key personnel within the team or organization who will be part of the research team. The team should be expert in ensuring that the protocols and methods are correctly designed and managed. In addition, these professionals will be responsible for following legal and ethical expectations.

- *Invest in the right tools and methods.* To do the best research possible, we need to have the best tools at hand to accomplish these efforts. Training on various tools such as media monitoring initiatives (e.g., Cision and Meltwater), media research (e.g., Nielsen), social media (e.g., Sprinklr, Salesforce, Crimson Hexagon, and Talkwalker), analytics (e.g., Microsoft and Adobe), customer relationship management tools (e.g., HubSpot), and specific platforms (e.g., Facebook Blueprint) helps us obtain the data we need. The tools we use to collect, analyze, and report research are going to continue to evolve and change. The channels in use will come and go over time, but the fundamental practices of collecting, gathering, and evaluating research will still remain.

- *Understand that reporting data and research is just the beginning.* If we simply report data, that is only 50 percent of the work. The insights that are gathered from research need to be presented like a story—with a beginning (problems that need to be addressed, current standing on the topic, history of the issue, etc.), a middle (action plan, method used, findings, and discussion), and an end (recommendations and next steps).

Obtaining Data and Other Challenges

It is important to note here that we face many challenges when it comes to conducting research. First, obtaining quality data is not cheap. Companies such as Facebook, Google, and Amazon collect a lot of information about individuals, and they know that this information equals money. Access to the tools needed to analyze data, and to the data, can be very expensive. Data drive the "pay to play" game for social media professionals. This means that to get access to data and reach audiences for a campaign, we may need a hefty budget.

Second, although research is a key part of public relations, the practice is not always housed in the same part of the organization. Often, social media research and analytics is housed in its own specialized department or within a department that oversees the overall budget for PR efforts rather than in a PR department.

Third, a gap exists between the knowledge and expectations in the industry regarding new types of data and research analysis and what is covered in colleges and universities in traditional PR courses. Those of us who conduct or evaluate research must be able to *understand the data* we collect and produce. Being able to evaluate the content we create gives us a solid foundation within our organizations or departments. Brands and agencies look for professionals who understand how to collect relevant data from social media platforms, have the skills and insights to explain what the data mean, and know how to apply the results strategically. In addition, understanding research methods allows us to do a check and balance on the metrics and data collected by third-party resources or other agencies or consultants. This approach ensures we are all on the same page in regard to the data collected from the digital and social media ecosystem.

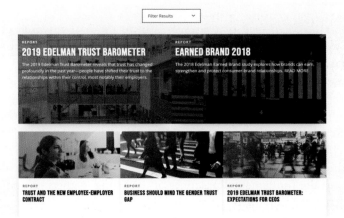

Lastly, there is a disconnect between the objectives we set and how we measure and evaluate them. Research must be interconnected with the objectives we set forth in our work. We need to determine the overall impact and significance of our data reports and insights on our day-to-day business and communication activities. These have to be aligned with the set objectives you have established for your campaign. Essentially, objectives are what you want to accomplish, and the metrics and analysis represent what you actually were able to accomplish. Ideally, you want to make sure these objectives follow the key SMART criteria (specific, measurable, achievable, realistic, and time-specific).

- How does this connect back to my objectives?
- Am I using the right method to answer the questions I am asking?
- How will this inform me about my social channels and online presence?
- Do I have the right tools (and knowledge) to collect and analyze this data set?

Knowing Where to Find Sources

In the challenging field of public relations, opportunities exist as well. More classes and other resources are becoming available, which means we can get the training we need to be skilled in using new research tools. Also, brands are recognizing the benefits of good research and are more willing to invest in it, which means we can more easily get the right tools for gathering the data we need for our campaigns.

Something to be aware of is that already-published materials (secondary research) can be found in sources beyond professional and academic journals. In fact, there are many ways in which public relations research is presented and formatted.

Agencies

Many PR agencies have featured research as one of their main areas of content creation and as a key service they offer their clients. Agencies have approached this in a variety

USCAnnenberg
School for Communication
and Journalism

News   Events   Alumni   Give Now   USC University of Southern California

Admissions   Academics ∨   Faculty   Research   Career Development   Students   About

RESEARCH » CENTER FOR PUBLIC RELATIONS » RELEVANCE REPORT

About the Relevance Report

The annual Relevance Report from the USC Center for Public Relations identifies emerging issues and forecasts topics and trends impacting society, business, and communications in the coming year. The book features contributions from public relations industry leaders, and USC academics and graduate students. The essays in the 2019 Relevance Report are brief, thoughtful, and cover a broad range of topics including media, communication, technology, marketing, and society. It is designed to give those studying and working in public relations a preview of what the coming year holds for the PR industry, society and people's careers. Authors include communication leaders from Best Buy, eBay, Hyundai, Nintendo and Sprint, and PR agency leaders from Edelman, Golin, MSL, Ogilvy, Weber Shandwick, and more. All are advisory board members to the USC Center for Public Relations.

Read from the Relevance Report

USC ANNENBERG RELEVANC...
Communication should bridge social divides
👤 Brad Neaton

USC ANNENBERG RELEVANC...
The reboot of tech PR
👤 Nirit Weiss-Blatt

USC ANNENBERG RELEVANC...
Leave the gate open for women gamers
👤 Cynthia Park

USC ANNENBERG RELEVANC...
The evolution of ethics, revisited
👤 Ron Antonette

of ways. For example, Weber Shandwick is known for its CEO of reputation research, and the firm has produced numerous reports, white papers, and webinars on the subject. Edelman has branded its Edelman Trust Barometer report for years as a key part of what the agency produces. The Edelman Trust Barometer has looked at the current state of trust not only in the PR industry, but in society as a whole, since 2001 (Edelman, 2020).

Analytics Companies

The social, digital, and traditional research companies are not only sharing their services regarding data they can collect; they also want to show the research they produce along with the tools they are promoting. Tools such as Talkwalker, a social listening tool, have been leading the way in producing free and accessible reports on various subjects. Talkwalker has integrated specific reports focusing on key trending specializations, such as influencer marketing, as a way to get audiences to review the research. In addition to free accessible reports on its research findings, Talkwalker provides insights that are covered in blog posts and webinars.

Universities

Research is at the core of a university's identity. The research that happens at a university includes the gathering and analysis of data that inform research articles that appear in peer-reviewed academic journals. It also includes the research that happens in various centers and by different groups on campus. For example, the University of Southern California features the Center for Public Relations, which is made up of faculty, staff, and students who are studying public relations and the various trends we face in the field. USC has produced several reports over the years, which is a way to share knowledge and information among those in the academic community and those in the PR industry as well.

SUMMARY

Research should not be a scary area for PR professionals. Yes, the field does deal with numbers, and the amount of information can be somewhat overwhelming. However, research brings forth so many opportunities that should outweigh any concerns or negative perceptions about the process. Research can be both theoretical and practical, and to address the challenges and opportunities effectively, a PR professional needs to have strong skills, experiences, and tools to help answer these questions.

APR EXAM

- Research
- Formal and informal research
- Research methods

KEY TERMS

Audience segmentation 93

Demographics 94

Evidence-based practices (EBPs) 93

Fieldwork 101

Formal research 99

Informal research 99

Mixed-methods research 102

Outcomes 96

Outputs 96

Persona 96

Primary research 99

Psychographics 94

Qualitative research 100

Quantitative research 101

Reliability 98

Research 89

Scientific method 99

Secondary research 99

Validity 98

DISCUSSION QUESTIONS

1. What is research? Why is this important in public relations?

2. Identify the key differences between quantitative and qualitative research. Are the methods the same?

3. Define evidence-based practices. What are the three areas that make up EBPs for PR research?

4. What are the ethical concerns related to research that PR professionals need to know?

ACTIVITIES

Building Your Portfolio

- *Research Audit*. You are working with a local business that has not done any formal research for its PR efforts.
  - Highlight in a short pitch (two or three sentences) why research is important for public relations.
  - Discuss the main methods the business should know, the benefits and challenges, and your recommendations.
  - Provide three resources for where the business can learn more about new research methods for public relations.

Building Your Brand

- *Research Your Brand*. You are applying for an internship but want to make sure you are able to put your best foot forward as a professional. You want to do primary research and ask your friends, family, and colleagues what your brand stands for.
- In this exercise, answer the following questions:
  - What questions do you want answers to? Write down two or three you want to explore.
  - Discuss the method you will use and why.
  - Create a game plan for how you will do this research and discuss how you will apply these insights to the internship application.

GAME CHANGER
Shahbaz Khan of the Minnesota Timberwolves

Courtesy Shahbaz Khan

How did you get your start in the industry?

Back in 2011, I came across a job vacancy at the Timberwolves and Lynx organization as a social media associate. Essentially, it was a full-time internship dedicated to running all things National Basketball Association/Women's NBA for the organization.

I applied that year, the year after, and a third time.

In every rejection, I took it as a means to bolster my experience, so I sought out as many remote internships in social media as I could, and by the third time I applied, I had six concurrent positions in social that strengthened my résumé and landed me my dream gig. From there I networked my way into a full-time role in Chicago, and later into a position with the Sacramento Kings.

What is your favorite part of working in the industry?

My favorite part about working in digital, specifically within the NBA, is the creative leeway we're allowed as teams and individuals to bring any and every topic to life through sport. Additionally, no day is the same—one day we may be creating content for a community feel-good piece, the next day leveraging a trending topic and intertwining it with our brand, and the next day doing anything from photography, to video editing, to running paid ads, to negotiating partnerships. The industry is so wide ranging in its reach that I'm hesitant to say I work solely in social— it's more a mix of social, digital, public relations, design, creative, sponsorships, and much more!

What is the most challenging part of working in your industry?

The most challenging part is also the best—every day is different. In the blink of an eye within social and sport, everything can change, so having a plan ready for something that's unplannable is always interesting, but also extremely fun.

Who do you think are the biggest game changers for your industry?

From a team perspective, I think what the Atlanta Hawks did in the early years of Twitter set the groundwork for what so many teams, brands, and organizations try to emulate now. Not everyone can be sassy, and the Hawks didn't do it just to do it but grew their fan base while also making a concerted effort to change the way their brand was perceived through their work in social. Nowadays, there's too many to name, but the Chicago Bears led by Jen Tulicki have transformed their social brand, and the Los Angeles Chargers have done a great job as of late, as have many NBA teams, most notably the Philadelphia 76ers in how their brand story has been told throughout the past few years.

What are some things you wish you knew when you were starting out in the industry?

Starting out, I wish I had become more familiarized with some of the tools that are an integral part of today's digital landscape. While I took time learning design through class and on my own, the level of animation, design, creative photography, and more that have become integral pieces to social and digital is astounding. Becoming more well versed in general in a wide array of skills would've helped expedite my knowledge and eased the learning curve in many areas!

Shahbaz Khan currently serves as the senior manager of digital content for the Minnesota Timberwolves and Lynx. For three consecutive seasons, Shahbaz's digital teams have earned the NBA's Digital Innovator of the Year Award, while also earning a top 10 spot among the media-voted "NBA's Best Twitter Accounts." When he isn't covering a game alongside his team, he spends time on his podcast, Social on the Sidelines, where he dialogues with fellow strategists about the business aspect of sports. Additionally, Shahbaz owns a social media consulting agency, and has recently launched an urban Minnesota-focused apparel line. You can find him most active on Twitter at @ShahbazMKhan.

CASE STUDY

*Amazon's Second Headquarters Campaign:
A Lesson on the Value of Research*

Amazon, one of the world's biggest brands, created a campaign inviting cities around the United States to apply to be considered for the location of its second headquarters. Cities submitted their bids to be part of the process and waited to see if they would be chosen as finalists. In 2019, Amazon announced that the company's second headquarters would be split between two cities: Arlington, Virginia (near the location of the *Washington Post*, which is also owned by Amazon CEO Jeff Bezos), and New York City.

Why did this case generate buzz?

- Amazon created an integrated campaign to determine where to build its second headquarters.

- Amazon at the time was one of the largest global brands, which was attractive to many cities given the possibilities of new jobs, revenue, and growth.

What are the ethical and legal issues?

- There were some concerns related to the reputation Amazon has for employee culture, which raised some concerns about how this could impact the image of the chosen city.

- Some experts felt the campaign message generated excitement and enthusiasm across the country, but the end results were not what many expected. Some felt the campaign was more of a "bait and switch" kind of a campaign, which was misleading in the original message the company sent out (Streitfeld, 2018).

What are some takeaways from this case?

- Amazon decided to divide its headquarters between Arlington Virginia, near Washington, DC, and New York City. However, due to the negative reactions and press from New York, the company decided to focus on the Washington, DC, area.

- Amazon provided the following statement on its website:

  After much thought and deliberation, we've decided not to move forward with our plans to build a headquarters for Amazon in Long Island City, Queens. For Amazon, the commitment to build a new headquarters requires positive, collaborative relationships with state and local elected officials who will be supportive over the long-term. While polls show that 70% of New Yorkers support our plans and investment, a number of state and local politicians have made it clear that they oppose our presence and will not work with us to build the type of relationships that are required to go forward with the project we and many others envisioned in Long Island City. (Day One Staff, 2019)

- If Amazon did research to explore the challenges, concerns, and issues that emerged from the New York City community, it could have saved money and negative media coverage.

- There were many missed opportunities here for Amazon, such as engaging more with small businesses rather than politicians, focusing on understanding its reputation in the New York City community, and discovering how it is perceived as a brand (Arenstein, 2019).

BRANDING

··

LEARNING **OBJECTIVES**

- Understand the concept of branding (branding of clients, corporations).

- Know how brands are created and supported.

- Define personal branding and its value (branding of an individual).

- Know how to create an effective personal brand.

- Be able to apply best practices in client branding and personal branding.

Introduction

Every organization, agency, and person has a brand today. To be effective in public relations, we must each be our own best advocate, whether we work as part of an organization or as a brand of our own. This means promoting our organizations, our presence in the industry, and ourselves as thought leaders and voices in the profession. Branding is not limited to marketing or advertising strategies: It is very much a key part of our work in public relations.

What Is Branding?

While branding and related tasks are often handled by marketing and advertising professionals, these groups do not hold the trademark rights to branding. In fact, branding has a natural connection to public relations: We build relationships with our key publics and tell the stories of our clients and their products. **Branding** can be defined as the strategic promotion of a product, company, or person through various visual, written, and design capabilities. Branding goes beyond visual messaging and storytelling. It requires our commitment to showing key audiences that we and our clients are different from our competitors. The practice of branding requires us to separate ourselves and our clients from the rest of the crowd by amplifying our messages in emotional, entertaining, and persuasive ways.

Branding follows principles of visual design that need to be part of an effective plan for a client or individual:

- A digital presence, including websites, social media content, blogs, and newsletters

- A distinct, memorable logo

- A color palette that represents the attributes of a brand

Now, it's important to have strong visual elements for branding purposes, but we must make sure our visuals have substance and tell a clear story. So our branding efforts must also articulate written, spoken, and visual content that we will create:

- *A brand voice.* What personality traits define the brand? How are those traits communicated through messages and all associated content?

- *A vision statement.* How do the people behind the brand see its place in society, the community, or industry, now and in the future?

- *A statement of purpose.* What is the client brand's mission and purpose in the industry?

- *A diversity and inclusion statement.* To what extent does the client brand embrace diversity and inclusion?

- *Brand pillars.* What are the values and characteristics that separate the brand from others?

- *Reputation.* What do others say and feel about the client brand, through testimonials, case studies, and other avenues?

How Do We Support Clients' Brands in Public Relations?

A brand, simply defined, is a product that is linked to a company or other client. In other words, a brand may be attributed to an actual product, as is the case for Tide, which is a brand product for Procter & Gamble.

Supporting a Brand for a Client

In public relations, brands are created and supported in various ways. First, we might work with clients to create a brand (product, idea, or service) that can be distinguished from others and promoted in a given industry and marketplace. In some cases, those brands already exist. Then, we invest in the tools, resources, and talent needed to create the visual, written, and branded content that will support the brand. These efforts help us create awareness of the story, features, and differences that this brand has compared to others. The next part of the process is promoting the brand and its story to the audiences we want to reach. These channels of communication, whether traditional, digital, social, or emerging, allow us to engage in a conversation with audiences about the brand, its features and benefits, and what it offers that related products do not.

Examples of Clients' Brands

Following are examples of how branding is applied in the PR context.

Oreo

One way that brands try to distinguish themselves from the crowd and invite a new wave of fame and fandom is through social media. With the power of social media, those behind a given brand can share updates and inject some personality into the mix, attracting existing

BRANDING

A personal brand is a collection of various attributes, expertise traits, personality characteristics, and insights for an individual person based on online and offline interactions. What makes personal branding relevant and important for public relations professionals is the fact that it allows users to be able to create their own brand voice.

Here is how a public relations professional can create their own personal brand:

TIME, ENERGY, AND RESOURCES

Know that personal brands don't happen overnight. Personal brands take time, energy, and resources to manage and create. They are lifelong investments for your future career in the field.

RESEARCH

Research to better understand your brand. It is key to determine how you present yourself, what attributes and personality characteristics others associate with you, and what makes you different from other professionals in the field. Conducting an audit of your personal brand is a great way to determine this.

BE UNIQUE

Decide what makes you "you." It is all about showcasing your unique perspectives, experiences, and stories as well as what you can offer that no one else can in the public relations field.

IDENTIFY EXPERTISE

Identify areas of expertise you can offer. What are you passionate about? What are the areas in which you want to establish yourself as a public relations professional? Each person has to ask themselves what makes them unique and special.

COLLECT SOCIAL PROOF

It is key to have social proof (evidence documented online by others validating your brand) to have on hand. By showcasing your level of expertise through evidence (e.g., testimonials, endorsements, quotes, work samples, etc.), public relations professionals are able to combat the "fake" professionals who are saying they are an expert, when, in fact, they do not have the evidence to back up their claims.

SHARE QUALITY INSIGHTS

Produce quality insights, content, and perspectives that add to the conversation. Share your personality, experience, and thoughts with the community to help grow your presence and community. There are no "right" answers here – but you want to be comfortable in sharing your ideas and content with the industry.

Oreo and *Game of Thrones*

MediaPost.com

and new audiences. Several have had success in this arena by integrating different takes on brand voice, including Wendy's (snarky), Aviation Gin (smooth), MoonPie (witty), and Steak-umm (millennial humor). Oreo, the iconic cookie brand, is no stranger to the social media world after its "Daily Twist" campaign and infamous viral tweet during the 2013 Super Bowl. By tapping its brand image and presence on social, the cookie brand has been able to tie into various pop culture moments. Oreo created a video featuring its cookies in a *Game of Thrones* promo for the show's last season in 2019 (Lukovitz, 2019). By doing so, the brand was able to integrate its voice and identity across channels in an entertaining way that sparked audience engagement and sharing.

Patagonia

The clothing company Patagonia has positioned itself as a strong leader in the retail business. Those behind the brand convey its value by showcasing the quality of their clothing products—and by taking a stance in support of environmental issues. This is an example of how brands can represent more than just the products and services they provide. Patagonia also promotes its brand by connecting with customers and addressing the issues that the company and its customers stand for and support.

Wegmans

Not only does the northeastern grocery store Wegmans have a strong reputation, but it also has an almost cult-like consumer following for its products, services, and experiences. The people behind the Wegmans brand pride themselves on their consumer-focused values, fresh products, and the positive shopping experiences they create for their customers. They confidently identify their brand as a contrast to other grocery stores. Their tagline states, "Food you feel good about," which communicates simply their overall purpose and position in the industry.

Examples of Client Branding That Involve Personal Branding

Client branding can also involve personal branding.

JuJu Smith-Schuster and Likeable Brand

Some of the best branding work has come from the sports industry and teams, especially the creation of personal brands for individual athletes. Many consultants and agencies such as Opendorse have been created to address this growing need. Athletes, like PR professionals, need expertise and talent to do their jobs, but they must also be strategic in marketing themselves to teams, brands, and their fan base. Jeremy Darlow, a consultant and former global lead of marketing and branding at Adidas, stated his overall goal is to "teach athletes how to build personal brands that set them up for success in life, regardless of what happens in sports. Too often athletes are defined entirely by their athletic careers without developing influence in other areas of passion. My goal is to change that" (Heitner, 2018a). One of the athlete brands that has gotten a lot of attention is Pittsburgh Steelers player JuJu Smith-Schuster (Tesfatsion, 2018). As a *Bleacher Report*

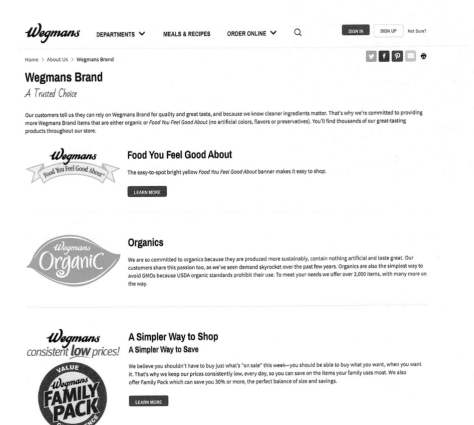

article discusses, Smith-Schuster shares his friendly and relatable personality with all key audiences in the National Football League (NFL) and humanizes his own brand on his social media platforms (Tesfatsion, 2018).

Politicians Running for Office

In the current age of "relatable" branding for politicians, PR professionals help candidates create personal brands that distinguish them from their competitors. The last few presidential elections have revealed a trend toward personal branding through the use of strategic messaging, innovative approaches, and new ways of engaging audiences. For example, President Barack Obama was part of the first "social media" election in 2008, and President Donald Trump ran with the message he was an Washington "outsider." in the 2020 election, several Democratic candidates used the strategy of extending their personal brands to be more "knowable" by their audiences. Examples include Senator Elizabeth Warren taking part in a TikTok challenge on *Saturday Night Live* and Beto O'Rourke going to the dentist. These practices tie into the personalized brand kit trend seen in personal branding.

What Is a Personal Brand? How Do We Create One?

An area of growth in public relations is the movement for individual professionals to create a personal brand that allows each of us to stand out in our industry. It is not only what you know in public relations that matters in the industry, but who knows you as a professional. Having a personal brand is becoming a key factor in the job search process and can be the deciding factor for whether you are hired.

Defining a Personal Brand

In the age of digital and social media, creating a personal brand should be as simple as setting up an account on a few platforms and calling it a day, right? Not quite. Building a personal brand requires more than throwing together a LinkedIn account and posting content that lacks a clear strategy. A **personal brand** is a collection of a person's various accomplishments, expertise, personality characteristics, and insights that take place both on- and offline. One of the great things about building a personal brand is that any of us can do so, not just the celebrities, sports figures, and other influencers of this world. Anyone can create a personal brand and present it to professional and personal networks to bring forth praise and new opportunities. However, while creating a "picture perfect" image may be tempting, it may not be the most authentic strategy or truest representation of who we are and can raise concerns among those in our communities about transparency. This brings forth the importance of having a strong **alignment balance**, which means having a consistent, authentic, and true representation of who we are in various circles and communities.

Examples of Personal Brands

When it comes to personal brands, there are individuals who have identified themselves as voices in their industries, then ventured out to other industries, sometimes going more mainstream. It's important to note that personal brands evolve over time: If we inhabit one role and then move to another, we'll need to brand ourselves in a new way.

Jimmy Fallon

Tonight Show host Jimmy Fallon has used various channels to grow his presence online and his standing in the entertainment industry. Fallon, a comedian and actor of *Saturday Night Live* fame, became the host of the late-night show in 2014. He has distinguished

Reese Witherspoon speaking at Adobe Summit
AP Photo/Jeff Bottari

himself from other late-night hosts by going directly to his audiences via social media, updating the show features and guests, and bringing the show out to fans in different cities such as Orlando and Los Angeles.

Lilly Singh

Lilly Singh is a very popular YouTuber known for her creative and entertaining video sessions with celebrities including Selena Gomez and Dwayne "The Rock" Johnson. Because of her impact and the growth of her community, she transformed her online success through exclusive brand partnerships with Sephora, Skittles, and Coca-Cola (Horn, 2016) and in 2019 became the first Indian Canadian late-night host with her new show *A Little Late With Lilly Singh* (Schomer, 2019).

Reese Witherspoon

Oscar-winning actor Reese Witherspoon has ventured into new arenas. She has rebranded and become entrepreneurial, establishing a production company called Hello Sunshine with the goal of empowering women in the entertainment industry (Ferrante, 2018). Witherspoon funded the company for five years (Tribbitt, 2019) while also forming a new partnership with Elizabeth Arden and overseeing her clothing brand, Draper James. Witherspoon has reinvented the notion of "staying in your lane" by moving successfully among different roles and industries.

Features of Personal Brands

Most of the time we focus on our clients' brands when in fact we should also focus on our own personal brands.

Personal Brand Voice

When we create a personal brand, we also create our own brand voice through which we communicate our personalities, messages, and tone. Some professionals use a positive and polished voice on social, viewing each post and update under a microscope to stay attuned with how their interactions affect their reputations. Others, however, are unfiltered in communications with audiences, sharing everything, sometimes unedited, in the name of authenticity and transparency. But most often, individuals with personal brands fall somewhere near the middle of the continuum, wanting to be seen as authentic and human while also staying on top of audience perception.

Personal Brand Reputation

Our reputations, on- and offline, are our most priceless possessions, and we must maintain and remain invested in them by thinking through how we present ourselves and how others perceive us (Rahmaad, 2018). Being a strong presence in our social communities is a good way to build and maintain our reputations. In public relations, we come together online for a variety of causes (e.g., nonprofit work, community efforts), professional interests (e.g., section groups in the Public Relations Society of America), community initiatives (e.g., thought leader seminars), and personal interests (e.g., specialized areas of sports or entertainment public relations). Such participation allows us to build our authority on a subject and to share resources and ideas that can help others and increase influence in a group. Influence, which often is covered by influencer marketing principles and practices, is not limited to Instagram stars or celebrities. Anyone can be influential and a voice of authority, but this takes time, energy, and resources to do over a period of time consistently.

Alignment

In public relations, people get hired not only because of what they have done and created, but also for how much they are "known" in the industry. As marketing professional and author Mark Schaefer (2017) writes in his book *Known*, we must foster sustainable interest in our personal brands and know where we are, and where we want to be, in the industry. However, if we focus on promotion without merit or substance, we will not succeed. The alignment and balance of personality and promotion with expertise and experience are what make a personal brand successful.

Creating a Personal Brand

You may be asking yourself: How do I create a personal brand that is relevant, unique, and powerful? There are certain perspectives and elements to keep in mind when you begin to create your own brand.

What Makes You "You"

Your personal brand should be owned, created, and controlled by you. If others are deciding what your personal brand is, that's a problem. Ask yourself the following questions:

- What unique qualities do I have that differentiate me from others?
- What life experiences can I showcase?
- What unique industry, professional, and personal connections do I bring to the table?
- What perspectives do I have that set me apart?
- How do I describe myself in my personal, professional, and social circles?

Planning your brand is not about checking all the boxes for what it takes to be a "typical" PR professional. Now more than ever, agencies and brands are looking for talent with varied experiences, perspectives, and stories.

Expertise

As Goldie Chan (2018) discussed in *Forbes*, personal brands must have a focus. One way to establish your focus is to identify the core areas that you have authority in and a passion for. Dennis Yu of BlitzMetrics discusses the Topic Wheel framework (see Figure 6.1), which shows that individuals have six topic areas about which they can speak with authority

▼ FIGURE 6.1

Topic Wheel Framework Using the BlitzMetrics Model

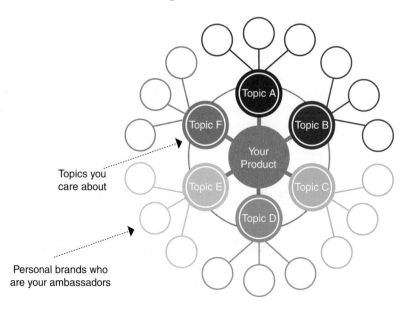

Topics you care about

Personal brands who are your ambassadors

and evidence based on work experience, stories, and expertise (Stukent, 2018). Within each Topic Wheel are six areas to cover and a layer of people (three per topic) in a given network who function as ambassadors for the topics and can endorse and advocate for the individual behind the personal brand. This brings forth the importance of having **social capital**, or endorsements based on expertise and validation from a community. These items are key to marketing and promoting a personal brand on- and offline.

When sharing expertise, you need to have **social proof**, which is evidence of your expertise that is documented online by others who endorse you and your personal brand. By showcasing your level of expertise through evidence (testimonials, endorsements, quotes, work samples, etc.), you can combat the "fake" professionals out there who say they're experts but who do not, in fact, have the evidence to back up their claims. More than ever, brands and organizations want individuals who not only talk a good line of their work and expertise but are able to show them they know what they are talking about.

Deirdre Breakenridge, founder and CEO of Pure Performance Communications, is a PR professional with decades of experience. She's been able to extend her personal brand into new areas. What Deirdre brings to the table with her personal brand is not just her expertise as a PR professional, but also her expertise in the following roles:

- Host of the *Women Worldwide* podcast

- Host of a live video show for Nasdaq

- Professor at New York University and Rutgers University

- Instructor for LinkedIn Learning on topics related to public relations

- Keynote speaker

- Author of several books including *Putting the Public Back in Public Relations* and *Answers for Modern Communicators*

- Creator of the popular Twitter chat for students, professionals, and faculty called #PRStudChat

As shown, Deirdre is active and present across multiple areas within public relations, but she also has expanded her reach and brand to other avenues and areas that have not been as populated by PR professionals. As a result, she has been able to create new channels and extensions for her personal brand to new audiences and formulate new opportunities for collaboration and networking.

Personality

A winning combination is having a level of expertise and insight in a subject area and also having a strong personality. This does not mean you have to be upbeat and charismatic 100 percent of the time or present yourself as something you are not. It means showing others your personal take on things, what motivates and inspires you, and how you see the world. Personality also shows your humanity, which is especially important.

Sarah Evans, otherwise known as PRSarahEvans online, is a PR professional who has worked with brands such as PayPal, SAP, Walmart, and Adobe over the years and has become a thought leader and speaker in many circles within the PR community. What Sarah has done to stand out and show her personality is to use a fashion accessory to distinguish herself from others when it comes to branding. Sarah's main accessory is a pair of oversized glasses, which are always present and accounted for in her talks, interviews, and professional sessions. By adding a unique and memorable accessory as part of a digital and physical brand kit, Sarah has been able to establish herself as a brand to be remembered.

Scott Monty is another professional who has used fashion as part of his personal brand. Scott, who was the lead in establishing a social media presence for Ford Motor Company and has worked with brands including Coca-Cola, IBM, and Google, uses a bow tie as part of his consulting logo and wears one all the time for talks, workshops, and professional engagements. For a personal brand, sometimes it just takes a fashion statement to create a memorable impression for audiences.

Quality Content and Stories

To establish a voice and presence in the industry, you must produce content that you can showcase in a consumable fashion. By creating and sharing content, you establish yourself as a resource for others. It also helps you establish new relationships with audiences and new partnerships with clients. Many professionals maintain blogs for this purpose. Table 6.1 shows some blogs written by PR professionals and the topics they write about in their content.

But what defines quality content—and how much of it should we provide? As Jason Falls (2019) points out, instead of focusing on creating as much content as possible, it is best to produce content that is of quality and substance. While it may be tempting to focus on creating the mass amount of content for the masses, quality trumps quantity for audiences.

This is somewhat of a different take from that of other professionals in the industry. For example, entrepreneur Gary Vaynerchuk has an entire team working at VaynerMedia dedicated to producing numerous pieces of content for his personal brand. The vast amount of

▼ TABLE 6.1

Sample of PR Practitioner Blogs

PR Professional	Blog Title	URL	Topics Covered
David Armano	Logic+Emotion	https://darmano.typepad.com	Public relations, social media
Deirdre Breakenridge	PR Expanded	www.deirdrebreakenridge.com	Public relations, modern communication, social media
Gini Dietrich	Spin Sucks	https://spinsucks.com	Public relations, PESO model, agencies
Jason Falls	Jason Falls	https://jasonfalls.com	Social media, public relations, content marketing, influencers
Scott Monty	Timeless & Timely	www.scottmonty.com	Public relations, social media, marketing, technology trends
Christina Nicholson	Media Maven	www.mediamavenandmore.com/blog	Public relations
Peter Shankman	Peter Shankman	www.shankman.com/blog	Public relations, technology, society and personal life

content produced by Gary and his team is not just for one dedicated channel, but for many other associated channels to get the most reach for his brand and audience (Vaynerchuk, 2019a, 2019b). For example, if Gary is going to be doing a keynote talk, he will record the video and post it through YouTube for his daily vlog (*GaryVee*), but then repurpose the content to be shared in short audio clips on Instagram and post the entire audio clip on his podcast. The overall goal is to engage audiences through various channels to get the most reach.

While owned media is a key branding hub for PR professionals to have on hand, it is important to create extensions of your personal brand to other channels, similar to what Gary Vaynerchuk has done. Creating these physical and digital touch points for your audience to reach you is crucial for getting as much exposure for a personal brand as possible. However, with each of these extensions, the overall goal is still to drive audiences back to the hub of the personal brand through channels owned and controlled by the individual.

Table 6.2 lists some types of content that PR professionals can create, host, and share to help amplify a personal brand to key audiences.

Some professionals gravitate toward owned media platforms and channels for presenting websites and blogs because they can control the content, structure, and look. Whatever we create and however we distribute it, our content must be relevant for our audience and personal in nature (highlighting the unique perspectives and attributes of the author), and it must have a long shelf life (otherwise known as **evergreen content**). Evergreen content allows us to be relevant over a period of time, not just for the duration of an updated blog post or brief article.

Another focus of content is storytelling. Brian Solis is a keynote speaker, digital anthropologist, author, and Altimeter analyst who has established his name in many PR and social media circles. Brian was one of the early adopters of digital and social media strategies and ebooks, which brought him to the spotlight as an innovator and global keynote speaker. *Lifescale*, a book Brian launched in March 2019, focuses on taking back control over digital connections and habits in society. In *Lifescale*, Brian integrates personal stories, and he further shares them in interviews, talks, infographics, blog posts, and social media posts. By taking this approach, Brian has been able to connect with his audience on an emotional level, strengthening his connections and presenting a human side to his already established brand.

▼ TABLE 6.2

Personal Branding Content Ideas for PR Professionals

Expertise	Earned Media	Resources and Education	Owned Media Promotion	Partnership Efforts
Awards	Curation of ideas and resources	Downloadable assets	Introduction videos	Documenting influencer experience
Blog posts	Endorsements	Ebooks	Promotion videos ahead of events	Exclusive interviews and experiences
Certifications	Featured interviews	How-to guides	Speaker reels	Guest blog posts
Courses	Media coverage	Infographics		Twitter chat guests
Papers	Social proof (evidence saved from social media)	Video guides		Webinar guests
Presentations	Video testimonials	White papers		
Reviews				
Testimonials				

What Are Best Practices for Client and Personal Branding?

Apply the following practices when implementing client branding and personal branding.

Best Practices

1. *Be yourself.* Each person or brand has unique qualities, characteristics, and stories that make each individual special. The goal is not to be like everyone else in the marketplace or applicant pool for a job. Being confident in the expertise, stories, and experiences you have to offer that no one else has can result in many opportunities.

2. *Be authentic and transparent.* As mentioned in previous chapters, ethics and having a strong etiquette code of conduct are more important than ever for PR professionals to have on hand. This does not mean sharing every daily aspect of your life and what you had for breakfast, but it does mean being honest, fair, and truthful to what is going on. Being able to share your emotions and ideas shows the human side of your personal brand, which many audience members can relate to.

3. *Be your best spokesperson.* The best person who can tell your story is you. When it comes to personal branding, the same principles we would give for clients who want to establish themselves as leaders in their industry can be applied toward individuals. With that being said, to get partnerships and opportunities, you have to get the word out about yourself. Formulate stories and features you can send out to blogs, media outlets, and brands you feel would be most aligned with your personal brand. Invest in creating a brand kit (logo, brand assets, media kit, press releases, templates, photography, etc.) to make your personal brand elements professional and unique (Ross, 2017).

4. *Invest in quality exchanges, partnerships, and collaborations.* Major corporations and nonprofits are not the only ones who can formulate partnerships and opportunities. When evaluating the overall nature of your personal brand, along with identifying key individuals who can endorse your brand as far as your expertise goes, an additional element could include looking at organizations and brands to align yourself with that fit these topic areas. For example, when exploring the brand of The Rock, one personal branding topic of his is working out, and he has aligned himself with Under Armour. The same goes for Karlie Kloss, who is a model and entrepreneur but also a fan of fitness, so she partnered with Adidas, which integrates athletics with lifestyle branding.

5. *Collect social, digital, and physical proof of your expertise.* Endorsements and testimonials are great, but to demonstrate the impact of a personal brand on the larger stage of industry and society, there has to be evidence to support this. Tweets and other social media updates that mention you, blog post mentions, news articles, features in magazines and blogs, and video testimonials are all pieces of content that can be collected and integrated into a personal brand media kit.

6. *Be consistent across all channels on- and offline.* Presenting yourself online one way and then doing something that completely contradicts the image presented results in a negative impression. How you present yourself online needs to be reflective of the behaviors and actions you take offline. When there is a disconnect, issues will come up for the individual.

While these are some best practices to consider, there are also some things you do not want to do as you start working on your personal brand.

Things to Avoid

1. *Not having a strategy in place for your brand.* Not having a strong stance for your personal brand and overall purpose could bring forth some challenges moving forward in the industry. Like all client and campaign work, a brand needs to have a strong strategic foundation for the individual to have an idea of the next steps to take and the challenges and opportunities that need to be addressed (Kaludi, 2014).

2. *Focusing on vanity metrics, quantity, and being everywhere.* It is important to note there are some things PR professionals do not want to do when it comes to creating and maintaining a personal brand for themselves (Arruda, 2019). While it is tempting to create the artificial illusion of being popular or "influential" on social media, for example, it is best to focus on the quality of the community, exchanges, and relationships that emerge from these connections.

3. *Faking it till you make it.* Unfortunately, with social and digital media it is very easy for others to "take the spotlight" and claim a position in the industry they did not earn. While it may be tempting to present yourself in a glamorous and high-profile stance online and in person, it is very easy to determine whether people are real or just trying to mislead others in believing they are experts when they are not. These actions violate the core principles of authenticity and trust, which are attributes needed in public relations now more than ever. There are huge reputation risks here if an individual is caught misleading audiences in this way, so the best advice to take is to be truthful about who you are.

SUMMARY

Creating and managing a personal brand is one of the most important components a PR professional needs to have for the modern industry landscape. Understanding the core attributes, stories, experiences, and expertise you have to offer your personal and professional community takes time, investment, and commitment over the long term. Having a personal brand does not mean you have to be like every other PR professional. In fact, it means it is crucial to own your narrative and story and to advocate for why you are unique compared to others. This does not happen overnight—you cannot wave a magic wand or rub Aladdin's lamp and say, "I want to have the best personal brand ever!" and have it immediately. This is not the way things work. A personal brand is a long-term investment of time, energy, resources, and effort. It is our most priceless possession, so we have to protect and build on it each and every day.

APR EXAM

- Personal branding

- Professional etiquette and branding practices

GAME CHANGER

Leo Morejon, Founder of Build & Inspire

Courtesy Leo Morejon

How did you get your start in public relations?

Working in public relations was an unexpected, pleasant surprise. My career in social media marketing began before Facebook, YouTube, Twitter, and the popular channels of today were part of any business conversation.

I was on Myspace learning to use the platform to create and spread content, but back then social media wasn't considered to be a PR tactic by most. But as social media became a vital part of any business's growth plan, I found myself working in the PR field.

What is your favorite part of working in public relations?

It's about relationships. Public relations, today more than ever, is about humanizing companies and allowing them to have relationships with whole groups of people as well as individuals.

What is the most challenging part of working in public relations?

The challenging parts for me are also some of the most exciting parts. No matter how much research, emotional intelligence, and other factors you can put into a response, campaign, or website, you never really know how people will react. You can have the best strategy and tactics, but until it's live, you really do not know how things will go. It's equally exciting but can be scary, especially during high-profile situations.

Who do you think are the biggest game changers for the PR industry?

The biggest game changers are companies that understand and practice emotional intelligence in their public relations. The most important part is "practice." At JWT we had a saying: "Cool is

cool and never tells you it's cool." This means that you can't be cool by just saying you are. A lot of companies project a vision or story that they themselves never practice. Everyone, every employee, has a voice today and will impact your public relations, so the companies that do first and speak later are the best. These may not always get the most press, but they do get quality press. Some that come to mind are Trader Joe's and Airbnb. They understand themselves, showcase it well in their public relations, and practice what they say internally.

What are some things you wish you knew when you were starting out in public relations?

Public relations and social media should never be siloed from the rest of the organization or looked at as an ancillary to your business. They need to be at the core of your business and should be leveraged to inform your decision with consumer insights and support your goals beyond just marketing. So, I wish I had known earlier on that things work best when you consider the business as a whole, and not just look at things tactically from one direction.

Leo Morejon, part of the social media team at Applegate, is an award-winning marketer (Clio, Cannes Lions, and others), sales leader, speaker, and content creator, and he attributes his success to always valuing people and relationships and focusing on being a trusted advisor above all else. His career began in the Emerging Media department at JWT's New York offices, before joining the Brand Strategy and Emerging Media department at 360i. There he pioneered real-time social media marketing with his work on Oreo, securing the first social media Guinness World Record and the famous Oreo Super Bowl blackout tweet, among other notable campaigns. Leo's professional focus is on how the intersection of different technologies can be leveraged to support both businesses and people. The passion for this space led him to a position at global professional services company Accenture and leadership positions at Sysomos Expion (an enterprise software as a service social media management and research platform). He worked across marketing, change management, and sales. Using his own unique sales methodology focused on storytelling, active listening, and being a trusted advisor, Leo secured millions of dollars in business from industry leaders such as Mondelēz, Subway, and the Estée Lauder Companies and trained over 200 salespeople. He also spent time in sales and marketing leadership positions for artificial intelligence and blockchain start-ups. Today, Leo combines his marketing and sales knowledge to help people in both fields reach their full potential by speaking around the world, mentoring, consulting, blogging, and podcasting. Leo also teaches at West Virginia University and Iowa State University.

KEY TERMS

Alignment balance 116

Branding 111

Evergreen content 121

Personal brand 116

Social capital 119

Social proof 119

DISCUSSION QUESTIONS

1. Describe what a personal brand means to you. What are three components that are necessary to have in a personal brand?

2. Identify the core components of a personal brand. Which one do you feel is the most important? Explain and share your rationale.

3. Describe what social proof means to you. Why is this necessary to have for a personal brand?

4. Review the best practices for personal branding. Are there any best practices you would recommend adding to the list? What about things to avoid doing when crafting a personal brand? Explain your positions on both cases.

ACTIVITIES

Building Your Portfolio

Building your brand kit. You are in preparation for applying for an internship at Edelman in New York City, and you want to make the best first impression for the hiring managers and internship coordinators.

You feel having a brand kit to showcase what you have done in your academic studies, internships, and freelance work will be the best way to showcase your brand. However, you want to draft a proposal to share with your academic advisor before implementing these ideas.

In this activity, you will create a brand kit for your personal brand and provide a short rationale for each of the following items (two or three sentences):

- Logo draft design
- Introduction to your brand
- Proposal for a digital portfolio to host your work
- List of items you want to include in your digital portfolio to showcase your personality, expertise, and experience
- List of social proof items you want to include

- Other components you feel are relevant (photos, testimonials, etc.)

Building Your Brand

Creating your own topic wheel. Based on the example shown in Figure 6.1, from the textbook by Dennis Yu and BlitzMetrics (Stukent, 2018), create your own Topic Wheel listing out six topics you feel you have some authority over.

- Topic 1
- Topic 2
- Topic 3
- Topic 4
- Topic 5
- Topic 6

Once you have done this, make sure to list the following for each topic:

- Three professional and personal connections who can speak on your authority
- Content pieces that can be used as social proof of your expertise and authority on these topics

CASE STUDY

*Drew Brees, Quarterback of the New Orleans
Saints: A Lesson in Personal Branding*

Drew Brees of the New Orleans Saints

When it comes to professional football, one name that comes up a lot for the sport is New Orleans Saints quarterback Drew Brees. Brees, who has been with the Saints since 2006, was part of the team that won the Super Bowl in 2009. Along with having the NFL's passing record, Brees has gotten over $14 million in endorsements on top of his professional football salary (Russo, 2018). With his success on the field and on the team, Brees has extended his personal brand beyond football to the community he serves on- and offline.

He also has been a strong part of the New Orleans community with his foundation, supporting efforts to help cancer patients with care, education, and additional opportunities for their families. In addition, Brees and his foundation have supported other nonprofit organizations such as the Make-A-Wish Foundation, the National Wildlife Federation, and the United Service Organizations. Aside from the nonprofit work Brees is doing off the field, he has explored other entrepreneur opportunities to enrich the next chapter of his life after football, including becoming an investor for the clothing brand UNTUCKit, a brand that sells shirts focused on comfort rather than convention (Heitner, 2018b). This involvement and support by Brees allows the brand to expand to an even larger audience group, so this partnership and investment is a win-win for both parties.

Why did this case generate buzz?

- In a time when professional athletes and celebrities may not necessarily have the best reputation or may come across as having an ego, it is refreshing to meet an athlete who understands the power of a personal brand not just for a team or company, but also for himself.

- Brees is strategic in using different channels and angles for his personal brand that are different from what has traditionally happened for athletes and other professionals. Instead of just focusing on one industry, Brees has reached outside of his main area and industry to branch out his brand to new audiences and opportunities.

- Brees has gotten recognition in the media and industry for having a strong personal brand that is powerful both on and off the field, which has led to a number of professional opportunities for him.

What are the ethical and legal issues?

- There are not necessarily any legal issues involving this case. However, when it comes to ethical considerations, when creating a positive brand with many different components to it, it is important to understand these efforts have to be sustainable over a long period of time.

- In addition, reputations and personal brands take a lot of time to build and grow, and it only takes one incident for the brand to be impacted negatively. Celebrities and sports figures including Tiger Woods, Kevin Spacey, and Lindsay Lohan all have found this to be true with their respective situations and industries. With Brees, presenting a certain brand image to an audience is important, but if a crisis hits, this changes the game. If the members of an audience feel their expectations were violated in some way, they will be outraged, and the person in question will lose all credibility in the space. This is a risk and challenge Brees needs to keep in mind and be aware of.

What are some takeaways to learn from this case?

- Personal brands can help extend opportunities beyond an individual's area of expertise.

- Looking outside of the main industry to become multidisciplinary can add to the unique features that distinguish one personal brand from another.

- Understanding the key attributes associated with your personal brand and tying this into aligned partnerships creates a win-win situation. Brees has been able to do this very effectively with both his nonprofit work and his corporate endorsement deals.

WRITING

CHAPTER 7

LEARNING OBJECTIVES

- Understand writing in the context of public relations.
- Become familiar with types and features of PR writing.
- Identify PR writing challenges and opportunities.
- Learn some best practices for PR writing.

Introduction

Writing effectively is one of the most important things that we do in public relations. Because writing is the number-one skill required by employers, it is one that you, as a student, will need to develop so that you will be ready to enter the professional world.

While PR writing is not rocket science, it does take time and experience to master the art of persuading your audiences through the written word. As successful writers, we create messages that are relevant to others and that resonate with them on a personal and emotional level. At the same time, our messages must be professional and aligned with our brand's mission and core attributes. To write for public relations, we must be skilled in writing for different formats and channels.

As a developing PR writer, it is important that you keep in mind the following questions before you create content and stories for a campaign:

- Am I creating the right content for my audiences? Is my content achieving my purposes?

- Is the content I am creating aligned to the communication and business objectives of our client?

- Am I writing content that is inclusive and reaching all audiences?

- What is my writing style, and is it consistent across all channels that my organization uses? How do people feel about my writing style?

- How can I make my writing stronger and more effective for my audiences?

These are questions addressed in this chapter. In addition to showing you how PR writers compose messages that impact readers (and viewers and listeners), this chapter will introduce you to different types of PR writing, help you build writing skills, and prepare you to integrate best practices into your writing.

What Does It Mean to Write for Public Relations?

Writing is at the heart of every PR campaign and is a strong core requirement for PR professionals today (Commission on Public Relations Education, 2018). As a student, you will find that among the required courses in the PR curriculum, the Public Relations Writing course, which you will likely take after this one, holds the same status as Principles of Public Relations, Case Studies, Research Methods, Experience or Internships, and Campaigns courses. Regardless of how tools, platforms, and technologies may evolve, excellent writing is a constant. If you like to write, then public relations is likely a good fit for you.

Writing, like training for the Olympics or any competitive sport, improves with practice over time. A PR professional does not wake up one day and say, "I must be a perfect writer right now!" Instead, regular practice, such as writing your own blog, will gradually lead to stronger skills. Because you will create a significant amount of content, even as an entry-level professional, your writing will only get better over time and continue to improve.

Writing Styles and Purposes

Many different writing styles and formats are used in PR writing, including persuasive writing, creative writing, storytelling, and real-time writing.

Persuasive Writing

Persuasive writing is at the foundation of PR writing because it incorporates everything we are doing in public relations. The ultimate goal for PR professionals is to create stories, content, and messages that resonate with audiences at an emotional, logical, and practical level, motivating them to take an action or to think differently. PR professionals write stories and content that make audiences like them because they are able to relate to what is being said. The content provides a valuable overall experience and a sense of community that is not accessible to many people (Mireles, 2014).

Persuasive writing is at the heart of what PR professionals do in all aspects of their work, from promoting new products to handling crises. For example, persuasive writing comes into play when a reputation is at stake. For example, an effective crisis statement was needed when the 2019 Kentucky Derby winner was disqualified. Churchill Downs issued a statement that not only provided information related to the incident, but also persuaded unhappy audiences to think differently about the outcome. The statement provided context for the crisis and helped to quell the outrage that followed the race results. In addition, this statement was presented consistently in its messaging across different channels of communication for Churchill Downs. By informing audiences about how decisions to disqualify are made, Churchill Downs succeeded in handling the crisis.

Within persuasive writing are some specialized areas that are integrated in current PR writing practices.

Creative Messaging

Creative messaging, writing that goes beyond the simple transmission of information to engage and entertain, is an important element for PR professionals. Some people assume that the only discipline and profession in which **creative writing** takes place is advertising (perhaps inspired by television's *Mad Men* series). However, public relations is a very creative field in which we integrate a wide range of messages, creative content, and visuals to help amplify the essence of a campaign in a unique and novel way. For example, Clinique, the popular makeup company, created a campaign that focused on its newest innovation, the hydration system Clinique iD. Clinique partnered with influencers to create content and share their stories (Shorty Awards, n.d.), which sparked audiences to engage in large numbers and to take action (by purchasing the product) as a direct result. The campaign was creative in that it put a global twist on influencer marketing and also shared the control of messaging with those influencers. Writing content does not have to be a one-way experience for PR professionals. Instead, it can be a collaborative process that results in stories that make an impact.

Storytelling or Narrative Messaging

Storytelling, or narrative messaging, is a growing area of focus for PR professionals. The clients and brands we work with cannot simply inform their audiences and promote their products and positions. To succeed, they must also share the stories that happen behind the scenes—stories that must be first intertwined with the brand's purpose, messaging, and essence and then shared across all platforms. In public relations, we work with organizations to create unique journeys for audiences that shape perceptions, grow community, and invite publics to be part of the overall brand experience. The stories at the center of our campaigns, above all, have to be memorable. Whether we design our content to persuade based on logic, emotion, or something else, our content must motivate audience members to share it with their communities and colleagues.

Maxwell House's Mother's Day campaign showed how storytelling can be used to shine a light on a specific issue. The coffee company wanted to raise awareness of the "invisible labor" that mothers perform in the course of raising a family while they maintain jobs and professional lives ("Maxwell House Is on a Mission," 2019). This campaign engaged with families by sharing a focused message about the work that women do, but the coffee brand did not stop there. The company also mixed into the campaign some universal stories shared by mothers and daughters—stories that resonated with audiences as authentic, transparent, and real. This kind of messaging and audience buy-in is much less likely to be achieved through more traditional campaigns, such as those featuring a paid spokesperson.

Real-Time Writing

Lastly, **real-time writing** is a way to define the spontaneous writing that we do online when we must act quickly. To support our clients and brands through real-time writing, we must think on our feet. While we can prewrite articles and schedule out our campaign's every social media post, there are times when we must respond in the moment—or lose an opportunity. For example, Starbucks missed a potentially big branding moment, failing to respond in real time when one of its coffee cups appeared in an early episode of *Game of Thrones* by mistake. While Starbucks waited until the next day to respond, the company was able to engage belatedly with audiences on Twitter and managed to gain some attention and grab some news coverage. The people behind many other brands, including Oreo, Aviation Gin, Cinnabon, Wendy's, Steak-umm, MoonPie, and Vita Coco, have raised the profiles of their products by applying wit and personality. The brand Vita Coco generated news thanks to its response to a Twitter

Vita Coco ✔
@VitaCoco

#NewProfilePic

10:14 PM · May 15, 2019 · Twitter for iPhone

558 Retweets   **6.4K** Likes

Vita Coco's Twitter
response to troll
Twitter/@VitaCoco

user who had decided to bash the brand in a way that was—let's just say—memorable (Sung, 2019). Vita Coco posted back, but unfortunately, the reception of the coconut water company's tweet was mixed (Sung, 2019). Falling flat or failing altogether is a risk we take when we write in real time, charging ahead without the benefit of colleagues' input or the questions raised during a typical approval process. In some cases, real-time writing has benefited brands, but in others, it has not gone over well at all. For our real-time writing to truly be great, we need to be supported by a professional culture that specifies when, why, and how to respond in the moment to online messaging.

Qualities of Effective Messaging

Writing effective messages means creating concise, powerful statements that motivate individuals to take action or to consider perspectives that may be contrary to their own. Overall, when it comes to writing approaches in public relations, the content within each message should have each of the following characteristics:

- *Consistency.* Is our message aligned with the perception and branding of our client? Is it varying and contradictory, or is it clear and steady?

- *Strong voice.* Do the specific style, word choice, tone, and pacing associated with the brand come across in our message? Is the brand's voice clear, and does it have the same recognizable quality when broadcast through various channels and platforms?

- *Authenticity.* Does our messaging feel artificially created, or does it truly represent the brand's purposes?

Let's look at some examples that reflect these principles.

Consistency

Our messaging must line up with the rest of our campaign and with the ethos of our client and brand. For example, Coca-Cola is very consistent with its messaging across all channels and media, which audiences can recognize in any place. The company's stated purpose is to "refresh the world [and] make a difference."

A PUBLIC RELATIONS WRITING PROCESS

Writing effectively is one of the most important (and challenging) things we do as public relations practitioners. For evolving professionals, it's a fundamental skill to develop—and the one most requested by employers. Not to worry! Using a process for creating effective content will help do your best work. I recommend the following:

RESEARCH CLIENT & TOPIC

- Determine client's style for writing /presenting content. Review previous work for attributes, messaging, "brand voice," the unique personality conveyed in that content.
- Discuss existing content/campaigns. Request samples of most successful pieces.
- Ask about assignment topic, sources for learning about it.

EXPLORE
CLIENT'S AUDIENCES, PURPOSES, & TONE

- Discover target audiences; identify platforms used to share content.
- Ask client purpose of your writing (e.g., to persuade? inform?). What tone to convey (e.g., authority, humor)?

DETERMINE
CAMPAIGN SCOPE & TYPES OF CONTENT TO CREATE

- Ask will you write one piece? Several?
- Ask what you will write, such as press releases, feature stories, social media updates. Locate research materials such as videos, websites, facts, content models.

CREATE
CONTENT, REVISE (A LOT), & FORMULATE PUBLISHING STRATEGIES

- Draw on research to begin drafting. Refer to model (if you're writing text for video explaining a process, find an excellent example). Keep track of sources used; document as required.
- Share drafts with trusted professionals (who are not your client); explain feedback type desired (check for bias, etc.); draw on that to revise, finalize.
- Brainstorm how to promote, evaluate impact with metrics on engagement, sentiment.

CHECK
CONTENT FOR ERRORS, ACCURACY, & EVIDENCE

- Edit and fine-tune. Check for format, accuracy, professionalism.
- Provide credits, citations, references of evidence as required.
- Evaluate (again); ask trusted professionals to read final piece for errors. First impressions matter!

SUBMIT/PUBLISH
CONTENT & ANALYZE METRICS

- Send content to client or hit "publish" button on digital platforms.
- Evaluate impact of content using tools such as Cision, Meltwater, Talkwalker.
- Evaluate lessons learned for future assignments, samples for clients.

Starbucks Coffee ✔ @Starbucks · May 6
TBH we're surprised she didn't order a Dragon Drink.

○ 1.2K   ↻ 22.4K   ♡ 79K   ↑

Julieta @julimicheletti · May 6
What do Dragons drink, anyway?

○ 14   ↻ 551   ♡ 2.4K   ↑

Starbucks Coffee ✔
@Starbucks

Replying to @julimicheletti

Whatever they want.

1:32 PM · May 6, 2019 · Lithium Tech

1.8K Retweets   **11.9K** Likes

Starbucks's response to *Game of Thrones* coverage of its coffee cup in episode 4

Twitter/@Starbucks

Strong Voice

Brand voice—the injection of personality into the overall tone of a message—is a significant and effective tool for PR writers and our clients. Brands such as Popeyes® Louisiana Kitchen, Burger King, Steak-umm, and Aviation Gin have all established their brands in their writing based on the specific attributes they value as part of their company. Popeyes, for example, conveys a strong brand voice as illustrated by the Twitter campaign for its chicken sandwich released in 2019. The company's introductory post read: "Chicken. Brioche. Pickles. New. Sandwich. Popeyes. Nationwide. So. Good. Forgot. How. Speak. In. Complete. Sandwiches. I mean, sentences."

Authenticity

Authenticity, or the quality of being honest and transparent, is a key element that many brands have difficulty communicating. However, Steak-umm, a frozen-meat brand, has met this challenge through its social media presence, showing who the brand is in its posts, clap-backs, and videos that comprise its "Steak-umm bless" campaign. The brand's 20-something social media manager reflects the angst and humor of a generation in posts such as "The night is dark and full of beef."

What Types of Writing Do PR Professionals Compose?

As a PR professional, you will need to know the fundamental principles that guide effective and strategic writing. You will also need to know the types of content that you will create. PR professionals construct a wide range of pieces and types of content:

- Memos
- Emails
- Brochures
- Fact sheets
- Statements
- Speeches
- Scripts (TV, live TV, podcast, and radio)
- Q&A materials
- News and press releases
- Feature stories

- Pitches

- Infographics

- Media kits

- Websites, blogs, and social media

In the following sections, we will cover the details of the most common types of writing that we must produce: news and press releases, feature stories, pitches, infographics, media kits, and digital and social media content.

News and Press Releases

Because public relations has a strong foundation in and connection to journalism, news and press releases are two main areas of focus for PR professionals. There are some differences between a news release and a press release that you need to know: While both are formatted similarly to how a news article is written, a **news release** focuses on hard news, such as breaking news and announcements, while a **press release** focuses on soft news, such as news of partnerships and coverage of events.

News Releases

We create news releases with our client or organization's purposes in mind and share them with the media. Through news releases we communicate to the media our client's perspectives on hard news, with the expectation that journalists will use the release as a foundation for a story they write for their publications or outlets. Do not be surprised if you see a news release you have written printed verbatim without your name. This is a common practice, and the key thing to remember is that when this happens, we've succeeded in getting our messaging to our audiences and into publications we wanted to reach.

Press Releases

A press release (as shown in the KFC example on page 135) has the same characteristics as a news release—covering the who, what, when, where, and why of an event—but does not focus on "hard" news as news releases do. Most press releases are housed and shared via an organization's newsroom and presented in a dedicated location on its website. Such updates are aimed at interested journalists and media outlets who use the information to write their own stories.

We use press releases to communicate each of the following:

- A new partnership or product (e.g., Adidas and Beyoncé, as shown in Chapter 4's case study)

- Mergers between companies to combine forces (e.g., Sprint and T-Mobile)

- Events with celebrities (e.g., Kentucky Derby galas)

- The opening of new offices and headquarters (e.g., Amazon and New York City/ Arlington, Virginia, for its second headquarters, as shown in Chapter 5's case study)

- The hiring of a new professional to join a specific team, an agency move, or a new position for a senior representative

- The winning of prestigious awards in the industry (e.g., Shorty, Webby, or Cannes Lions award)

As is the case for most of the writing we do, we must follow a specific style when composing press and news releases, and that is the one used by journalists and set forth in the *Associated Press Stylebook*. "AP style" highlights specific ways to spell out or abbreviate certain words—for example, the use of "Oct." for *October*—and sets requirements for the overall format for writing a news or press release. For example, press releases are brief, usually one or one-and-a-half pages long. The *AP Stylebook* also gives us guidelines for grammar, spelling, and identifying factual errors. Making a factual error—that is, an error in which we present incorrect information (such as a wrong name, location, or time)—can result in our being fired. PR writers must be careful and factual, not only because it's the right thing to do, but because sharing incorrect information results in confusion, lost opportunities, and diminished credibility. So, if you get a bad grade for making an error in a PR writing assignment, rather than losing a job, you can learn, improve, and strive to be as careful as possible.

Let's move on to what makes a press release a press release. Each one needs to have the following:

- A *headline* that focuses on the main news that is the focus of the press release

- A *lead paragraph* that outlines the most important elements covered in the story

- *Quotes and supporting information* in the paragraphs that follow the lead paragraph

- A *closing* that provides contact information (phone and email) and a URL for readers who want more details

- A *final boilerplate paragraph*, no more than two to three sentences in length, that gives an overview of the person, organization, or brand discussed in the press release

For example, a writer for Kentucky Fried Chicken created a press release to discuss how the new Colonel Sanders is an actual colonel. The people behind the brand were able to add a unique twist to the company's iconic figure, Colonel Sanders, and the writer of the press release was able to provide some additional points of interest. The objective of the press release was to persuade KFC audiences and potential audiences that the brand is doing something new and innovative. As shown, the press release was not the only thing integrated in this HTML document. Images, videos, and additional resources were also included to achieve the writer's goals.

Whether a press release is sent directly to media outlets or posted online for the general public, the document gives writers and our brands the opportunity to share relevant stories, updates, and news that others, including the media, would find interesting.

When working on a press release, we need to keep the following crucial elements in mind:

- *Purpose and message: We must work to make clear why our story is a story.* Writing a press release requires a persuasive strategy that involves putting ourselves in the position of a journalist to ask: Why would I want to know about this story? Why

KFC press release

Retrieved at https://kfc.new-media-release.com/kentucky_buckets/index.html

Introducing the Kentucky Buckets— America's newest professional football team, and not just a cheap marketing gimmick the Colonel (now in the form of comedian Rob Riggle) thought up to help sell buckets of delicious, hand-prepared Kentucky Fried Chicken to football fans. Seriously, it's a real team—with uniforms and everything.

HOME

IMAGE GALLERY

VIDEO GALLERY

KFC Announces First Celebrity Colonel Who is Actually a Colonel

Coach Colonel Rob Riggle introduces the Kentucky Buckets, a real professional football team, sort of

LOUISVILLE, Ky. – September 8, 2016 – This morning Kentucky Fried Chicken's Colonel Harland Sanders announced the formation of the first professional football team fueled by fried chicken, the Kentucky Buckets. Actor, comedian and writer Rob Riggle has been named Coach Colonel and will star in advertisements as the coach of the very real Kentucky Buckets.

"As owner, general manager, head coach, defensive coordinator, offensive coordinator, marketing director, groundskeeper and scouting director of America's newest professional football team, the Kentucky Buckets, I've got one goal in mind," said Coach Colonel Rob Riggle. "To get buckets of delicious chicken across the goal line and in front of millions of fans on football Sundays. And Thursdays. And Mondays."

EMBED THIS

Taking the field in red-and-white striped jerseys, the Colonel's famous string ties and white helmets graced by delicious fried chicken, the Buckets are embodiment of America's finest gameday fare. When Colonel Coach Riggle dons his headset on the sidelines, he will be joined by his squad, Buckets cheerleaders and "Mr. Bucketeer" the mascot.

A retired Lt. Colonel in the United States Marine Corps Reserve, Riggle is the first actual colonel to take on the role of KFC's famous founder, Colonel Sanders. In other striking biographical similarities, Riggle hails from Louisville, KY, the home of KFC since 1966.

"Rob Riggle was the obvious choice for those on the internet calling for us to use the real Kentucky Colonel in our ads," said Kevin Hochman, Chief Marketing Officer for KFC U.S. "He was born in Louisville, Kentucky and served our country as a Lieutenant Colonel in the Marines. It doesn't get any more real than that."

might it matter to my readers? Which messages and details would I share with my audience? It's best to show journalists, rather than tell them, why a story is significant (Yonkman, 2017). Having a new roof put on an office and attending a conference are events that do not require a press release. However, it might be worthwhile to report on the use of a cutting-edge process that involves the community and sustainable materials or on the effect of a groundbreaking discovery presented at a conference. Attention and time are money for our media audiences, so we must spend these wisely when choosing what events warrant a press release.

- *Audience: We must conduct research on those we want to share our stories with.* Research pays off when it comes to learning about our audiences, including our media audiences (see also Chapter 5 for coverage of audience segmentation).

Understanding which audiences to reach and why, and exploring the stories and press releases our media contacts have written in the past, is central to pitching our stories effectively. Tools including Cision and Meltwater can help us with this task by showing us what given media professionals have written before, what type of stories they have produced, and how they want to be contacted. Sending our press releases to the wrong contacts or outlets causes problems. For example, you would not want to send a press release about a University of Southern California fundraising event for USC Annenberg to a die-hard University of California, Los Angeles (UCLA) vlogger.

- *Adaptation: We must tailor our stories for specific audiences as needed.* To be effective, we have to adapt our press releases so that they fit individual media outlets and the interests and sensibilities of their journalists. Showing them that we've done our research and we understand how a story ties to their mission is critical. Once we've informed ourselves about our media audiences and what they are most likely to write about, we can edit accordingly and reach out to individual journalists. As noted earlier, it is important to know what these journalists have written and how they want to be approached. For example, Taylor Lorenz, a *New York Times* technology reporter who has also written for *The Atlantic*, does not use email to correspond about stories, but prefers doing so through Twitter and Instagram direct messages (DMs).

- *Relationships: Remember, it's all about relationships.* Media professionals appreciate when we stay in touch in general. It's a good practice to reach out to our contacts to say, "Hi, hope all is well," and to see what they are working on. If journalists and others have an idea that we are genuinely invested in what they are writing about, they will be more likely to establish a proactive and substantial long-term relationship with us. Plus, you never know where a media professional will go next. Rather than going for the short-game pitch for a quick media hit, think of the long game.

- *Persuasion: We must support our stories and arguments with evidence and supplemental content.* To persuade journalists, we need to provide credible quotes and background information that paint a complete picture of our story beyond what we present in the press release. When pitching to the media, we need to think about how to make people's jobs easier, especially given the cuts to newspapers and other publications, because media professionals and journalists must now do more with less. If we include a link to a press release or attach it as a document, we should be sure to note the inclusion of any additional elements such as photos, social media updates, or video. The more we provide (readily and concisely), the easier it will be for the media to cover the story.

Best Practices for Writing and Distributing News and Press Releases

1. *Do not spam or stalk journalists.* These bad practices top the list of what journalists do not like. While we may pitch a story and send a press release to particular journalists, we may not hear back from them. This does not mean we should wait

an hour and then spam them with a follow-up email, or stalk them across different channels to see if they saw our email or got our 100th phone call about the press release. We need to be positive and empathic in our communications and relationships with media contacts.

2. *Know your media contacts.* Research is key. It's a very bad idea to pitch a story or press release idea to a media outlet that we know nothing about. Journalists want to know that we've specifically gone out of our way to discover who they are, what they do, and what they've written. For example, we wouldn't pitch a NASCAR story to a Sephora influencer.

3. *Do not assume.* The fact is that a given journalist or media contact may not write about our story. They are under no obligation. Yes, we may know it is the best story ever, but not everyone will share our enthusiasm. It's important to be relevant and convincing if we want journalists to understand why ours is an important story to tell and why it is essential for their audiences.

4. *Always assume.* We must work under the assumption that everything we say and do as professionals is documented and on the record, all of the time. Saying something meant to be "off the record" or overpromising something to a reporter usually comes back to get us. The media are all about getting a story—we need to make sure it is the story we want to tell. And while this seems obvious, we must never, ever lie to a journalist or media professional. Ours is a very small industry, and our reputations are our most priceless possessions. Word of a misstep, whether intentional or not, gets around quickly, putting not only our reputations at stake, but those of our clients and brands.

Feature Stories

As is the case when we write press and news releases, when we write feature stories, we follow the AP style guide that journalists use. However, one of the main purposes of writing a **feature story**, or a human-interest story, is for us to promote individuals who are part of a brand and in the news. Such stories profile those who are doing interesting things. Another goal of writing a feature story is to boost the "human side" of a brand or organization to persuade audiences of its value.

Qualities

A feature story is formatted as a long-form piece of content in which we tell a story using the tools of narrative writing, such as dialogue, detail, and creative thinking. The overall focus is not to provide hard news facts or statistics, but rather to present a unique angle of a person who may not usually appear in the news. For example, Emilia Clarke, who played Daenerys Targaryen in the HBO hit show *Game of Thrones*, was the subject of a feature story that appeared a few weeks before season 8 began. It reported that she had battled health issues during the first few seasons of the show, a story that was unique and that had not yet been reported. The story was also timely and relevant because the show was entering its final season. *Game of Thrones* audiences wanted to know more about the actors who inhabited the characters of the iconic show.

Best Practices for Writing Feature Stories

Among the best practices for writing feature stories are the following:

1. *Remember the objective.* We must keep in mind the overall purpose of our feature story, presenting it in a way that adds value for readers and information that has the depth to humanize or demystify the person or brand we're featuring. Key to the feature story are additional stories, perspectives, and quotes that create a strong impression that will be remembered, shared, and discussed.

2. *Use storytelling practices.* When we write features, we do not follow the inverted pyramid structure often used for press or news releases. The inverted pyramid structure, applied to a news release, involves beginning with the most important information about the event or news item (who, what, where, when, and why). This method is not as useful for feature stories, which focus on storytelling and require less set structure. Our goal in writing a feature story is to capture the attention of the reader, spark an emotional response from the reader, and motivate that reader to share and discuss what he or she gleaned from the story.

3. *Include supporting detail.* We use quotes and other personalized features to give the story substance and color. There is no word limit for feature stories like there is for news or press releases, so there is room to add rich content to illustrate our overall message and purpose.

4. *Show, don't tell.* As we do for press and news releases, we must show audiences why our story is important and deserves to be told. For a feature story, we can use all of our senses to do so.

5. *Remember the bigger picture.* Feature stories, which are human interest stories, must also be relevant and purposeful. We often publish them ahead of big promotions, events, film openings, or other timely happenings to give audiences a deeper level of understanding of the characters involved. These stories must also be factual, as must all of the content we create.

Pitches

A **pitch** is a short memo in which we outline what we want to accomplish in a piece of writing; its purpose is to show our plan to provide a win-win situation (Schick, 2018). Whether we are pitching to a writer for a *Forbes* piece or reaching out to an influencer about a potential partnership, we must be skilled in creating these documents. We must put ourselves in the shoes of the assignment editor or other person we want to persuade by asking ourselves: What would I want to see in a pitch? What additional information would help me create the story I'm proposing? This is a mindset that we must integrate and adapt as a situation requires.

Sample Pitch

For example, if I saw a PR pitch come through my email saying, "Hi Karen, I read your article about coffee, and I just know that #DecafPower coffee is the perfect brand for you and your audience to try," not only would this result in my swift deletion of the message (decaf is not coffee!); it would show me that the writer did not do his or her research. However, if I were to receive a pitch like the following, I'd likely respond more positively:

Hi Karen. I read your latest post on coffee. I appreciate the impact that coffee has on the daily lives of students and professors. What I don't understand is this: Why don't brands do more to engage with such a key audience, especially with final exams coming up? If you want to chat more about a coffee brand that's invested in students and educators, I have a contact I'd love to introduce you to. I'd be more than happy to send you some additional information and answer any questions you have.

This pitch is concise and reflects evidence that the writer has done his or her research about the context and media contact recipient (me). The pitch is brief, and at the same time it gives enough information to invite interest (Schick, 2018).

Best Practices for Writing Pitches

Among best practices for writing effective pitches are the following:

1. *Do the research.* As we saw in our discussion of press releases, we need to reach the right people in the media and know ahead of time what they will need and expect from us (Garrett, 2018).

2. *Write concisely.* When writing a pitch, which is usually just a few sentences long, we keep things brief and focused. In addition, we give readers a way to contact us in addition to our email addresses (Jennings, 2018).

3. *Make the lives of media contacts easier.* All of us who work in public relations or the media work under deadlines. In some cases, there is the added pressure of being understaffed. That is why we need to anticipate what our media contacts need and make background information or other appropriate materials readily available to them.

4. *Follow up when appropriate.* This does not mean that we should stalk journalists or other media professionals every 15 minutes to see if they need anything else from us. There is a time and place for approaching journalists to follow up. Proper etiquette is crucial in this stage, and checking in after 48 hours is appropriate.

5. *Use the phone.* No, this does not mean sending texts or DMs to our contacts. It means picking up our phones, selecting the phone app icon, and dialing a number to talk to another person. Yes, I am talking about calling our contacts directly. Cold calling people we don't know is a challenge, but often it is more effective than sending multiple emails. By calling, we can interact personally through a different channel. Plus, calling is even faster than relying on new technologies. Going old school may be the best way to approach things (Jennings, 2018).

6. *Share the article and coverage that results from your pitch.* As we've said, public relations is all about relationships, and it does not cost us anything to thank reporters, journalists, and other media professionals for their work. Sharing a quick note with an update and word of thanks across different channels can go a long way in solidifying relationships.

Infographics

The **infographic** is a form of storytelling that allows us to visualize content and present it to our audiences. In public relations, our overall purposes in creating infographics are to illustrate data (research), share knowledge (information), and capture attention (through visual experiences).

Qualities and Samples

While infographics vary in type, those designed to share information typically feature a strong headline that focuses on the topic, followed by three to five major and related points (see the "modern unicorn marketer" example from Larry Kim on page 141). Another type of infographic focuses on a specific image or graphic that demonstrates a key issue, such as the infographics that appear in popular news articles and reports for presidential elections. Yet another type shows a process, outlining specific steps that provide audiences with a better understanding of how things work. For example, this type of infographic allows us to describe how certain products are made (e.g., coffee). Others focus on the key parts that make up a product, as demonstrated in the image of the modern unicorn marketer. Finally, infographics can highlight comparisons, outlining key differences or similarities between two brands or competitors. These are present across the board, such as *Ad Age* infographics about what is hot and what is not for events such as CES®, SXSW®, and Cannes Lions. Ultimately, the overall goal is to provide information in a visual manner that is highly consumable.

Throughout this text, you'll find three different types of infographics that (1) show a step-by-step process, (2) illustrate a concept, or (3) present an image or document with analysis.

Infographics can stand alone, but they are usually part of something more substantial in a PR campaign, report, or story. We might use infographics to do any of the following:

- Report a visual of specific research findings (e.g., Edelman Trust Barometer)

- Frame a story (e.g., 2020 U.S. presidential election)

- Provide additional information related to a new product, process, or issue (e.g., iPhone X)

- Spark initial interest in a story being shared on social media

Infographics, while visual, are very much about writing. When we create an infographic, we first outline its overall purpose, determine the content we will use it to present and the best design for doing so, validate and confirm that our information is accurate, and identify the appropriate channels for showcasing this content.

Best Practices for Creating Infographics

Some best practices for composing and designing infographics include these:

1. *Be accurate.* While design is part of the planning of an infographic and the conversation audiences have around it, our content and messaging are the stars of the show. Our content must be 100 percent accurate, and all supporting evidence and sources must be of high quality. If we do not cite our information appropriately, our infographic will generate mistrust that will reflect badly on us, our clients, and the brands we represent.

THE MODERN UNICORN MARKETER

Modern unicorn marketer
from Larry Kim

Larry Kim, MobileMonkey, Inc.

HARD SKILLS

Analytics
Negotiating and interpreting a large pile of data to discern audience preferences and behavior, as well as evaluate campaign performance and ROI.

Content Strategy
The definition of goals with content, as well as using search engine optimization, link-building, and best practices in amplification to get as much exposure for content as possible.

Social Media
Compiling social data to help make business decisions on how to prioritize time and money spent on social channels based on audience behavior and engagement.

Mobile
Comprehending the connection between mobile and social media usage to determine how to optimize a mobile marketing campaign.

Ecommerce
Understanding customers through online marketing campaigns in social and mobile to see what new channels can be undertaken to boost the company's ecommerce efforts.

SOFT SKILLS

Creativity
Bringing new concepts and ideas to the table for solving existing problems through either images or words.

Resourcefulness
Utilizing all the tools at her disposal to seek the ripest sources of data to come up with the best analysis possible.

Adaptability
Changing plans and accommodating situations when new obstacles and challenges come about with a show of fortitude and an ability to endure hardship.

Collaboration
Working with other teams and specialists to help marketing efforts succeed, as well as provide data and insights that assists them in turn.

Leadership
Directing and inspiring a team towards achieving a common goal through experience, insight, and collaborative effort.

By: Larry Kim, MobileMonkey, Inc.
© https://MobileMonkey.com

2. *Write concisely.* We must choose our words carefully, saying a lot with a little. We must also generate a strong headline to attract audiences and for search engine purposes.

3. *Design purposefully.* Our choice of font and other visual elements matters. Good messages not only are clear and concise, but must also be readable and accessible to many. Identify clear fonts that are easy to read and that align with the brand's messaging and purpose.

To create his infographic, Larry Kim combined color and creativity with strong copy. He presents information in a clear, consistent way, while illustrating the "hard skills" and "soft skills" that marketers must have very simply with icons and brief text. Kim has managed to convey a lot of information in a small space that doesn't feel cluttered or overwhelming. Given his thematic choice of a unicorn, his approach is also playful and friendly, and designed to attract audiences, among whom are people learning the basics of public relations.

Media Kit

Another traditional form of content that we create is the **media kit**, a collection of premade promotional and informational materials that covers a brand, person, or cause and is targeted and distributed to media professionals. Over time, media kits have evolved from a package of print materials circulated at events and press conferences to exclusive experiences to be shared and discussed online. As shown in the example for Billboard on page 143, contemporary media kits integrate a range of multimedia components, statistics, and information available for others to download and use for their PR efforts.

This media kit is effective for a variety of reasons. First, it is visual and brand aligned with its brand colors and overall presence. Second, it combines multiple media and formats, making this a media kit fit for the modern age. This will make it easier for the media and others to consume the content and promote the stories and brand.

Parts of a Media Kit

Our media kits equip journalists and other media professionals with the content that they need to tell our stories as thoroughly as possible. Items typically included in media kits are the following:

- *Press releases* (see page 133)

- A **backgrounder**, which is an overview of the key players involved in a PR campaign

- *Biographies*, which are brief, focused life stories of key players involved

- A *brochure*, which is a trifold document outlining key points of information in a visual way

- *Infographics* that highlight details of research or product information (see page 139)

- A *fact sheet*, or one-page overview of a campaign with the major points highlighted

- *Visual elements*, such as photos, video clips, and B-roll footage (video coverage that is used during a voice-over in a video)

- *Social media*, including accounts and posts for brands and a hashtag for the campaign

- *Metrics and evidence of impact of work* including metrics of evaluation that are tied to a campaign or account

- *Contact information* for key professionals including the PR team

Of course, the people behind brands are not the only ones using media kits to engage with the media. Influencers, large and small, are creating their own media kits to engage with brands and others for potential partnerships. Media kits have evolved to not only provide information, but also integrate evidence of previous work. For example, the people behind Later, the Instagram scheduler and social media platform (Canning, 2019), advise that a media kit should include metrics from social channels, evidence of previous campaigns, and audience demographics that showcase the background of our audiences to others.

Best Practices for Creating Media Kits

When we write content for a media kit, the following guidelines can help us provide effective and comprehensive materials to media professionals and others on behalf of our clients and brands.

1. *Keep the materials up-to-date.* With each campaign and over time, we gain more opportunities to add to and update the information in our kits and to freshen their presentation for our audiences to consume.

BRAND OVERVIEW

BILLBOARD IS ONE OF THE MOST DYNAMIC, WIDELY VISITED MUSIC DESTINATIONS. ITS SIGNATURE ASSET, THE BILLBOARD CHARTS, REMAINS THE GOLDEN BENCHMARK IN MUSIC.

DIGITAL

18M U.S. UNIQUES

35 MEDIAN AGE

$90K AVERAGE HHI

51% MALE
49% FEMALE

The definitive source—read by fans and music industry insiders.

MOBILE

15M+ UNIQUE VISITORS

Website and chart experiences optimized for mobile devices so music fans can stay up-to-date wherever they are.

SOCIAL

26M FOLLOWERS

A highly engaged social following connecting music lovers everywhere.

PRINT

23,191 CIRCULATION

115K READERSHIP

47 AVERAGE AGE

$212K AVERAGE HHI

77% MALE
23% FEMALE

A weekly magazine is read by the most powerful people in music.

EVENTS

20+ EVENTS

Exclusive events targeting industry insiders and the music-loving masses.

2. *Showcase the content that best tells the story.* Our media kits should focus clearly on our objective and message and not overwhelm our audiences by including too much stuff. We want to provide just enough for our media contacts to gain a solid understanding of our story, background, and purpose and the actions we'd like them to take.

3. *Adopt a clear aesthetic.* Aligning the brand's voice with our overall presentation of information is a must for our media kits. If a person's media kit looks or sounds different from what the brand or individual is known to stand for, it will create confusion. Having a consistent look and feel across all materials in the kit is important.

4. *Check facts and fix errors.* Before uploading our kits online or heading to the printer, we need to make double-triple-sure that we're presenting accurate, current information. We must also check for errors in grammar, spelling, and punctuation. Such mistakes have a negative impact on how others perceive our material. It's key to make the best first impression.

Websites, Blogs, and Social Media

These days, we focus on digital-first efforts, meaning that the time that we invest in our online messaging and channels is a priority for us and our clients, organizations, and brands. Because digital and social media generate the most reach, attention, and conversations, we must be prepared to write for online channels such as websites, blogs, and social media.

Digital Media and Social Media

First, let's go over the difference between social and digital media. **Digital media** are all channels and outlets that are online, including discussion board forums, blogs, social media, and other aspects of the World Wide Web. However, **social media** involve only the platforms that bring communities and networks together, such as Facebook, Twitter, and Instagram. Writing for the Web includes creating content for **websites**, blogs (discussed next), social media, webinars, and more. Knowledge of search engine optimization, or SEO, the ability to tag the key words we want to have tied to our content on search engines, is key because we want our content to show up on the first page of results on Google and other search engines. Website content also bridges the divide between owned media (the content we own and control) and earned media (the content and coverage we earn but do not own).

Blogs

Blogs and other long-form content are considered to be the "traditional" pieces of digital content. Blogs provide the means to share updates, insights, reflections, and news related to an organization, professional, individual, or brand. Most blog posts are between 500 and 1,000 words in length, and they include various multimedia features that are integrated within each post.

Ideas for Writing Social Media Content

The ability to write effectively on social media is a fundamental skill emphasized in many job postings aimed at new professionals. Social media writing ranges from fast-form media, or the generating of content that is responsive and immediate (e.g., updates or tweets), to slow-form media, or the generating of content that takes time to plan, implement, and produce (e.g., podcasts, interviews, or videos).

For each social media platform, we should determine the type of message and content that is appropriate to publish on each individual channel. For example, Instagram may not be the best place to showcase business long-form content, the type that can be shared on LinkedIn, but it is a good place for posting short-form videos and testimonial features. See Table 7.1 for additional examples.

Best Practices for Writing Digital and Social Media Content

When we write for digital and social media, we are guided by the following:

1. *Think of keywords as your friends.* When we're writing content for a website, blog, or social media site, it's important to know which tagging words or hashtags will allow our content to show up on feeds and search results.

2. *Understand the client's brand voice, community, and business objectives and how they are aligned with the social and digital content.* Research ahead of time what are the key values, characteristics, and brand pillars for the company and how to integrate these into pieces of content. Be strategic in aligning content with the client's business and communication objectives.

3. *Create content that fits your audiences, but also your algorithm.* Sometimes we write content before thinking about the platforms through which we'll distribute it. However, we should not assume that what we write is appropriate and relevant for a given platform unless we understand how that platform works and how our content will appear and be available to our audiences.

4. *Be mindful of what you post.* Google and Twitter do not forget if we make a mistake online. Even after we delete a perhaps poorly conceived post, someone has already taken a screen shot that can be shared with others.

▼ TABLE 7.1

Content Format and Ideas for Writing Social Media Content

Platform	Content Types/Formats	Ideas for Writing Content
Facebook	Ads, updates, live video, video	Statements and information about events; live video coverage of an event or show
Twitter	Tweets, live video, collages, threads, Twitter chats, GIFs, Fleet (stories for Twitter)	Preplanned content related to brand message; live video coverage of an event, show, or announcement
Instagram	Instagram feed, Instagram Stories, Instagram Live, and IGTV (for video series)	Feed: aesthetic branded content; Stories: takeovers, events, features; Live: interviews, product demonstrations; IGTV: series coverage
Snapchat	Snapchat Stories	Storyboards, angles to film, takeovers, "day in a life," events
LinkedIn	Updates, LinkedIn Live, LinkedIn Pulse articles, LinkedIn Groups, LinkedIn Stories	Announcements, motivational thoughts, event coverage, interviews, features, LinkedIn Live shows and videos
YouTube	Video, live video	Vlogs, features, demonstrations, interviews, "day in a life," events
TikTok	TikTok Stories, ads, collaborations, challenges	Storyboard, brainstorm ideas, film
SoundCloud/ Apple Podcasts	Podcasts	Interviews, features

5. *Stay on top of platform changes and how they impact your content.* Subscribing to different media outlets to stay informed about updates or other changes that may impact the digital media landscape is a must. In the PR industry, we follow *The Next Web*, *PR Daily*, *VentureBeat*, *Digiday*, and *Social Media Today* to stay in tune with the platforms we use and how forthcoming changes may impact the content we're producing. In addition, it's a good idea to regularly check our platforms' blogs for announcements.

6. *Track people's reactions to your content, constantly.* We need to know what audiences are thinking and saying about what we've shared on social. Do people like what we are doing? What is and isn't working? How can we address any problems? We do not want to go on producing content that's not hitting the mark, and we don't want to be surprised or blindsided by any negative reactions. Using the metrics and research tools at our disposal, we can easily determine what content is resonating with audiences, as well as what content is not. Data do not lie.

What Are Helpful Tools for Writing in Public Relations?

As discussed in this chapter, our content takes many forms and can be formatted in different ways, depending on our contexts and audiences. To make the right choices we need the right tools such as the following:

- *Associated Press Stylebook* (www.apstylebook.com). This is the required book and resource for all writing activities. The *AP Stylebook* comes in printed and online formats and offers certain features that we can use to test our knowledge of the style guide. Exercises, quizzes, and other educational materials are highlighted and available for purchase.

- *Diversity Style Guide* (www.diversitystyleguide.com). In our industry, we must understand how to cover diversity and inclusion issues. Topics highlighted in this guide cover areas such as race, religion, society and politics, and more.

- *Acronym Finder* (www.acronymfinder.com). When we cover an event or work with an organization that uses acronyms and abbreviations, this resource comes in handy.

- *SEMrush* (www.semrush.com). This tool is helpful in identifying the key words that we need to include in our digital and social media content.

- *Grammarly* (www.grammarly.com). Spell-check on Word is good to a point, but Grammarly allows you to get feedback on your online grammar and spelling as you type. It is worth the investment to avoid the risk of making the wrong first impression.

- *HemingwayApp* (www.hemingwayapp.com). Edit, read, edit, and read again seems to be the natural process for being an effective writer. This app gives us feedback on our readability, grammar, and spelling, serving as a digital proofreader.

- *Canva* (www.canva.com). This tool helps us to create brand content on digital and social media, and can also be used for creating media kits. Canva provides different templates and formats such as a cover sheet, résumé, and pitch deck.

- *Adobe Spark*. Like Canva, Adobe Spark is a free tool for creating responsive pages, posts, and videos for our audiences to consume. Adobe Spark Page can be used as a responsive version of an online media kit.

- *Adobe Premiere Rush*. Adobe Premiere Rush is a video editing tool for creating videos for social and digital media content. This tool provides a way to share exciting news, updates, and introductions with our media contacts.

- *Muck Rack* (https://muckrack.com). This tool helps us find appropriate journalists to reach out to for a given story.

- *Prezly* (www.prezly.com). Prezly allows us to publish our content in one place for everyone to see and can be used for sharing published stories and press releases for a campaign.

- *BuzzSumo* (https://buzzsumo.com). When we publish our content, stories, and press releases, we want to monitor how these materials are doing metrics-wise; we also want to see the coverage we're getting from other sources, and exactly who is sharing our content. This tool allows us to do this monitoring from a PR standpoint.

- *Talkwalker* (www.talkwalker.com). Talkwalker is a social listening tool that offers a free quick search tool to use for mentions and hits. In addition, the Influencer One program is a media planning service that integrates influencers into the media planning model.

- *Meltwater* (www.meltwater.com). Meltwater is a media monitoring tool that allows PR professionals to see what content is trending in the news, being discussed online, and resonating with audiences. It is a great tool for discovering whom to reach out to for pitches, stories, and opportunities for collaborations (e.g., influencers) as a result of its partnership with the influencer tool Klear.

SUMMARY

Writing for public relations is fundamental to what we do in public relations, and like most activities that involve skill, it takes time, dedication, and practice. We create many different types of content, from traditional press releases and pitches to social media copy for items shared online. While writing types and formats will continue to evolve, some principles always stay the same. Knowing our objective and audiences, being accurate, formatting content to our media and channels, and using proper grammar and spelling are practices that we must always follow. Strong writing skills are among the most requested qualities that PR agencies and organizations look for in their future talent. The art of writing has been impacted over the years, and it is more important than ever to follow strong and traditional writing style guidelines. To become a better writer, you have to write and learn from writing over time. Olympic athletes do not decide the day before the Olympics they will compete in the event. They decide many years in advance. Similarly, writing takes patience and persistence as we hone our craft to create the right message, at the right time, in the right way.

APR EXAM

- Principles of writing

- Traditional forms of writing for public relations

GAME CHANGER

David Armano, Senior Vice President of Edelman Digital

Courtesy David Armano

How did you get your start in public relations?

I always like to say that I didn't find public relations; public relations found me. I had spent the majority of my career as a creative director for a number of digital agencies working on all kinds of brands like Adidas on the consumer side and Grainger on the business-to-business side. And before the days of Facebook, blogging was a thing and it made me really curious about the emergence of the social web, so I dove in headfirst.

And the next thing I know, I'm writing for the *Harvard Business Review* and *Ad Age* and being featured in *Businessweek*. At the time, I had tried my hand at one of the first social media consultancies (Dachis Group), which was ultimately acquired by Sprinklr, and that's where Edelman found me.

I didn't know much about public relations, but I knew that Edelman was taking social media very seriously, and I made my move there. I've learned everything I know about public relations at Edelman.

What is your favorite part of working in public relations?

I really enjoy the proximity to the CEO, not just the CMO. I also like how much of what we do in public relations is based in what we like to describe as "multi-stakeholder" or "multi-audience" communications. What that means is that much of the program work that we do has to be designed to make sense for multiple audiences—unlike in advertising where it's more focused on the end consumer or customer. We often need to think about all sorts of influencers from journalists to "cultural" influencers (like a social media star), to experts and thought leaders, to employees and shareholders. It makes the communications more nuanced and audience specific. Also, the reliance on earning trust and attention is attractive to me—it's more challenging especially when there are lean budgets and you can't just throw millions at TV, Facebook, and Google. It requires a great deal of ingenuity that I find intellectually stimulating.

What is the most challenging part of working in public relations?

Proving the value of public relations can be a challenge. Sometimes the value of what we do is crystal clear—like when we help a client during a moment of crisis—and you can literally measure what we do in valuation of the company. Many of the companies we help during crisis scenarios bounce back faster and better with our help, and CEOs especially understand this. On the marketing side, it can sometimes be more nebulous. Public relations operates at the higher end of the marketing funnel in areas like awareness, word of mouth, and reputation and while all play a role in actually purchasing a product, it can be challenging to show exactly where that impact is. Public relations is still relationship driven, and sometimes it takes leaders who understand the value of the relationships people have with brands to fully understand the value that public relations brings to the table. None of this is an excuse for not advancing our practice in the literacy of data and analytics. It's something we can't do fast enough.

It's the balancing act public relations has with doing what we've always done and staying in our "swim lane" and advancing our capabilities and influence within the company. We've seen the communications teams for many of our clients consolidate in some cases and in other cases lose influence they once had. But in reality, we're operating in a world where the integration of public relations has never been more important. People are skeptical, wary of fake news, and increasingly unsure of whether or not what they are reading in their social newsfeeds is accurate. Public relations is inextricably linked to the idea of trust—we are champions for it. Our challenge is to be stewards of trust both in our organizations while influencing how they communicate and in the actions they take. We must be at the table at the moment of decision making rather than brought in to react to a situation. But to do this, we need to speak the language of business, data, and culture in addition to storytelling.

What are some things you wish you knew when you were starting out in public relations?

I wish I had a crystal ball for understanding just how much social media would end up looking like traditional advertising and how much of an impact that was going to have in the world of news media. Journalism standards are in peril as the business models of media companies scramble to keep revenue streams alive. Looking back, I did see some of this, but the speed and scale, I think, surprised even the best of us. I was a vocal advocate for the power of social media, and these days I find myself advocating for its reform. I still believe in the power of connectivity and all the benefits that come with it, but with that power comes accountability. So I am taking that lesson forward—it's on all of us as individuals right down to the practitioners of public relations. We must remind the brands, platforms, advertisers, and purveyors of power that with that power comes great responsibility (and accountability).

As global strategy director for Edelman, David Armano focuses on planning and activating integrated marketing efforts that are purpose-led and social by design. Armano also leads various strategic partnerships across Edelman, as well as the firm's digital transformation efforts. In addition to being a seasoned practitioner in digital and integrated marketing, Armano has published articles in publications including Harvard Business Review, Forbes, Bloomberg Businessweek, Ad Age, Adweek, CMO.com, *and* Digiday, *among others.*

KEY TERMS

Backgrounder 142

Blog 144

Creative writing 128

Digital media 144

Feature story 137

Infographic 139

Media kit 141

News release 133

Persuasive writing 128

Pitch 138

Press release 133

Real-time writing 129

Social media 144

Storytelling 129

Website 144

DISCUSSION QUESTIONS

1. What is the current state of PR writing?

2. Identify the four areas of writing to consider for public relations. What are some of the concerns that arise with real-time messaging?

3. Define *press release*. Outline the pros and cons of using press releases in public relations today.

4. Do you agree that digital and social media have changed the focus for PR writing? Explain your rationale for why or why not.

ACTIVITIES

Building Your Portfolio

Media kit. You are asked to create your own brand media kit as a PR professional. You are tasked with having at least five different pieces of work that you want to include as part of your internship package.
- With this information, identify the five pieces of work you want to have on hand for your media kit.
- Discuss the rationale for having these pieces on hand, and outline the steps you will need to take to create your own personalized media kit.
- Bonus: Start creating a media kit with these materials and information using either Canva or Adobe Spark.

Building Your Brand

Collecting writing samples. For most PR jobs, you will be asked to create a writing assignment for a specific time allotment, or to have samples of work on hand. Identify pieces of work you have created so far that you might want to include in writing sample submissions. Writing sample examples could include any of the following:
- Guest blog posts
- Newspaper articles
- Sample classroom writing assignments
- Social media updates for internships and fellowships

CASE STUDY

Uber Driver Stories: A Lesson in Shifting the Focus

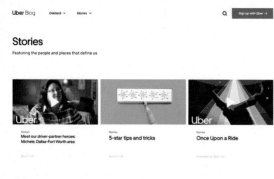

Uber blog for Uber driver stories
Uber.com/blog/oakland/stories

Uber, the global ridesharing company, is no stranger to news or coverage. The difference is the brand has not necessarily been viewed positively in the news due to crises it has experienced over the years internally as well as externally. Sexual harassment accusations, leadership changes, driver boycotts and protests, and driver safety concerns are some of the issues the company has had to deal with. However, Uber partnered with Giant Spoon, *Ad Age*'s breakthrough agency winner, to launch a new campaign to provide a view of the human side of the brand and focus on a group that is usually not highlighted or seen: Uber drivers (Giant Spoon, 2020). The campaign, titled "Going Beyond 5 Stars: Driver Compliments," shares the stories of the most complimented drivers for Uber in a social and digital series.

Why did this case generate buzz?

- In light of what was happening for the ridesharing company, this story was able to connect to the human side of the brand and focused on telling the stories of Uber's "employees," so to speak— those who are on the front line for the brand.

- Uber had not shared the experience of what it was like from the driver's perspective, so this was a way for drivers to share their story and why they are part of the Uber driver community.

What are the ethical and legal issues?

- While these stories were focused primarily on the drivers with the most compliments, they might not have been telling the complete story of what was happening with the brand and with other drivers. Uber did not disclose how it selected or recruited these drivers, or what their compensation was for participating in this program.

- In light of everything that was going on with Uber and its various challenges, this could have been viewed as a campaign to "spin" the image of the company to a more positive light. It could have been viewed as not being transparent or real to key audiences.

What are some takeaways from this case?

- The power of human stories will always resonate with audiences. If people are able to see there is a real human behind a brand whom they can relate to, they will be more likely to respond and engage with the brand accordingly.

- This campaign employed a digital- and visual-first approach, but also integrated traditional forms of PR writing components including press releases, articles, and additional materials in the media kit. This campaign shows while traditional writing formats are not necessarily dead in public relations, they just have to be integrated with other components that will resonate with audiences more. The key element is that the content in the package must be most appropriate to ignite the response you want from your audience.

APPLICATIONS

PART II

STRATEGIC CAMPAIGNS

Introduction

One of the most important areas of expertise a PR professional can cultivate is a strategic understanding of what it takes to create, manage, and execute a PR campaign. There are many ways to plan a campaign, but there are also some universal core principles to follow. In this chapter, we will discuss what a PR campaign is and what core principles and steps are involved, and we will look at some examples of how brands have used creative innovation in successful campaigns.

What Is a PR Campaign?

A **PR campaign** is a systematic, thorough, and brand-aligned document that outlines from start to finish what an individual or client brand wants to accomplish creatively and strategically. For example, the professionals behind a brand may need to address a problem or explore a fresh opportunity. As practitioners, when we create a PR campaign, we outline a plan for achieving such a goal and give specifics on what innovative strategies and communications will be most effective.

To carry out a successful campaign, we do a lot of work behind the scenes. We create press releases, stories, social media updates, and other communications that are part of our larger plan. We also set forth certain guidelines, procedures, and applications (tools, tactics, visuals, programs, and branding, to name a few) that allow us to take the necessary steps to achieve our set goal. Our goal, whether it is to improve a negative reputation or identify new business, helps us determine a framework for how to go about accomplishing it. A strong campaign plan can be repurposed, meaning that we don't

CAMPAIGN AND MEDIA

One of the most important areas of expertise a public relations professional can bring to the table is their strategic understanding of what it takes to create, manage, and execute a public relations campaign. There are many ways in which one can plan a campaign; here are some universal core principles that must be followed:

BACKGROUND The background section (research section for the ROPE and RACE models) is one of the most important steps that a public relations professional needs to take. Providing a background on the client and overview of their industry is key to understanding where they stand, as well as what the current challenges and issues are.

SITUATIONAL ANALYSIS This section allows the public relations professional to combine the findings and takeaways discovered during the external scanning, background research, and communication audit phases to set up the overall picture of what is going on for a brand, organization, or person.

COMPETITIVE ANALYSIS This analysis helps the PR professional evaluate what they are doing as far as their communication efforts go. Use of specific tactics and strategies, influencer marketing initiatives, and campaigns to address crises all have to be taken into consideration.

SWOT Strengths, Weaknesses, Opportunities, and Threats.

GOALS All of an organization's functions must revolve around its missions, goals, and objectives, which in turn are assessed with measurements that are definitive and quantifiable.

OBJECTIVES All objectives must fulfill certain SMART criteria to be effective. Using SMART criteria is an established way to categorize effective objectives into five different categories. (SMART: Specific, Manageable, Achievable, Realistic, and Time-specific)

STRATEGIES A strategy identifies how the client will be implementing the objectives set forth in a campaign.

TACTICS Tactics are the tools and applications that you will be using to accomplish your objectives and fulfill your strategies. For example, using a branded hashtag is a type of tactic.

EVALUATION The set objectives that were made in the campaign have to be reviewed in this section to determine whether or not the PR efforts in the campaign helped accomplish these tasks for the client.

CALENDAR Formulate a timeline for the campaign and how long each strategy, media placement, and tactic will take.

BUDGET Budgets are also necessary for tracking all of the associated costs for a campaign. Accounting for the cost of time (staff), resources, research, and out-of-pocket expenses is key to note.

FUTURE STEPS + RECOMMENDATIONS This is the part of the campaign process where you provide your commentary and key takeaways that you want to highlight for the client. This is an opportunity to provide additional recommendations and note suggestions for the future.

need to reinvent the wheel each time we undertake a new one. It can serve as a road map that can be tailored with each client and campaign.

A successful PR campaign achieves our business and communication goals, but can also help foster stronger relationships between our clients or brands and their key publics. In addition, a successful PR campaign achieves the following:

- Stronger brand awareness and equity

- Stronger relationships among key publics

- Building a stronger emotional connection with the client

- Sparking innovative approaches in experiential activities for audiences

- An increase in desired behavior (sales, traffic, impact, share of voice, etc.) among key publics

- Financial and emotional goals that contribute to both business and communication objectives

In this chapter, you will learn about the RACE and ROPE models that we use to set up a PR campaign, the differences between these models, and how the Strategic Model incorporates the best of the traditional models while adding steps that position us for the future.

What Are the Steps for Conducting a Successful PR Campaign?

PR campaigns require us to take clear steps. This section covers the following:

1. Conducting research

2. Identifying purpose and audience

3. Planning

4. Developing content and persuading audiences

5. Experimenting with innovative ideas

6. Evaluating success

1. Conducting Research

As discussed in Chapter 5, research is a key part of most PR efforts. Before we do anything in regard to generating ideas and creative executions, we need to conduct research. Research for campaigns can be done through primary methods, such as conducting focus groups and surveys and interviewing internal and external publics about brand awareness. We can also obtain information through secondary sources, by reviewing published articles and media monitoring and social reports and analyzing campaigns from previous years. The important factor is to create an evidence-based and complete picture of where our clients have been, what opportunities and challenges they face, and what gaps or opportunities we can make the most of through our PR campaign. These insights serve as the springboard to the ideas and actions that we carry out when conducting a PR campaign.

2. Identifying Purpose and Audience

First, we need to identify our overall purpose or goal in conducting a campaign. Do we want to engage with a new target audience, or perhaps with more diverse audiences? Do we want to address and promote the rebranding of an individual client or client organization? Is our client in crisis and in need of reputation assistance? What do we want to persuade our audiences to think or do? In addition to identifying our purpose, we need to ask ourselves:

- What is our message, and what audiences will receive it?

- How will we communicate our message?

- What are the best ways to reach our audiences?

- How will we involve our audiences in our campaign?

- How will we work with advertising, marketing, and other professionals to ensure that our efforts will pay off?

- What else might we need to do to meet our client's needs and bottom line?

Aviation Gin response video to Peloton by Ryan Reynolds
Twitter/@VancityReynolds

All of these questions can be answered and addressed through the PR campaign we create. To be effective, we must also be aware of client expectations, agreed-upon focus points, and the type and quality of deliverables—such as an increase in sales, number of customers, traffic to stores or to a website or online store, and brand coverage in the media—that we will produce.

For example, let's take the brand Aviation Gin, which has an investor *Deadpool* actor Ryan Reynolds. The gin company has been very aggressive in creating brand awareness for its product in a highly competitive marketplace. However, the brand was able to respond immediately to the commercial featuring the "Peloton wife" and integrate the product into a sequel commercial, sparking many discussions of how this move toward agility in responding to a trending topic proved this was a strategic and innovative way to drive brand awareness and sales for the company. Reynolds worked with his team (including Senior Brand Marketing Manager Adrian Molina) and stated that the reason why their work was successful was a combination of speed, flexibility, and trust—all elements that come from having a strong goal and purpose for a campaign (Griner, 2019). Since this commercial was launched, Aviation Gin has continued building the momentum for the brand with other creative campaign approaches, like partnering with the Westminster Kennel Club Dog Show and showcasing Arlene Manko on Leap Day to celebrate her 21st birthday (in reality, she is 84 years old, but only celebrates her real birthday every four years).

Having an objective and overall purpose creates a solid foundation for a campaign. However, it takes more than that to succeed, as Aviation Gin has found. Further, it is essential that we integrate into our process the core principles built into each of the steps outlined in this chapter (see "What Are the RACE and ROPE Models for Conducting Campaigns?" on page 158 and "How Does the Strategic Model Benefit Campaigns?" on page 160).

3. Planning

There is no substitute for excellent planning. Planning a step-by-step process keeps us aligned with our business and communication objectives and allows for creative thinking. A plan helps us connect the dots between our overall challenge or problem and the ways we can meet or solve them, using strategic, imaginative, and evidence-based practices. Planning is not just about coming up with the big idea. You can have the best idea out there, but if it is not backed by sound research and clear takeaways, you cannot properly execute it. Big ideas are not just about creativity—they are rooted in facts and insights and strategic execution. As shown in the previous section, planning was essential for the success of Aviation Gin's brandjacking of Peloton's controversial ad.

Planning involves the following steps:

- *Conducting research.* As mentioned previously, research—whether it is primary or secondary—is at the forefront of all things. Ryan Reynolds and his team at Aviation Gin realized that people were talking about the Peloton commercial that sparked controversy and discussion, and used this as a basis in their overall decision to move forward with their response ad. In addition, they conducted research to determine which medium and outlet to use to get their message across.

- *Innovating.* We pay attention to elements that are different and unique, not to things that are routine or systematic in nature. Audiences want to be entertained and dazzled, and to do this with a PR campaign, creativity has to play a part in the planning process. When the *Today* show invited Monica Ruiz to the show to address the Peloton ad, Reynolds surprised her and came on the interview. This move sparked conversation and buzz for the brand and topic at hand, but most importantly, people paid attention to the topic and talked about it. That's a key return on investment there for a creative idea.

- *Executing.* You can have the best idea, but if you cannot execute the plan, the idea is lost. Aviation Gin not only was able to have the best idea, but executed in a way that made it stand out from other brand activations and campaigns, making the brand worthy of its 2020 *Fast Company* ranking as one of the top innovative brands in the industry.

4. Developing Content and Persuading Audiences

To be effective, a campaign needs strong content that promotes our message to target audiences through visual, audio, and written media. While some pieces of content will be created by others, we need to have a strong content-driven narrative that ties each piece together. Through that narrative, or story, we unite the content under our overall objective. Further, there must be consistency throughout each step and across all content and messaging that we put out through our campaign. If we move forward with one message, one look, and one medium for our campaign for our client and then do something completely different in another aspect of the campaign, we will not communicate our message as effectively as we should. For example, as Dunkin' moved to change its name from Dunkin' Donuts to Dunkin', the professionals behind the campaign had to make sure they were consistent with their content, messaging, and overall look when communicating about the brand through various outlets.

As PR writers, we must connect with our audiences by appealing to their emotions. We are all human beings who crave authentic stories and experiences. The stories that we tell through our campaigns—the stories that mean the most to our audiences—really do help to forge a stronger emotional connection between our audiences and the brand we are promoting. Such stories can also persuade audiences to feel even more positive about a brand they already care about. This has been demonstrated repeatedly. One case involved Budweiser and its partnership with National Basketball Association star Dwyane Wade. Wade, who decided in 2019 that he was going to retire from the NBA, was known for exchanging various jerseys with fellow players over the years. Budweiser invited Wade to a basketball court in its commercial, where he was able to meet people he had inspired over the years and they were able to give him various gifts as thank-yous. What made this an emotional experience for audience members were the personal stories that individuals shared with Wade about how he had made an impact on their lives.

Dwyane Wade sharing his Budweiser partnership at Cannes Lions
Getty Images Entertainment

5. Experimenting With Innovative Ideas

Ideation is the strategic process of formulating ideas or concepts to be executed. It is a key part of sparking the creativity that makes for a successful campaign. Ideation allows us to focus on the overall process of developing, creating, and communicating new ideas. We can develop our ideas in various ways, from brainstorming to mind mapping or even getting inspired by what we see in our environments, on- or offline. For example, the bourbon company Wild Turkey wanted to do something unique to celebrate its product and the founder of the company, and found its inspiration not from brainstorming sessions but from the idea of sending one anniversary tweet (McAteer, 2019). Heat, a Deloitte media company, had Jimmy Russell, a distiller at Wild Turkey, read on video the tweets that people had written that communicated their negative perceptions of the brand. Then, each of the negative comments was etched on the insides of Wild Turkey Bourbon barrels, set on fire, and burned through the process of making the bourbon. The barrels then were sold. This was a unique, novel approach for a traditional brand in an established industry, but it produced a great response and strong connections with audiences (Heat, 2020).

6. Evaluating Success

At the end of the day, we have to be like Jerry Maguire and make sure we are "showing them the money"—that is, the impact we have made on behalf of our clients through the campaigns we initiate. PR professionals have to identify key performance indicators (otherwise known as KPIs) that help us determine whether we've been successful through our campaign. Aviation Gin and created an ad to respond to the Peloton commercial for $100,000, and the global media coverage and increased sales of their product provided strong measures of success. Wild Turkey Bourbon gained press coverage and awareness as a result of the brand's novel campaign. Dunkin' saw an increase in sales and brand equity even after rebranding. These measures of success have to be determined before a campaign is launched, but be integrated and evaluated throughout. This is a key part of a PR campaign to which senior management and others involved with the client will pay attention.

What Are the RACE and ROPE Models for Conducting Campaigns?

Traditionally, we choose from several possible models, including **RACE** and **ROPE**, for initiating, organizing, and carrying out a successful campaign. The RACE and ROPE models (see Table 8.1) share some universal points, such as the emphasis on research and evaluation, but there are subtle differences between them. For example, RACE focuses on integrating strategies and tactics in the *communication* stage, whereas ROPE uses the term *planning* instead. You say *to-may-to*, I say *to-mah-to*, but the differences between these approaches lie in the way they are framed.

Most PR programs follow one of these two models, but in this book, we propose that our campaigns should take a more detailed and enhanced strategic approach, one that ties in more with related disciplines (see "How Does the Strategic Model Benefit Campaigns?" on page 160).

Like all things in public relations, the models for planning and carrying out a campaign are described in acronyms. Table 8.1 lists some of the organizational models that guide our PR efforts. The most common ones in use are RACE and ROPE, but to determine which models to use, we have to be aware that there are several to choose from that are practiced in the field and around the world.

▼ TABLE 8.1

Identifying PR Planning Models

Model	Parts	Qualities
RACE	Research, action, communication, evaluation	• Focuses on tying in the action steps and planning for public relations • Endorsed and used by the Public Relations Society of America
ROPE	Research, objectives, planning, evaluation	• Addresses the different steps in the PR process
PACE	Planning, action, communication, evaluation	• Puts planning as part of the first step with research and gathering insights
RPIE	Research, planning, implementation, evaluation	• Identifies implementation as a key step that needs to be emphasized with strategy
ACE	Assessment, communication, evaluation	• Ties research into two major steps in the planning model
Strategic Plan	Background, situational analysis, goals, objectives, strategies, tactics, evaluation, recommendations	• Focuses on tying in more micro steps

The RACE and ROPE Models: Similarities

As noted in Table 8.1, the RACE and ROPE models are different acronyms outlining each of the steps in a PR plan. RACE focuses on research, action, communication, and evaluation, whereas ROPE focuses on research, objectives, planning, and evaluation. These models focus on major areas within the steps for carrying out a PR campaign.

Conducting Research

First, both the RACE and ROPE models highlight the important step of research. As PR professionals, we need to identify the potential problem or opportunity that will establish the purpose of our campaign. We also need to identify our target audiences. This step provides us with a clear foundation for what is happening with the individual client or organization we are representing, what the campaign will focus on, and what we will address with key audiences.

Evaluating Success

Second, both models emphasize evaluation, which allows us to determine whether we achieved the goals of our campaign.

The RACE and ROPE Models: Differences

The two models differ in regard to objectives, strategies, and tactics.

Objectives and SMART Criteria

Objectives are statements of what we and our clients want to accomplish. Such statements must meet certain criteria, such as **SMART criteria**, which help us to write an objective statement that is specific, measurable, achievable, realistic, and time-specific. Each objective has *specific* elements that have to be achieved, and they must be *measurable* so we can determine whether or not we have accomplished these tasks. They have to be *achievable*—can we actually do this, and is it *realistic* for us to do? Lastly, we have to *specify the time* when we want to accomplish these objectives. For objectives to be effective, they must have all of these components.

Strategies and Tactics

Strategies are broad statements in which we discuss how we, either with or on behalf of our clients, will accomplish our stated objectives. Related to strategies are **tactics**, the specific communication tools and activities that we will use to carry out our strategies. For example, if Dunkin' wanted to raise awareness of its recent rebranding, one strategy could be to revitalize the look and feel of the brand both on- and offline, and tactics for doing so could include the presentation of new product designs in stories or videos (e.g., on Instagram or TikTok) with updates to social media that reflect the rebranding, as well as the circulation of press releases and fact sheets that articulate the brand's changes, to key audiences.

When it comes to strategies and tactics, the ROPE model features a designated step where we can identify the objectives we want to accomplish. Under the RACE model, the process falls under the category of an action plan (or the *A* in the model).

But the RACE model has shortcomings. One weakness is its simplicity. PR campaigns are more integrated and thorough in nature than just a four-step process. Further, we must ask: To what extent does the RACE model contribute to what we want to achieve in the 21st century? Some concepts, listening and monitoring, and new forms of media and audience/competitor analysis need to be integrated into existing models in order for campaigns to succeed.

While the Public Relations Society of America, the largest PR professional organization, endorses the RACE model as the recommended approach for conducting PR campaigns, ongoing changes to our industry and media landscape indicate that it's time for something new.

How Does the Strategic Model Benefit Campaigns?

The Strategic Model for a PR campaign is a systematic plan outlining in detail the key steps for achieving our goals. Such a model focuses not only on planning, but on the micro steps that help us succeed in telling the detailed story of a campaign. For example, the Strategic Model takes other related discipline perspectives and business components into account. Further, it allows us to align our campaigns, language, and documents with those of professionals in related areas, such as marketing.

The Parts and Steps of a Strategic Model

As PR professionals, we outline and implement a **strategic plan** for conducting any PR campaign by creating the following parts (or steps) of that plan:

- Background research

- Situational analysis

- Competitive analysis

- SWOT (strengths, weaknesses, opportunities, and threats) analysis

- Objectives

- Audience and messaging strategies

- Evaluation

- Calendar

- Budget

- Future steps and recommendations

In the following sections, we'll discuss several of these components of a campaign plan: background research, situational analysis, SWOT analysis, objectives, and audience and messaging strategies.

Creating a Background Research Section

We need to consider research before we begin a campaign, and include it as an ongoing part of our process. This is where we provide an overview of our clients, their challenges and opportunities, and any additional notable internal and external factors. Further, creating this section of the plan helps us understand our clients' past and present situations, their main challenges, and their advantages and opportunities. Creating a background research section involves conducting an **environmental scan**, also known as an **external scan**, or an overview of the factors that are happening outside of our clients' internal environment that can impact their work.

Conducting an External or Environmental Scan

This work helps us and our colleagues to evaluate the current landscape within which our clients operate. When we carry out an environmental scan, we take into account political, legal, and economic factors:

- *Political factors.* Political elections, social activism cases, and regulation by governing agencies such as the Federal Trade Commission can impact our clients. These influences operate at the local, national, and even global levels. Elections and changes, perhaps in different countries (e.g., Brexit and the European Union), are an example.

- *Legal factors.* Understanding legal challenges that pertain to PR efforts, such as fake news and new laws and bills including the California privacy law and the General Data Protection Regulation in the European Union, can impact how consumers interact with brands.

- *Economic factors.* We need to understand the current financial landscape that affects our clients, such as spending habits related to technology, information, and content creation. Further, we need to be aware of key trends happening in the workplace, such as industry hiring or layoffs, employee satisfaction, or financial barriers to entry (barriers that are set forth so only those who earn or make a certain amount can be included).

Once we've identified these factors, we create a **client overview**.

Creating a Client Overview

A client overview is a brief section introducing our clients and where they stand presently before a campaign. In this section of our strategic plan, we research and write about the following:

- *Client history, background, and key players.* We give a brief overview of the history of our client, including successes, significant moments, and key players (CEO, CMO, CFO, CCO, etc.).

- *Industry position.* We also identify where our client organization sits in the competitive landscape of the industry. Is our client an industry leader? A newcomer? Or has our client dropped in rank because of a crisis?

- *Products, services, and issues.* We find out what products, services, or issues (e.g., social justice, diversity and inclusion initiatives, and other social issues) most interest our client. What is the status of our client in relation to these entities and concerns? What is working, and what areas need to be improved?

- *Ethical and legal conduct.* It is a good idea to evaluate and be fully aware of any ethical and legal challenges that our client may be facing. What is positive, and what areas can be improved?

- *Diversity and inclusion programs.* What is our client's standing in regard to diversity and inclusion? For example, we might look at the representation of races, genders, sexual orientations, cultures, and perspectives represented by our client's employees, campaigns, causes, and initiatives. Is there room for improvement?

- *PR history.* We take a look at our client's previous campaigns and the media channels used to promote them. For example, if Under Armour were our client, we would need to know about its previous campaigns, including the "Protect This House," Misty Copeland and Stephen Curry, and Michael Phelps campaigns, as well as the launch of The Rock's product line.

- *Communications audit.* Conducting a communications audit of our client organization is one of the most crucial things we do before carrying out our strategic campaign plan. In this case, we analyze all communication elements including our client's existing content, brand messages, and media channels, as well as any relevant communications that take place among personnel within our client's organization. Examples of the items we look at include emails, memos, leadership statements published in the media, white papers, social media posts and updates, websites, and other digital communications.

- *Competitors.* When we consider our client's competitors, we study their backgrounds, standing in the industry, and current and past PR campaigns. We can learn a lot by evaluating their communication efforts—their use of specific strategies and related tactics, their influencer marketing initiatives, their campaigns that address crises, and more—from a business and PR standpoint. In this process, looking at what our client's competitors are doing well is equally important to what they are not doing well. Evaluating competitors also allows us to identify any gaps (using specific channels to engage with audiences, creating certain activations, formulating new partnerships, etc.) in the industry that may give us an opportunity to promote our client.

Asking Deeper Questions About Our Client

While these elements typify the client overview section of a PR campaign, it is important to dive even deeper to understand our client and the areas that may need to be enhanced or improved upon in preparation for the campaign. Several questions help us build our knowledge of what we need to address in our PR campaign:

- Who are we as a brand, company, or individual?

- What is our mission statement and overall purpose in the industry?

- What are the issues, causes, and groups we want to support?

- What is our diversity and inclusion policy as a company?

- Who are our audience members? Are we reaching and including everyone in our community?

- What are our goals presently?

- What is our role as a brand, and are we best advocating for and with our audiences?

- What is our leadership style like?

- What is our ethical and legal philosophy (basic beliefs, values, ethics, etc.)?

- What are our core skills and competitive advantages?

- What are we not doing that our competitors are doing?

Writing a Situational Analysis

A **situational analysis** allows us to organize the data we have collected, creating a clear overall picture of what is going on for our individual client or our client's organization. In this section of our strategic plan, we combine the findings of our background research, such as the details that emerged from our environmental/external scan and our client overview, especially from the communication audit phase. This approach helps us to determine the next steps of our strategic plan. Because our research is only as good as our ability to identify what is happening, why things are happening, and how we can apply findings to construct sound strategies, we must organize our efforts so that we can see the full picture of what we know and what we need to do.

In most strategic plans, we outline a single main problem that we need to address in a PR campaign. We communicate that problem in a **core problem statement**, which is a one-sentence statement summarizing the big issue that needs to be addressed. A core problem may be that we need to figure out how to address an ongoing issue for our individual client or our client's organization. For example, we might need to restore the public's trust in our client after a crisis, such as the Boeing 737 MAX disasters, Facebook's privacy problems, and the failure of the Fyre Festival. So, if we were to write Boeing's problem statement, it would go something like this:

> *Due to negative press and uncertainty of internal safety precautions of the 737 MAX model, Boeing is facing a reputational crisis at a global level.*

Further, because we sometimes overlook the need for a strategic plan that can address new opportunities rather than just solving existing problems, our strategic plan might highlight efforts to take advantage of positive relationships with a community or increase sales and exposure.

Writing a SWOT Analysis

The SWOT analysis section of a strategic plan focuses on a client's strengths, weaknesses, opportunities, and threats. SWOT analysis is a traditional part of our communications and marketing processes, but it is essential to our strategic plans as well. We can use a SWOT analysis to identify solutions to problems, take advantage of new opportunities and ventures, decide which steps to take to rejuvenate a community or brand, or brainstorm new ways to engage online through social media. All four aspects of SWOT are important, but we have to make sure that we form bridges between these components and the other parts of our strategic plan.

Identifying Strengths

This is where we outline in detail the strengths we observe in our clients in current practices. These could include strong internal culture, awards for work in the industry, or strong credibility for leadership internally or externally.

Identifying Weaknesses

Our clients' weaknesses are the practices that hinder or challenge their ability to accomplish their objectives. Sometimes clients' weaknesses are the complete opposite of their strengths. These could be that internal culture is not positive or there is a break in communication internally between leadership and others in the company.

Identifying Opportunities

An opportunity is a set of ideas or circumstances that are external to a client. When we take note of such opportunities, we may persuade our client to try new approaches and behaviors. This part of our SWOT analysis also presents a list of creative ideas to jump-start brainstorming and new initiatives that will benefit our client.

Identifying Threats

Threats to our client, which arise from negative events and experiences, represent a classic external factor. For example, competitors could attack the client, or there could be rising protests outside of the client's organization, new external regulations, activists going against the client, and so on.

Writing About Strategic Implications

The **strategic implications** section is a fifth component of our SWOT analysis in which we look at the "so what" factor, which helps us figure out how to move our clients forward. A strategic implication is simply outlining the main challenge and opportunity that needs to be addressed.

Writing an Objectives Section

All of an organization's functions must revolve around its missions, goals, and objectives, which in turn are assessed with measurements that are definitive and quantifiable. To be effective, the goals and objectives of our strategic plan must be simple, understandable, and connected with measurable achievements. We must also update them throughout our planning period to ensure they continue to serve our clients' needs and purposes.

To carry out a strategic plan for a PR campaign, we use the approach known as **management by objectives** (MBO). We use this to address the key things that we want to accomplish based on the challenges, problems, or opportunities we have identified through our research. The objectives of our strategic plans can take many different forms, but to be effective, they must fulfill certain criteria, such as the SMART criteria discussed earlier in this chapter (see page 159). Our objectives must certainly be specific, stating clearly what we need to address in our plan. They also must be measurable and provide specific guidance on questions such as how much we want to increase or decrease a certain element in our plan.

Writing an Audience and Messaging Section

As discussed in the next chapter, an essential part of a strategic plan is figuring out how to communicate to our audiences. Understanding their underlying characteristics, motivations, and perceptions; learning what communication channels they use; and exploring what issues and causes they are invested in and want to support are just some of the components to consider. Audiences want to be talked to in a way that is personable, not promoted at.

Types of Audiences

Two types of audiences will be outlined in your strategic plan. **Primary audiences** are those you want to target directly and that have a meaningful relationship and connection to the client. **Secondary audiences** are those who are supportive and potentially viewed as influencers by the primary audience members. With both types, outlining emerging audience members is very useful. Emerging audience members are not necessarily on the radar yet but could and perhaps need to be.

Understanding audiences means painting a picture of these groups of individuals, which we saw in Chapter 5. *Demographics* are a basic way to categorize a group of individuals. They involve the basic population data that are easily collected, such as age, education level, ethnicity, and location. *Psychographics* also allow PR professionals to categorize audiences based on their attitudes, opinions, and values, but this higher-level approach to categorization narrows down the groups into specific audiences based on psychological characteristics and attributes. More details on other categorizations and insights on audiences from Chapter 9 should be included and highlighted in the audience analysis section.

Types of Messages

There are two types of key messages: primary and secondary. **Primary messages** are broad statements that you want to communicate to your key audience members. The primary message should be simple, concise, and to the point. This is not the time to be elaborate. The primary message should be one sentence long. It captures what you want to accomplish and communicate to your audiences if you only have a certain amount of time. If you want to expand and elaborate on key messages, this is where the secondary messages come into play. **Secondary messages** provide evidence to support the primary message. Secondary messages use facts, statistics, and additional information to build on the point outlined in the primary message. These messages can incorporate evidence and additional information regarding what the client has already done in a campaign. There is no magic number for how many secondary messages you need to support your primary message, but you want to be thorough in your explanation of these points to avoid audience confusion. A rule of thumb is the more information you can provide to your audiences to guide them regarding actions they should take, the better off you will be.

Writing a Strategies and Tactics Section

Strategies and tactics are the heart of a strategic plan. However, you can have the best ideas for a strategic plan, but without proper execution of your strategies, nothing is gained. A strategy identifies how the client will implement the objectives set forth in a campaign.

Tactics are the tools and applications that you will be using to accomplish your objectives and fulfill your strategies. Tactics are the nuts and bolts of your social media plan. For example, using a branded hashtag is a type of tactic. A Facebook Live video showcasing a question-and-answer session with a senior-level manager discussing a new initiative or promoting a giveaway of an exclusive opportunity is another example

Popeyes Chicken ✓
@PopeyesChicken

Don't eat the art. Even though it's delicious. Go see our masterpiece "The Sandwich" at @Sanpaulgallery for #ArtBasel.

Toasted brioche bun, two pickles, fried chicken, mayo, duct tape on canvas. $120,003.99 🤤 🎨

♡ 569   6:32 PM - Dec 6, 2019   ⓘ

Popeyes
Twitter/@PopeyesChicken

of a tactic. As you can see, tactics are very specific and very focused. Each tactic needs to be aligned with the strategy. Managing tactics well is a way that you can impress employers and clients and use your creativity to stand out among your peers. Tactics allow you to experiment with new trends, tools, and platforms. At the same time, tactics must be used strategically and systematically, not just for fun.

There are several ways in which we can see this playing out.

The Nike Campaign

One case involved Nike. The focus of this campaign was to create awareness of an ongoing issue related to a key audience or topic that is happening in society. Nike, which has been a powerhouse brand for decades, decided to create a campaign that tied into its audience base of female athletes. In Nike and "Dream Crazy," the company wanted to celebrate its Just Do It tagline with stories highlighting how women athletes, across different sports, came together to challenge the limits and prove that it is not "crazy" to imagine a future where females can succeed at the level of their male counterparts in their sport. The launch of this campaign originated not from the brand itself, but from one of its biggest sports figures and supporters, Serena Williams. She was the one who first shared the video with her voice-over on all of her own dedicated channels, bringing forth the new activation and implementation strategies for how a campaign can be launched by someone other than a brand or company. The strategy was used to increase awareness of Nike's support for female athletes, and the tactics involved having Williams share the video on her social channels and then amplifying the video and message on other platforms.

The Popeyes Campaign

Another example is Popeyes® Louisiana Kitchen's response to the banana art piece at the San Paul Gallery at Art Basel. In this art exhibit, a banana was duct-taped to a white wall, and the artist was charging $120,000 for it. Someone actually ate the banana, which of course sparked a viral discussion online among audiences. Based on the analysis and media coverage, brands like Popeyes felt they needed to be part of the conversation so as to be top of mind for audiences and their biggest fans. So, one tactic the chicken brand decided to take was to jump into the conversation surrounding the banana art exhibit and create its own version.

Let's take another example of a brand that focused on a strategy to create unique partnerships using influencers to spark engagement.

The Wendy's Campaign

Wendy's is not new to the creative activations and partnerships realm for PR efforts. Following the fast-food company's snarky interactions on Twitter and partnership with Spotify to create a mixtape, Wendy's wanted to do something to target the up-and-coming generation of potential audience members, Generation Z. One characteristic of Gen Z members is that they are engaged and active in various gaming communities, watching gamers like Ninja play games through Twitch. This was the inspiration for the Wendy's and *Fortnite* collaboration. Wendy's realized that Twitch, which has become a rising online streaming platform for young consumers, would be a perfect way to engage audiences with *Fortnite*. Many brands have tried to interject themselves into a game to spark a conversation with key audience members, but it has not gone over that well. However, Wendy's wanted to be in *Fortnite* as a player and fellow community member, not as a brand advertiser. It took the strategic approach of playing and engaging rather than paying to play. The player, which was designed like the Wendy's iconic character on the brand's logo, was able to play and answer questions about Wendy's products while livestreaming the interaction in *Fortnite* on Twitch. Since this had not been done before, Wendy's was able to demonstrate that approaching audiences through engagement, rather than pushing key content messages that are perceived as advertising, created a more authentic exchange that helped foster some new relationships with Twitch users and *Fortnite* gamers.

Creating a Budget and Calendar Section

The **budget** and **calendar** are two important elements for any PR campaign. One focuses on the timeline for the campaign and how long it will take, and the other focuses on how much you have as far as resources go.

Each campaign is going to have different timelines. Some are just a few months long, and others are more long term. Timing has to come into consideration in terms of not just resources, but also placement of key messages. For example, while some channels can be implemented very quickly, others take more time to get the content into circulation

▼ FIGURE 8.1

Sample Gantt Chart

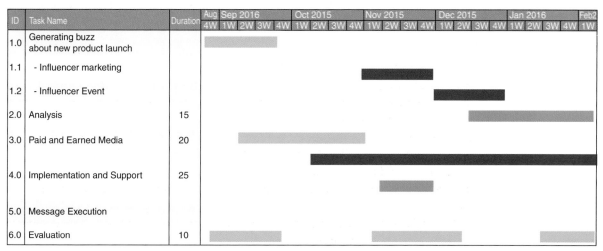

(e.g., magazines). Along with media placement and execution, PR professionals have to identify when each of their associated tactics and ideas will be implemented during the campaign. This is usually done throughout the campaign, but it depends on the overall scope and resources. Timing is everything when it comes to creating an effective and successful campaign. As mentioned previously, you can have the best idea out there, but if it is not properly executed, then it may fall flat. For example, there have been some cases over the years where a brand has sent out an inappropriate message during a time of crisis (e.g., Epicurious and the 2013 Boston Marathon bombing), which could have been prevented if the PR professional had worked with the social media community manager to pause any automated and scheduled posts that would go out during the crisis. While some protocols have been set for the most part to address these concerns ahead of time, it is still essential to be proactive in the effort to avoid these mistakes.

One way to present your calendar is through a Gantt chart (see Figure 8.1), which allows you to see when each strategy, tactic, and measurement component will be implemented.

Budgets are also necessary for tracking all of the associated costs for a campaign. There are several categories to consider for a PR budget:

- *Resources.* These are items that need to be accounted for when creating content for the campaign. While this may sometimes be listed under staff time, there are still programs, tools, and materials that need to be included.

- *Measurement and research.* This seems to be one of the things that are often missing in both the calendar and the budget sections. Research is not free and does not grow on trees—and it has to be accounted for in terms of the staff time to conduct, analyze, and report the findings for the campaign. In addition, there are specific costs associated with certain methods (social media monitoring, data management and analytics, etc.) that need to be accounted for in the overall cost for the campaign.

- *Staff time.* For most campaigns, there has to be a note of how many people are a part of the campaign and how many hours they work over a given time. Some campaigns are based solely on the project (the PR professional and team get paid on fee for the completion of the product), on retainer (the agency or team is paid the same rate per month for a project), or by the hour (this depends on who all is working on the client account). For example, a vice president is going to charge more per hour for his or her services compared to an intern working on the account.

- *Out-of-pocket expenses.* As they say, things happen. A hurricane may come to your outdoor event during the summer in Florida. What happens if you are at a conference, like SXSW, and need to cancel due to the coronavirus? Or the Stay Puft Marshmallow Man may end up walking down to Times Square for your big product launch on *Good Morning America* in New York City. Calling the Ghostbusters to help you fix this issue would be pretty expensive, and you don't want to try to find this money in a time of crisis. You have to be prepared for the unexpected. Assuming everything will go without a hitch is unrealistic, so it is best to account for some part of the budget to be allocated to addressing things if changes emerge. Traditionally, 8 to 10 percent of the budget is usually a safe buffer for PR campaigns to manage and have on hand. In addition, make sure insurance is part of the equation in case an event, activity, or issue comes up. Building this into the budget is essential to have in PR campaigns.

Writing a Measurement and Evaluation Section

Measurement and evaluation have to be considered as key parts of the campaign and planning process from start to finish. There are a few things that PR professionals need to keep in mind regarding these processes. First, measurement metrics have to be taken into consideration. In addition, tools and services to be used have to be accounted for in the budget and calendar. One of the areas that are somewhat missing from most campaigns is the realization that (1) research takes up time and money and (2) various evaluation methods use various services and programs to collect, analyze, and report the findings for the campaign. Traditional research methods are often used for measurement purposes, but there are, of course, new tools as discussed in Chapter 5 of this book.

As stated earlier in this chapter, the measurement components of the SMART objectives (specific, measurable, achievable, realistic, and time-specific) are so important. Without knowing what or how much we want to increase what we are looking for (reputation, impressions, awareness, engagement, etc.), PR professionals will not have clear and actionable variables to present to senior management. In addition, most of the time, senior managers want to see hard numbers that clearly illustrate the growth, impact, and results from public relations, marketing, reputation building, and sales. What PR professionals have to do in this case is be able to connect the dots with evidence to support each of their points of insight and make recommendations and assessments accordingly. To do that requires a clear analysis from the insights and data gathered that are reported in a way that discusses how this campaign helped the client increase sales, improve its reputation, and generate action by audiences based on the creative strategies and activations that were initiated.

Writing Recommendation for the Future

You will wish to conclude your strategic plan with a summary of your findings and recommended next steps. Along with the executive summary, which is present in strategic plans, this is where you provide your commentary and key takeaways that you want to highlight for the client. This is an opportunity to provide additional recommendations and note suggestions for the future. This section allows the strategic plan to come full-circle while also providing a stepping-stone to the next plan the organization, agency, brand, or person wants to pursue in the future.

How Does the PESO Model for Media Promote Campaigns?

One of the areas that have constantly been changing for public relations is the media landscape. As discussed in Chapter 2, public relations has had a strong relationship with the media landscape. **Media** has been traditionally defined as the means to broadcast information to the masses. Of course, this information can be visual, audio, written, or all of the above.

Starting with traditional methods of communication like town halls, press conferences, and events, public relations now enjoys many more choices for media channels for communicating messages to audiences. Changes in the media landscape offer new challenges, niches, and opportunities for the PR field.

To give you an idea of the complex media landscape, the illustration on page 170 outlines the breakdown of the landscape and the many different channels, tools, and media specializations. This can be somewhat overwhelming as more niche media outlets and communities emerge.

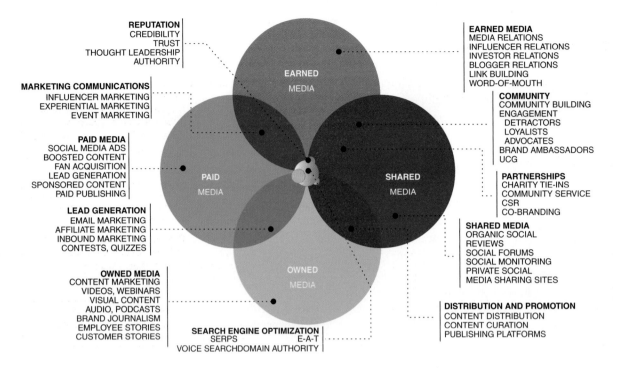

REPUTATION
CREDIBILITY
TRUST
THOUGHT LEADERSHIP
AUTHORITY

MARKETING COMMUNICATIONS
INFLUENCER MARKETING
EXPERIENTIAL MARKETING
EVENT MARKETING

PAID MEDIA
SOCIAL MEDIA ADS
BOOSTED CONTENT
FAN ACQUISITION
LEAD GENERATION
SPONSORED CONTENT
PAID PUBLISHING

LEAD GENERATION
EMAIL MARKETING
AFFILIATE MARKETING
INBOUND MARKETING
CONTESTS, QUIZZES

OWNED MEDIA
CONTENT MARKETING
VIDEOS, WEBINARS
VISUAL CONTENT
AUDIO, PODCASTS
BRAND JOURNALISM
EMPLOYEE STORIES
CUSTOMER STORIES

SEARCH ENGINE OPTIMIZATION
SERPS   E-A-T
VOICE SEARCHDOMAIN AUTHORITY

EARNED MEDIA
MEDIA RELATIONS
INFLUENCER RELATIONS
INVESTOR RELATIONS
BLOGGER RELATIONS
LINK BUILDING
WORD-OF-MOUTH

COMMUNITY
COMMUNITY BUILDING
ENGAGEMENT
  DETRACTORS
  LOYALISTS
  ADVOCATES
BRAND AMBASSADORS
UCG

PARTNERSHIPS
CHARITY TIE-INS
COMMUNITY SERVICE
CSR
CO-BRANDING

SHARED MEDIA
ORGANIC SOCIAL
REVIEWS
SOCIAL FORUMS
SOCIAL MONITORING
PRIVATE SOCIAL
MEDIA SHARING SITES

DISTRIBUTION AND PROMOTION
CONTENT DISTRIBUTION
CONTENT CURATION
PUBLISHING PLATFORMS

EARNED MEDIA

PAID MEDIA

SHARED MEDIA

OWNED MEDIA

PESO model 2.0 by Gini
Dietrich

Spin Sucks

The **PESO** model helps us understand the media landscape by outlining the associated channels that can be used in PR efforts. Developed and created by PR professional Gini Dietrich (2020) of *Spin Sucks*, the PESO model focuses on breaking down the types of media: paid, earned, shared, and owned (see Table 8.2).

Paid Media

Paid media includes content the organization has paid for to be placed at a certain time, on a certain platform, and before a certain audience (e.g., sponsored ads). Paid media focuses not just on the paid aspects of media buying or paying for content, but also on investing in the time, placement, and tools that are needed to get the content to the intended audiences in question. This is sometimes confusing since public relations has traditionally been a profession that gains media coverage without paying for the content. Examples include print and television advertisements, search key words, ads and promoted social media content (see "Shared Media" on page 171), and paid influencer content (Waddington, 2020). Paid media is not just designated to traditional media channels (commercials, advertisements, etc.), but can also include sponsored posts on platforms like Facebook. Facebook, one of the early adopters of the "pay to play" model, realizes that to reach audiences on the platform, brands have to sponsor, boost, or even pay for their content to appear in the newsfeed. As shown in the new PESO model, paid media components can be tied to earned media as well, such as experiential marketing and event marketing. These are two areas that are paid, but the overall goal is to attract earned media coverage, which will be covered next.

Earned Media

Earned media includes content you have shared, created, or pitched that has arrived on another platform without charge (e.g., a feature on a blog post). Earned media is at the heart of what public relations has traditionally done over the years. This is content and

Descriptions of PESO

Type of Media	Characteristics	Benefits	Challenges	Examples
Paid	Low trust, high scale	Reliable, placement will be guaranteed	High cost, perception may not be as credible	Sponsored posts, promoted videos, digital ads and banners, search engine optimization, native advertising, lead generation, paid publishing
Earned	High trust, medium scale	Low cost, high credibility	High time commitment, hard to break into the noise	Blog posts from influencers and news outlets, influencer marketing, event marketing, brand ambassadors, user-generated content (UGC)
Shared	High trust, low scale	Low cost, mid-level credibility	Platforms that have been considered shared platforms are now moving toward paid	Shared content on social (shared articles, posts, videos, etc.), reviews, forums, private messaging
Owned	Low trust, low scale	Low cost	Not viewed as trustworthy	Websites, email newsletters, blogs, printed materials, media kits, voice search

types of channels that feature your client or yourself in their publication for free. These placements are based on relationships formed by building connections and opportunities with the media professionals. However, these relationships are not limited to reporters and journalists, but also include bloggers, influencers, community-based publications, and websites. On the same scale, there are lots of options for what is considered to be earned media, but some examples include media relations, blogger relations, and organic influencer content (Waddington, 2020).

For earned media, the ultimate goal is to get press and media attention, and many brands have been able to do this successfully. In fact, one example of a successful buzz generated through creative activations and word-of-mouth communication comes from a brand that wanted to change its identity and name completely. This was the overall focus for the "IHOP turns IHOB" campaign. The people behind the popular restaurant International House of Pancakes wanted to generate some buzz related to their brand, so they decided to announce to the world they would be changing their name from IHOP to IHOB. Everyone was trying to figure out what the *B* stood for until IHOP announced the *B* was for burgers. Eventually, the company came out saying it had not really decided to change the name from IHOP to IHOB, but did it to spark a conversation and gain attention.

Shared Media

Shared media is the essence of social media and consists of content that has been distributed to others (e.g., repost content or shared videos on Facebook or retweets on Twitter). Shared media is somewhat confused with earned media. Earned media is focused more on universally traditional roles and outlets sharing content (e.g., publications, bloggers, influencers, and media professionals) whereas shared media focuses on individuals sharing the content within their community, such as organic reviews, social forums, and private messaging platforms (WhatsApp, GroupMe, etc.). Traditionally, shared media has been classified as social media since, in essence, it involves sharing

Black & Abroad's "Go Back To Africa" content hub

Retrieved from https://gobacktoafrica.com/

content, stories, and other materials on social media channels. Sharing has been a popular way to generate buzz, excitement, and drive for a story or news topic. However, what has made this a bit challenging for PR professionals is that many social channels are realizing that they have a powerful presence in reaching audiences. With this in play, many platforms including Facebook and others have made this landscape to become a "pay to play" situation.

Shared media can provide a powerful word-of-mouth communication channel for campaigns, as demonstrated by Black & Abroad's "Go Back To Africa" campaign. One of the issues that are facing society today is racial tension, and this was quite apparent in this campaign created by Black & Abroad. Online, there have been many instances of racially radicalized language directed toward African Americans along with the slur "Go Back To Africa." However, Black & Abroad, a travel brand that serves members of the Black community, wanted to take back this phrase and address the trolls and haters. In this campaign, the people behind the brand wanted to create a positive narrative of travel for the Black community, which they were able to do through an integrated approach in which they hijacked the slur, redacted the racist context, and created ads that highlighted the beauty of traveling to Africa. The platform (GoBackToAfrica.com) focused on commercial photos, influencer content, and other curated items that were driven by artificial intelligence technology. There were no paid media efforts behind this campaign. Instead, the campaign focused on curated content from users to present on their platforms along with influencers to share the messages and stories with others.

Owned Media

Lastly, **owned media** is the content you personally own and control. Your website, blog, and internal assets are examples. These items allow you to control the message, the updates, and the design of the media. For example, Adobe has a blog where the company is able to control what stories, news, and features to highlight as part of its brand. This has been a way for the brand to create awareness of not only what the company is doing, but also interesting features that may be of interest to Adobe's key audiences.

Applying the PESO model to public relations requires consideration of certain elements. First, PR professionals have traditionally not been in the business of buying content for media (Ochieng, 2018). Advertising and marketing professionals have been the professionals buying content for their clients, and this role has not been a typical part of the obligations and tasks for PR professionals. Yet, due to the social media landscape, more platforms are realizing they are in a situation where they can call the shots and charge businesses and others for getting messages to the right audience. Second, Ochieng (2018) discusses how the PESO model focuses on what PR professionals do not do since it leads with *paid*. Again, the challenge of what we are supposed to be doing and what we have not been doing as part of our profession comes into question. Ochieng (2018) discusses how the paid version of PESO should be classified more as a subset of shared media than anything else. In all of these cases, it is important to note that public relations, like other fields, has to evolve and change with the times. If platforms and technology channels are starting to force audiences to pay for access to their content, then that needs to be considered when developing a campaign. PR professionals have traditionally been "paying" for placement of their content already through the services of Cision, PR Newswire, and other press release and news services. This is just a transition to using new ways to get stories and key messages out to the media.

Stephen Waddington (2020) states that public relations has its roots in both earned and owned media, and yet, with the changes happening in the media landscape and emphasis on paid media, public relations is getting closer to what marketing is doing. This is why in this book we are taking the strategic plan approach to make sure the core components that have been communicated and initiated within the different models are still in place, while integrating key characteristics that are aligned with overall business communication and marketing goals.

SUMMARY

Creating, executing, and planning campaigns for public relations is one of the most important central areas of expertise we bring to the table for the business and communication fields. These plans serve as a guide to explore the journey our clients have had so far, their historical background, what challenges and opportunities they are facing, and what they need to address now. These plans are not just a one-and-done document—they serve more as a living plan that continues to grow and foster new ideas and possibilities. Each plan brings forth key lessons and takeaways of what worked and things to note for the future. PR plans require a strong foundation in sound research insights, with the blended integration of creative innovations in messaging, strategies, and tactics. With all of these features and steps, PR strategic plans evolve over time and must continue to adapt to the changing expectations and needs in the industry and workplace.

APR EXAM

- Management by objectives
- PR programming and implementation
- RACE
- ROPE

KEY TERMS

Budget 167
Calendar 167
Client overview 161
Core problem statement 163
Earned media 170
Environmental (or external) scan 161
Management by objectives 164
Media 169
Objectives 159

Owned media 172
Paid media 170
PESO 170
PR campaign 152
Primary audiences 165
Primary messages 165
RACE 158
ROPE 158
Secondary audiences 165

Secondary messages 165
Shared media 171
Situational analysis 163
SMART criteria 159
Strategic implication 164
Strategic plan 160
Strategies 159
Tactics 159

GAME CHANGER

Gini Dietrich, Founder of Spin Sucks

How did you get your start in public relations?

Courtesy of Gini Dietrich

That's a funny story. I got an undergrad degree in English, with a minor in statistics. I figured with both of those on my résumé, I could go to law school. I wanted to do contract negotiations for athletes. But life, as life does, had other plans for me. My mom got sick my senior year in college, and I found myself having to look for a job and postponing law school. I wrote for the *Omaha World-Herald* (the weddings and obituaries) my junior and senior years in school, so I figured I would either stay there full-time or write for another paper.

Then a girl who lived next door to me in the dorms called to say she'd interviewed at a PR firm in Kansas City and wasn't really interested in the job, but that she threw my name into the ring. At that point, I was willing to take almost anything so I could be near my mom and help her out financially. I interviewed for the job, and during my last interview, the general manager asked me where I saw myself in five years. I looked around his office and said, "This office looks good to me."

I may have been a bit full of myself, but he thought it was funny and I was hired on the spot. Not to say it was a fun job to start. I spent many a day making color copies of all of the media placements the account teams had secured. And back then, it took *forever* for color copies to print. The copier did five full runs—first the red, then the yellow, then the blue, then the black . . . and then one final pass to mush it all together. As I stood there, waiting for them all to copy, I would read the stories. I learned a ton about our clients that way, and it's what got me my first promotion about six months into my new role.

And the rest, as they say, is history.

What is your favorite part of working in public relations?

I love, love, love that it's ever-evolving. What we did 20 years ago is no longer what we do—to a certain extent. The strategy and thinking remains the same, but the tools we have to use to achieve results—*real measurable results*—change all the time. It's a fun time to be in this industry!

What is the most challenging part of working in public relations?

While we have an opportunity to prove that the work we do is an investment, not an expense, the industry does not have a standard way of reporting results, which is a pretty big challenge. In some cases, we borrow from our marketing brethren to measure marketing- and sales-qualified leads. And in other cases, we seem to be okay with media impressions, advertising equivalencies, and social media followers (it's *not* okay, by the way). Without an industry standard, we'll continue to fight for a seat at the proverbial table.

Who do you think are the biggest game changers for the PR industry?

Oh, this is a fun question! I have several:

- Martin Waxman—he's doing some crazy smart things around artificial intelligence and public relations.

- Deirdre Breakenridge—she continues to move the industry forward with *Women Worldwide* and her LinkedIn Learning courses.

- Michael Smart—he's the foremost expert on media relations and how it still works effectively today.

- Betsy Cooper—she has created a crazy smart virtual agency that encompasses more than public relations, which allows her and her team to showcase results in new and interesting ways.

- Rob Biesenbach—he's your one-stop shop for all things presentation skills and public speaking in this industry.

- Melissa Agnes—the work she is doing to influence how organizations get crisis ready is enviable. I love watching her brain work.

- Alex Sévigny—his writing/research on data is forward-thinking, and he approaches it from a communications (versus marketing) perspective.

What are some things you wish you knew when you were starting out in public relations?

I really wish I'd known three things: (1) how to think strategically; (2) how to negotiate—with clients and with bosses; and (3) the business side of public relations.

On every review when I worked for someone else, I was always told, "You need to think more strategically," but *no one* taught me what that meant or how to—I don't know—think strategically. Of course, I eventually learned it, but I had to do a ton of self-study to figure it out.

One of the things I've noticed as I grow my own business is, when offered a job, men always negotiate, and women never do. It breaks my heart!

There is a lot of research that shows women are typically very bad at negotiation. If I had one wish for young women coming into the business world (public relations or not), it's that they learn to negotiate early on. No one is going to be mad if you negotiate your job offer. If they do get mad, that's a major red flag, and you should run before you're trapped.

And, having run a business for more than a decade now, I really, really wish I'd learned the business side of what we do. Without those lessons while I worked for someone, it was a very expensive and harsh experience doing it on my own. Even if you think you'll never run your own agency, learn the business side anyway. If nothing else, it'll teach you how an organization makes money, and you'll be better at reporting results that matter.

Gini Dietrich is the founder, CEO, and author of Spin Sucks; *host of the* Spin Sucks *podcast; and author of* Spin Sucks *(the book). She also has run, built, and grown an agency for the past 14 years. She is co-author of* Marketing in the Round, *co-host of* Inside PR, *and co-host of the* Agency Leadership *podcast.*

DISCUSSION QUESTIONS

1. There are many different PR models. What two areas are commonly identified in the models?

2. What is the difference between the ROPE and RACE models? What are the similarities?

3. What are the key components of a strategic plan?

4. Identify the key benefits and challenges for each component of the PESO model. Which ones bring forth the most trust for a client?

5. Measurement is a key component to tie in with key objectives. Why is this the case?

ACTIVITIES

Building Your Portfolio

Creating a PR strategic plan proposal. You have been asked to create a proposal for one of the following companies:
- Burger King
- Cheetos
- Denny's
- Facebook
- Glossier
- KFC
- Lush Cosmetics
- Mountain Dew
- Netflix
- Patagonia
- Peloton
- White Claw

In this proposal, collect and analyze the information about the company and its current PR efforts through a SWOT analysis and situational analysis, and propose a new idea for the company to implement. Note the key audiences, messages, strategies, and tactics you want to share.

Building Your Brand

Build a strategic plan to get your dream internship. Strategic plans are not limited to PR clients and agencies. Evaluate your efforts to apply for your dream internship by conducting a SWOT analysis for your own personal brand. Write out a one- or two-sentence strategic implications statement. Write out your goal statement and objectives you wish to accomplish (following the SMART criteria) and discuss three strategies (with two associated tactics) you want to initiate to move forward with the objective of getting your dream internship.

Insta Novels from the New York Public Library's Instagram page

Instagram/@nypl

This case study addresses the issue of the younger generation of audience members in society not reading books as they used to. There are several possible reasons why this is happening, but some believe it is due to the increased use of technology and social media. It is a concern among libraries— how can they engage with the younger generation as well as be creative in how to reach this group?

The New York Public Library wanted to enhance engagement through the creation of Insta Novels, where the library would create stories from books to be shared on Instagram Stories. As a result, audience members on Instagram were able to read and follow along with popular stories in a medium that they were used to, and the New York Public Library was able to create a new way to present e-reading for a new generation. These stories were then saved on the library's Instagram profile as highlights so audiences can go back and enjoy the content.

Why did this case generate buzz?

- This case and campaign addressed a growing concern about the fact that younger audience members are not reading books or going to libraries as they used to. This also presented a new way of engaging with audiences through a channel in which they are used to consuming content.

- This was also a sustainable approach and strategy for the library as it was able to tie in the features and visual elements that were aligned with not only the books, but the library brand.

- This had not been approached or done before on Instagram, so the novelty of the activation and implementation was something that drove a lot of awareness and press to the campaign.

What are the ethical and legal issues?

- The issue of author copyright and ownership of the books that were turned into Insta Novels is something to note. It is not clear if the library got permission from the book authors who were highlighted to let them know it was doing this with their creative work. Understanding the terms of service agreements on platforms like Instagram and what they mean for copyright and ownership should be noted.

How did this address diversity and inclusion in the library's PR efforts?

- The New York Public Library addressed this by making its content accessible to audiences on Instagram and featuring diversity within the content on its main feed as well as Stories, including a range of authors from different backgrounds.

What are some takeaways from this case?

- There was no paid engagement or promotion for this campaign—it was driven all on earned and owned media initiatives for the New York Public Library.

- The Instagram account for the New York Public Library increased its follower base by 80 percent, which allowed more than 155,000 people to see the library's content. In addition, since this was a new approach to using Instagram, the library is taking action to work with the platform on promoting and creating features that support more long-form and long-term content.

CHAPTER 9

AUDIENCES AND RELATIONSHIP MANAGEMENT

LEARNING OBJECTIVES

- Distinguish between publics and audiences and between influencers and creators.

- Understand how we identify audiences through segmentation.

- Define relationship management and know how we apply it to audiences.

- Understand our relationships with clients, and their relationships with stakeholders and other audiences.

Introduction

Public relations consists of two important elements. The first is the "public" part—the audiences with whom we, as well as brands, agencies, and other organizations, engage. As professionals, we need to focus on our public audiences and recognize that they grow and change with the times. Brian Solis and Deirdre Breakenridge, in their book *Putting the Public Back in Public Relations*, make this point:

> The very people we had always wished to reach through traditional channels are now the very people we need to convince and inspire directly. . . . This is a new era of influence and in order to participate, we have to rewire our DNA to stop marketing "at" audiences in order to genuinely . . . connect with real people and the online communities they inhabit. (Solis, 2009)

While their book was published in 2009, these principles ring true today more than ever in PR circles. Instead of pushing content and hoping our audiences will react to what we say, we must embrace the co-creation aspect of our audiences. Today's audience members are creators and consumers of media and content. Storytelling in public relations is not about pushing messages to the masses, but rather about tailoring for individual audience members the content that is relevant to them and inviting them to participate.

The second element of public relations is "relations." Relations in the context of PR practices focus on the (potential, current, or in some cases former) connection someone has with the client in question. Engaging in mutually beneficial relationships that create a win-win situation for all involved is our ultimate goal. We make this happen by listening and making sure we understand what needs, expectations, and issues need to be addressed and what steps need to be taken to do this in a timely manner. To best understand our publics and our current relationships with them, we must understand our audiences through segmentation strategies. Doing this, as well as looking at audience relationship strategies, will allow us to identify new audience groups, such as creators and influencers, with whom to partner.

In addition to reviewing the key principles of strong relationship management (first presented in Chapter 1), this chapter will explain the features and types of relationships we participate in—and show how we manage these relationships for maximum benefit.

How Do We Identify Audiences?

To be effective in our PR efforts, we first have to understand to whom we are talking. If we do not understand our audiences, we will not be effective in persuading them to change their attitudes, listen to our perspectives, or behave in a certain way. There are different ways of understanding our audiences, and this section will cover these approaches in more detail.

Identifying Audiences Through Segmentation

Audience segmentation, as described in Chapter 5, refers to the process of categorizing people into groups based on specific criteria. These criteria can be broad in nature, organizing audiences based on demographics and population data, or they can be narrowly focused (or niche), organizing audiences according to specific categories, such as their industries or interests, or how visually driven they are. Basically, when we use an audience segmentation strategy, we identify subgroups within a larger target audience so that we can develop stronger connections with clients, brands, and the public (Mailchimp, n.d.). The more information that we have about the people with whom we communicate, the more effective we will be in crafting our messages, proposing and applying creative campaign strategies, and understanding the journey that individual audience members have gone through to get to where they are presently.

Using audience segmentation strategies, we and our clients, as well as other organizations and brands, collect information to create a profile of an audience with which we want to engage. We can create broad targets to prioritize those we want to reach first, or we can identify specific people to receive our messages and content. The more we segment our audience, the more focused we can be in narrowing down the people we really want to reach for a campaign. Of course, we don't want to reach everyone—we only want to target those who have a vested interest in learning more about what we are doing and in formulating a stronger relationship. Audience segmentation strategies also help us identify new audiences who may not be on our radar, but who may bring new opportunities to the table.

AUDIENCE AND RELATIONSHIP MANAGEMENT

Public relations professionals have to understand their audiences in order to craft effective messages, stories, and experiences. There are some rising audiences that are becoming a key part of any public relations strategy, but they are not all the same or created equally.

INFLUENCERS are individuals who have built an audience, naturally and over time, and are viewed as authority figures on a certain subject, area, or perspective in the online space. In addition, an influencer has the trust of a community, which allows the influencer to persuade audiences to take a specific action based on what is shared. Influencers bring their experiences, unique perspectives, and brand voice to the table, which makes it difficult to categorize influencers in a consistent way.

Influencers and creators have different types that need to be noted based on focus area, experience, cost, and size of their community.

CREATORS are a subset of influencers who focus on creating original content in their own voice for brands rather than just sharing brand-created content. They view their creativity as the most important element of their contribution to their partnership with the brand. Creators want to create a story, experiment in programming, and allow themselves to organically and authentically integrate themselves with a brand in their content.

ACTIVISTS are individuals who educate, promote, and engage in a variety of different channels and circumstances to reach their intended audiences. Individuals who are active and engaged in supporting different issues, causes, and areas of focus have been a topic of conversation for public relations for many decades. Activists today are not only engaged in supporting issues and causes on their own, but they also partner with brands that support their causes.

HERO

- 1+ million followers
- Big name in the creative industry
- Known for strong partner deals with brands
- Not viewed as authentic due to $$ payouts
- Posts on a regular basis, but very conscious of aesethic and brand image
- Example: Casey Neistat and Ryan Reynolds

MACRO

- 100,000+ followers
- Have an established following
- Partnered with large brands
- Posts frequently with brand image in mind
- Example: Amy Landino and Taylor Lorenz

MICRO

- 10,000+ followers
- More brands are working with these audiences since their audience is more interested in the content they are creating
- Posts frequently and engages with audiences
- Example: Matthew Kobach and Kerry Flynn

NANO

- 1,000+ followers
- More niche in focus, but community is highly engaged
- Posts very frequently and is extremely active in the community
- Example: Truth Pug

Using Categories for Segmenting Audiences

When we create an audience analysis, there are a few major categories that we typically use to organize our audiences (see Table 9.1). First, as we saw in Chapters 5 and 8, *demographics*, the statistical qualities of a population, give us a way to identify our audiences through data that include age, language, race or ethnicity, gender, income level, job type, and geographic location (Mailchimp, n.d.). On the other hand, *psychographics*, or psychological categories of attributes, come into play "when [we] have access to insights about [our] audience's personality types, values, attitudes, and beliefs" (Mailchimp, n.d.). This type of segmentation allows us to better understand our audiences based on their mental preferences and lifestyle characteristics, which gives us more detailed information than demographics.

Behavioral segmentation, which focuses on analyzing the actual behavior and actions individuals take, goes beyond psychographics, allowing us to consider how an audience has behaved or acted in relation to our client or brand (Mailchimp, n.d.). For example, if our audiences are looking for a holiday vacation, individuals who travel frequently will have certain expectations for the messages they receive from us, compared with those who travel less frequently. In addition to gaining an analysis of buyer habits, behavioral segmentation allows us to see which audience members are loyal and active members, which are long-standing customers, and which are former customers. Behavioral segmentation helps us determine our best overall message strategy, one that will engage each of our different audiences.

A last type of audience segmentation that we use is **communication channel segmentation**, which looks at the channels (media, individuals, communities, devices, platforms, influencers/advocates/creators, and sources) our audiences interact and engage with. To sort our audiences using channel segmentation, we may ask: What accounts or influencers do our audiences follow? What content do they like on digital and social media channels? How much time do they spend on each of these channels? Do they consume or create content on these channels? These insights can provide a finer perspective of focused behaviors and actions of audiences on specific channels.

Audience segmentation informs us of the following:

- *Niche audiences are more important than large audiences.* Our efforts should not target the 7+ billion people on the planet. Instead, it's more important that we focus on the unique qualities that make up our smaller and highly engaged audiences. While niche audiences may not be large in numbers, they are more likely to participate in a conversation with our client's brand than are broader audiences. Niche audiences are not cookie-cutter audiences. Rather, they require from us personalized messages and activities that are relevant to them specifically.

- *Data are our friends when we segment audiences.* New media channels, platforms, and tools provide us with deep insights into our audiences. For example, brands such as Facebook are essentially global databases of segmented audiences. Facebook not only knows who its audience members are but also has insights into what they like, what they follow, with whom they engage, and much more. As we gather information about our audience segments, we need to use our data analysis skills to understand, interpret, and apply our findings to create effective messaging (Gee, 2017).

Key Categories for Audience Segmentation and Their Characteristics

Demographics	Psychographics	Behavioral Segmentation	Communication Channel Segmentation
• Age • Gender • Occupation • Race • Location • Language preference • Relationship status	• Attitudes • Behaviors • Interests • Opinions • Lifestyle • Connections	• Buyer habits • Frequency in purchases • Loyal or active members • Former clients or customers	• Creating or consuming content • Communities audiences belong to • Influencers, creators, advocates, and personalities audiences follow • Individuals (thought leaders) audiences follow and respect • Devices and other media tools used to create and consume content • Other similar interests or brands audiences follow

- *Insights about our audiences inform our strategies.* Our failure to understand our audiences can be devastating for the success of our campaigns. To be effective, before going forward with a plan, we need to first segment our audiences (Gee, 2017). In addition, we must take advantage of the more sophisticated tools and solutions at the enterprise level (e.g., Salesforce) that are available to us and that can integrate different types of data to tell a story about the who, what, where, and why aspects of key audiences in question (YouGov, 2016). The amount of data that we collect for individual audience members—such as which bands they like, where they shop, what sites they visit, where they check in, and which apps they use—can paint a very clear picture of who they are (YouGov, 2016).

- *Relevance is the new reach.* Relevance means that it is important to the individuals or publics in question—they are more motivated to engage with clients, brands, and others they wish to interact with than those who are trying to reach them without an established connection. Reach, or how many people are exposed to our message, is a primary area to address when segmenting audiences. Pushing out content that may not be relevant to our audiences, including press releases, videos, and more, in the hope that something will "stick" in their minds is no longer an effective practice. Rather, we need to share what is relevant to our key audience segments.

Is there a right or wrong way to segment our audiences? The answer is no, but it's important to strike a balance: Having too few categories will not help us distinguish each audience as unique, and having too many can be so focused that we end up targeting only one individual (Patel, 2019). A best practice is to make sure that each audience that we segment and analyze is relevant (aligned with our campaign), unique (having uncommon distinguishing characteristics), significant (having an impact on the overall success of our campaigns or brands), and locatable (easy to find) (Patel, 2019).

Identifying Audiences Based on Characteristics: Grunig's Theory

Another tool for segmenting our audiences is the **situational theory of publics**, created by James Grunig, professor emeritus at the University of Maryland. Grunig's theory guides us in the task of organizing our audiences according to certain characteristics. Grunig states that in this theory it is important to classify audiences based on these attributes to better group them into different categories. He outlines the following areas for segmentation:

1. Problem recognition

2. Constraint recognition

3. The level of involvement of an audience, which includes those who seek information and those who process information

Grunig's approach goes beyond the typical segmentation strategies such as considering demographics and psychographics, as discussed previously. Grunig's situational theory of publics helps us figure out what will motivate our audiences to listen, act, and engage in a conversation with us and our client. Following are the major principles of the theory.

1. Problem Recognition

Problem recognition refers to how well an audience member recognizes a problem that needs to be addressed versus a situation that is not important enough to require action. When audiences have a vested interest in a situation, they are more likely to recognize any problems that arise. Typically, people don't perceive something as a problem unless it has an impact on their lives.

2. Constraint Recognition

Constraint recognition refers to how well an audience member identifies any obstacles that are in the way of achieving a certain goal. Constraints may be physical, emotional, or mental in nature.

3. Level of Involvement

An audience member's level of involvement is the degree to which that person wants to identify and participate in addressing a problem. Some members are active (**information seeking**) in wanting to understand and fix the problem, while others are passive (**information processing**), preferring to wait for information to come to them.

Who Are Our Audiences? How Do We Interact With Them?

Some of our audiences are focused on internal activations and correspondence (communication) and are considered internal audiences, while others are more external in terms of their engagement and relationship activities. Thinking of an audience as internal or external is a way for us to organize individual members into groups. That said, with the current media landscape, there are many different characteristics and niche areas to consider.

Following is an overview of the relationships that we have with our audiences. Some are standard, such as our relationships with media and customers, while others are emerging, such as our relationships with influencers, discussed later in this chapter.

The Media

Even if some people think that traditional media is "dead" or no longer relevant, it is still a primary audience for us. When we practice media relations, we work with professionals in the media industry, which includes newspapers, radio, and broadcast stations, and coordinate stories. In media relations, we rely on a middleman, the media, who communicates with us and with audiences. When we work with the media to promote our clients, we use "different media outlets and coverage to tell [a] company's story, rather than directly engaging with the publics and key stakeholders" (Sabourin, 2014).

The media industry has grown and evolved tremendously, as has the field of public relations. We now work with online news outlets and blogs, such as *The Next Web*, *Morning Consult*, *Bleacher Report*, and *Digiday* to name a few. To showcase stories and other features on these platforms and channels, we need to have strong relationships with media professionals, something that takes time and the dedication of both parties. A current challenge is that the traditional media are facing financial problems and many publications and outlets are cutting staff due to budget constraints. In 2019, more than 7,800 employees at major organizations such as CNN, BuzzFeed, Verizon, and Gannett lost their jobs (Goggin, 2019). This compression affects how we pitch, engage, and share stories about our clients with the media and their audiences. In some cases, the ratio of PR professionals to journalists is staggering, with one report stating that there are six PR professionals for every one journalist (Schneider, 2018). One effect of this imbalance is that we face more competition for journalists' attention. In addition, many brands and agencies are becoming their own media outlets, something that we discussed in Chapter 8. Many of us now work more directly with individuals who have their own communities and networks, such as creators and influencers. Media relations, our relationships with those who oversee a community and platform, are still prominent, but as is true for all specialized areas, we must adapt to the growing changes and expectations in our industries.

Fellow Employees, Vendors, and Customers

Other audiences that are engaged with clients are operating external to the client, as discussed in this section of the chapter.

Employees

Employees, our colleagues at our organizations, are an important audience for us as PR professionals. This internal relations aspect of what we do is sometimes overlooked. Because our focus on what external audiences think and feel tends to dominate, we sometimes forget about the significant internal relationships that can emerge within our organizations.

Because employees experience the natural balance of being connected within their organizations and also with their organizations' external audiences, they can see both internal and external perspectives. When we foster these relationships over time, we can produce great benefits for our companies, such as building communities that persevere through good times and in crises and developing cultures that attract new and emerging talent. Southwest Airlines is an organization that sees its employees as an important audience. Known for strong customer service, the management at Southwest makes its employees its number-one concern by first focusing on communication efforts and then addressing external audiences (Martin, 2015).

Employees who leverage their own loyalty as a currency are known as **ambassadors**. Ambassadors are engaged, transparent individuals who are willing to share their stories and insights with communities both on- and offline. As ambassadors, employees can help answer questions from other groups and foster stronger relationships for their organization's brand by being approachable. Employee ambassadors are more relatable than paid spokespeople since they are viewed as being more trustworthy and authentic, and they are not perceived as being paid to promote a brand or company in question—something that can even help to reach new audiences.

Meltwater, the media monitoring company, recommends the following steps to establish an employee brand ambassador program (Heald, 2017):

- Conduct an internal audit to determine the level of commitment and engagement among employees. If the culture is strong and engaged, this program will be successful. If not, then it will not be.

- Select and review potential employee candidates for the ambassador program.

- Set up protocols, best practices, and clear expectations for the employees who are part of this program.

- Create regular training sessions and meetings with these team members to determine strategies and to identify additional collaborative measures to make the program a success.

- Evaluate the team's performance and highlight leaders who are active and engaged with the community.

In addition to employees, we need to be aware of other business audiences.

Vendors

Vendors, or other companies doing business with us and our clients, are an audience with whom we can forge strong relationships. When businesses work with each other, that is called business-to-business, or **B2B**. Traditionally, PR professionals work with businesses that relate to consumers, or **B2C**. Relationships with vendors, or any suppliers who work with other businesses, are valuable to us, especially when they are long-standing, forward-looking, and mutually beneficial. Sometimes, powerhouse brands come together for a common cause to take on an emerging competitor. For example, Adobe, a global technology program company, partnered with Microsoft in 2019 to announce a partnership to take on Salesforce, a dominant social management and listening company. The partnership will focus on providing access to key learning platforms, data analytics, and content marketing tools for both brands. This relationship was built over time and could not have happened without the dedication and support of both companies working together. Brands should look to potential relationships and partnerships that can help foster and grow the community they have built. Adobe has done this exceedingly well with its strategic acquisitions of brands such as Magneto (ecommerce features and platform) and partnerships with other specialized companies such as social media tools Hootsuite and Talkwalker.

Customers

Customers are another key audience with whom we should build strong relationships. Among our customers are supporters and fans, and then there are the haters—every brand, team, and organization has experienced this. That is the nature of public relations: There will always be people who love whatever you share and post, and there will always be others who hate it. To engage all audiences, we need to cultivate transparency and authenticity.

To be transparent and authentic with our customers, we have to be real with them. Allowing customers to know you and your company, and to appreciate that they could go elsewhere, helps foster a strong relationship. Creating memorable experiences that surprise and delight is one way to forge a more powerful relationship with customers. One brand that has done this very well is Coca-Cola through its "Open Happiness" campaign. By creating experiences through grassroots efforts and featuring vending machines giving out amazing prizes, Coca-Cola's campaign not only taps into the brand's key messages about happiness; it also produces memorable impressions for its audiences.

Consider the following points before attempting to launch a successful "surprise and delight" campaign (Expert Panel, 2019):

- *Research your customers and determine their needs.* In 2017, WestJet, a Canadian airline, wanted to surprise audiences by activating their visions for Christmas in "12 flights of Christmas" for customers (WestJet, n.d.). The airline brought children's ideas to life by gathering ideas submitted to the company and activating them in real-life situations for the children to see in person. This was unexpected and brought forth a strong positive reaction from customers.

- *Share things that are not on your audience's radar.* Surprise makes people remember their experiences. Determine things that your customers need, but also things they do not expect to have at a particular time. Doing this can spark creative strategies and make a memorable connection for your audience members.

- *Tie your strategies back to your brand and overall relationship.* Remember that any strategy or campaign must connect back to your client's brand. Coca-Cola reinforced its brand through the "Open Happiness" campaign, and WestJet focused its campaign to surprise and delight during the holiday season when travel is heaviest.

- *Always overdeliver.* When you think you have done enough, push ahead and give a bit more to your audiences. Generosity is always appreciated, and to make an experience iconic and memorable, it has to be special. Exceeding expectations and focusing on the quality and uniqueness of the audience experiences you have created can foster an even stronger relationship with customers.

Activists

Activists, individuals who support different issues and causes, have been a topic of conversation in public relations for decades. Activists educate, promote, and engage in a variety of different channels and settings to reach their audiences. Activists today are not only engaged in supporting issues and causes on their own, but they also partner with brands that support their causes.

Traditionally, activists have worked with nonprofit organizations, such as St. Jude Children's Research Hospital and Metro United Way, and government agencies, but many now look for other opportunities for getting their messages out there. Melissa Dodd of the University of Central Florida has pointed out that corporations support activists because of the public's growing expectations that they need to take action on issues (Data Freaks, 2015). Some organizations have integrated brand activism into their mission statement and purpose, such as Delta Air Lines, which severed ties with the National Rifle Association; Dick's Sporting Goods, which no longer sells guns in stores; Patagonia, which is working to save national parks; and Airbnb, which lobbies for marriage equality in Australia.

Younger Generations Are More Likely to Be Activists

The generations defined

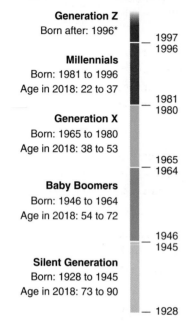

Generation Z
Born after: 1996*

— 1997
— 1996

Millennials
Born: 1981 to 1996
Age in 2018: 22 to 37

— 1981
— 1980

Generation X
Born: 1965 to 1980
Age in 2018: 38 to 53

— 1965
— 1964

Baby Boomers
Born: 1946 to 1964
Age in 2018: 54 to 72

— 1946
— 1945

Silent Generation
Born: 1928 to 1945
Age in 2018: 73 to 90

— 1928

*No chronological endpoint has been set for this group. In this analysis, Generation Z includes those ages 13 to 21 in 2018

"Generation Z Looks a Lot Like Millennials on Key Social and Political Issues"

Fry, Richard, and Kim Parker. "Early Benchmarks Show 'Post-Millennials' on Track to Be Most Diverse, Best-Educated Generation Yet." Pew Research Center, Washington, DC (November 15, 2018) https://www.pewsocialtrends.org/2018/11/15/early-benchmarks-show-post-millennials-on-track-to-be-most-diverse-best-educated-generation-yet/

The activist trend is different across generations. Generation Z, the cohort emerging past the millennials, is a purpose-driven and highly engaged demographic that is focused on activism more than any other age group in recent history ("Getting Gen Z Primed to Save the World," n.d.). These activists participate in more causes, engage in more volunteer work, and want to do more with what they have for the community and world. They are also more involved with diversity and inclusion issues, political campaigns, protests, and gender identification.

Brands such as Nike have been on the forefront of engaging in politically driven campaigns, and also partner with activists as their key spokespeople to bring more awareness to these issues. Along with Colin Kaepernick, Nike has partnered with younger activists such as Deja Foxx, a Gen Z activist focused on diversity and inclusion. More brands are trying to establish relationships with Gen Z activists because they already have a focus in their community. Many have also gained influence on social media.

Influencers and Creators

A new group of audience members who are transforming themselves into their own media outlets are influencers and creators. These are two different groups of impactful audience members to note, and they continue to rise in both popularity and numbers. This section will go over the similarities and differences between these two groups.

Influencers: Celebrity, Mega, Micro, and Nano

What do we know about influencers? An **influencer** is someone who has built an audience, naturally and over time, and who is viewed as an authority on a certain subject, practice, or perspective in online spaces. In addition, because an influencer has the trust of a community, he or she can share content that persuades this audience to take a specific action.

Influencers bring their experiences, unique perspectives, and brand voices to the table, which makes it difficult to categorize them. Some influencers enjoy a strong standing based on their role and profession, such as sports figures, pop stars, and media professionals, but for the most part, influencers are regular people with a specific interest and passion, as well as the dedication to create a name for themselves within their industry and community.

As far as platforms go, creators usually tend to lean toward video content, which makes YouTube one of their top choices. Influencers today are most likely to be found on Instagram, but more are gravitating to other platforms for more exposure and brand opportunities, such as the Chinese-based platform TikTok or video content creation platforms including YouTube. Most influencers use more than one designated platform to house their content and engage with their audiences—for example:

- A website

- A blog

- A social media presence on Facebook, Twitter, Instagram, YouTube, LinkedIn, TikTok, and other channels through which they cultivate their audiences

- An email marketing newsletter

- A show, such as a live or recorded broadcast or podcast

- A YouTube channel for vlogs, tutorials, and daily videos

- A strategy to have multiple lines of income driven by their influence (product deals, partnerships, etc.)

More brands are investing in influencers for their work than ever before. According to a 2019 Talkwalker report, 69 percent of respondents ranked influencer marketing as their top priority for the year, and 61 percent stated they will increase the amount of money they invest in the practice. Characteristics that influencers showcase that make them successful in the public relations space include the following:

- *Authenticity* is a critical part of what makes an influencer influential. It's crucial that influencers are able to share parts of their real lives in a transparent way—and offer their perspective on life and their profession, as that is what audiences crave (Sharma, 2018).

- *Relevance* is another characteristic that is key for influencers. Do they have the necessary level of expertise and insights to matter to audiences? Or are they all about "faking it till they make it"? This is why many brands look for evidence to support the decision to invest in one influencer over another.

- *Personality* is a must. To be memorable, influencers must reveal their humanity and share their charismatic personality. Certain influencers have been successful in creating a brand for themselves online through certain personality characteristics (Freberg, Graham, McGaughey, & Freberg, 2011).

- *Engagement with audiences*—or the actions that influencers take when audience members respond to an update, post, or other online conversation—is an important measure (Sharma, 2018). Influencers who engage their audiences are active and present on their accounts; they are sure to answer questions, communicate with community members, and create content that connects with their viewers or listeners. Level of engagement is one metric that brands look to as a way to evaluate their position in the market and their relationships with influencers.

- *Reach*, or the degree to which influencers connect with audiences, and the associated numbers, is an important factor. However, there are some caveats: Reach needs to be real and organic, not forced or artificially created. Reach is based on "real followers" versus paid followers or bots (artificial programs that are programmed to like, comment, and engage with an account or influencer to create the illusion of influence and popularity).

Celebrity endorsements, product placements, and statements of support are some of the ways we can employ influencers in our PR efforts. When we include influencers as part of a campaign, we compensate them in a variety of ways. Of course, to some we pay fees based on what they share and post for their various audiences. The more followers and reach individual influencers have, the more they are able to charge. However, there are other ways to compensate influencers. Many times, brands and companies send influencers free products and gear with the hope they will be willing to share their experiences with the goods on their channels. Yet one of the most effective ways we can compensate influencers is to provide them with an experience they can then talk about with their communities. Exclusive events, sessions, and insider information are just some of the ways in which influencers are compensated for their time. An example of this involves Adobe Insiders. This group is made up of professionals from marketing, digital, social, and public relations who are actively using Adobe products in their creative and business work. Adobe has brought these individuals together to help cover events such as Adobe Summit, a large marketing conference in Las Vegas, and exclusive events at Adobe headquarters. In return, Adobe Insiders share their experiences through news articles, videos, and blog posts.

There are different types of influencers to evaluate for a PR campaign (see Table 9.2). *Celebrity, mega, micro,* and *nano influencers* are frequently used terms in public relations. **Celebrity influencers** hold a prominent status that allows them to influence others. Celebrities including Dwayne "The Rock" Johnson, Ryan Reynolds, Kylie Jenner, and Will Smith are all examples of prominent celebrity influencers who have their own online spaces and channels. While these individuals have a strong online presence and voice in their respective industries, they may not be as credible on campaigns that are not directly related to their brands. In addition, the cost of having a celebrity influencer post or comment online, or be part of a campaign, is very high. However, celebrity influencers know the benefits that participating in a PR campaign can have for them and their careers. Actor, producer, and wrestling professional Dwayne Johnson has been ranked as the top influencer in the entertainment industry, and he owes much of his success to what he does on social media (Robehmed, 2018). Johnson was quoted in a *Forbes* article as saying this:

> Social media has become the most critical element of marketing a movie for me. I have established a social media equity with an audience around the world that [knows] there's a value in what I'm delivering to them. (Robehmed, 2018)

The Rock and his lucrative partnership with Under Armour
Instagram/@therock

Mega influencers are influencers who have a prominent status on social media and a broad appeal that puts them on track to reach celebrity status. These individuals shape culture and industries and make a direct impact on their communities by driving sales of products and services. Such influencers may not be celebrities in the Hollywood sense, but they are prominent in their respective industries, such as Gary Vaynerchuk, a mega influencer among entrepreneurs. Vaynerchuk, who owns VaynerMedia and is a best-selling author, has established himself as a leading voice in the industry by making connections with audiences outside the normal business landscape (sports figures, rappers, musicians, etc.) and created his own products (e.g., a shoe partnership with K-Swiss). Going outside of the box, creating impactful content across different channels, and strategically communicating how he's different from other entrepreneurs has helped him gain a large global audience and become a dominant influencer in the media landscape. Working with mega influencers can be financially challenging, but it's especially beneficial when they impact a brand by creating a sponsored post, a shout-out, a mention, or a story (Mediakix, n.d.). In addition, mega influencers do not need media training or oversight, unlike other influencers (such as micro or nano influencers, covered in the following paragraphs), because they are prepared, have experience, and know the expectations for working with the brand.

Micro influencers, who have smaller audiences than celebrity or mega influencers, are the source of considerable buzz. These influencers have generated significant attention over the past few years because of their ability to cultivate strong communities around particular interests (Mediakix, n.d.). They also have strong engagement rates, which is a key metric that we and our brands may look for instead of high follower counts. Still, there are risks associated with working with micro influencers. For example, they may lack brand awareness, media training, and preparation. They also have less reach than celebrity or mega influencers. However, the many benefits include higher engagement rates, lower commission costs when compared with celebrities, and access to focused and niche communities.

Nano influencers, influencers with the fewest followers, with audiences even smaller than those of micro influencers, were first introduced in a 2018 *New York Times* article titled "Are You Ready for the Nanoinfluencers?" As discussed in the article, nano influencers' "lack of fame is one of the qualities that make them approachable. When they recommend a shampoo or a lotion or a furniture brand on Instagram, their word seems as genuine as advice from a friend. Brands enjoy working with them partly because they are easy to deal with. In exchange for free products or a small commission, nanos typically say whatever companies tell them to" (Maheshwari, 2018). While nano influencers can be effective, a challenge is that audiences may see them as inauthentic and not a part of their community. If a community feels a nano influencer is being "bought" or has allowed a brand to take over his or her account for a campaign, they may not trust the influencer again.

Creators: A Subset of Influencers

A new type of audience, **creators** are a subset of influencers who create for brands original content in their own voices. They don't simply share brand-created content. Rather, they view their creativity as the most important part of their contribution to a brand. Creators

Types of Influencers

Celebrity	Mega	Micro	Nano
• Have 10+ million followers • Prominent in the industry • Huge reach and exposure • Trained and prepared to work with media and brands • Expensive and may not be perceived as credible due to payment	• Have between 1 million and 9+ million followers • Specialized presence and leadership in specific industries • Effective for sponsored content • Experience working with brands and media • Somewhat expensive	• Have 10,000 to 50,000 followers • Highly engaged and cultivate strong community with accounts • Ability to tap into more niche and focused communities • There is a lot of benefit	• Have 1,000 to 10,000 followers • Lack of fame makes them approachable • Easy to work with for brands • Exchange is usually a small commission or free product

Shaun McBride, otherwise known as Shonduras, is an example of a creator who has gone mainstream with his YouTube and esports team Spacestation

Getty Images Entertainment

want to tell a story, experiment in programming, and allow themselves to authentically integrate with a brand through the content they write (Goldberg, 2018).

Creators are also successful in making videos and other forms of content that end up going mainstream. Mike Meltzer, a popular creator on Snapchat and now part of the Covina analytics team, has been known to partner with brands such as the Ultimate Fighting Championship, NASCAR, and Reese's. James Charles, the focus of this chapter's case study, started out by creating makeup tutorials and is a spokesperson for CoverGirl. Shaun McBride, a creator on Snapchat, emerged as an influencer through his creative illustrations; he later moved to YouTube and then esports with his brand. As their personal branding deepens and expands, creators have room to grow their relationships with their communities and other audiences.

Creators and influencers are similar in many ways, but they differ in approaches and characteristics. A creator focuses more on creating and producing content for a specific platform, such as YouTube, to be shared to the masses, whereas an influencer focuses on a specific area of expertise, such as fashion or local food, across various platforms (Hakim, 2015). Many influencers also claim to be creators because they produce videos, images, or other content that can be consumed on blogs and other online locations. In the current social media environment, creators are perceived more positively than influencers since they have not had the negative press or associations influencers have gotten over the years.

As is the case for influencers, creators come in different size categories—in this case, micro, macro, nano, and hero (creators who are transparent and authentic in how they produce content and manage their communities)—based on how large their following is on designated platforms. In Table 9.3, each category is outlined based on certain features and criteria. While it may be tempting to go for the creators with the largest following, more brands are engaging with micro creators because they are viewed as more authentic and are more inspired by the content they create (Expert Commentator, 2018). Another element to consider for micro or even nano creators is the fact that these individuals are more engaged with their audiences than the hero creators or macro creators. These individuals, with their smaller yet more concentrated audience groups, have the time to respond, chat, and help their members on a more regular basis.

The one universal foundation that all creators share with each other is why they are in the positions they are in. They have collectively built a level of trust with their audiences over time, making it a win-win situation for their relationships, by being real with their community through authentic conversations.

Influencers and Creators: Differences

Something to keep in mind is that the term *influencers* is not always thought of positively by audiences. Because of the crises and other problems surrounding some influencers—such as the failed Fyre Festival, the discovery of fake influencers, and bots—the term is sometimes perceived negatively. Creators, on the other hand, are viewed more positively due to their emphasis on being true to their brand and partnering with brands not "just for the money," but rather for their established connection and being able to co-create and collaborate with a brand or client they believe in. This is something that has led some influencers to rebrand themselves as creators. However, as mentioned previously, creators and influencers have a different focus in mind, as illustrated in the next point. On the other hand, *creator* as a term "implies one who is not defined by their marketing utility but by their desire to create content that adds value to those who engage with it" (Goldberg, 2018).

Creators want to collaborate with brands, whereas influencers want to take from brands. Creators want to tell a story through their creative lenses and share their insights with others. Influencers are more interested in receiving perks than creating. Free perks such as hotel stays, paid speaking engagements, and new products are all part of the package. Creators, on the other hand, want to create a story and experience that is new and relevant for their audiences with the brand in question (Goldberg, 2018).

▼ TABLE 9.3

Types of Creators

Nano	Micro	Macro	Hero
• 1,000+ followers • More niche in focus, but community is highly engaged • Post very frequently and are extremely active in the community • Examples: Vincenzo Landino, Goldie Chan	• 10,000+ followers • More brands are working with these creators since their audiences are more interested in the content they are creating • Post frequently and engage with audiences • Example: Taylor Lorenz	• 100,000+ followers • Have an established following • Partnered with large brands • Post frequently with brand image in mind • Examples: Amy Landino, Roberto Blake	• 1+ million followers • Big name in the creative industry • Known for strong partner deals with brands • Not viewed as authentic due to payouts • Post on a regular basis, but very conscious of aesthetics and brand image • Example: Casey Neistat

Source: Adapted from Smart Insights, "Micro, Macro, Nano, and Hero Creators," 2018

With so many brands tapping into this space, brand deals are thrown to this genre of talent left and right. More and more, creators are maintaining a defensiveness about their content and what they love. Being approached by so many brands, they reserve the right to do what is most authentic and are able to truly tell a story versus producing a one-off opportunity. When strategizing the best programming for your client(s), think about the ways these creators can work beyond video integration (Hakim, 2015). Creators don't just share a review or picture on Instagram featuring themselves with the product, but they bring a creative and unique brand voice to the table to create a story that has not been featured before for the brand (Goldberg, 2018). Here are some case studies that involve creators and what public relations can learn from them:

- *Onboarding influencers to the team.* Kellogg's has shifted things around in the industry by changing the game in its relationships with influencers. First, instead of having a one-off partnership with influencers by having them post an update on social media, Kellogg's is integrating them into the conversation, which is creating an opportunity for the influencers to be part of the collaboration and creation process. This has not been done before by Kellogg's (Joseph, 2019). Influencers are able to share a collaborative document with the team at Kellogg's and bounce around ideas. What is changing is that instead of a "pay to play" model, influencers are being treated as members of the team or even as part of the agency or creative side of a campaign (Joseph, 2019).

- *Loopholes and endorsements.* This has been one of the biggest challenges for PR professionals when it comes to influencers. Influencers need to disclose whether they have been sponsored for a promotion, update, or contest. The Federal Trade Commission has strict guidelines for what should and should not be done when it comes to influencer marketing. However, like all of the different angles and new tools out there, there are always loopholes. Philip Morris, the tobacco company, discovered one of these. The company had used influencers to promote its product on social media, using the hashtag #IQOS. This was brought to attention by the Campaign for Tobacco-Free Kids, and resulted in Twitter and Snapchat taking down these posts (Kary & Wagner, 2019).

- *Being the target of the "cancel culture."* What happens if your PR client is rejected or "canceled" by audiences based on the client's actions? Being *canceled* is a term that rose up in society to essentially dismiss or "cut someone down" out of the media or high-level status of being perceived as influential. Many celebrities and influencers have fallen victim to being "canceled," such as YouTube beauty influencer James Charles, comedian Kathy Griffin, and Olivia Jade. Jade, a YouTuber with a cosmetic line, was part of the Operation Varsity Blues crisis that hit college campuses in 2019. Jade was involved due to her parents, Lori Loughlin and Mossimo Giannulli, paying the University of Southern California to get her admitted to the university. Jade has since left USC, but the scandal and being "canceled" still follow her brand off- and online.

Both creators and influencers must be successful community builders. Community is at the heart of what drives audiences to listen, engage, and stay with one influencer or creator versus another. Online communities are made up of people who are invested in a particular issue, brand, or area of expertise. The following characteristics define a strong community:

- *Relevance.* Is the information being shared relevant to the growing interests of the community? To matter to their audiences, influencers and creators must anticipate and respond to what their audiences want.

- *Exclusivity.* Being in the know is powerful. People want to feel like they are getting something that not everyone else is. Being able to get information and updates first is one of the main reasons communities in social media exist. Influencers and creators must be sure to provide valuable insider information.

- *Safety and tone.* We all want to be part of communities that are positive and engaging. However, because some community members don't follow the basics of respectful interaction, influencers and creators must be proactive in sharing policies for dealing with such individuals. They must outline expectations for what is acceptable and what is not and share clear statements about what will be done if policies are not followed. This helps assure audiences of their safety, the tone of their interactions, and their expectations for each other.

- *Consistency.* People do not want to be part of communities that are all over the place. Communities need a centralized mission, goal, or purpose.

- *Sustainability.* Communities are not formed and immediately abandoned. They are constantly maintained and invested in by hosts and administrators. If audiences know a video will be uploaded every day, they will change their behavior to make sure they are there to see it.

What Is Relationship Management?

Relationship management is a strategy that allows us to focus on our connections with audiences, especially on the strategic communications between our client organizations and their key publics. Relationship management is behind all of our professional practices, guiding the choices we make whether we're conducting research, seeking new opportunities for business, or carrying out campaigns.

Professor Mary Ann Ferguson of the University of Florida sparked a conversation about the importance of relationship management in a conference paper in 1984 on the subject, which in 2018 was reprinted in the *Journal of Public Relations Research*. The main premise of this article was how this perspective for PR scholarship would greatly enhance the probability of productive theory development (Ferguson, 2018). This paper helped initiate a shift to a better understanding of how relationships in public relations evolve and impact our practices and message strategies with our key audiences.

Relationships in Public Relations: Personal, Emotional, and Cultural

In our field, relationships are personal, emotional, and cultural in nature, making them multidimensional. The relationship management that is so integral to our work is embedded in a movement in the field from the very beginning. It places, at the center of our practices, the relationship between our client organization and its stakeholders—audiences with a vested interest in that organization (Broom, Casey, & Ritchey, 1997). Because relationships are at the core of everything we do, good relationships reflect good public relations, and bad relationships reflect bad public relations. If our client organization somehow breaks the trust of our audiences or fails to meet their expectations, those audiences will respond negatively. That is, their perceptions and confidence in the organization will deteriorate, and the relationship will falter.

Relationships are not stable connections, nor are they consistently positive or negative. Rather, they are dynamic and take time and resources to nurture and invest in for the long term. The history of their relationship with an organization affects how stakeholders interpret current events and how they interact, whether on- or offline. A stakeholder's investments with the organization can be financial (similar to being a stockholder or employee) or emotional (such as being a fan of a sports team). For us, understanding the nature of the stakeholder's investment, whether it's financial, emotional, or something else, is a key element in determining the basis and overall quality of that relationship.

As PR professionals, one of the most important things we do is to establish strong and lasting relationships with our clients' stakeholders (Kent, Taylor, & White, 2003). Building these relationships is crucial to "gaining and maintaining [a] competitive advantage" for our clients (Hillman & Keim, 2001, p. 128). The way that we achieve this is by showing stakeholders examples of how our clients engage with audiences proactively and conduct their business ethically (Kent et al., 2003).

Features of Managed Relationships

Researchers have explored the different features that make up relationships in public relations. Professors Linda Hon of the University of Florida and James Grunig of the University of Maryland investigated the outcomes of managed relationships and how they can benefit us, our clients, and the key publics with whom we are engaged (Hon & Grunig, 1999). Following are the features of such relationships:

Controlling Mutuality

Mutuality refers to how much power individual audiences have within a given relationship to influence each other.

Trust

Trust is the level of confidence each party (the client and its audiences) has for the other, which is influenced by perceived transparency and authenticity.

Satisfaction

Satisfaction is the favorable result of a win-win exchange with the organization.

Commitment

Commitment refers to how much of an investment (in money, emotion, energy, and time) both the organization and its audiences are willing to put into a relationship.

There are many different types of relationships that PR professionals manage, foster, and create.

Types of Managed Relationships

Exchange Relationships

An exchange relationship is one in which the parties involved have specific expectations of each other. What does (or will) one party do for the other? How well has this worked over time? In an exchange relationship, one party may benefit more than the other. The relationship gets evaluated periodically, and the parties decide whether continuing the relationship is worthwhile.

Communal Relationships

Unlike exchange relationships, communal relationships allow both parties to benefit equally. This is the type of relationship that is most valued by PR professionals. Both communal and exchange relationships, however, are key components for PR professionals to note. There are going to be cases where the relationship expectations are equal in nature (e.g., brand partnerships such as Beyoncé and Adidas) to name it a win-win situation, but there will be other cases where there is an exchange to perhaps gain a competitive advantage over competitors in some areas (e.g., Disney buying Marvel and Lucas Films to get the Star Wars franchise to compete with brands like Universal Studios, or Disney launching Disney+ to compete with streaming services like Netflix). Ultimately, these relationships do not happen overnight. A lot of planning, communication, research, and effort needs to be placed and invested in to make these relationships successful for the long term.

SUMMARY

Relationship and audience segmentation strategies are at the heart of modern-day PR efforts. With emerging trends and new audiences coming to the forefront, PR professionals should be aware of the growing changes, expectations, and approaches that need to be taken into consideration when formulating these new ventures.

While some of the long-standing best practices are consistent in this new age of social and digital media, additional elements should be integrated into current practices. First, authenticity and transparency are more valuable than ever before, and this goes for the relationship that audiences want to have with organizations and brands, as well as the type of content and experiences they are craving. Raw content that is viewed as being genuine will foster a stronger connection for the audiences and create stronger brand affinity (Subramanian, 2019). In other words, there will be a stronger emotional connection and preference between the audience members and the brand. In addition, the times for paid spokespersons sharing information without any context are over. Ambassadors and creators are audience members who will help tell the story through their perspective, bringing more diverse and creative approaches to the table (Subramanian, 2019).

These new relationships and audiences raise new challenges and obstacles. As mentioned in the influencer audience segmentation section, there is a lot of room to present a false view of influence, resulting in a lack of trust and credibility. Verification and other key criteria will need to be included and addressed before partnering with an influencer or creator for a PR campaign (Subramanian, 2019). Research and metrics will continue to be a key part of the equation to evaluate the current return on investment of relationships and partnerships.

APR EXAM

- Audience segmentation
- Key publics
- Relationship management

GAME CHANGER

Rani Mani, Head of Global Employee Advocacy and Influencer Relations for Adobe

Courtesy Rani Mani

How did you get your start in influencer marketing?

I was the director of social support in the customer experience organization at Adobe when the head of influencer relations role was created within our global marketing organization. My leadership team was aware of my aspirations of becoming Adobe's chief community officer and offered me this job as a step closer to my dream job.

What is your favorite part of working in influencer marketing?

I *love* the relationship aspect of the job—getting to know people and what makes their hearts sing and designing a "give to get" plan so that I can ensure they are benefiting from their affiliation with Adobe.

What is the most challenging part of working in influencer marketing?

The most challenging part is to educate influencers on the benefit of looking at the long game and not settling for transactional activities as they might be accustomed to doing with other brands.

Who do you think are the biggest game changers for the industry?

The members of our #AdobeFam community are the biggest game changers in the industry that I have seen to date. I'm specifically referring to the way we support one another's endeavors and crowdsource answers to important questions, as well as network and give one another a hand up.

What are some things you wish you knew when you were starting out in the industry?

I wish I knew that audience doesn't equal influence. It's so easy to be bamboozled by the big, socially impressive follower numbers and not realize that doesn't translate into subject matter expertise, authority, or influence.

Rani Mani is the head of global employee advocacy and influencer relations at Adobe. She's passionate about cultivating and nurturing communities and coaching others to do the same. Rani is currently working across Adobe teams to drive understanding, excitement, and advocacy among the global workforce to enable and empower all employees to be the company's biggest brand ambassadors. Nicknamed the Velvet Hammer, Rani has a mantra to make the impossible seem possible through her humor, grace, and passion. When she's not asking provocative questions and making declarative statements at work, Rani is making magical memories with her husband and four kids as they continue to visit the many wonders of the world.

KEY TERMS

CASE STUDY

James Charles's Fall From YouTube Grace:
How Not to Treat Your Followers

Fairfax Media/Getty Images

James Charles became a global influencer in beauty and fashion when he started uploading his makeup tutorials on YouTube. Charles went viral when he shared his 2016 yearbook picture and the world saw someone who wanted to bend gender roles and expectations in the beauty and fashion industry. Since then, Charles has become the first male celebrity endorser for CoverGirl, and was able to attend the Met Gala in 2019 as a celebrity (Safronova, 2019). Charles was on his way to becoming a household name not just among YouTube influencers for the Generation Z audience, but for the fashion and beauty industry as a whole.

However, in May 2019, fellow YouTube influencer Tati Westbrook went online and accused Charles of mistreating others and going against their friendship, as well as exploiting straight male YouTubers for the world to see (Sands, 2019). This resulted in each influencer responding in back-and-forth videos, posts, and updates.

Why did this case generate buzz?

- Community is everything. This is a core component for PR professionals. Communities come and go, and people will leave if they feel their expectations are violated.

- If brands have partnered with an influencer and they have experienced a crisis, they have to determine whether or not they wish to pursue this partnership and venture further.

- Subscribers and likes—which are key components for social media influencers—are

becoming the new currency that influencers are looking for. Attention is the ultimate form of value for an influencer, whether the attention is for positive circumstances or negative ones.

- Many people were focused on how many followers and subscribers Charles would lose due to this crisis. At its height, Charles had lost over 3 million subscribers to his YouTube channel (Safronova, 2019).

What are the ethical and legal issues?

- Several issues can be raised here. First, defamation could have happened and been addressed if these accusations were fake. A lot of false news stories emerging from this case went viral on social media, which could have had devastating effects for Charles's reputation in the industry (Sands, 2019).

- A lot of memes were created on sites like TikTok regarding the incident. These memes are a powerful way to talk about current issues, but some ethical and legal aspects to these are hard to police and monitor for reputation purposes.

What are some takeaways from this case?

- The rise of rumor mill accounts and "tea accounts" for influencers needs to be taken into consideration as part of the PR strategy and seeing who all is watching, listening, and viewing these accounts. According to Taylor Lorenz of *The Atlantic*, **tea accounts**, "so called because the word *tea* is slang for juicy information, are like online gossip magazines on steroids. They are networks of Instagram pages, YouTube channels, Twitter handles, and Facebook groups, many of them run by young fans and observers, though some tea-account admins are in their 30s or even 40s" (Lorenz, 2019). These accounts need to be evaluated as do sources that people are going to for information and whom they trust as part of an audience segmentation practice.

- Being prominent and relevant for an audience and brand is not guaranteed. Influence is not a stable characteristic that can be called in or viewed as if it will always be there. Relationships are based on

(Continued)

(Continued)

consistent trust, credibility, and authenticity. While Charles's reputation suffered a bit with these accusations, he was able to restore the number of his subscribers by making statements and being upfront with his responses. Westbrook also took some heat for her role in these accusations, and some have shifted the blame from Charles to her instead.

DISCUSSION QUESTIONS

1. Identify the key elements of audience segmentation. Why is this important for PR professionals to master?

2. How does the situational theory of publics apply to emerging audiences for public relations? Discuss your rationale.

3. What are the differences between a creator and an influencer? Provide your explanation and examples of each.

4. What are the opportunities and challenges for each type of influencer? What about creators?

5. What is the impact of having an exchange relationship for a client? What about a communal relationship?

ACTIVITIES

Building Your Portfolio

Creator and influencer identification. You are asked to produce a creator and influencer report for a brand of your choice, and you can choose from the following brands:

- Adidas
- Applegate
- Charmin
- Dawn
- Disney+
- Popeyes®
- Sephora
- Sharpie®
- Walmart

Identify the audiences you will be focusing on for this initiative based on the audience segmentation categories:

- Behavioral
- Channel
- Demographics
- Psychographics
- Relationship

Evaluate the type of influencers you feel you will need to reach out to and why. Discuss what they have done before and where they stand with their social channels, and articulate potential pieces of content or stories they could collaborate on with the brand.

Building Your Brand

Identifying your own influence. Evaluate your own brand as a potential influencer. Determine what type of influencer you are, and why, based on your online and digital presence. Explore this type of influencer. Examine what type of content you are sharing, and what you may want to create in the future to showcase your personal brand online. Identify three brands you want to work with in the future, and explain why it would be beneficial for them to work with you based on your analysis.

CREATIVE CONTENT

CHAPTER 10

LEARNING OBJECTIVES

- Understand the importance of creative content and content marketing.

- Evaluate content using the marketing funnel and Flywheel models.

- Understand message strategies and how to adapt content pieces for different platforms.

- Evaluate the range of creative content, including textual, visual, audio, and multimedia.

Introduction

What is **creative content**, and how is it different from the more traditional types of writing we do as PR professionals? Creative content is a type of content that we compose through innovative approaches. As discussed in Chapter 7, we craft unique stories and strategic messages into consumable content that is entertaining and high-interest and that sparks the interest of key publics. For example, social media updates, such as what Disney+ has done with Baby Yoda, or creatively executed videos, such as the ones Dwayne Johnson and Kevin Hart made to promote their friendship, are a form of creative content. A related concept is content marketing, which refers to a way of positioning and presenting content so that it appeals to audiences.

Following are some myths about creative content and content marketing in the field of public relations:

- In public relations, the only types of content that matter are press releases, fact sheets, and social media updates.

- Making creative content is strictly the job of advertising professionals.

- In public relations, we do not "market" content.

None of these statements are true. Developing creative content and determining how and where it will appear are absolutely among the most important things that we do for clients. Presenting information in a consumable fashion is central to supporting our clients' brands. To do so, we rely on content marketing—the strategic application of content with the goal of motivating audiences to take an immediate action in response. This strategy involves creating, sharing, and evaluating content so that it can make the greatest impact.

How Do Marketing Tools Connect Our Content With Our Audiences?

Measuring impact and success, as we will see in Chapter 12, involves looking at how well a goal, message, or specific piece of content worked in the context of a PR effort, such as a strategic campaign. To determine whether we have achieved our goals, for example, we use measurement metrics, which include *engagement* (how do audiences interact with, and respond to, the content we share?), *shares* (how many people share our content with their communities?), and *mentions* (how many times have our clients or brands been cited for their work?; Gynn, 2018).

Content creation, introduced in Chapter 7 along with marketing and the strategic execution of campaigns and stories, is essential to public relations. We all need writing skills to create meaningful, high-interest content, to market that content, and to run successful campaigns. We need writing skills so that we can create, edit, and adapt copy (the written content created for any visual or multimedia piece) that is on-message and fits our audiences and media channels. The content that we share with audiences informs their first impressions, so if our writing is lacking in depth, boring, or filled with errors, spelling mistakes, or jargon, we will negatively impact how our clients and audiences will perceive the branding and messages we are trying to promote.

The Funnel and Flywheel Models

One of the marketing concepts that we embrace in public relations is how marketing professionals create and share content that resonates with audiences. HubSpot, the customer

▼ FIGURE 10.1

Traditional Marketing Funnel Model

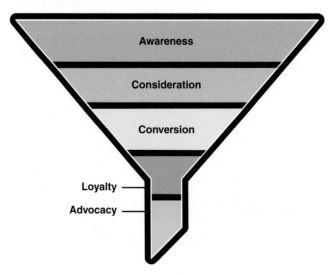

relationship management software company, created the marketing **Flywheel**, a model that challenges the traditional marketing funnel model that's been in use for decades ("Flywheel," n.d.). Marketing models have traditionally helped professionals determine the content that needs to be created to achieve communication and business objectives; that is, specific messages, visuals, and multimedia content are created to move individuals through certain steps to ultimately come to the desired action by the client (e.g., advocating for the brand to key audiences, continuing to invest in and purchase products, or being a key influencer for the client among new potential audiences). The traditional marketing funnel is a systematic top-down model that focuses on moving audience members down the path from awareness (being introduced to the brand or message); to eventual buy-in to the product, message, or campaign; to becoming an advocate for and loyal member of the community around that brand or message (see Figure 10.1).

The HubSpot Flywheel has three main areas: attract, engage, and delight (see Figure 10.2). At the top of the wheel is content that's designed to *attract* audiences. This content also breaks down any barriers that may keep audiences from gaining access to what we want them to see. For example, Adobe created an attractive resource for educators and students. The company's easy-access Education Exchange page provides tools and content for courses and internships. Examples of content designed to attract audiences are fact sheets, press releases, websites, and blog posts, to name a few.

The lower right side of the Flywheel refers to content designed to *engage* audiences. Engaging through content is not just about going for the "hard sell." Instead, we focus on the relationships and dialogue with customers that take place on various channels. Customer service communications are a type of engagement. For example, airlines

▼ FIGURE 10.2

HubSpot's Marketing Flywheel Model

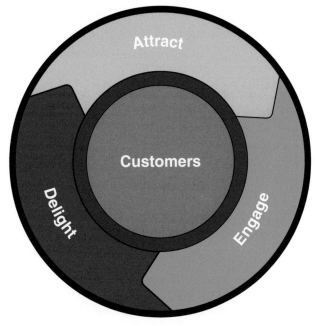

HubSpot, https://www.hubspot.com/flywheel

such as Southwest are praised for their timely and personalized conversations with their passengers. Examples of content designed to engage are Twitter and social media replies, email exchanges, live video comments, and review comments.

The lower left side of the Flywheel refers to content designed to *delight*. To delight audiences, we create content and experiences that are meaningful to them on a personal level. Creating pleasant surprises for our customers, making extra efforts on their behalf, and showing them our appreciation takes our overall messaging to the next level. Ideally, when we create content, we should look at this model as a guide for not only what to create for our campaigns, but how and why we should pursue these efforts to foster strong relationships with customers.

Media Platforms

Another consideration for marketing content relates to media platforms. We must provide professional and unique content on each media platform we use—while keeping in mind that there are differences to consider when posting from one channel to another. What works on Instagram may not work on LinkedIn or as a blog post. Each piece of content needs to be evaluated based on our audience or community and our brand, message, and channel. We must also account for the life span of the content we share on each platform. For example, on social media, there are many channels, each of which is constantly evolving. New features, channels, and algorithm and format changes, as well as media trends and updates, shape the content marketing landscape on a daily basis. In essence, we need to be students of the media landscape, vigilant in studying and reviewing, and creative in experimenting and applying new insights into our work.

How Do We Describe and Share Content?

In public relations, we have extensive terminology for content and what we do with it. For example, *content marketing* is different from *content curation*, and *content creation* is something completely different. In the world of public relations, sometimes these terms are used incorrectly; it's important to understand their different definitions and functions. Here is a list of the main content terminology that we use:

- *Content creation.* **Content creation** refers to the development of original materials made up of relevant information, stories, and other pieces that have not been produced previously. Stories in this case focus on the client's narratives, the client's background and values, the personalities of those who work with the client, and other material. Many brands such as Southwest Airlines, United Airlines, FedEx, Starbucks, and Papa John's have used this approach in sharing their stories in various capacities. In addition, many brands such as Guinness have created content to reassure their fans they will be back after the coronavirus canceled their St. Patrick's Day festivities in 2020. All of these brands focus on providing value and messaging that resonates with their intended audience directly through various media and channels.

- *Content curation.* **Content curation** is the search for relevant articles, resources, and materials that others (fans, customers, brands, media personalities, influencers, creators, etc.) have composed. This is done to amplify user-generated

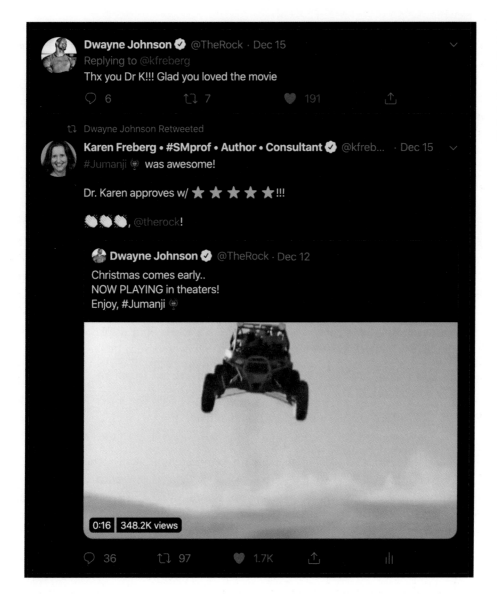

Dwayne Johnson ✔ @TheRock · Dec 15
Replying to @kfreberg
Thx you Dr K!!! Glad you loved the movie
💬 6   🔁 7   ♥ 191   ⬆

🔁 Dwayne Johnson Retweeted

Karen Freberg · #SMprof · Author · Consultant ✔ @kfreb... · Dec 15
#Jumanji 🌴 was awesome!

Dr. Karen approves w/ ⭐ ⭐ ⭐ ⭐ ⭐!!!

👏👏👏, @therock!

Dwayne Johnson ✔ @TheRock · Dec 12
Christmas comes early..
NOW PLAYING in theaters!
Enjoy, #Jumanji 🌴

0:16   348.2K views

💬 36   🔁 97   ♥ 1.7K   ⬆   �hii

Dwayne Johnson is known for his presence and content curation on his accounts, and occasionally responds and shares content from other people (such as the author of this book!).
Twitter/@TheRock/@kfreberg

content not attached to the brand (i.e., content that the client in question has not created, but someone else has) to either help build a community, show awareness of the brand, or foster new communities. Celebrities, such as Dwayne Johnson, have done this for their fans on social media to help build their network and influence in the industry.

- *Content marketing.* **Content marketing** is the process of promoting our content to audiences. This gives brands and audiences new ways to make connections, start dialogues, and reinforce perceptions. Why create content if our audiences don't know about it? Content marketing is key.

- *Content amplification.* Distributing content to audience feeds and accounts is just as important as being creative when we are composing our messages. In essence, if we see a piece of content that's been shared within our networks, whether online or by email, and we then share that content, we are boosting the exposure and reach of that content, or engaging in **content amplification**.

- *Content ideation.* At the heart of all strong content is a great idea. That great idea, or great ideation, allows us to see the big picture of our writing situation and to strategize how to bring our concept to life. We can generate fresh ideas by researching what's already been done in the field, identifying what is missing, and exploring other fields for ideas to try. More strategies for **content ideation** include hosting hackathons and brainstorming sessions internally to determine which new ideas to implement.

- *Content strategizing.* When we devise a **content strategy**, we look at how and why we create and manage our materials, as well as how to update them for future use. To do so, we consider any internal guidelines that our organization has that will help us stay consistent and on message.

- *Content execution.* **Content execution** focuses on how and where we'll deliver our materials to our audiences. This involves identifying the media channels, platforms, and other outlets that we will use to package and display our content. Other elements that must align when executing content include the following:

  1. *Timing.* When are we launching our content relative to other activities in our campaign?

  2. *Tone.* What characteristics, such as confidence, humor, or emotion, are tied to our message?

  3. *Treatment.* Is our content aligned with our branding? Is this done visually and professionally?

We need to consider these elements before we can execute and distribute our content effectively.

What Is a Message Strategy?

Without content, there is no storytelling, engagement, community building, or relationship management. For our stories and interactions to succeed, we must align our planning and composing processes with evidence-based practices (as covered in Chapter 5). Further, we must focus each piece of content around a strong central message—one that we then tailor for our specific audiences and platforms.

Primary and Secondary Messages

A **message strategy** highlights the key points that we want to communicate. As outlined in the Chapter 8 discussion of strategic planning, message strategies take various forms, including primary messages, which are the key ideas that we need to articulate, and secondary messages, which are the points of evidence that support our primary messages. One way to approach message strategies is to think of them as brief sound bites that give the details we most want people to notice and remember. We want our audiences to recall not only our messages, but also the brands (our clients) that are behind them. We may have the best content out there, but if our audiences do not remember our message, why it's important, and who presented it, our whole campaign is a bust and we've wasted time and money.

Best Practices for Creating a Message Strategy

Generally speaking, our messages should resonate with audiences on an emotional and intellectual level. Following are some best practices:

1. *Be direct.* Our audiences cannot read our minds. Our messages should be concise and easy to comprehend. They should not contain jargon or terminology that our audience cannot relate to—for example, don't use "tween" slang when communicating to a baby boomer audience.

2. *Develop content that has substance.* Our audiences, which include journalists and influencers, do not have time for messages that lack substance. All fluff and no meat is a waste of everyone's time. Our messages must be interesting, newsworthy, and relevant.

3. *Put effort into your content and message strategies.* Taking the time to craft quality content with the right message pays off well. While we may at times feel rushed or under pressure, it does no good to put content out into the world for its own sake. Conducting a successful campaign with strong content takes time and effort.

4. *Make meaningful connections.* Good content is a start, but there are additional questions to ask ourselves. Why are we creating this content, and how is it aligned with our messages and goals? How is this content going to resonate with our audiences? How are we creating authenticity and transparency for our actions with this content? Are we inclusive and diverse in how and why we are presenting this content to our audiences? It's crucial to think through how we will share our content, something that is part of the implementation stage of our campaigns.

5. *Strategically execute and promote your stories.* As TopRank points out, "Facts tell, stories sell" (Odden, 2015). At our core, we are storytellers, and if we create and share content that persuades and resonates with our audiences on a personal level, we have a win-win situation. The value we bring to our campaigns is more than creating excellent content—it's also about determining what messages, channels, and relationships we can work with on behalf of our clients. Content marketing can frame the substance of our content, but true PR expertise lies in how we execute our content plans and align them across channels to impact those who receive our messages.

6. *Stay audience-focused.* What types of content do our audiences want to see? For example, if we wanted to move people to long for a product or initiative, we would not try to persuade them with a white paper that discusses benefits. A better choice might be making a video that is visually interesting and memorable. Today's content needs to be both entertaining and unforgettable.

7. *Create social proof.* Social proof, introduced in Chapter 6, refers to evidence that shows our expertise, experience, and testimonials as a brand, client, or person (Cyca, 2019). Ultimately, it serves as a recommendation for others when they're deciding whether to buy a product, try out a new restaurant, or donate to a cause.

8. *Take advantage of different perspectives.* Creating content should not be the role of one person involved in a PR campaign. Instead, we need to include those with different perspectives, ideas, and experiences in our content brainstorming sessions. Otherwise, we might overlook ideas that may be transformative and innovative. While working with teams within our organization, we evaluate team members' ability to create, execute, and evaluate content. Some team members will be strong writers while others can create beautiful videos. It all comes down to how to best use the talents, experiences, and strengths of each member to create the best content together (Expert Commentator, 2017).

9. *Amplify content.* We should strive for a balance between sharing content created by others (content curation) and creating our own content to promote and share (content creation). Promoting only our own work does not help to foster community or relationships (Valat, 2018).

10. *Be consistent in brand messaging.* Having a strategy around the creation and execution of content will ensure a cohesive and aligned message strategy that is consistent across the different channels. For example, Wendy's had to make adjustments once the decision was made to become snarky in its Twitter responses. Initially, Wendy's was promoting traditional advertisements that were focused on its products except on Twitter. Fast-forward to 2019, and we can see that the fast-food chain went all in on the snarky message strategy to be consistent with its brand message strategy and overall presence in the industry.

What Types of Content Are Best for Different Channels?

To be successful in our campaigns, we need to think through the types of content available to us in relation to the various channels through which we disseminate that content. Not only should we choose our channels strategically, but we must also choose our content strategically so that each piece is shared on the best channel for our purposes.

When we strategize and plan how and where we'll promote our content, we need to think about whether we will use a website, a microsite dedicated to a specific campaign, or both. For example, while Spotify has a constant brand website that anyone can access online, the music streaming company has also created microsites for specific campaigns such as "2019 Wrapped." This campaign used user data to determine which songs, artists, and genres each Spotify user streamed over the course of not only the year but also the decade heading into 2020. The microsite will be accessible to people, however, only for a limited time. In most cases involving a website or microsite, a mixture of various pieces of content helps us tell a story, provide opportunities to create a conversation with customers, and give audiences information on how to take action. The question is not whether we will use traditional types of writing or new media pieces to get our messages out there, but rather where to present that material so that it is most effective.

In this section of the chapter, we will cover the types of content that are created for PR efforts, including traditional pieces and new forms of content. Best practices and recommendations for how to approach each type of content will be discussed as well.

Short, Long, and Slow Forms of Content

Writing, as discussed in Chapter 7, is a giant part of what we do as PR professionals. Writing press releases or fact sheets may be viewed as "traditional" or "old school" when compared with the proliferation of video content and the rise of snackable entertainment clips like TikTok videos. Nonetheless, writing and editing skills are requirements for making strong video content.

Many people in public relations have a stake in writing content for the field. Interns often work on pitches (written content to persuade others to cover their stories and content to gain press or media attention for their client) and use them to reach out to journalists about potential opportunities. Account executives develop briefs (a one-page document providing an overview of the strategic plan to the account and creative teams) to present an overview of what needs to be done for a client account. Senior managers produce the final details that go into a strategic campaign plan. We use additional written content to engage with certain external audiences as well as internal marketing teams when we integrate our market research (research dedicated to a specific industry in which the client operates) and competitive analysis into a strategic campaign, the focus of Chapter 8. We also engage with influencers through proposals (laying out creative and aligned ideas for a strategic campaign to create a win-win situation) and contract initiatives. At the heart of all of this content creation is the written form. Without it, the spark of creativity and innovation of ideas that comes from video, visual, and new forms of media is not grounded in the foundation of strategy and planning.

Content comes in various specific types, such as videos, audio, live video formats, and textual pieces of content, but we also break content out by size and length. **Short-form content** is the content that we usually present on social media. These are short snippets of information that are consumed quickly and effectively. A 280-character-long tweet with an image is just one example of short-form content. Based on our audience and the platform we're using, short-form content does not require the sustained attention of the audience and is useful for conveying key messages in a short amount of time. Some examples of short-form content include the following:

- Twitter updates on breaking news

- Facebook announcements on new webinars to sign up for (e.g., Stukent)

- Livestreaming concerts on Instagram (e.g., John Legend)

- Updates related to the coronavirus from the Centers for Disease Control and Prevention

- Audio statements from teams on significant announcements (Tom Brady leaving the New England Patriots)

Long-form content expands a message in greater detail, which helps showcase the expertise, insights, and education opportunities of our brands. Long-form content can range from blog posts (500–1,000 words) to even longer forms of content like ebooks, webinars (recorded or online video hosted sessions on a given topic to register for with panelists or guests), research reports, and online guides, to name a few. Another important content type is **slow-form content**, which is content that takes a long time to create but has a long shelf life. Slow-form content moves at a slower pace than other types of content. Some examples of slow-form media include podcast episodes, vlogs, and extra-long blog posts (2,000+ words).

Traditional forms (which have been used in public relations for decades) of written content for public relations include the following:

- Press releases

- Fact sheets

- Feature stories

- Advertisements

- Annual reports

- Testimonials

- Guest blog posts

- Reviews

- Ebooks

- Webinars

- Sponsored posts

- Interviews

- Media kits

- Statements

- Website content

- Blog posts

- Email marketing initiatives

- Social media updates

Among these content types are traditional pieces that are now created and shared in new ways. For example, a traditional press release over the past few decades was simply presented as written text, whereas now written text is accompanied by hyperlinks to other sites, video samples to be used for stories, and social media and image content to be shared and distributed along the way. In addition, these items are not produced and then left alone and forgotten. Many have a "real-time" engagement factor as well, such as number of views, shares, and comments tied to the press release and announcement. For example, Star Wars announced the updated news of merchandise availability for The Child (aka Baby Yoda) for fans on a website with a press release that included all of these components. The press release had more than just information to it—additional visuals, hyperlinks, and the ability to share this content with audiences in different online platforms.

Content Types That Spark Conversations With Audiences

When we create content, we should also realize the power of engagement and interaction over our audiences when they receive our messages through various channels and platforms. Creating opportunities for *conversation* is another factor in ensuring that our audiences connect with our messages. People do not want to be advertised to or promoted to all of the time. If they feel pushed, or that a brand is trying too hard to get their attention, they are more likely to tune out and go on to the next thing. Conversation is not just responding to someone's content by saying, "Thanks for sharing!" Rather, we need to bring our conversations with customers to the next level by asking questions, discussing key issues, responding to inquiries in a personalized way, or discussing current topics that may spark a dialogue with more audience members and their communities. A case in point is the messaging of the brand Steak-umm. The brand's PR efforts have featured some very successful content on social media that includes entertaining updates. However, Steak-umm decided to change things up when the brand's social media writers discussed the issue of mental health on Twitter, a topic that sparked discussion and engagement with their community. The content appeared to be more than what typical brands would say; it added a personal touch to a topic that has gained a lot of attention in the industry. This approach has made the brand Steak-umm one to watch as far as how it integrates official brand content with content that appears to be more personal in nature. This is a balance that is hard to achieve in public relations, but when it is done well, it helps build more of a stronger connection with audiences on- and offline.

There are several best practices to remember when writing content aimed at having conversations with audiences. First, we need to research what our audiences want to read and consume. We need to know what truly matters to the people we are trying to reach. We also need to know what they find useful. Today's audiences are bombarded with tons of content and messages, and they do not want to be spammed or marketed to the point where they might unsubscribe from your email newsletter or email list, or unfollow you on social media. Second, we must evaluate the overall tone of our messages. Is it friendly? Or does the tone come across as inauthentic or spammy? Promotional pushes without a hint of personality or substance can rub people the wrong

Steak-umm ✓
@steak_umm

the past year this thread has been referenced in numerous discussions about brands exploiting mental health for advertising. prior to the backlash, we had frequented the content style because it came to mind, was different, and our followers enjoyed it

Steak-umm ✓ @steak_umm · 9/26/18
why are so many young people flocking to brands on social media for love, guidance, and attention? I'll tell you why. they're isolated from real communities, working service jobs they hate while barely making ends meat, and are I...

Show this thread

5:10 PM · 7/9/19 · Twitter Web Client

Steak-umm social media messages
Twitter/@steak_umm

way, so it's important to review each message with our content teams to make sure it is aligned appropriately with the brand and overall campaign. Third, our written content must always be professional. In addition to message and tone, correct spelling and grammar are important contributors to making a strong impression.

How Does Visual, Audio, and Multimedia Content Work?

PR professionals have traditionally been focused on written content for their work, but times have changed. PR professionals have to plan, execute, and evaluate all forms of content for their campaigns, which includes visual, audio, and multimedia. This section will cover each of these types of content for public relations.

Visual Content

Visuals are among the most powerful elements that we can create for our initiatives or campaigns. Sometimes they are more powerful than words given our ability to understand images immediately (Pant, 2015). Visuals contribute to the ways people consume our content and comprehend our messages. Further, visuals are adapted for individual devices, whether a phone, laptop, or television screen. Because audiences consume so much content on their phones, many messages are tailored to that device on which people spend the most time consuming, creating, and sharing content.

Visual Formats

Visual content comes in many formats, including posters, electronic images, and videos. This type of content is one of the fastest-growing areas in public relations, and having graphic design skills will make you a very marketable content creator. However, you still need to be aware of the complete picture, which means you must have the necessary written and strategy skills, too.

A visual is not simply an image or video that we create and share; it's also a piece of content that reveals to audiences how it was created and who created it.

Visual elements created in public relations include these:

- Media kits (a collection of materials to be sent to the press such as press releases, fact sheets, backgrounders, videos, and photos)

- Lookbooks for products and services (visual books showcasing products and services)

- Question-and-answer sessions

- Behind-the-scenes tours

- Case studies

- Tutorials

- Product design, demos, and fact sheets

- Infographics (visual representation of knowledge, information, or stories)

- Images (white papers, media kits, blogs, etc.)

- Data (graphs, charts, etc.)

- Video infographics

- Slide decks (presentations given at conferences, luncheons, and events)

- Vlogs (video blogs)

- Video reviews

- Influencer takeovers (an influencer taking over an account on social media)

- Documentaries

- Instagram Stories

- Snapchat Stories

- Short video clips on Facebook, Twitter, TikTok, and LinkedIn

- Live videos

- Memes (e.g., images to be shared on social media, as GIFs, or for TikTok challenges)

As you can see here, visuals range from very specific pieces of content that are created for certain platforms (e.g., Instagram or Snapchat Stories) to universal pieces that are shared and distributed for various platforms (e.g., vlogs).

Integrating Visuals With Text

Let's take an example of how to integrate a visual with strong copy. Halo Top, an ice cream brand that is growing in popularity, emphasizes the fact that you can have a great ice cream product that is also low in calories. Those who create Halo Top's campaigns choose to target adult audiences with their brand, making sure that their content is visual and relevant to those customers. While the messages align with the Halo Top brand, they are also memorable and entertaining, playing on the issues and topics that resonate with grown-ups. Halo Top integrates innovative product designs for its offline actions, such as product displays, and showcases these designs through images distributed on social and digital media platforms.

Another way to convey messages through visuals is through real performances that are shared by video and other means. The brand Skittles, for example, went a different route with its content for the 2019 Super Bowl battle of commercials. Instead of showing a traditional commercial during the broadcast of the football game, Skittles decided to create a full-on 30-minute Broadway musical. This musical included original songs such as one titled "Advertising Ruins Everything."

Social Media Content

The previous examples highlight visuals that suit long-form and even traditional channels. However, other platforms are empowering creators, brands, and PR professionals to think creatively about engaging our audiences in new ways.

CREATIVE CONTENT

Content, as well as the context in which the content appears, is absolutely a key factor that plays a huge role in public relations. Content marketing has a strong place in public relations. It is one of the most important things that we create for our clients. Public relations is about establishing relationships and building on these connections and, in order to do this, you must create information in a consumable fashion. Here are some steps to consider while creating content in public relations campaigns and efforts for clients.

1 RESEARCH TO DETERMINE INSIGHTS FROM DOING A CONTENT AUDIT

What is the color palette being used? What pieces of content have been created and used before? What has worked and what has not? These questions will help evaluate which content to use and create based on previous work and success.

2 STAY AUDIENCE FOCUSED

What types of content do our audiences want to see? For example, if you want to move audiences to feel an emotion about a product or initiative, you would not want to share with them a white paper discussing the benefits.

3 DEVELOP CONTENT THAT HAS SUBSTANCE

Journalists, influencers, and audiences do not have time for messages that have no substance. All fluff and no meat is not going to go over that well for audiences today. Messages should be newsworthy and relevant for an audience.

4 PUT EFFORT INTO THE MESSAGE STRATEGY AND CONTENT

Quality content and spending enough time to craft the right message for a campaign pays off very well. Public relations professionals may feel they are rushed or have to get something out there for the sake of getting something out there.

5 AMPLIFY CONTENT

We should see a balance between sharing content from others (e.g., content curation) and creating your own content to promote and share (content creation). Making sure the right people see the content is going to make it effective and successful. You can have the best content out there, but if no one sees it, it won't bode well for the client and campaign.

6 EVALUATE

Determine what the overall responses, metrics, and engagement actions have been for the content. Evaluate to determine what worked, what did not, and lessons that can be taken into future content initiatives.

Social media also requires a strong content strategy and plan for creative execution. Some of the pieces of content that can be created on social include the following:

- Updates (Facebook, Twitter, and LinkedIn)
- Long-form updates
- Audio files
- Threads
- Posts
- Videos
- Images
- Collages
- Ads
- Live videos
- Storyboards
- Stories

The Pillar Approach

On social media, brands and professionals use various platforms and features to engage and share stories. Let's take entrepreneur Gary Vaynerchuk as an example of how to create content for social media. Gary uses the "pillar approach" (focusing on certain channels as pillars and creating content from that) of creating pieces of content that are then shared and repurposed for other platforms (Vaynerchuk, 2019b). For example, Gary and his team, designated "Team GaryVee," may create a long video for his vlog, *DailyVee*, but then convert this content to a blog post to share on his website, short edited videos for TikTok, some small video sound bites that can be shared through an Instagram Story on his main account, and an image with a direct quote to be shared on LinkedIn, Facebook, and Twitter. Along with producing creative content that resonates and ties back to his brand, Gary is also effective in executing his content so it is consistent, on brand, and appropriate for his audiences and media channels. What is also important to explore when using the pillar approach is the creative execution and specific purposes for what content goes where. Based on the HubSpot Flywheel model, we can evaluate how Gary has used specific pieces of content tied to each characteristic of the Flywheel, as demonstrated in Table 10.1.

Emerging Apps and Platforms

While some channels are more established in the social media industry, it is still important to keep an eye out for new channels that are emerging. One platform that has caught the attention of brands engaging with the Generation Z audience is the social media platform TikTok. TikTok, which began in Asia, is a dominant platform that helps creators make short videos to share within their community and has about 1.2 billion users per month

▼ TABLE 10.1

Gary Vaynerchuk's Social Media Content

Platform	Types of Content	Creative Execution
Facebook	Updates, blog posts, news, videos, live videos, interviews	Engagement
Twitter	Updates, images, videos, live videos, stories (Fleets)	Interaction and real-time conversations with audiences; surprise and delight
Instagram	Instagram Stories, feeds, live videos, quotes, images, audio quotes, series (IGTV)	Engagement and attracting content
YouTube	Vlogs, documentaries, talks, Q&A sessions	Informational content
LinkedIn	Updates, blog posts, articles, live videos, videos, stories	Informational content

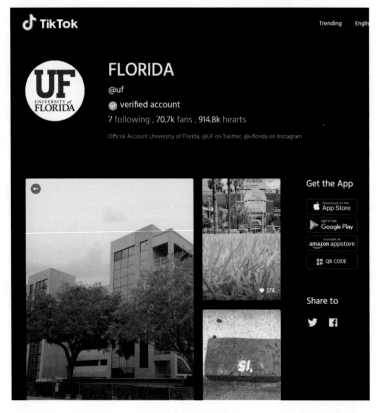

University of Florida on TikTok

TikTok/@uf

(Lorenz, 2019). Users can create content that includes lip-syncing acts and dance moves. They can also create and edit short videos with music and participate in certain challenges by creating videos around a designated theme (Sehl, 2020). Duets, reaction videos, and influencer collaborations (collaborations with one or more influencers) are just a few things that users have created through the app.

Another brand, the University of Florida, has successfully implemented TikTok in a content strategy to showcase the life of a UF student in Gainesville. The account features students on campus doing various tricks and has creative video features that align with the university's brand voice. By experimenting with a new platform and executing it through a strategic lens, the University of Florida TikTok account is the only verified university account on the platform.

Content for Augmented, Virtual, and Mixed Realities

Three interesting areas for which creators are making content are augmented reality (AR), virtual reality (VR), and mixed reality (MR). Augmented reality sometimes gets confused with virtual reality, but it is slightly different. Augmented reality adds virtual elements into the real world whereas virtual reality purposely interjects a user into the experience, tapping into more of the emotional cues and responses that may come out of it. These are among some fresh, strategic formats through which we and other social media professionals can invite users into the stories we create, allowing them to have a meaningful experience. Mixed reality is "blending the physical world with the digital world. Mixed reality is the next evolution in human, computer, and environment interaction" ("What Is Mixed Reality?," 2018). MR is different from AR in that it integrates real, augmented, and virtual realities all together. Microsoft is very active in promoting this technology, including its HoloLens products that integrate MR with AR and VR for creating and interacting with content. One such partnership is that between innovative fashion brands and products and the London College of Fashion to explore the future of fashion (Roberts-Islam, 2019). This area is rich with the potential for creating experiential content, but the investment in the education, training, and resources to create this content is still in its infancy stage. When innovative content is executed well, the outcome is worth the investment. For example, to celebrate the news of LeBron James joining the Lakers, an AR mural was created and made accessible through Snapchat. Snapchat, another dominant social media platform, is investing time and energy in campaigns for marketing and PR efforts in the AR space, in particular through branded lenses and AR features, as shown next.

Audio and Vocal Content

Audio tools give us the power to create podcasts and pieces of content for listening. A lot of podcasts are on iTunes and other app-based platforms, but SoundCloud is the most popular platform for hosting podcasts for brands and professionals. Anchor is another product that allows us to create **audio content**.

Traditional uses of audio in public relations include these:

- Interviews with clients, customers, employees, media professionals, influencers, creators, and others

- Radio ads

- Features

- Jingles

- Podcast episodes

- Audio content shared on social media in the form of podcasts on Spotify, Audible, SoundCloud, and other platforms

Our ability to create and listen to audio content has been expanded by voice-activated devices such as Alexa, Siri, Google Home, and Cortana, to name a few. Voice is a popular medium through which brands engage and talk with consumer audiences, especially through Amazon's Alexa (Koksal, 2018). As PR professionals, we must focus on how we can integrate voice into our brands' technologies, search features, recommendations, and sponsored ads. The integration of voice technology has tremendous potential, as illustrated by Project Revoice. Project Revoice, which has partnered with the ALS Association, uses voice technology to give a voice to those who have lost the ability to speak because of a disease (Project Revoice, n.d.). This initiative was launched after the famous Ice Bucket Challenge of 2013, a viral campaign on social media where people would dump ice water over their heads to raise awareness of amyotrophic lateral sclerosis (ALS) and encourage others to donate to support research to address the disease, and the organization states that it can re-create any voice and build a clone for a person if it can get recordings of the person's voice pre-ALS.

What Are Best Practices for Creating Content?

As we review the types of content that we create and execute for our campaigns and initiatives, we need to review how this all applies in the larger content creation matrix. Earlier in this chapter, we discussed the integration of our practices with HubSpot's marketing Flywheel model. However, we can also apply that model to our content strategies. Table 10.2 discusses each of the elements of the Flywheel, and which pieces of content are aligned with those elements.

For our content to be innovative and strategic, we must align and balance it with all three aspects of the Flywheel model—attract, engage, delight—across the board. While it's important to create and execute content that is purely focused on attracting audiences, we must also have a plan for sustaining our engagement with them and fostering our mutually beneficial relationship. In addition, there must be some reward for audiences for being part of a community. Those rewards may be connected with entertainment, positive interactions, and the delight of experiencing a piece of content. What is unique about the Flywheel model is it is not the straightforward, top-down model that has been used for decades in the communication and marketing professions. It is tailored so that we can first prioritize our goals, and then adapt or evolve our content to fit a different situation or audience relationship.

▼ TABLE 10.2

Applying the Flywheel Model for PR Content

Element of HubSpot Flywheel	Examples of Content
Attract	White papers Fact sheets Press releases Testimonials Infographics Digital media (blogs, websites, emails, etc.) Radio and video ads
Engage	Social media updates Responses to comments, reviews, and posts Comments on live videos Interviews and podcasts
Delight	Feature stories Testimonials Videos (short and long) Vlogs Video documentaries Voice focused content Entertaining videos (Instagram, TikTok, etc.) Takeovers on social media AR/VR/MR experiential content

In looking toward the future, it is important to consider ways in which we can improve and grow our content creation and execution efforts. Here are some best practices to remember when it comes to content strategy, creation, and execution:

1. *Review previous case studies and stories for inspiration.* Sometimes, the most brilliant content idea has already happened, but in a different industry, channel, or situation. We can always learn from others, and by taking an idea from somewhere else and seeing how it can be used in a different setting—that's the root of what creativity is all about.

2. *Create and share a universal style guide for our content.* This is key to making sure that content is consistent with our brand, aligned with our messages, and universal across all channels, platforms, and types of content. In a brand style guide, we outline our overall goals and mission statement, the overall tone and voice we want to present to our audiences, which audiences we are targeting, and some key points to remember as we create content. Many brands have their own style guide for branding purposes, story format, and more, so it is essential to implement such a guide before asking a team to create content.

3. *Create content that our audiences want.* Want to know what your audiences are looking for when it comes to content? Ask them! None of us are mind readers, and unless we ask people what they want, we won't be able to build a community or engage in conversation. A way to do this is to conduct a survey or other thorough audit of the type of content that your audiences will be happy to receive, and of what you need to create, curate, or revamp.

4. *Get feedback.* It's important to ask others for feedback on what we write and also on our strategies for getting that message out into the world. Ask other writers as well as other colleagues with expertise in content creation and execution.

5. *Edit, edit, and edit some more.* Once it goes public, our content will be seen under a harsh light. So it's crucial to take the time to edit, revise, review, and edit some more. We must also be aware of the timing and schedule of our content and when it needs to be ready to go. While we may strive for perfection, it can keep us from completing our work. It's important to remember that our content won't help or reach anyone if we never hit the "publish" button.

SUMMARY

Content creation and execution has a strong place in strategic PR efforts. To make the most of connecting with audiences to build strong relationships, the content that is created and distributed has to be relevant and aligned with the expectations of the audience from the brand's perspective.

Public relations is no stranger to content creation. This has been a fundamental part of our work and contribution to the business and communication industry. While we are still being asked to create and execute the traditional forms of content, new forms are emerging that have opened new opportunities

GAME CHANGER

Goldie Chan, LinkedIn Content Creator

Courtesy Goldie Chan

How did you get your start in your current position and industry?

I got started in marketing and social media after I had my first big failure. I had an interesting journey—from published geneticist at Stanford to fashion designer to being utterly confused about what I was doing with my life. After a protracted period of moping, my friends staged an intervention where we agreed that I needed to get a real job instead of playing video games, and the first job I landed was in marketing with a focus on social media. I had over a decade of experience in a head of marketing position and was on a one-month sabbatical when I got into the LinkedIn video beta and started creating videos on LinkedIn.

What is your favorite part of working in content creation?

I love the creative ideation and collaboration aspect of content creation. Being able to partner and work with others—often spotlighting them in interviews or working with them on more complex projects—has been transformative for helping to create bigger and better projects.

What is the most challenging part of working in content creation?

I often speak on the loneliness and exhaustion that comes with creating content. I have the longest-running daily channel on LinkedIn (over 650 consecutive videos), and burnout is real. I think it's incredibly important to support other creators and to build community so people feel less lonely and more connected.

Who do you think are the biggest game changers for the industry?

I believe that livestreaming is making a resurgence in content types. There's a push for more authenticity, and livestreaming helps the audience feel closer to the subject of the stream. This also includes short unedited videos in Instagram Stories and other short burst content.

What are some things you wish you knew when you were starting out in the industry?

I wish that I knew that everyone gets trolls. There's a great quote by Dita Von Teese—"You can be the ripest, juiciest peach in the world, and there's still going to be somebody who hates peaches." Even with the most kind and loving brand, there will be someone who finds fault with your brand. That's why it's best to develop a tough skin early and ignore the naysayers.

Goldie Chan is the top LinkedIn video creator, global keynote speaker, and digital strategist. Her video channel won LinkedIn Top Voice and is the longest-running daily show on the LinkedIn platform with over four million views and counting. She's known as the "Oprah of LinkedIn" by HuffPost. Her current partnerships include global brands. She also runs Warm Robots, a social media strategy agency based in Los Angeles, and writes for Forbes *on "personal branding and storytelling in the digital age."*

In 2018, she represented the United States in the United Kingdom as part of an inaugural Women in Tech delegation through the Mayor of London's office and was a Forbes Fellow. A Stanford University graduate, she is a proud member of the Producers Guild of America New Media Council and has been featured as a fresh voice in Forbes, Fast Company, *and more.*

for public relations to take advantage of. These new content forms can help create more effective stories, experiences, and opportunities to build and foster relationships. However, without taking the time to understand the strategies and goals for how and why we want to create certain pieces of content for our PR efforts, it will be all for nothing. The content possibilities are endless and full of potential for PR professionals. Being open to new ideas, types of content, and channels is what makes working in public relations exciting and never dull. You will always be able to learn something new each and every day.

APR EXAM

- Communication channels
- Content creation
- Message strategy

KEY TERMS

Audio content 215

Content amplification 204

Content creation 202

Content curation 202

Content execution 204

Content ideation 204

Content marketing 203

Content strategy 204

Creative content 199

Flywheel 201

Long-form content 207

Message strategy 204

Short-form content 207

Slow-form content 208

Visual content 210

DISCUSSION QUESTIONS

1. What are the current myths related to content marketing and public relations? Do you agree with these statements, or have you heard these before? Explain your rationale.

2. What are the main components of the HubSpot Flywheel? How are they applied to PR efforts?

3. What is the difference between content creation and content execution?

4. Why is a content strategy important for public relations?

5. In public relations, what visual types of content should be implemented?

ACTIVITIES

Building Your Portfolio

Analysis of written, visual, and audio content. You are building on your portfolio of work for your internship application, and you want to make sure you make the best first impression. Review the types of content outlined in the chapter (written, visual, and audio) and determine the main types of content that are tied to each category. Propose and create a piece of content for each area to add to your portfolio with a rationale for why you feel this demonstrates your brand.

Building Your Brand

Create your own content list based on the HubSpot Flywheel. Think about how you want to present your brand as you enter the industry as a PR professional. Brainstorm at least three pieces of content for each element (attract, engage, and delight) you will want to have to be able to engage with your community based on the model. Provide a rationale for why you have chosen these types of content for your brand.

CASE STUDY

Gary Vaynerchuk and the K-Swiss Shoe Launch: A Creative Content Strategy

Gary Vee and GV004

Retrieved at https://www.youtube.com/watch?v=mi6J54Xvgdk

Gary Vaynerchuk, entrepreneur and owner of VaynerX, has been a dominant force in the technology and social media industry for years. Along with investing in start-ups like Snapchat, Uber, and Venmo, he is also a best-selling author and owner of multiple brands such as Empathy Wines and ONE37pm. However, Gary has ventured to extend his growing presence and develop a new relationship for his brand, and that involved the shoe company K-Swiss. Gary and K-Swiss partnered to create a range of shoe lines for Gary over the past few years, and each shoe had a designated theme and message. The latest shoe Gary and K-Swiss launched was called Positivity and Optimism.

Gary says this message is key to remember in a time when technology and society are showing some of the negative sides to life:

> I've always felt that the small minority of people who are mad, angry, hateful, and dark are much louder than a large percentage of us who are happy, excited, and feel great. And because of the way technology works today, that small minority is much, much louder than they've ever been before. As somebody with an audience, I feel a sense of responsibility to get louder about positivity and optimism and encourage other happy people to do the same. That's what the GaryVee 004 is about. (Vaynerchuk, 2019a)

Why did this case generate buzz?

- Gary Vaynerchuk has been a successful entrepreneur and voice in the industry, and has always pushed the envelope when it comes to trying out new ways of branding and creating content. He was one of the first entrepreneurs to really embrace the merchandise market, and by partnering with K-Swiss, he was able to break out from the noise with a new product around which he could then create more content.

What are the ethical and legal issues?

- Gary has been a polarizing viewpoint in the industry for being engaged in the "hustle" mentality of working 24/7 all the time and then is shown in this campaign as promoting positivity and optimism. There have been some issues and concerns about the mixed messages this has brought forth in the PR space.

How did this case study promote diversity and inclusion?

- In this particular campaign and initiative to promote his latest shoes called Positivity and Optimism, Gary brought together various activists, speakers, and professionals representing all aspects of society. These individuals were coming in with a different background and life challenge they had to overcome from gender issues, disabilities, and social issues.

What are some takeaways from this case?

- Gary has partnered with K-Swiss to create not only a new product, but movement through content that taps into the HubSpot Flywheel model highlighted in this chapter. Gary and K-Swiss have produced attractive, engaging, and delight-focused content that is on brand, but also tailored to fit the platforms, channels, and audiences that are being targeted.

- This is the first time Gary has partnered with other speakers, professionals, and individuals in a campaign like this. In addition, the diversity and inclusion that is presented in this campaign shows the emotional connection and delight this will bring forth among his audiences.

MANAGEMENT AND BUSINESS ACUMEN

Introduction

Over the years, the relationship between business and public relations has been described as "complicated." This stems from a basic misunderstanding of the role of public relations. For example, sometimes marketing professionals, and professionals in other fields of business, do not take our field seriously. Sometimes they assume, quite simplistically, that our role is to place content in the media, host events, and hang out with celebrities. However, this picture is far from complete. Our work has more direct alignment with business goals than ever before, which sparks the need for both fields to work more effectively together.

In truth, we can do better to advocate for ourselves in the wider business field, but first we need to educate ourselves and each other. For many years in higher education, the study of business and business practices has been missing or underrepresented in the PR curriculum. The result is that PR graduates may lack the business skills and savvy needed to enter and function in the professional workplace. The study and practices of business, management, and public relations should be integrated and balanced. Ideally, as we move forward, business professionals will appreciate the growing importance of building relationships on- and offline through effective PR strategies, and we in PR will embrace how our actions, messages, and relationships contribute to the bottom line for finance, sales, and an organization's return on investment.

The changes we are making now as a field to align and integrate more items from other fields into our work (e.g., business metrics and objectives that tie into what we are doing in our communication practices) are allowing us to build a more

Importance of
understanding business
for public relations
iStock.com/undrey

independent business-focused field in which we come together to form common goals and mutually beneficial relationships. This chapter covers these changing roles, discusses business acumen (powerful and in-depth understanding with keen problem-solving and decision-making abilities), addresses the alignment of our work with related business specializations, and looks toward the future.

What Myths Exist Among Business and PR Academics and Professionals?

A number of myths have evolved over the years regarding the relationships between business and public relations, and they need to be addressed. What's true is this: To succeed in the business world, we need to prepare by studying business. To move forward as a profession, we need to understand any assumptions about business—and creatively integrate business practices into what we do.

Myth 1: PR students do not need to study business

This has been a growing area of frustration for PR programs at colleges and universities. While it's understood that students of marketing and sales need to study business, most students who major in public relations are not required to do so. In response, PR students may decide to pursue a minor degree in business or take on a double major in marketing to gain an understanding of business principles. Students need to know not only what business principles are, but also how to connect them to PR practices (Ragas & Culp, 2014).

Myth 2: Business lingo is all we need

This is certainly not true—while it is important to know the key terms commonly used in marketing and business circles, to build and enhance true business literacy we need to understand and apply them to our own strategic work (Duhé, 2013). To succeed, we must be business fluent; that is, we must understand and apply key concepts of business and combine them with our own communication strategies so we can all work together (Duhé, 2013).

Myth 3: Only senior leadership needs to carry out business practices

One assumption has been that only the CEO, CFO, and CCO (covered under "Public Relations and the C-Suite" later in this chapter) need to understand finance and business protocols. This is not true. To be an effective member of a team we need to be able to navigate the business and communication landscape. To offer sound, strategic insights to our teams, it's crucial to have knowledge of business foundations and practices (Ragas & Culp, 2014).

Myth 4: PR metrics and business metrics are the same

Metrics are great, but they are not universal in nature. Business metrics focus on what makes an impact on a brand, while PR metrics focus on both output and outcome metrics (as discussed in Chapter 6 on branding). Business metrics are more tangible because they're based on areas such as sales and financial investments and they prompt specific actions in response to an initiative. On the other hand, PR metrics are less tangible because they measure less concrete things, such as values, attitudes, opinions, and desires. However, if business and public relations were able to collaborate and share metrics, we could determine, for example, whether individual audience members were influenced by a specific message that they responded to by taking action and making an investment.

What Do We Need to Succeed in a Business Setting?

As we've discussed, the myths about business practices and public relations are not true. Having a strong business acumen is not only essential for us—it's now an expectation to master. According to the Commission on Public Relations Education (2018), business acumen is one of the areas that needs to be enhanced in the PR curriculum. Strengthening this focus will allow students to become professionals who understand the complete picture of their work, especially how it impacts business revenue and financial and reputational measures. Duhé (2013) outlines the need in public relations for business literacy and acumen (discussed next) as well as skills and knowledge sets.

Business Literacy and Acumen

In the business world, we need to be informed, fluent, critically minded, and decisive. We need to understand business principles, possess marketable business and PR skills and experiences, and have the acumen to conduct ourselves with confidence.

An Understanding of Business Principles

Going forward without a clear understanding of business principles and how they interconnect with PR communication practices is like going with Harry Potter into the forbidden forest without any resources. You do not want to face the Acromantula Aragog unprepared! You need business savvy and experience to advise, guide, and help your client or organization navigate the changing industry waters smoothly and capably. Otherwise, you will be sprinting out of the woods with Ron at your side, followed by lots of terrifying spiders. Avoid this by being prepared.

Marketable Business and PR Skills

Higher expectations and additional skills are appearing in job placement ads, internship postings, and fellowships. Long gone are the days when these postings were restricted to PR areas of expertise. As we will see in Chapter 13 on careers, more organizations require experience, training, and education in business and public relations. As students who hope for a range of job offers to choose from, we need to evaluate both our communication and our business skills to see where we stand and what we need to become the most marketable candidates out there.

Business Education and Real Experience

As noted in the Commission on Public Relations Education (2018) report, business needs to be integrated into all courses. PR coursework tends to shift away from business altogether, especially in capstone or campaign classes. Further, in many cases, a nonprofit organization is chosen as a client to give students the opportunity to gain real-world experience. Yet, while these organizations do have financial statements and provide some

MANAGEMENT AND BUSINESS ACUMEN

Business acumen focuses on the understanding of certain business principles like accounting, finance, marketing, and sales. As the public relations professional is promoted to higher ranks from manager-level positions that are focused more on the bigger picture and on strategy, they are expected to have more understanding of business practices for their work. There are some ways in which public relations professionals can work on getting a seat at the table and present themselves with knowledge, expertise, and experience in business practices.

1 BE A STUDENT OF BUSINESS AND MANAGEMENT

The beauty about learning more about business and management is the fact there are a ton of resources out there at your disposal. Subscribe to business and trade publications (e.g., *Harvard Business Review, Forbes*, etc.) for the latest news regarding business trends. It is also good to invest in books and resources by professionals who are in these fields.

2 TAKE ADDITIONAL BUSINESS-FOCUSED CLASSES AND WORKSHOPS

These courses could be done in person or online. Workshops on key areas focusing on business are also encouraged. Organizations such as the American Marketing Association and others often have free and paid webinars and courses to take advantage of.

3 ADD IN BUSINESS INSIGHTS IN YOUR PUBLIC RELATIONS WORK

As you are working on your content for a brand or writing materials (e.g., press releases, media kits, blog posts, etc.), evaluate and see what are some insights that may be of value for audiences that pertain to the overall business. Use this opportunity to educate the audience on the business side as well. Make sure these tie back to both communication and business objectives for the client.

4 EMBRACE THE STATISTICS

Statistics are a way for us to understand what is happening, and while they consist of numbers, they also reflect a strong story behind how and why things are happening. Statistics are an invisible language that needs to be mastered in modern public relations practices. Invest in workshops, courses, and online resources on statistics to be able to integrate this level of understanding into your toolkit.

5 EXPAND YOUR NETWORK TO INCLUDE BUSINESS PROFESSIONALS

Network with other professionals at business functions and conferences, join groups online dedicated to marketing and business, and even participate in Twitter chats on the subject.

▼ INFOGRAPHIC 11

Spotlight on Four Business Principles: Accounting, Finance, Marketing, and Sales

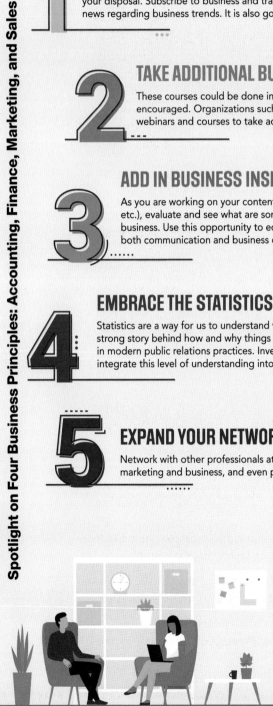

practice, students upon graduation are likely to choose a sector other than nonprofits to work for. Therefore, we need to have experience working with businesses on tasks such as analyzing financial reports, conducting market and database research, and creating reports that tie communication objectives to business objectives.

Business Acumen

To work effectively with business and management colleagues, we need to develop a **business acumen**—that is, an understanding of business principles such as accounting, finance, marketing, and sales (Jones, 2016). As PR professionals are promoted to higher ranks, we are expected to have a more complete understanding of business practices. Further, the expectation for integrating business and communication goals will be higher with each promotion (Gillis, 2009). We are doing a lot of this already. First, we need to have a clear idea of the costs to be incurred and the revenue to be generated in relation to our initiatives and campaigns (accounting and finance). We can have the best ideas for a campaign, but if they cannot be covered by our budget, this is a problem. We must also be able to align our efforts with our organization's overall marketing and business objectives and bottom line (marketing). Lastly, while our goals may not necessarily be focused on driving sales, we must show that our work on creative activations, messaging, and relationship-building strategies moves us toward increasing business and market share for our clients (sales).

Business Skills and Knowledge Sets

Public relations is a complex, evolving field that is a practiced and integrated profession, discipline, and industry all around the world (Grunig, 2001). It is a field rooted in strategic relationship management, with a dash of creativity and innovation thrown in.

Public relations is practiced in different ways and in various settings. One of the beauties of the profession is that it doesn't limit us to working for an organization or agency. In fact, we can be our own bosses and serve as consultants, which allows us the flexibility to be independent and self-sufficient. Yet, if we are our own bosses, we must still manage our time, budgets, investments, marketing, sales, and promotions. We must have a firm understanding of marketing and sales, not only to establish a presence in the industry, but to survive.

New, Emerging Skills

As the expectations and responsibilities of the profession continue to grow, new skills are being added to the tool kit of today's PR professional (Ragas, Uysal, & Culp, 2015). These skills include the ability to work with others to achieve the following:

- *Advocacy marketing*, which requires integrating advocacy efforts (e.g., supporting key social and local/global issues, topics, and publics) within an organization's internal campaigns to promote certain causes and efforts

- *Corporate governance*, which requires working with a legal team to discuss policies, procedures, and protocols for addressing key communication efforts

- *Corporate social responsibility*, which requires tying together the social, environmental, and financial efforts to support specific campaigns and causes aligned with a brand

- *Database marketing*, which requires tying data to PR insights

- *Financial relations*, which requires engaging in PR efforts within the financial industry

- *Issues management*, which requires identifying potential threats, crises, and early warning signs that could turn into crises

- *Social research*, which combines the data collected from traditional methods and digital and social platforms to answer questions and provide guidance on how to address opportunities tied to business and communication objectives with key audiences

Skills Related to Public, Government, and Nonprofit Sectors

Traditionally, public relations has been practiced in three areas: public (business, private sector, organizations, and brands), government, and nonprofit (Avidar, 2017). With changes emerging from society and communication technologies, the areas in which we practice have not only grown but blended together and even produced new areas of focus, such as entrepreneurship and consulting (Avidar, 2017). These changes have brought new demands for fostering even more creative and strategic relationships, urging us to tie our work in with the business's bottom line (Avidar, 2017). For more on entrepreneurship, see page 229.

Skills Related to Managers and Technicians

PR professionals usually take on one of two different roles. One is that of a PR **manager**, who oversees the strategic implementation, counseling, and overview of the campaign for a client (Neill & Lee, 2016). Senior account executive, senior vice president, and director are just some of the roles that fit this category. The skills required for the role of manager are to provide more of a strategic viewpoint on the tactics, messages, and other key elements in a campaign for a client. Personnel management, budgeting, creating pitches and proposals, and directing the strategic research and creative executions are some of the duties managers seem to be designated with.

On the other hand, a PR **technician** will focus more on the technical aspects of the work involved, such as the creation of posts for social media, the pitching of stories to media professionals, and the running of analytics and insights for campaigns. These specific assets are created for reports that will then be presented to the client by the manager. Interns, account executives, and assistant account executives are some of the roles that are more technical in nature for public relations. The skills required for the role of technician are to create the tactical components in a campaign or client account, such as researching influencers, creating materials to add to media kits and pitches, writing press releases and social media updates, and conducting media reports to be shared with the team. Compared to managers, technicians are asked to create the content, tactics, and materials that are designated and agreed upon by those in the manager's role.

Business Acumen Skills and Knowledge Sets

As Gillis (2009) notes, certain knowledge and skill sets exist relative to business acumen for PR professionals. We obtain knowledge sets through education, workshops, and exercises. Certain areas of specialization, such as investor relations and crisis communication, require specialized coursework and management training. On the other hand, skill sets are the hands-on technical skills required to apply the combined efforts of business and PR communication practices. We can acquire these skills through classroom exercises, internships, and real-world experiences. Table 11.1 combines skills that are dominant in

Business Acumen Knowledge and Skill Sets for PR Professionals

Knowledge Set	Skill Set
• Media relations • Marketing communication • Employee relations/internal relations • Executive communication • Community relations • Issue management • Investor/donor relations • Consumer/customer relations • Client relations • Government relations • Crisis communication • Negotiation skills • Change management • Corporate social responsibility • Advocacy relations	• Writing and editing • Relationship building • Presentation • Visual communication • Business acumen • New media acumen • Communication planning • Measurement (research and evaluation) • Communication management • Project management • Special events planning/management • Human resource management • Cultural literacy diversity • Vendor and agency contract relations • Leadership • Professional development • Foreign language • Business development • Fundraising and grant writing • Ethical concerns • Recruitment and training • Request for proposal process management • Management of volunteers

Source: Gillis, 2009.

PR practices (writing, relationship building and management, etc.) with business practices that are not as common in PR circles (e.g., vendor and agency contracts, project management, and business development). This list serves as a blueprint for pursuing the necessary areas of education and mastering the skills to succeed in combining PR and business efforts.

Whom Do We Work With in the Business Setting?

Much of the time, the assumption is that PR professionals work separately and in our own silo. This could not be further from the truth: Public relations is more integrated with business disciplines than ever before, and the expectations are growing for more equal collaborative efforts on all sides to create a win-win situation for the business or client in question. This section will discuss specifically where PR fits in the business setting within specific disciplines and departments.

Public Relations and Marketing

Some people say there is a love-hate relationship between public relations and marketing. That's not necessarily true. While there are differences between the ways in which professionals in public relations and marketing approach our disciplines, we have a lot in common. An apt comparison is that of the Starks and the Targaryens in *Game of Thrones*: They share similar goals, but their approaches are very different in nature. For example, marketing's overall goal is to promote an organization or client's products in a way that conveys value but also drives revenue (Allison, 2014). Public relations, on the other hand, is more involved with managing communication channels, message strategies, relationships, and the reputation of clients (Allison, 2014). Marketing and public relations also have a different sense of timing. Those in marketing often want things done immediately, whereas in public relations, we need to take time for certain tasks, such as building relationships.

Universal characteristics that bring public relations and marketing together include the following:

- *Both public relations and marketing value the essence of stories and content.* Professionals in both fields understand that to make an impact on audiences, we have to connect with them on an emotional level. The bridge between these two disciplines is consumer behavior, the study of the actions, attitudes, and beliefs audiences have toward a brand or organization.

- *Both public relations and marketing value digital and social channels.* While marketing may view social and digital media as more of a tool to sponsor and push certain content, in public relations these channels help build powerful relationships. However, both disciplines realize that social media can be a tool for amplifying a brand message and that listening and monitoring tools provide the means to measure effects (Frantz, 2018).

- *Both public relations and marketing transmit information to audiences.* While marketing might prefer media channels that drive clear metrics, such as paid media, public relations may target specific media outlets, professionals, and influencers to help generate awareness.

Public Relations and Sales

As Cathy Summers, the vice president of SHIFT Communications, points out, "PR is a sales job. We're in the business of selling clients' stories and ideas to publications" (quoted in Penn, 2013). This makes us a great fit with sales professionals in achieving common goals.

As shown in Table 11.2, professionals both in public relations and in sales look at new opportunities such as new customers, products, and channels for communicating messages, as well as whom to target. However, the two fields often use different terminology (Penn, 2013). In sales, customers are prospects, whereas in public relations, they are audiences. The fields also disagree about the ultimate outcome and goal for each task. Sales is focused on completing a deal or sale, whereas public relations focuses on placement of a story in a media channel (Penn, 2013).

▼ TABLE 11.2

Comparing Sales and Public Relations

Sales	Public Relations
Audience	Audience
Prospects	Prospects
Leads	Leads
Opportunities	Opportunities
Closed Deals	**Placements**

Adapted from Shift Communications

To be effective as salespeople and to integrate selling principles into public relations, we should do the following:

- *We must continue to be the source for consistent messages about the products, ideas, and services we offer.* This is especially important on social media where professionals and brands actively search for leads, approach new customers through social media channels, and advertise based on searches and key words. This approach, called **social selling**, uses all social media channels to promote certain sales and campaigns online. While this may be effective in reaching people, the key thing to remember is the fact people do not go on social media to be sold to. They come online to communicate with friends, family, and colleagues. However, based on these networks and connections, brands are able to use insights to approach potential customers in a more systematic way to strike up a conversation and build a connection.

- *We must make sure audiences have the information they need to make choices.* We want to make it as easy as possible for customers to make a decision about the product, idea, or service we offer. Creating supplemental materials such as a media kit comes in handy in any sales pitch or promotion effort. Customers want to have as much information as they can to make an informed decision, and do not want to go looking for these materials (Huntly, 2017).

- *We must know the difference between hard sell and soft sell approaches.* Selling is not about starting off with the pitch for what we want to promote, but rather is about the relationship that is built with audiences over time. A hard sell approach focuses on driving home the point of the sell first, while leaving out the simple pleasantries of a conversation. A soft sell approach focuses on building a relationship over time, and then bringing up the selling points. A soft sell approach is usually more successful than a hard sell. More than ever, people are more responsive to the soft sell approach since they do not want to be viewed as just a "number" or an account for a business. They want to know their feelings, opinions, and relationships are unique and important to businesses, so taking the time early on to establish this approach before the selling point is very important to the overall success of this venture.

Public Relations and Advertising

Advertising, a very traditional avenue of focus for many students over the years, is a nonpersonal form of communication that persuades audiences to take action by buying a product, service, or idea. A designated sponsor provides the paid content, which can come in many different forms and functions. Advertising has had its own revolution over the years in which television, outdoor billboards, magazine articles, and radio public service announcements are giving way to content that is more digital.

Public Relations and Entrepreneurship: Working for Ourselves

One of the fastest-growing movements within public relations today is for recent graduates to become their own bosses instead of applying to agencies or brands for entry-level work. Becoming an entrepreneur, someone who creates and markets a product or idea, is a very popular course of action among young professionals.

The Entrepreneurial Approach

While this is a new trend for public relations, **entrepreneurship** is not new to society. Professor Howard Stevenson of Harvard Business School, considered to be the "godfather of entrepreneurship," has been cited for coming up with the universal definition of what it means to be an entrepreneur (Eisenmann, 2013). Stevenson defines entrepreneurship as "the pursuit of opportunity beyond resources controlled" (quoted in Eisenmann, 2013). This means that entrepreneurship focuses on strategically and persuasively going after funds and support that are controlled by others (businesses, venture capitalists, investors, etc.), while at the same time others pursue these efforts as well. While most people feel entrepreneurship is a specific stage for a start-up or other business, Stevenson presents it as an approach to managing a business and its resources. This approach is quite different from the "glamorous" approach and outcomes of entrepreneurship that the mainstream media tend to showcase.

Certain skills are needed to be a successful entrepreneur:

- *Ambition.* If we are our own bosses, then we must have a strong sense of responsibility and drive to make things happen for ourselves and our teams (e.g., start-up).

- *Persistence.* There are a lot of lessons and tough times to be had by entrepreneurs, and not all that happens or is created is successful. This is where being able to learn from an experience and pick ourselves up to take a new approach is very important.

- *Empathic listening.* Being in tune with what people are feeling and saying is crucial in determining which messages, facts, and points will be most influential in any business venture.

- *Creativity.* Entrepreneurs have to be creative in all of the things they do. This is true in regard to our business pitches to investors, our presentations to clients, and how we distinguish ourselves from other entrepreneurs in the same market.

- *Strong leadership skills.* Taking ownership of what needs to happen and mentoring members of our team (if we are managing a team for a start-up) are important as well. To drive change and make things happen as an entrepreneur, we have to embrace the role of a leader.

Entrepreneurial skills can provide many opportunities for PR professionals. They allow us to

- create a culture of innovation,

- foster decision making,

- master client-side negotiating and sophisticated communication skills,

- train emerging PR pros through mentorship, and

- promote the industry as a whole. (Lukitsch, 2016)

Stevenson identified three different aspects that make a successful entrepreneur: pursuit, opportunity, and "beyond resources controlled" (Eisenmann, 2013).

Pursuit. **Pursuit** is the specific focus and dedication needed to accomplish a set goal for the launch of a new product or service. Timing is of the essence, and if an entrepreneur misses a window, it will be gone forever. For example, start-ups that provide home delivery food kits such as Blue Apron and HelloFresh are plentiful because many people are jumping on the subscription-based model. Will this be sustainable, or is it worthwhile to focus on some other need or related product or service?

Opportunity. **Opportunity** is the idea that a product or service being offered is unique in a variety of ways; perhaps it represents an innovative product, a newer or cheaper version of a product, the targeting of a new audience with a product, or the use of a new business model. The features of an opportunity are directly aligned with what we already manage. For example, LinkedIn launched the LinkedIn Live feature in 2019, presenting it to a select group of creators, including Goldie Chan, Chris Strub, and Brian Fanzo. All three were able to go live as entrepreneurs, but they had to do so through a third-party tool and platform. Of the three companies that were given access to go live through LinkedIn, one was a start-up called Switcher Studio. Switcher, which has been around for years as a video camera operating platform for social media channels, was able to jump on the opportunity with a new exclusive offering of its product to a growing community in social media.

"Beyond resources controlled." This refers to the constraints that must be evaluated as someone considers a possible new venture. These constraints can be social, financial, emotional, and/or time-based. Some of these **resources** are out of the control of the entrepreneur, but in control by others involved. Entrepreneurs must be able to pitch to potential investors the reasons why an investment is sound and how and in what quantities it will return benefits to them.

For PR professionals to move forward in entrepreneurship, we must have strong problem-solving and leadership skills (Zundel, 2018). To invest in the right opportunities with limited resources, we must be able to identify the various issues involved and take action to address the challenges and turn them into opportunities. In addition, leadership, a valuable attribute in business, is a highly sought after asset for public relations as well (Lukitsch, 2016). If change is going to happen, someone needs to take ownership and lead by example. One professional who has established herself as a successful entrepreneur is Deirdre Breakenridge. Breakenridge, a PR professional and author, hosts a podcast called *Women Worldwide* and has her own business through which she advises clients in the United States and all over the world. Deirdre's work is an example of how a PR professional can build her own business and be her own boss (see pages 238–239).

Public Relations and Human Resources

The professionals behind human resources (HR) departments deal with the hiring, managing, and firing of employees within an organization. These individuals are in charge of communicating changes within an organization that impact employees financially, emotionally, and/or culturally. For example, we in public relations must work with HR to make sure the corporate culture is in good standing as far as communication, correspondence, climate, and team dynamics are concerned. For a strong brand to be successful among external audiences, the culture within the organization must be strong as well. HR also evaluates and responds to internal inquiries, complaints, and promotions. For example, if there are any concerns related to employee disagreements, this is where HR comes into play. In addition, as PR professionals, we sometimes fit into these roles, especially those of us who specialize in **employee relations** (also known as **internal relations**). When we participate in employee relations, we engage in PR practices not with outside clients but with employees, staff, and others who work inside our organization or brand.

Public Relations and the C-Suite

The major leaders of an organization are often known as a **C-suite**. This group of managers represents the company at the highest level and fills the following roles:

Chief Executive Officer (CEO)

The CEO is the face of an organization and leads the C-suite team of professionals. This person has several years (or decades) of experience either with the company or with others to move up in the ranks.

Chief Financial Officer (CFO)

The CFO reports to the C-suite on the organization's accounting, financial, and investment relations. This individual has experience primarily in the financial sector, within accounting, finance, and other related fields.

Legal Counsel

The legal counsel is an attorney or group of attorneys who manage an organization's legal challenges, opportunities, and status. The legal counsel works directly with all members of the C-suite team to make sure everyone operates legally.

Chief Operating Officer (COO)

The COO oversees internal processes such as recruitment, training, and legal and administration services.

Chief Marketing Officer (CMO)

The CMO manages marketing aspects of the organization including sales, marketing, branding, advertising, public relations, and other communication functions. CMOs often coordinate these functions with a CCO (described next). This person has a background primarily in the marketing field with several decades of experience.

Chief Communication Officer (CCO)

The CCO oversees communication channels, usually in conjunction with the CMO. More brands and organizations are bringing in a CCO as part of their C-suite, but it has been challenging for communication and PR professionals to get a seat at the C-suite table. This is the area in which PR professionals usually work if they do have a position in the C-suite.

Chief Information Officer (CIO)

The CIO is responsible for the technical areas of an organization (information technology, programming, coding, project management, online technical components, tool investments, etc.). Alternatively, this position can be referred to as the chief technology officer (CTO).

How Does Our Approach Benefit Business?

After reading the previous sections, you may be asking, "Can't we all be friends?"

The answer is, "Of course." What is interesting about the different work relationships discussed in this chapter is that one discipline unites everyone together. Which discipline does that? Public relations. In the PR field, we embrace and integrate all of the different principles and practices into our own understanding to make sure our messages, strategies, and ideas are on the same page as everyone else's. Public relations is the glue that connects and aligns business practices together with communication applications.

This is why, more than ever, public relations needs to be in the C-suite when it comes to high-level and managerial business decisions. We must embrace today's C-suite, which is integrated and represents the whole of business and communication. In public relations, we've earned a place in the C-suite, and the following sound evidence supports that argument.

Public Relations and a Data-Focused Approach

First, more than ever, data is the name of the game for organizations and brands, and public relations is getting more involved in this space (Brasche, 2017). We have many quality tools at our disposal for collecting, analyzing, reporting, and gathering insights. The tools for evaluating media data are endless and quite effective in providing insight. In addition, media data can help us determine overall reputation measures that impact sales, how consumers think and feel, and which individuals drive conversations online. Not only are these tools able to report insights and behavioral metrics; some can provide numerical value data for these exchanges. For example, TapInfluence, a social media and influencer tool, provides the financial value of influencers on their respective platforms. These insights are valuable for marketing and advertising purposes, but also for showing a company the value of partnering with an influencer for free instead. Data should not be housed in one discipline or department, but should become a hub where everyone comes together to analyze the overall impact of the media conversations. Some brands have already implemented this approach, such as General Motors with its Center of Excellence department. More companies and agencies follow this method.

Public Relations and Crisis Expertise

Crisis management is a specialized area in public relations. We can use media data to identify early warning signs of emerging issues and potential crises that we need to address (Brasche, 2017). We make sure that messages are appropriate and sent out in a timely fashion, and work in loose contact with the C-suite to do so. We have our fingers on the pulse of what is happening, and can counsel our teams on how to address situations effectively and calmly. Tools including Zignal Labs, Talkwalker, Cision, Meltwater, and Zoomph all have media data features integrated in their platforms, a valuable addition to our PR tool kits.

Public Relations and Audience Analysis Expertise

To be effective in our marketing, advertising, and business activities, we must first understand the importance of what our audience is thinking about (Jansen, 2017). We contribute to communications by marketing to audiences based on what we know about those audiences. In addition to our clear understanding of key audiences, we share expertise in crafting effective, strategic, and clear messages that are personalized and tailored for each audience.

Public Relations and Strategic Planning, Research, and Analysis

Not only do we contribute a strong foundation in strategy and planning, but we interconnect these areas together (Brasche, 2017). As discussed in previous chapters, PR professionals are generalists in understanding what other disciplines can offer in terms of insights and perspectives into the work we do. However, we do more than host parties and work with the media: We are specialists who combine the creativity of big ideas for a client with a scientific formulation that resonates at an emotional level for our audiences, and base all of this on thorough research and analysis.

What Common Goals Do We Pursue With Business and Management?

As we have seen, PR professionals have many ways to move forward and work together with our business colleagues. In this section, we will discuss the vast number of opportunities for public relations to collaborate with other fields.

Corporate Social Responsibility Campaigns

The practice of **corporate social responsibility** (CSR) ensures "that companies conduct their business in a way that is ethical. This means taking account of their social, economic, and environmental impact, and consideration of human rights" (University of Edinburgh, 2017, quoted in Wilden, 2017). While there are many different reasons why brands integrate CSR measures into their business plans, the overall purpose is to show audiences, both internally and externally, that the company and brand are investing in their community and world for good.

Table 11.3 outlines some types and goals of CSR actions along with examples of recent campaign efforts. Some campaigns have been well received by audiences, such as Starbucks's initiative regarding plastic straws and cups.

Starbucks

In July 2018, Starbucks decided to phase out plastic straws and develop a new lid that is more environmentally friendly (Warnick, 2019). Andy Corlett, a packaging engineer for the coffee company, stated, "We're bringing new technologies to our company that we've never thought of before. It's very exciting times as we look forward to our journey of being the most sustainable company we possibly can" (quoted in Warnick, 2019).

Microsoft, charity: water, and *Minecraft*

Microsoft partnered with a specific nonprofit, called charity: water, to address the global crisis regarding the availability of clean water. Microsoft and charity: water created a

▼ TABLE 11.3

Types of Corporate Social Responsibility

Type of CSR	Company CSR Statement (quoted directly)	Example
Social issues	Through our disaster relief efforts, our brands bring the comfort of home to those who suffered the effects of natural disasters. This year, we responded to more than 25 disasters around the world. (https://us.pg.com/community-impact/)	Tide and disaster relief
Economic	Many companies have value statements, but often these written values are vague and ignored. The real values of a firm are shown by who gets rewarded or let go. Below are our real values, the specific behaviors and skills we care about most. The more these values sound like you, and describe people you want to work with, the more likely you will thrive at Netflix. (https://jobs.netflix.com/culture)	Netflix and paid parental leave
Environment	What is the role and responsibility of a for-profit, public company? We have always believed Starbucks can—and should—have a positive social impact on the communities we serve. One person, one cup and one neighborhood at a time. (www.starbucks.com/responsibility)	Starbucks and plastic straws
Human rights	The majority live in isolated rural areas and spend hours every day walking to collect water for their family. Not only does walking for water keep children out of school or take up time that parents could be using to earn money, but the water often carries diseases that can make everyone sick. But access to clean water means education, income and health—especially for women and kids. (https://my.charitywater.org/global-water-crisis)	Microsoft, charity: water, and *Minecraft*

new map for the popular game *Minecraft*. For every download, Microsoft would donate to charity: water, resulting in a fund of $100,000 for the cause (Stone, 2019). What worked was the fact that these brands were aligned with their cause and able to collaborate together in a creative way to raise funds among a key audience group.

Ambassador and Advocacy Programs

Ambassador and advocacy programs are created most often by PR and marketing teams to help external audiences (ambassador programs) and internal audiences (advocacy programs) come together to share stories, information, and education.

Ambassador Programs

Ambassador programs are focused on audiences of loyal supporters outside of the company who have a strong affinity for the company. Organizations including lululemon and Sephora have been active in recruiting individuals to be ambassadors for their brands. For example, Sephora launched a rebranding program called #SephoraSquad, which allows users to obtain free products, discuss new product ideas with the brand, and participate in content collaboration opportunities. Ambassador programs are not financially incentivized; they are experience incentivized, meaning the experience participants are able to have is payment for their contribution. Many ambassadors aim to have these experiences so they can share them with their communities and networks. Most ambassadors want to be able to say they work with brands and companies they respect, and are willing to tell their stories with others.

Advocacy Programs

Partnering with those who are strong supporters for a brand in a professional capacity is the focus of **advocacy programs**. The people behind brands are realizing, more and more, that audiences are not gravitating to traditional media resources or even to online influencers for their updates, but instead are relying on people who are like them or who have a vested interest in the company. In many cases, for internal audiences, this means other employees. **Employee advocacy programs**, used by brands such as Adobe and General Motors, have been successful in building an advocacy culture through which those within an organization communicate with the rest of the world. Employees (senior to lower-level management) help with recruiting (engaging with potential job seekers), social selling (i.e., chatting about the services offered), managing reputation (the qualities and views of the people behind the logo), and sharing news about the organization with others. At Adobe, employees share their views through an employee advocacy portal that connects with their social channels in a centralized place with the hashtag #AdobeLife. At General Motors, employees share their views and news with the hashtag #IWorkAtGM. Both organizations do this to create transparency about employee advocacy and sources for brand information.

What Are Best Practices for Conducting Business?

In public relations, we need to understand business and management and integrate these practices into our activities and education. There are certain expectations and best practices we can consider in moving forward in this direction (Jones, 2016):

1. *Be a student of business and management.* The beauty of learning more about business and management is the fact that there are a ton of resources out there at our disposal. Subscribe to business and trade publications (*Harvard Business Review*, *Forbes*, etc.) for the latest news regarding business trends. It is also good to invest in books and resources by professionals who are in these fields. Mark Schaefer, a well-established marketing professional, has several marketing books such as *Marketing Rebellion* that should be on everyone's digital and physical bookshelves. Professors Matt Ragas and Ron Culp from DePaul University have a series of business-oriented books for PR professionals.

2. *Take additional business-focused classes and workshops.* The best way to learn about business is to take additional courses and to talk with others in the field. These courses could be taken in person, online, or virtually. Workshops on key areas of business are also encouraged. Organizations such as the American Marketing Association often offer free and paid webinars and courses.

3. *Add business insights into your PR work.* As you work on your content for a brand or writing materials (press releases, media kits, blog posts, etc.), evaluate insights that may be of value for audiences that pertain to the overall business. Use this opportunity to educate your audiences on the business side as well. The best way to learn about a subject and see if you know what you are talking about is to teach someone else.

4. *Embrace statistics.* Yes, you must understand the numbers relevant to business. This is not an option to consider, but a necessity. Statistics provide a way for us to understand what is happening, and while they do consist of numbers, they also reflect a strong story behind the how and why of things. Statistics is an invisible language that needs to be mastered in modern PR practices. Invest in workshops, courses, and online resources on statistics to be able to integrate this level of understanding into your tool kit.

5. *Expand your network to include business professionals.* One thing we seem to be missing in our field is time spent talking with each other. Network with other professionals at business functions and conferences, join online groups dedicated to marketing and business, and participate in Twitter chats on the subject. The best way to get insights into a field is to foster relationships with those who are part of it. We understand the power of relationships when it comes to clients, but we have to take our own best advice and apply it to ourselves.

SUMMARY

Building business acumen and working with other disciplines should not be intimidating for PR professionals. They are some of the expectations that professionals in the field must have to be successful in their ventures. While PR professionals need a growing list of business practices under their belts, they also need to make sure this is not a one-way street. PR professionals are the best advocates for the profession, and the way for everyone to get on board and be on the same page is to educate others on what we do, what we can offer, and what we can do together.

APR EXAM

- Business acumen
- Management

KEY TERMS

Advocacy program 236

Ambassador program 235

Business acumen 225

Corporate social responsibility 234

C-suite 232

Employee advocacy program 236

Employee relations (also known as internal relations) 232

Entrepreneurship 230

Manager 226

Opportunity 231

Pursuit 231

Resources 231

Social selling 229

Technician 226

DISCUSSION QUESTIONS

1. What is the current state of business acumen in public relations? Identify three trends PR professionals need to be aware of.

2. What is the role for public relations in marketing? Sales? Entrepreneurship? Discuss the current relationships for each.

3. Define the difference between knowledge and skill sets for public relations. Determine which areas are similar and different.

4. What is the difference between advocacy and ambassador programs?

GAME CHANGER

Deirdre Breakenridge, Author, Educator, and PR Practitioner

Courtesy Diedre Breakenridge

How did you get your start in public relations?

When I won an essay contest for a New York radio station, my guidance counselor suggested a career that involved writing. He said, "You can go into journalism or public relations." I had never heard of public relations before, but knew it was right for me as soon as I learned I'd be writing, working with the media, and building relationships with different constituent groups. Then, what really "sealed the deal" was my first internship. My fourth-grade teacher's husband, who is still a well-known PR expert, introduced me to an agency with a small New York City office. Within the first couple of days, I remember creating media lists and calling reporters about events. Within a month, I was on the phone pitching the *Chicago Sun-Times* and WOR Radio. I landed a few good stories and media appearances for our client. My senior vice president decided to send me out on a New York City media tour with that client. Just the two of us! To this day, I've joked that my supervisors were seriously understaffed to have the intern accompany the client on the media tour, or they knew the client would be in good hands. My love of public relations only grew from there. Because I raised my hand for new experiences, even when I was far outside of my comfort zone, these new opportunities led me down an incredible PR path. I guess you could say I was hooked from the get-go.

What is your favorite part of working in public relations?

Every day in public relations is a day of stepping out of your communications comfort zone. There is learning around every corner and through many new channels. You have to step into your "uncomfortable zone" often. In public relations, the media landscape continues to evolve, technology is advancing, and consumer behavior is always shifting. You are sharpening your knowledge and skills and also learning new competencies at the same time. When I started out in public relations, the "hot" technology was the fax machine. Can you imagine? Faxing a news release was considered tech savvy, and news releases were also the main mode of communication through newswire services.

Today, there are many different ways to share a story with the media. With social media, you move beyond journalists to bloggers, to new influencers, and even directly to your customers. PR professionals have to be flexible and adaptable to all of these media changes. My book, *Social Media and Public Relations: Eight New Practices for the PR Professional*, discusses the PR Tech Tester. Being a PR Tech Tester means you must be 10 steps ahead of your audiences' needs. PR Tech Testers are ready to learn new technologies every day. They also help others understand how technology adds value to their communication, creating better experiences for the people they serve.

What is the most challenging part of working in public relations?

Measuring public relations has always been challenging for PR professionals. I remember when my marketing communications firm was the agency of record for JVC Professional Broadcast Company. We relied on launching broadcast camcorders and equipment to obtain trade magazine features, product reviews, and user case studies. The more coverage we could get to fill a news clipping book, the happier the JVC executives were with our performance. We would present the CEO with a large binder of JVC product news clippings after each big annual conference, and that was the "value" of our work. Today, measuring PR value goes so far beyond clip books and other older methods of measurement, such as advertising value equivalents (AVEs).

Now, public relations is integrated with marketing and other areas of the company to gauge what happens after the media coverage is published. It's the brand awareness and the company links that drive traffic to a company's site. You're able to see what consumers do and how they behave from there. Technology helps you to track far beyond impressions right to a conversion or an action, whether it's a registration for an event, a review of a product, a download of an ebook, sign-ups for a promotion, or tracking a lead to a sale. However, challenges will always exist. With an abundance of data, companies need resources to capture, filter, analyze, and report on their findings to demonstrate how public relations is tied to higher-level goals for the company and business value.

Who do you think are the biggest game changers for the PR industry?

There are so many outstanding professionals who are game changers for the PR industry. The first shout-out goes to Brian Solis for coining the term *PR 2.0*. I met Brian when I was writing my book *PR 2.0: New Media, New Tools, New Audiences*. With an instant connection and passion for public relations and social media, we wrote *Putting the Public Back in Public Relations*. Brian, along with JESS3, was also the creator of one of my favorite infographics, the Conversation Prism, which helps PR professionals to understand and navigate the social media landscape. After many updated iterations, the infographic is still used in PR classrooms today. The second shout-out goes to Todd Defren, CEO of SHIFT Communications, for creating the social media release. At a time when storytelling was evolving, Todd developed a social media press release template showcasing an interactive blog format. It was a new way to share news with many different audiences, in a much more engaging way, and without distributing your story through a newswire service. The third game changer and shout-out goes to Katie Paine, who is known as the "Queen of Measurement." Katie has been working with PR professionals to advance their measurement strategy and to move measurement beyond website hits, impressions, and AVE to business value and measurable communication outcomes.

What are some things you wish you knew when you were starting out in public relations?

Starting out in public relations, I wish I had asked more questions when I felt unsure, especially when I faced rejection. There were quite a few times that journalists were impatient with me, or even hung up the phone when I was in mid-sentence. In my book *Answers for Modern Communicators*, I shared some of these earlier, challenging experiences. I was embarrassed to let anyone at my agency know how I was feeling. However, what I also realized quickly was that rejection was not limited to pitching and relationship building with the media, and I needed to develop a tough skin, in general. Public relations involves relationship building, changing public opinion, problem solving communication concerns, and dealing with reputation issues and crisis. It's not supposed to be easy, and there were days that I went home feeling really tired and "beat up."

Of course, once I learned to share the ups and the downs of public relations with other professionals, and I was open to receiving help from these giving colleagues, I found more strength and success in public relations. For me, it really helped to have mentors who were there to say, "Don't worry, it happens to the best of us." Having a shoulder to lean on or an ear to listen, or even better people who can share their stories and tips, makes all of the difference. My advice to young professionals is to ask questions early and always share your knowledge with others to "pay" what you've learned forward.

Deirdre Breakenridge is an award-winning PR practitioner, educator, and author. Deirdre hosts several shows on Nasdaq and has a regular podcast supporting women professionals around the world called Women Worldwide. *She can be contacted via Twitter @dbreakenridge, and her website is www .deirdrebreakenridge.com.*

ACTIVITIES

Building Your Portfolio

- *Creating a CSR pitch*. Research a particular issue or cause about which you are passionate, and write up an overview of what PR efforts have been taken on behalf of the cause. Evaluate whom advocates for the cause have worked with, and identify missed opportunities for the nonprofit/cause/issue you are supporting. Outline three potential brand partnerships you would recommend and discuss why. Highlight at least three creative and innovative strategies for how this collaboration would work using both PR reasoning and business principles.

- *Designing an ambassador program*. You have been tasked to create an ambassador program for your favorite company. Provide an overview of the company, discussing what an ambassador program is and why it can be helpful for a brand, and create a pitch to launch one.

CASE STUDY

Orangetheory Fitness: A Lesson in Business and Collaboration

Brandon Klein /Alamy Stock Photo

The fitness and well-being industry will continue to grow as it hits a $30 billion value (Midgley, 2018). More professionals are recognizing the benefit of their mental and physical well-being, which has helped brands like Orangetheory Fitness rise in the rankings.

Orangetheory, a fitness studio that focuses on measuring your heart rate to determine the number of calories burned during and after your workout, has grown rapidly over the past few years since the company was founded in 2015. The brand has over 1,500 studios around the world in 17 different countries, and it was estimated to hit the $1 billion value mark in 2019 (Monllos, 2018).

Why did this case generate buzz?

- Orangetheory Fitness partnered with the Tombras Group in Knoxville, Tennessee, to focus on a hyperlocal and data-driven approach for generating word-of-mouth communication. The Tombras Group practices in advertising, marketing, social media, and public relations.

- By using data on social and digital media, the agency was able to target specific ads for key audiences around the Orangetheory studios, and to help spread word among customers attending the classes. Kevin Keith, Orangetheory's chief brand officer, stated the campaign focused on elevating the brand as a whole, and he and his team were able to accomplish this by using new technologies like artificial intelligence, data, and public relations (Monllos, 2018).

- This case combines the marketing emphasis of sales, data-driven marketing approaches, and public relations all together. To get the word out, Orangetheory needed to have the data to know where to be for its marketing efforts. Yet the company also needed to have public relations come in to promote, engage, and tell new customers and audiences the story of what makes Orangetheory different from other fitness studios.

What are the ethical and legal issues?

- While this campaign was successful for Orangetheory in identifying new customers, improving sales, and increasing brand visibility, there are some issues pertaining to how the campaign was approached from a marketing side.

- Using data in this campaign without the consideration of the privacy issues audiences may have may bring forth some concerns among certain audience members.

What are some takeaways from this case?

- Once members were able to come to the Orangetheory studios, they were able to use the power of word of mouth to recruit new members.

- This case shows the collaboration needed between PR and business professionals. PR professionals need to understand the business angle and determine what metrics are needed. Brand visibility and awareness are key objectives for PR professionals, but ultimately, the goal was to generate new customers and increase sales for the fitness studio brand.

○ Outline the key audience to target, key characteristics, what the overall ambassador program would entail, how to recruit ambassadors, and how you would evaluate this program's success.

Building Your Brand

Investigating business education resources. To build up your understanding of business principles, conduct research to determine what areas you will invest in to further your understanding.

- Highlight at least two examples of resources you will use on a regular basis to further your business acumen education and apply it to your PR practices.

- Resources may include books, websites, publications, online communities, Twitter chats, and courses (webinars, etc.).

MEASUREMENT AND EVALUATION

....

CHAPTER 12

LEARNING **OBJECTIVES**

- Understand the importance of measurement and evaluation in public relations.

- Identify the core principles of measurement in public relations.

- Compare and contrast methods of evaluation used in public relations.

- Understand various metrics used in measurement and evaluation practices.

- Be familiar with best practices for measurement and evaluation in public relations.

Introduction

Do you recall our discussion in Chapter 5 of the need for PR people to embrace data and numbers? Well, we need to have a similar chat now that focuses on the importance of using measurement in public relations. Although the terms *measurement* and *evaluation* are often aligned with simply reporting numbers and facts, there is much more to these processes that can benefit us.

While measurement and evaluation involve math, finances, and other numerical data and may seem less exciting than, say, creating a glittering campaign, applying these tools allows you to see the results of your campaign. You can determine and share which strategies and messages worked, which things you might do differently next time, and to what extent you accomplished what you set out to do. Measuring and evaluating can be creative and strategic, depending on how we approach it. If we use only traditional methods that have been around for decades, we may as well embrace living as we did back in the stone age, using fax machines, physically clipping media snippets, and being on #TeamAVE (advertising value equivalents, discussed on page 249). PR measurement practices in the 21st century have evolved to align with current business trends and expectations, but there still is much work to be done.

You can help make it happen.

In this chapter, we will learn that measurement and evaluation in public relations involve more than simply reporting back to a client or organization. Measurement and evaluation practices also help us understand the results of a campaign or initiative. For example, when Impossible Foods partnered with Burger King and KFC, respectively, the company was able to measure the increase in sales for its plant-based meat products *and* the number of stories written and shared in response as well as how many audience members vowed to try the products and share their experiences. Measurement and evaluation bookend the first part of the PR plan process, identifying what you want to accomplish in a campaign. (For more on planning strategic campaigns, with evaluation as a step in that process, see Chapter 8.) **Measurement and evaluation** make up the systematic assessment of PR initiatives; they determine whether PR professionals and our clients have been held accountable for our efforts in a campaign. Essentially, evaluation is the truth test that shows whether we've delivered, or over- or underdelivered, on what we promised to our client.

Why Are Measurement and Evaluation Important?

First, being able to measure the overall value of PR efforts is one of our biggest challenges today, and one that is likely to grow in importance in the future. It's paramount to be able to tie our efforts to our brand or organization's overall bottom line. Compared to marketing and advertising, which have strong metrics that focus on behavioral measures and conversions based on actions taken, what we measure in public relations is largely intangible, as pointed out in Chapter 11 on management and business acumen.

Showing Value

Evaluating our efforts also allows us to prove our worth to our organizations and show the impact that we contribute on behalf of our clients and campaigns. When investing time, money, and personnel, we need to validate that these costs are worth it over the short and long term for our clients. As discussed in Chapter 5 on research and evidence-based practices, evaluation is part of every campaign model for public relations. We cannot propose objectives and ideas to initiate a campaign without a strategy for how to measure them appropriately. A good rule of thumb is if you cannot measure it, don't do it! Even if it is the best idea ever in the history of the field, it has to be measurable and evaluated to determine its value for our clients. Otherwise, how can we show the impact of our work on business and communication objectives? Public relations as an industry needs to validate the work that we do through real measures that can also show that what we do contributes to the overall success of a client's presence in the industry, financial standing, and reputation in society.

Evaluation has evolved over the years from collecting and counting press clippings and media impressions to applying more sophisticated data analysis and behavioral and systematic approaches. That said, some old-school but accurate metrics, which we will discuss in this chapter, are still being used, such as the reach, frequency, and tone of the message (Watson, 2012).

Making Strategic Plans

The Public Relations Society of America (2019) discusses how we need to use measurement as part of our ongoing practices to help "make the case" for our work and to justify internal and client investment and support. According to PRSA, good measurement practices can do all of the following:

- Validate the results of PR efforts

- Link our results to business outcomes that further our organization's goals

- Promote, credibly, the impact of our results to those who fund our programs

- Allow organizations to set smarter objectives and use more compelling strategies

- Enable mid-program or mid-campaign adjustments and corrections

- Allow us to adapt our measurement practices over time in light of changing objectives, new competitors, and emerging best practices

When constructing the measurement and evaluation section of a PR strategic plan, you will want to ask yourself:

1. How do these metrics align with my set objectives?

2. What research methods do I need to use to evaluate the metrics and my set objectives?

3. How easy will it be to calculate, collect, and analyze the data gathered from these research methods?

4. Are these metrics and insights universally used across different departments (marketing, public relations, strategic communications, etc.) or not?

5. Will these metrics and insights provide insight to help future decision-making processes?

6. Which metrics align with the outcomes we've set forth for our campaign?

Businesses, agencies, and PR professionals sometimes forget about the measurement and evaluation step in the strategic planning process. This step holds the key to figuring out whether we have been successful in our efforts to engage our audiences, accomplish our short- and long-term objectives, and provide value (emotional, financial, and social) for the intended parties. Without measurement and evaluation, the success of our social media campaigns cannot be assessed. That's important because while social media initiatives are often launched by other departments or disciplines, we need evidence to show to others (e.g., senior management, clients, and the industry) what we are able to achieve in this area.

Explaining How and Why We've Succeeded

Tying in what we wanted to accomplish, and determining whether or not we did so, is important. In public relations, to determine our success, we need to connect the objectives we set forth in our campaigns with the measured results of those campaigns. The measurement component of the SMART objectives—specific, measurable, achievable, realistic, and time-specific—introduced in Chapter 8 (page 159), is so important. Without

MEASUREMENT AND EVALUATION

In all PR campaigns, public relations professionals have to report whether or not they have achieved their set objectives for the campaign in their measurement and evaluation section. Below is a sample report from Georgia Power for their 2019 Silver Anvil Award winning submission.

Georgia Power tracked more than 150 media stories that included the company and its restoration efforts. More than 95 percent of media stories were neutral or positive in tone, and the majority of the stories included one or more of the company's key messages on restoration progress, safety, scam awareness or resources for customers.

Georgia Power experienced a 22 percent month over month boost in Positive/Neutral media sentiment from September to October (74 percent positive/neutral to 96 percent positive/neutral). On social media, Georgia Power recorded a 594 percent increase in month over month engagements (likes, comments or shares) from September to October (41.6K to 288.8K), a 107 percent increase in month over month impressions from September to October (1.5M to 3.1M) and 2K new followers across all social channels.

Customer feedback was very positive on social media when discussing new infographics used to visualize damage assessments and ERTs. Internally, Georgia Power has approximately 7,500 K employees. The company recorded over 133K total employee views for internal stories and emails related to Hurricane Michael.

There needs to be an acknowledgment of the tools that have been used for the measurement and evaluation.

Evaluating the output of content (ex. stories) is one way to evaluate the effectiveness of engaging with the media on what is happening in this crisis.

Taking a step further in analyzing the overall tone of the news article is a key factor to consider. Positive media stories are better than negative ones, but what is missing is the overall breakdown in numbers. It is important to be able to review items by humans because the evaluation/measurement tool could mark it differently without reviewing the context of the situation. For example, if someone says that the latest movie with The Rock is #%%@ amazing – the software program may view this as a negative statement, when in fact it is positive.

Sentiment is another metric that is used here for traditional and social media platforms.

This is good to have an internal commitment as a brand, but it may be important to note this for their external audiences (ex. customers, vendors, partners., etc) as well.

Impressions are again not the best metric to use – it shows that key publics had a chance to see the content on social media – but more advanced metrics on what people did in response to seeing the media message is necessary.

Need an analysis of the content effectiveness of the infographics. How many users shared these infographics? The sentiment and tone in sharing these infographics?

There needed to be a timeline for when these views occurred.

knowing what we want to achieve, such as increasing audiences or engagement, we will not have clear and actionable variables to present to senior management. Those in leadership positions want to see hard numbers that clearly illustrate the growth, impact, and results of our work, which may include marketing, reputation, and sales-based numbers. We must be able to connect the dots and support each of our insights with evidence to make recommendations and assessments accordingly.

Measurement is more than just collecting data and analyzing it. It requires creativity as well. There is an art to analyzing and discovering insights gathered from the data to best tell a story of what happened and what we can do for the future. We do not want to simply report what we did and whether it was successful. Instead, we need to explain why our efforts were successful, and what we need to do in the future based on our findings.

What Types of Measurement and Evaluation Do We Use?

When it comes to measurement, we have a range of tools, metrics, and analyses at our disposal. All of these measurements are important as they align to communication and business objectives, but some aspects of our efforts are harder to measure and achieve than others. The following sections discuss each of these points in detail.

Output and Outcome Measurements

There is a common misunderstanding about whether we should focus on the measurement of *outputs* (the production of materials for a campaign) or the measurement of *outcomes* (what actions the audience takes in response to what we created), as discussed in Chapter 5. Output measurements focus on the items created by audiences (customers, fans, media, etc.) in response to messages and media coverage about an ongoing story. Some examples include press releases, social media updates, videos, press kits, and other promotional items that PR professionals or their teams create. This is a way to measure our work during the course of a campaign.

However, is measuring outputs always a wise use of time and money? For example, would it be better for Paramount Pictures to send out tons of press releases about the release of *Top Gun: Maverick*, or would it be more effective for Tom Cruise to share the movie trailer on his own Twitter account? If you said you feel the need for speed and went with Cruise's Twitter account, you are correct. Allowing the star to tweet the news drove audiences to engage and share in response and paid off for Paramount in terms of promoting the film. A press release would not have driven as much engagement, and the movie house would have missed out on achieving certain objectives of the launch campaign.

Sentiment and Exposure Analyses

Outcome measurements focus on actions and statements made by the audiences in response to what is presented. So, going back to the *Top Gun: Maverick* example, among Paramount's goals would be to measure **sentiment analysis** (an evaluation of the overall tone of the messages, as positive, negative, or neutral) of what people had to say about the film so far (e.g., based on social media updates and shares), to measure media commentary and influence scores, and, then, ultimately, to measure how many people saw the film and wrote their own reviews.

Second, we need to differentiate between measures of message sentiment and measures of **exposure** (how many people were able to see a message). Sentiment analysis evaluates the overall tone used by audiences in relation to what is being said by the brand or client in question. Some messages are clearly positive in nature, but others are less so. For example, if someone says, "Damn. *Top Gun: Maverick* is the $%@#!," you might consider it to be a negative response. However, in this context, it's a positive one. This is why it's important to have a human (aka a PR team) evaluate such responses for tone and sentiment. Exposure, on the other hand, is a measure of response that generally does not take into consideration the tone of the response.

An Analysis of the *Top Gun: Maverick* Launch

Let's continue with the example of *Top Gun: Maverick*. Media monitoring companies evaluate, collect, and analyze the results of media coverage for certain events and items during the course of a campaign. Among the metrics that are analyzed are mentions (how many stories the event is mentioned in), influence (how popular the media outlet is), and sentiment (what people have to say about it). Companies such as Meltwater and Cision specialize in these areas. Let's take a look at the two stories shown in Table 12.1 covering the release of the *Top Gun* trailer. Based on the headlines, each story has a different angle and tone to it. The first story, from *Business Insider*, relays how *Top Gun* changed Maverick's jacket to appeal to the Chinese government, something that diminished the overall message that Paramount Pictures wanted to portray. The second article, from *Inc. com*, describes how Paramount Pictures was able to create some exciting buzz for the film and discusses the ways the movie house did this. These two separate stories cover the same news (the film), but approach it through different lenses. In the measurement

▼ TABLE 12.1

Media Clip Snapshots of Stories About *Top Gun: Maverick*

Snapshot		Story URL
BI Business Insider **'Top Gun' appears to bow to China's communist party by changing Maverick's jacket** The sequel to "Top Gun" appears to have bowed to China's powerful Communist party by changing the jacket of its titular character, Maverick, played by Tom ... 23 hours ago		www.businessinsider .com/top-guns-maverick-appears-changed-to-please-chinas-communist-party-2019-7
I. Inc.com **The New Top Gun Maverick and Cats Trailers Show Why Expectations are Everything in Creating Buzz for Your...** You might have noticed that the trailers for two highly-anticipated movies dropped this week. One is a sequel of maybe the best fighter jet movie ... 2 days ago		www.inc.com/jason-aten/the-new-top-gun-maverick-cats-trailers-show-why-expectations-are-everything-in-creating-buzz-for-your-brand.html

Source: Aten (2019); Lockie (2019).

and evaluation phase of a strategic campaign, it is important for us to note these trends so that we can review and make any adjustments before the next campaign is launched.

What Methods Do We Use for Measuring and Evaluating?

As discussed in Chapter 5, we have many options from which to choose for determining whether our PR efforts have been a success.

Surveys

Our choice of evaluation method depends on the question or objective we are putting forward. For example, if a PR professional has an objective focused on changing the public's perception of a CEO from negative to positive following the CEO's poor handling of a crisis, the PR professional may want to propose benchmark surveys (surveys that are conducted over spans of time) to measure the improvement of perception during the course of the reputation management or branding campaign. What is great about surveys is that we can send them out to large audiences and receive quick responses in various formats. Surveys can be administered in many formats, such as by mail, online, over the telephone, and on paper. Certain challenges and benefits are associated with each of these. While surveys offer a chance to reach a huge audience, the response rate for surveys is challenging. For example, if you want to get 100 responses to a survey at a 10 percent response rate, you may have to send out 1,000 surveys. In many cases, professionals behind a campaign may use what is known as a pretest–posttest survey: A (pre)survey is done before the campaign to evaluate the current attitudes and behaviors of key audiences, and a similar (post)survey takes place after the campaign. The post-campaign survey is used to determine the extent to which audiences changed their perceptions of a message, brand, or brand reputation, for example, between the launch and close of a campaign.

Focus Groups

Another popular measurement and evaluation method is the focus group, which allows researchers to recruit and assess the free responses of participants (usually in groups of five to seven). Focus groups can be conducted before and after a campaign to determine whether any changes or new trends have emerged as a result. Focus groups allow us to see if audiences have feedback on our message design, product launch, or product redesign. They also help us understand audience response to the brand's statements and messages following a crisis. Focus groups work well to help us explore issues in depth, but we cannot generalize our findings because of the small size of the group sharing insights.

Attendance and Sales Records

Creators and promoters of pop-up events, conferences, festivals, and other happenings need to determine whether their events are a success. Measuring attendance records from one year to the next can be a way to determine an event's success. Attendance analyses could also cover the different groups who attended the event and any increase or decrease in the presence of certain groups including sponsors, media, and influencers. Sales records, including information about customers and what they purchased, are also part of this method of analysis.

Content Analysis

Media coverage and analysis remain important elements to measure and evaluate for a PR campaign. This type of analysis includes noting the number of stories that were written, how many were shared in the traditional media outlets, and where they were featured specifically in the particular publication (e.g., specific sections of a magazine or newspaper). Also, the overall tone of the story should be analyzed to see if it was a positive, negative, or neutral piece. Tools such as Cision and Meltwater are able to help in this analysis and provide PR professionals with insights on the response to content and coverage of the story.

Communication Audits

An evaluation of the work created for past campaigns helps us see what worked and what did not, allowing us to revise our plans as needed for the future. Exploring all of the pieces of content and evaluating their overall success also provides beneficial insights.

Requests and Follow-Ups

This measure taps into what actions audience members are willing to take in response to the content of a PR campaign. Audience response can be measured through phone calls, direct messages (DMs), email requests, contact requests, and other contact touch points.

What Metrics Do We Use to Evaluate a Campaign?

We need metrics to determine the impact of our data reports and insights on our day-to-day business and communication. We also need metrics to help us see what's working when it comes to our PR efforts. First and foremost, we must align the metric we'll use for analysis with the set objectives we established for the campaign we want to evaluate. Our set objectives might have been to increase brand awareness, to restore relationships online after a crisis, or to generate excitement and buzz for an upcoming product launch or partnership.

Essentially, our objectives are what we want to accomplish, and the metrics for analysis that we select represent what we actually are able to accomplish. Ideally, our objectives follow the key SMART criteria; that is, they should be specific, measurable, achievable, realistic, and time-specific. When choosing our metrics, we should ask ourselves the following questions:

- How does this metric connect back to my objectives?

- Is this metric really applicable to what I want to accomplish?

- Which category (outcomes or outputs) does this metric represent?

- Do I have the right tools and knowledge to collect and analyze data using this metric?

- Is this metric universally used across different departments (marketing, advertising, etc.)?

We will review the tools and methods available for evaluating a campaign, beginning with the metrics commonly used to evaluate PR efforts. This set of metrics can be tricky and occasionally controversial. Some metrics are considered strong candidates for effectively measuring and evaluating PR efforts, and there are other metrics that "shall not be named." No, we are not going to bring Lord Voldemort into our PR efforts, but some metrics are just not appropriate for use in modern PR practices.

Advertising Value Equivalent

One of these less desirable metrics is called the **advertising value equivalent**, or AVE. AVE was first implemented by advertising firms in the 1940s with the overall purpose of evaluating the effectiveness of message exposure (Meg, 2018). AVE is calculated by multiplying the size of an article by the advertising rate of the publication (Boyles, 2018). So, if we had a full-page story on the front cover of a big-city newspaper, we would record millions more in publicity dollars than if we'd placed the same article in a local community newspaper, based on subscribers and audience reach. However, the time has come to retire AVEs for PR efforts in measurement and evaluation. AVEs have been noted over the years to demonstrate "the success and value of [individual] PR efforts," but ads are not the same as stories, and should be measured accordingly (Meg, 2018).

As demonstrated in Table 12.2, there are some pros and cons to using AVEs in public relations. The pros simply focus on what we call **vanity metrics**, or metrics that look good but do not really show anything other than high numbers. In addition, AVEs are used and understood by other disciplines such as advertising and marketing. Yet there are many cons to using AVEs. First, advertising metrics are not the same as the metrics for PR efforts, and should not be used to evaluate what we are or do through our initiatives. Public relations focuses on driving certain efforts forward, such as production and impact, and these are not part of what AVEs capture. In addition, AVEs have been used more typically in traditional media outlets, such as print media (magazines and newspapers), making it a less-than-ideal metric for today's channels, such as measuring and evaluating website traffic, sentiment, tone, mentions, influence, and reach (Boyles, 2018).

Impressions

Impressions are also frequently cited in regard to evaluating our digital and social media efforts. An **impression** is simply "any interaction between a piece of content and an audience member" ("PR 101," 2017). This metric can be used in many different formats and circumstances. For example, if you open up the *New York Times* newspaper or read it online, you can be counted as an impression. Seeing a tweet from Tide about its product during the Super Bowl is an impression. However, the risk associated with these types of

▼ TABLE 12.2

Pros and Cons of Using AVEs in Public Relations

Pros	Cons
Metrics look "good." Metrics are also understood and used by advertising and marketing. AVEs are persuasive, especially if our budget is tight.	Advertising metrics are not the same as PR metrics. Other disciplines don't report PR efforts. AVEs do not measure outputs, outcomes, and impact. AVEs are not relevant for today's media landscape.

Source: Adapted from Wallace, n.d.

metrics is that they do not show whether an audience member actually did something in response to a story, social media update, or video.

Other key metrics include engagement (how many people in your community are interacting with your content, as discussed in Chapter 1), and **sentiment** (how people feel about your content—positive, negative, or neutral). These metrics help determine the overall scope of a community. Advocacy, audience engagement, and influencers are just a few metrics that can be collected and analyzed for identifying your different audience segments. These metrics are somewhat more challenging to categorize and collect, which may mean you need to get specific tools to analyze them.

Monitoring and Listening

Two measurement and evaluation tools are commonly used in public relations, particularly when looking at digital and social media conversations: monitoring and listening. These practices are often confused with each other. **Monitoring** is the systematic process of analyzing and reporting online insights and conversations on a brand's reputation, position, and community, and the opinions of key audience members. This sustainable method focuses on objectives and tying in metrics and key performance indicators (KPIs) to the data being collected and analyzed. This information has to be connected to current business and communication objectives within an organization or brand. Monitoring, in essence, is more reactive because, in this case, you know the key metrics that are consistent for reporting to your client and senior management. **Listening** is about uncovering emerging trends, opportunities, activities, and issues that could impact an organization either positively or negatively. This means brands may listen to key individuals (e.g., media outlets and professionals, influencers, and other audiences) to see what is trending and what trends they can jump on to boost their relevance. For example, Dolly Parton, the famous singer from Tennessee, created the #DollyPartonChallenge, sharing four portraits of herself in a collage to illustrate how she would represent herself on the social media platforms Facebook, LinkedIn, Instagram, and Tinder. Brands, including Aviation Gin and Applegate, and celebrities such as Jack Black jumped on the challenge as a way to engage with audiences and show their relevancy in relation to current trends. In other words, listening is a proactive strategy for identifying potential challenges and possibilities. In terms of measurement and evaluation, monitoring uses standardized metrics for reporting, while listening requires PR professionals to report metrics based on the opportunities they receive. Both monitoring and listening are essential to PR measurement practices.

New Metrics: Analytics

The days of collecting press clippings, gathering and reporting impressions, and relying on AVEs are over for public relations. These practices are in the past; they distract from the now (quoting Edna Mode from the movie *The Incredibles*).

New metrics will move our field forward, not backward. To do our best work, PR professionals must *invest in the right tools*, especially management tools for social media. Management tools allow us to collect and sync up all of our various platform accounts (Facebook, Instagram, YouTube, Twitter, LinkedIn, etc.) into one single space. Tools such as Hootsuite, Sprout Social, Buffer, and Sprinklr can handle these tasks. PR tools come in different sizes, metrics, data collection capabilities, and prices. The more data, filtering, and reporting measures we want to have, the more expensive our tools are going to be.

We should ask some questions before exploring the newest measurement approaches:

1. Do the KPIs being used in these new measurement approaches align with the set objectives of our campaign?

2. How easy will it be to calculate, collect, and analyze data through digital and social analytics programs?

3. Are these methods universally accepted in other related disciplines and by the measurement organizations in public relations?

4. Have we conceptualized the metrics so that we can make them work for our audiences, clients, and team members?

Types of Analytics

Analytics is an integrated approach for collecting data, interpreting data patterns, and applying data insights to actionable strategies. To make informed decisions, we need analytics to tell us what is happening, what major trends and issues are emerging, and how we can use analytics to predict behavior and spark creative ideas for future campaigns and audiences. The Commission on Public Relations Education (2018) highlighted analytics as an area that PR students need to grasp so they can understand current measurement expectations in the field. In many PR situations, and in the context of our roles and duties, we can apply various types of analytics:

- *Market analytics.* These compare a market, industry, and position of a brand in relation to its competitors. Market analytics are aligned with what marketing professionals do to determine where to invest their efforts in promotion, product development, and consumer outreach. General Motors, for example, would want to know how Chevy is doing in relation to competing brands such as Ford, Toyota, Honda, and Tesla. This is also true for other industries, including direct-to-consumer (DTC) brands such as Peloton and the fitness company Orangetheory. It is important to know where you stand compared to your competitors, and what opportunities and challenges are happening for you and your industry.

- *People analytics.* An organization's dynamics and hiring practices, along with how people function in a specific work culture, can be handy facts for figuring out a brand's internal success. People analytics can identify areas that a company needs to improve upon, such as diversity and inclusion efforts. These analytics also give us information that can help us set up an employee advocacy program. People analytics are also combined with artificial intelligence (AI) for talent management purposes, to identify individuals who could become a leader, a CEO, or even a general (in the case of the military).

- *Web analytics.* When you think of web analytics, you may think of Google. Web analytics is the practice of collecting, analyzing, and discussing the findings of interactions that happen on the internet. Website visits, key word search terms, and time spent on various pages based on location are all elements to consider. Web analytics involves looking at the bounce rate—that is, the percentage of people coming to our website or blog and immediately leaving. This is a common metric used to determine the success or failure of a campaign microsite or other website. Web analytics also determines conversion rates based on the actions audience members take in response to content shared online. Did a customer sign up for a webinar? Download a white paper or ebook after seeing an email we sent? Purchase our product based on a message we shared online? Donate to support a particular cause or nonprofit organization on GoFundMe? To gain a strong conversion rate, we must provide a strong call-to-action statement on our website or blog for audiences to see. A call-to-action statement focuses on the actions we want our audience to take in response to our message, such as "Learn more," "Sign up here," or "Register for this event." These calls to action allow us to implement conversion effectively.

- *Social media analytics.* Social media analytics, which are somewhat similar to web analytics, collect data from various social media platforms. There are many tools for collecting social media data, but the useful ones have access to a platform's application program interface (API). Without such access, third-party analytics tools are unable to gather the data coming from the platform. The leaders at Facebook, Twitter, and other platforms are realizing that their data are extremely valuable, so they are beginning to cut ties with third-party tools. Companies including ManageFlitter (Twitter) and CrowdTangle (Facebook) have experienced difficulties as a result of this trend. ManageFlitter had to rebrand itself as ManageSocial after losing access to Twitter's API, and CrowdTangle lost its access to Twitter, too, even though it is a Facebook-owned company. However, other brands (e.g., TikTok and Snapchat) are integrating more work in providing metrics and analytics to users so they can determine what is working and what is not.

Analytics Versus Analysis

We need to distinguish between analytics and the analysis of the data collected. While analytics predicts what is going to happen in the future, **analysis** determines what happened in the past and what we can learn from that experience. Let's apply these concepts to a brand. In 2019, Taco Bell announced a pop-up hotel in Los Angeles that would be available for check-ins for a limited period of time. Taco Bell likely conducted an analysis of previous events, pop-up sessions, communications, and PR efforts to determine what worked in the past, what didn't, and what to note for the future. On the other hand, by using certain types of analytics, Taco Bell could determine what to do in the future based on reviewing data and gathering insights from people and organizations, as well as the behaviors of social media audiences. For example, the company could discover how many audience members shared the news of the pop-up, how many visited, what other content they shared, and the actions that others took in response to that shared content. The pop-up hotel campaign was deemed a success. By using a combination of analytics and analysis, Taco Bell can easily do something similar in the future and enjoy success. In summary, analytics and analysis are both parts of the equation that makes up social

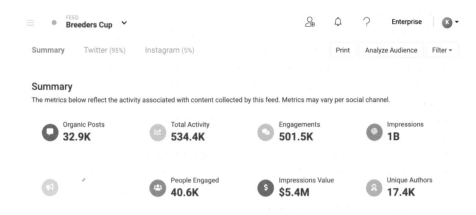

Zoomph dashboard
showing Breeders' Cup
event analytics
Zoomph

research, which ties together the insights gathered from both areas and provides PR professionals with results they can share with their team and use to guide their evaluation of the campaign in question.

Metrics of Analytics Tools

Analytics can do different things and offer various types of specialization. So, it's important to understand the pros and cons of each so we can choose one that matches our specific approach and needs. Several key metrics are associated with the analytics that are important to our PR efforts. For example, many analytics tools report vanity metrics (follower count, impressions, etc.), while others provide advanced analytics that are more comprehensive. These tell us about the behaviors of our audience members and what actions they take in response to our message. The more features and advance metrics that an analytical platform offers, the more expensive it will be. As shown here, Zoomph outlines basic summary points for social media data collected during the Breeders' Cup, a popular horse racing event that travels to different states such as California and Kentucky. While these tools provide impressions and **impressions value** (the value of how much the exposure would cost you if you had to pay for this coverage), they also provide data about unique authors (how many individual people participated in the conversation about an event), engagements (how many people interacted with a comment, share, or specific action), and organic posts (posts that were not promoted or sponsored).

Resources for Applying Metrics

You may be wondering: Are we finished talking about data yet? While there is a lot to grasp, gathering and analyzing data is one of the fastest-rising specializations in our industry. Brands, agencies, and other organizations are looking for ways to bring on more professionals who understand (1) what to measure and evaluate and (2) how to apply these insights to strategic plans.

Many resources are available to further our education in this area, and to help us meet industry needs. Most of these programs are free and allow professionals and students to learn how analytics, measurement, and evaluation are tied together in PR efforts and to put knowledge into practice.

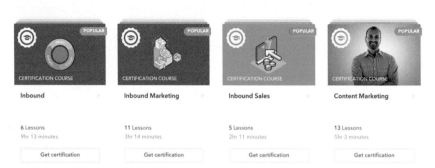

HubSpot

This software company offers various customer relationship management (CRM) tools that are aligned with PR and marketing efforts. HubSpot is also known for issuing free certifications in various topics related to measurement and evaluation, including certificates in social media and content marketing. This third-party brand offers these services to customers, but also has strong relationships with major brands including Facebook, Google, and Twitter.

Google Analytics

Google is a dominant platform that offers a free program for professionals to learn about analytics, from basic principles to more advanced ones. Google's certification covers the basics in digital and web analytics, which is helpful for most of the measurement and evaluation that we do.

Facebook Blueprint

Some platforms have their own education portal that offers their most updated features, KPIs, and measurement practices. Facebook Blueprint offers lessons that are free and accessible. However, there are some differences between this certification and others. First, this certification focuses only on Facebook's products and features, which is

Google Analytics

Retrieved at https://analytics.google
.com/analytics/academy/

different from what other certifications do (HubSpot, etc.). Second, it's one of the only certifications that uses an industry standard testing service for the exam, which is a positive. The testing makes certification a rigorous experience that is held in high regard across the industry. Having a Facebook Blueprint certification is a benefit to those of us working in public relations and social media.

Brandwatch

If you are interested in combining efforts for digital and social analytics, then Brandwatch is a program to integrate into your studies. Brandwatch offers a certification for students, but the course must be part of a class that a professor has signed up for. This program highlights some of the main web and social metrics associated with analytics, and discusses how to apply them strategically into various campaign situations.

Stukent

This organization provides students and professionals with the opportunity to take part in simulations with analytics, rather than having participants apply them in the real world, without training. Stukent offers several measurement programs that test participants in the areas of marketing analytics, social media analytics, and even influencer analytics.

While these programs may seem a little daunting, they are some of the most respected brands in the industry in terms of testing and effectively educating us on new methods of measurement. In addition to being familiar with these educational and professional development resources, it's handy to know some of the measurement standards that are set by PR organizations, which we will discuss in the next section.

What Are Industry Standards for Measurement and Evaluation?

Professional organizations for public relations (e.g., PRSA, AMEC, and Barcelona Principles) in the United States and beyond have set objectives and standards for dealing with measurement and evaluation. As our field evolves, so too do these objectives and standards. Our professional organizations set forth guidelines, key metrics to evaluate, and even statements on metrics that should *not* be used (e.g., AVEs).

Standards: Public Relations Society of America (PRSA)

The Public Relations Society of America has worked with several PR organizations to determine the best ways to create a consistent and sustainable model for measurement and evaluation practices in our industry. PRSA has partnered with the Council of Public Relations Firms, the Global Alliance for Public Relations and Communication Management, and the Coalition for Public Relations Research Standards. PRSA has also worked with the Institute for Public Relations in setting standards and protocols for effectively measuring PR efforts in both academic and industry research.

Framework: International Association for Measurement and Evaluation of Communication (AMEC)

Many professional associations (PRSA, American Marketing Association, etc.) have presented their views on the importance of measurement and how it ties directly to social media practices. AMEC (2020) has its own framework for the key areas that need to be covered in social media:

- **Inputs** include who our target audience is, what the current situation is, and what resources are available to understand them.

- **Activities** make up the strategies and tactics portion of our campaign plans, including what content and messages we will create and disseminate out to our audiences.

- **Outtakes** are the reactions and behaviors (discussed by AMEC) that occur as a result of our messages, content, and actions and involve the likeliness that others recall our content with others.

- **Impact** concerns the high-level objectives that contribute to social media protocols and actions, and to the well-being of the entire organization; these objectives reflect brand reputation, changes in policies, or improved business practices.

The AMEC framework also includes two concepts that we covered in Chapter 5:

- *Outcomes* involve how well the audience receives our messages, and the extent to which audience members change their views or attitudes.

- *Outputs* are the specific measures that we are able to collect and evaluate, including likes, comments, reach, impressions, and engagement.

Standards: The Barcelona Principles (AMEC)

The Barcelona Principles were created by AMEC to help us measure and evaluate our social media and PR efforts.

List of Principles

AMEC (2020) recommends several principles for PR, communications, and social media professionals to follow:

1. *Set goals* and measurement practices for our communications and campaigns. This is fundamental to communications and PR efforts.

2. *Measure outcomes*, not just outputs, of our communications and campaigns.

3. *Measure the impact* of our work on the performance of our brands, clients, and organizations.

4. *Measure social media* consistently with other media channels.

5. *Do not use AVEs*; they do not address the value of our communications and campaigns.

6. *Be transparent*, consistent, and valid in our measurements and evaluations.

There are several important elements to note here regarding these six principles and how they apply to public relations. First, integrating the importance of setting goals and objectives way before a campaign happens is essential. Evaluating whether we've been successful in our measurement venture is crucial to determining the overall impact of our work on the performance of our brand or organization. Second, the emphasis on outcomes (behavioral actions of audiences) rather than outputs (our production of content and information) is a shift in the industry. In the past, we've measured how many press releases, social media updates, and other pieces of content have been produced in response to our campaign. In these cases, our "success" had no ties to what audience members actually did in response to our content. In addition, AVEs are a form of metrics that we should avoid for our PR work. (That said, these principles are significant to related disciplines, such as marketing and advertising.) Lastly, our emphasis on social media measurement and evaluation needs to be consistent with that of our other channels and media.

Challenges of Measuring Success in Certain Areas of Public Relations

In addition to the principles just discussed, we must be aware of professional and ethical challenges when it comes to measuring specific aspects of PR efforts, such as social media. For example, Convince & Convert (Baer, n.d.) noted the following challenges that we encounter when measuring the impact of our social media work:

- *We do not know what to measure.* Social media channels and platforms come and go, and so do the metrics used to determine what we need (or don't need) to evaluate and monitor. For example, in 2019, Instagram hid the ability to view "like" counts on the platform in several countries (Wong, 2019).

- *We do not have the right tools.* In public relations, our budgets can be decided on sometimes by other departments or factors we cannot control. If we do not have the right tools to measure, evaluate, and analyze our work, there will be a limitation on what we can provide to our clients. This is especially true with regard to digital and social media tools, which can cost hundreds of thousands of dollars each year. PR professionals have to persuade and advocate for the right tools in order to effectively measure and evaluate their work.

- *We have limited data.* Depending on our budget for investing in measurement, what we can measure comes down to how much data we have available to evaluate, analyze, and report on. Each platform has its own ability to host analytics and insights, but when our resources are limited, we get what we (can) pay for.

- *We are not looking at our impact on business.* We sometimes focus on metrics that "make us feel good," otherwise known as *vanity metrics*, which make all of us feel really good but don't really tell us anything useful. For example, the number of people who subscribe to your YouTube channel, follow you on Twitter, or have liked your Facebook page is considered to be a vanity metric. Impressions are also a vanity metric—impression numbers sound great, but do they really show the actual impact of our campaign on our clients or business? We cannot truly measure that without being able to see what specific actions audience members take in response to our message, story, or other content.

What Are Best Practices for Measurement and Evaluation?

When integrating measurement and evaluation efforts into our PR campaigns or plans, there are some best practices to keep in mind as we move forward in this venture.

1. *Evaluate the "why" of measurement.* If you cannot measure what you want to do, then do not do it. Always question how your tools actually work with and measure the concept or campaign efforts in question (known as *operationalizing*). For example, if you decide that you want to measure audience engagement, then you can choose which tools to invest in and which ones to pass on. This also means you have to evaluate how you want to measure the success of your efforts, another factor in choosing tools. For example, social media platforms and measurement tools change frequently. You want to make sure you have the best tool to do the job, and this means constantly determining which tools and methods will help you accomplish your measurement strategy duties.

2. *Check your methods on a regular basis.* Conduct a regular audit of the methods you use for your PR efforts. Set up a realistic timeline for when you want to collect, report, analyze, and discuss data. This shouldn't be a once-a-year activity.

3. *Be willing to learn and grow in your understanding of measurement.* Once you evaluate what you've accomplished in terms of your objectives, it's time to

reassess and see what worked, what didn't, and which items and measurement tools you want to keep or delete. Measurement and evaluation protocols should not go backward, but instead should help us move our efforts forward to explore new challenges in creative spaces and in research and practical practices.

4. *Note the limitations in the measurement methods and tools you use.* You will not use just one method to evaluate the entirety of your campaign efforts. Most likely, you will use a lot of different methods. In each case, you will need to acknowledge (a) challenges and benefits of each method along with the rationale for why this method or tool was used, (b) what KPIs were collected and how they were analyzed, and (c) the rationale for why certain tools were *not* used. You might also put together an overview of how the data were collected, cleaned, and used in your campaign. In contexts where digital and social tools are used, it's key to outline the features and limitations of these tools. For example, if your budget for measurement is zero dollars, you will be limited in your choice of tools. That affects the amount and quality of the data and insights that you can gather and present to others. This is why it's essential to persuade senior management and your clients that a part of your budget should be dedicated to the research and measurement of your campaign.

5. *Invest in measurement training and education.* The expectations of what we can measure constantly change as digital platforms change. While many certifications are free, it is key to look at workshops, webinars, and other programs that can get you the tools, experiences, and applied insights you need to be effective and competitive in this area. Your education in the area of measurement should be on par with the training you've gotten for content creation and the creative execution of that content. Taking part in the various analytics and measurement certifications (see pages 254–255 of this chapter) is a great way to invest in your future education and training.

SUMMARY

The measurement and evaluation section of a PR plan is critical for conveying the success of our campaigns. Measurement and evaluation will become more prominent and important as our field evolves and grows. More tools, methods, and resources than ever are now accessible and integrated into current PR practices. Further, certain measurement practices (AVEs, impressions, etc.) are becoming something of the past, and the PR field is moving forward with more aligned metrics, methods, and analytics to evaluate our efforts for our clients and campaigns. There is still much to do to address the challenges we face in this area, but with each step, the field continues to improve.

APR EXAM

- Analytics
- AVEs
- Evaluation
- Impressions
- Measurement
- Methods

GAME CHANGER
Dennis Yu, CEO of BlitzMetrics

How did you get your start in the industry?

Courtesy Dennis Yu

I started building websites in high school over 30 years ago. Does that make me a dinosaur? LOL. My mom was a programmer and my dad was a quant jock, so I was lucky to have access to the very first personal computers. Back then, it was bulletin boards via dial-up, dominated by hackers. Some of my friends went to jail for breaking into government systems or changing their grades at school. I wasn't quite so adventuresome, since I didn't feel getting straight As was that big of a deal.

Building websites sure was more fun and profitable than being a paperboy or mowing lawns, which I did to get exercise. I was making $20 to $50 an hour making ugly websites for lawyers, baby clothing stores, musicians, and even a major defense contractor. I hired friends to help me out and soon had my own agency. We named it E-Motion Internet Solutions and made a few thousand dollars a month—a lot for a teenager.

Word of mouth, largely via mentors and clients, got me a role at American Airlines and then as an executive at Yahoo! And it was around 2000 that the industry shifted from the technical focus of building websites to the current PR and marketing focus on branding and traffic. My programming background served me well at what was the number-one search engine at the time and gave me a front-row seat into how Silicon Valley founders behaved. Many of the stories aren't of the variety we could publish in a book. But let's just say that it was a male-dominant culture, focused on relentless innovation.

What is your favorite part of working in the industry?

There is a cold, egalitarian beauty in digital marketing—in that if you have a strong campaign, you can make a lot of money. It's not a matter of opinion or feelings. I once found myself making $80,000 a day from Facebook ad campaigns. But just as easily, I was losing $10,000 a day on campaigns that I thought were just as good.

I know people who have made over $100 million by themselves—no boss or client involved, just them alone putting stuff out there on the internet and having a better product with better execution. My friend Markus Frind built an online dating site all by himself and sold it for a few hundred million dollars. There is something beautiful, yet tragic, about a few super hardworking geniuses who make a killing, but most of us are squeaking by on a salary, despite our talent and good nature.

The internet doesn't give you extra credit for effort or humanity, since it's a scale, much like the stock market. But my hope is to change that by creating mentorship and training systems that reward people for helping others via employment and leveling up.

What is the most challenging part of working in your industry?

For sure, it's the multifaceted skills that modern PR and marketing professionals need to succeed. In the "old days," being good at one thing was enough. You could be killer at copywriting, building websites, running Facebook ads, selling, editing videos, or whatever. Now, you need to know at least two different skills, since teams have to be more nimble and work cross-functionally. Graduates now are more likely to work at a smaller company, where a smaller group of people have to wear multiple hats.

This change is happening so fast that traditional academia can't keep up. Textbooks and classroom instruction can't replace on-the-job training. Thus, we all need mentors—not just to get going, but at all stages of our careers. How many of us are actively seeking, receiving, and providing mentorship?

Who do you think are the biggest game changers for the industry?

At risk of sounding cliché, AI, whether through machine learning or general AI, is disrupting digital marketing. My friend Walter Burch, CEO of Envoy

Media Group, held a brainstorming session with his top executives to see what jobs are immune from AI—where an algorithm or computer couldn't do their job. And the group concluded that nearly every job could be significantly replaced by an algorithm.

It's not just self-driving cars replacing truck drivers or self-check-outs replacing cashiers. The majority of sports recaps are written by AI, done so well that you can't tell if a human wrote it. And most of public relations and marketing is mundane stuff that the algo actually should be doing, like sending out cold emails, generating reports, scheduling meetings, and making PowerPoint presentations.

RadiusAI has technology that scans customers at gas stations to serve them up personalized offers while they are waiting at the pump. The technology knows how often particular customers come back, the license plate number on their vehicle, approximately how old they are, the mobile identifier of their phone, and so forth. Imagine what is possible in public relations and marketing with all this data and what we need to do to adapt to it—to be smarter about marketing, while also protecting ourselves.

The internet of things is just the beginning of a massive explosion of smart, connected devices, creating more channels for us to manage.

What are some things you wish you knew when you were starting out in the industry?

I wish I knew that relationships are far more important than skill or money. Starting out, I had the mistaken idea that employers and clients hired me because of my skill. So I studied like crazy to get the best grades possible. I'm not saying to let your grades fall or not to go to college—rather, take the time to build industry relationships, venture out of your comfort zone to seek mentors, and prioritize people over opportunities.

Today, when I have a question, I can ask Google or ask a knowledgeable friend. And it's my connections that drive my career, not my knowledge.

Dennis Yu is the CEO of BlitzMetrics, a digital marketing company that partners with schools to train young adults. Dennis's mission is to provide education at no cost to students. Dennis's program centers on mentorship, helping students grow their expertise in digital marketing to drive leads and sales by managing ad campaigns for enterprise clients like the Golden State Warriors, Nike, and Rosetta Stone. He's an internationally recognized lecturer in Facebook marketing and has spoken over 730 times in 17 countries, spanning 5 continents, including keynotes at L2E, PubCon, Conversion Conference, Social Media Marketing World, Gulltaggen, and Marketo Summit. Dennis has been featured in the Wall Street Journal, New York Times, *and* Los Angeles Times *and on* National Public Radio, TechCrunch, Fox News, CNN*, and* CBS Evening News, *and he co-authored* Facebook Nation, *a textbook taught in over 700 colleges and universities. He is a regular contributor to* Adweek's *SocialTimes column and is published in* Social Media Examiner, Social Media Club, Tweak Your Biz, B2C, SocialFresh*, and* Heyo.

You can contact Dennis at dennis@blitzmetrics.com.

KEY TERMS

DISCUSSION QUESTIONS

1. What is the overall perception of measurement in public relations?

2. Why is measurement and evaluation key for PR efforts?

CASE STUDY

Pittsburgh Knights and Zoomph: An Analytics Partnership

Pittsburgh Knights × Zoomph
Twitter/@KnightsGG

When it comes to partnerships and sponsorships, many people think about Coca-Cola and the Olympics, the Goodyear Blimp for college football games, and Home Depot for home improvement shows on HGTV. However, measurement and analytics companies are the latest to jump on the sponsorship and partnership train and branch out in their industry to reach new audiences, such as esports.

Zoomph, a data analytics platform that integrates social and digital metrics for various brands, sports teams, and other companies, announced a new partnership with the esports team Pittsburgh Knights (PR Newswire, 2019). This is a new partnership for both parties that will allow the Knights, a rising gaming esports team, to use Zoomph's measurement and analytical capabilities to evaluate their efforts across digital and social channels in real time, including Twitch. Twitch, the live gaming streaming platform, is one of the more prominent channels used by this audience and industry.

Why did this case generate buzz?

- This is one of the first sponsorships emerging in the esports industry featuring a partnership with an analytics company, which brings forth the possibility for other companies, industries, and partners to do the same.

- Zoomph has offered services both in digital and in social, but has also integrated AI capabilities to help the Pittsburgh Knights to understand and apply data to creative and innovative practices.

What are the ethical and legal issues?

- When it comes to data and measuring data, it is key to be transparent about how the data are collected and measured and how each KPI is operationalized. These items need to be transparent and accounted for in all cases.

- The access to the various platforms from a third-party company like Zoomph has to acknowledge both the ethical issues (where the data are stored, how much data are collected, how the data are analyzed, etc.) and the legal issues that could come up. For example, access to particular social platforms is decided not by the third-party vendors, but by the platforms themselves. There has to be some discussion on the contract side of what can happen and what steps will be taken if issues occur.

What are some takeaways from this case?

- Analytics, measurement, and evaluation are not only prominent areas in public relations, but they continue to evolve and grow in our industry. We are in a data-driven society, and the more information we are able to gather and use to create new and innovative ideas, the more our industry is going to evolve.

- Measurement can also be used as a strong skill and selling point to market and promote a brand to reach new audiences. Measurement is growing from something that is done for campaign ventures and PR initiatives, to a skill and service that can be offered as a form of sponsorship and new partnership opportunities. With this new trend, PR professionals and agencies can offer their services and reach new audiences and industries, increasing their reach and potential presence in the market.

3. Name and discuss two traditional methods and how they are used in PR measurement.

4. What is the difference between output and outcome metrics for public relations? Which is most acceptable in PR practices?

5. Are AVEs acceptable metrics to use in PR measurement practices? Explain your rationale for why this is or is not the case.

6. Impressions are commonly used in new and traditional measurement methods. Why is this the case?

ACTIVITIES

Building Your Portfolio

Evaluating measurement tools and methods. You have been asked to evaluate various new tools and methods in your internship, and you have to create an audit for your managers of which tool you recommend they use to evaluate their PR efforts. You will need to create a table and evaluate the following tools for this assignment:

- Meltwater
- Cision
- Talkwalker
- Brandwatch
- Sprinklr
- Salesforce

You will then have to evaluate the tools based on the following criteria:

- Date the company was founded
- Cost
- Features
- Data collection procedure
- Key metrics the tool is able to collect and report
- Key metrics (how the company defines them, such as by influence, engagement, impressions, etc.)

- Diversity metrics (data translated in different languages, accessible for all audiences, etc.)
- Benefits and challenges of using this tool
- Companies that are using this tool

Be prepared to provide your rationale for which method and tool you recommend and why you feel this is the best investment and method to use.

Building Your Brand

Measuring your personal brand. As they say, you are your most important client, and you can apply everything you have learned in this chapter for your personal brand. As you look toward graduation, there are certain objectives you want to achieve before you graduate and enter the workplace. Set up some objectives you would like to accomplish (getting an internship, studying abroad, etc.) and list the things you will do to accomplish these tasks. As you are setting your objectives, determine the methods (traditional or new) you will use to evaluate whether or not you have accomplished these tasks. List the steps you will take to make sure you do accomplish them and are successful.

CHAPTER 13

CAREERS

LEARNING **OBJECTIVES**

- Identify the current employment landscape in public relations.

- Explore skills needed to work in public relations.

- Understand your options for working in public relations.

- Discuss emerging new expectations for PR professionals.

Introduction

In the previous chapters, we've covered an overview of public relations, its history, and the ethical and legal matters we must consider when practicing in our field. In this chapter, however, we'll explore what it is really like to work in public relations. But first, let's pause to note how pop culture portrays public relations as a glamorous career in which we throw decadent parties, chill with celebrities, and handle crises with style, all while wearing Louboutins.

Okay, so public relations is not Olivia Pope–level glamorous, but that doesn't mean we can't succeed in our work while wearing a fabulous shoe style!

You may be asking yourself: What *is* it like to work in the field? What qualifications do I need to succeed? What experiences will employers look for? Should I develop a personal brand? Does that matter? These are the same questions that professionals already in the PR workplace are asking themselves. This chapter addresses some of these questions and covers what you need to know as you enter the PR field.

What Skills and Experience Do We Need to Work in Public Relations?

The general perception of what it means to be a PR professional has evolved over the last few years. More businesses, corporations, and individual consultants are taking notice of the growth areas in public relations, specifically around social media. Our job market, careers, and specific roles are changing and growing along with the shifts taking place in our industry. This may mean that your future job has yet to be created. In other words, there are numerous opportunities ahead. In such a landscape, we must continuously educate ourselves and adapt our skills, experiences, and expectations. Further, we need to have a serious commitment to learning and growing our skills as we go along. This capacity is not only expected—it's necessary for us to be relevant and valued in our field.

Skills and Literacies

To apply and be qualified for any position or internship, we need to have certain skills and knowledge in our tool kits.

Business Literacy

We need to be able to go into the boardroom with a solid background in finance, accounting, marketing research, and business communication practices. Most PR departments work with and are in sync with these related disciplines, so it is important to be able to understand and integrate their practices into our work.

Creative Thinking

Being able to think outside of the box while bringing forth new ideas is something that many agencies, brands, and organizations look for in job candidates. It's too easy to keep doing the same things, the same way, for clients, just because "this is what we've always done." This attitude does not spark innovation. That is why diverse perspectives, fresh ideas, and evolving applications of messages and stories are all highly sought after by organizations and brands.

Critical Thinking

Seeing the underlying elements at play in a given situation, evaluating the credibility of a source (e.g., determining what is real or fake news or influencers), and thinking through ethical and legal implications are key skills for PR professionals.

Data Analysis

Along with the expectations related to research, we need to know how to collect and analyze data. We must be able to identify factors that may impact our strategies, messaging, and design and the impact of our campaign or brand, whether positively or negatively (e.g., reputation management and crisis communication).

Diversity Literacy

Diversity literacy means that we embrace those with different ethnic and cultural backgrounds, experiences, and schools of thought. Working together in this way brings in fresh ideas that represent and reflect our colleagues and audiences.

Media Savvy

It's key to be informed about the latest media trends, technology issues, emerging channels, and changes in audience behavior across media. The ability to forecast and experiment with new channels and educate others on these trends is a skill that is highly sought after by PR businesses and agencies.

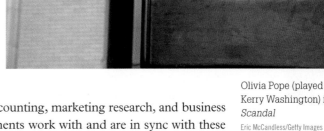

Olivia Pope (played by Kerry Washington) in *Scandal*
Eric McCandless/Getty Images

Multimedia Composing Skills

Content creation is not just about writing content, but also about being able to create graphics, videos, audio clips, and emerging content (e.g., augmented and virtual reality).

Research Skills

We need research skills to uncover data and interpret the results of our efforts, but also to provide guidance on how to apply these insights.

Social Media Skills

Knowing the latest trends, tools, and features for understanding what's going on in social media is crucial. We need to use these platforms strategically for brand messaging, relationship building, and the creative execution of our plans. Also important is knowing how people of different age cohorts (e.g., baby boomers and Generation Z) consume and create content on a given platform. This brings together our research and creative thinking skills.

Storytelling Skills

We must embrace our brand's voice, tell its story, and connect with all audiences in a variety of different formats.

Writing Skills

Creating content—and presenting it creatively in different media and contexts—is one of our biggest responsibilities. We also need to keep up with relevant writing formats and styles, such as those presented by the Associated Press. Most internships and job postings require writing samples, and some also give timed writing tests to evaluate our skills.

Experience

In some fields, you can get away with learning on the go after graduation. Public relations is *not* that field. You must not only talk the talk in public relations; you must show that you know what you're doing. Experience is the first thing that employers want to see, and they will ask how many internships, projects, and clients you've had before considering you for a job. Additional expectations are that you have a dossier or online portfolio that showcases your work. You need to show future employers your abilities, your creations, and your commitment to lifelong learning. The most common way to gain experience is through internships.

Internships

Some internships are a semester long, while others last only a few days. For example, many PR agencies, such as Golin and Edelman, offer semester- or even yearlong internships. In addition, at Churchill Downs, there are internships for those dedicated to carrying out PR initiatives during the Kentucky Derby, which lasts for just one day (with a few days in preparation ahead of time).

While internships can be paid or unpaid, it's important to note that paid internships are fairer and more valuable. **Internships**, which are offered for class credit or no credit, boost our experience levels and our résumés. They give us the opportunity to determine which areas in public relations we most enjoy, as well as those we don't like and would not pursue, career-wise. For example, you may think you want to become the next Andy or Emily of *The Devil Wears Prada* and work in fashion and consumer public relations. Your experience as an intern might reveal that the work is everything you hoped it would be, or it might reveal the complete opposite. At least you know going forward what to expect if you pursue a career in this area after graduation. On the positive side, some PR internships can evolve into full-time, paid entry-level jobs. Internships come in many forms, from traditional (face-to-face) to online or virtual internships. The experiences all contribute to great learning and professional opportunities navigating, engaging, and working in the PR field.

There has been a lot of discussion and controversy over the issue of unpaid internships in the PR field. According to *The Guardian*, about half of the 1.5 million internships available in the United States annually are unpaid (Kasperkevic, 2016). Many have called this "exploitation" of young talent, suggesting that to get this "experience" while going into debt is unfair and uncalled for (Kasperkevic, 2016). In addition to the issue of not being paid, there may be other challenges to doing an internship, depending on the culture of the organization you work for. For example, the work you are tasked with may not feel meaningful or provide the "real-world" experience you signed up for. These are just some of the elements to consider when exploring the types of experience that internships provide, as shown in Table 13.1.

When the topic of internships comes up, think about those that might benefit you, not just locally or nationally, but internationally as well. Most PR firms including Edelman, Golin, and Weber Shandwick offer international internships for students to take during a semester or over the summer. These types of internships provide real-world experience and show employers and others that you (1) understand we are a global society now, (2) are willing to explore new opportunities and ventures, and (3) are willing to go outside your own comfort zone to learn, grow, and expand your viewpoint of the field.

In addition, international internships sometimes provide opportunities you would not have otherwise, like giving the fashion director of Prada a call regarding the official launch of the company's product for the first time in South Africa on your second day

▼ TABLE 13.1

Pros and Cons of Internships

Internship Pros	Internship Cons	Elements to Consider
• Getting real-world experience • Networking and making connections • Adding content to our portfolios and résumés • Determining what we like and don't like about the field and/or workplace • Having a potential opportunity to go from an internship to a full-time job • Having the option of a face-to-face or virtual internship	• Lack of meaningful experience in the field (e.g., getting coffee or making copies instead of helping with a campaign) • Lack of control over time and responsibilities • No guarantees that an internship will turn into a full-time job • Unclear focus and sense of responsibilities • The need for clear guidelines, responsibilities, schedule/deadlines, and expectations to be placed on virtual or online internships	• Whether the internship is paid or unpaid • What the end goal is and if there is potential for advancement and a permanent position • Culture within the organization • Deliverables for the internship • Hours dedicated to the internship • Overall history of internship culture and mentorship support

on the job (side note—this was me!). I was tasked with making sure the fashion director knew of the promotion content we would need to engage with the media and fashion trade publications. Would this be an opportunity designated to an intern in a local PR agency? Most definitely not. Experiences like this provide you with a vast array of lessons learned. International internships teach you many skills—thinking on your feet, working in another country, learning a different culture—but also can provide you with opportunities you may not have in most cases.

The overall purpose of an internship is to get experience in the field, to be mentored by a professional in the industry, and to create samples of work that can be used for future professional opportunities.

Fellowships

Fellowships are a great way to learn about the profession through a quick, real-world experience. Organizations such as the Plank Center for Leadership have fellowships through which they send students to workshops and conference sessions on PR leadership. The Plank Center also places PR professors in agencies and companies to gain real-world experience through its Educator Fellowship Program.

Speaking and Presenting

Speaking engagements, presenting at conferences, and hosting workshop sessions are not limited to the high-level professionals in our industry. In fact, anyone can organize, launch, and conduct a speaking event or workshop session. Educating others on a topic that is relevant to the community is a great way to not only build up a professional network, but also establish a presence in public relations. In addition, learning and teaching boosts our own understanding of the PR field. Some ideas for speaking and presenting as a way to gain experience are hosting a workshop at a local event for the Public Relations Student Society of America, volunteering at a local business to present new trends in social media, or hosting your own live video session on Instagram or LinkedIn Live that focuses on a topic you're passionate about and want to share with others. All of these experiences help us gain exposure, awareness, and connections in key online and offline communities.

Memberships in Professional Organizations

Being active in professional organizations is a key factor in building a network within the industry. One major organization to connect with is the Public Relations Society of America (PRSA), which offers workshops, webinars, resources for students and professionals, and local, regional, and national conferences. In addition, within PRSA are groups of people with specific areas of specialization and interest (e.g., entertainment and sports), including a group for new professionals in the industry. There is a group for everyone! Other PR programs to consider joining are the Arthur W. Page Society, the Plank Center, and any local professional groups focused on communication.

Personal Branding

Our personal brands—basically, our reputations—are part of how others in the profession see us. As discussed in Chapter 6, being your own best advocate will help you distinguish yourself from other candidates vying for the same internships and jobs in the field.

What Types of Careers Does Public Relations Offer?

Something to consider when applying for jobs in public relations is that PR jobs are not always labeled as such. In fact, they may be listed and framed in a variety of ways. For example, if we apply for jobs in the military or government sector, most positions are labeled as "public affairs," whereas in corporate settings, the PR positions may be titled as jobs in "corporate communications" or "internal communications." It is important to be aware of the different titles out there for work in public relations. Table 13.2 discusses the different roles for PR professionals and the industries in which they appear.

Traditional Roles and Job Titles

Public relations is a fast-paced field that generally allows us to find work quickly and, even better, to advance our roles throughout our careers. The potential for career growth within an agency or other organization is exciting, but the skills required, and the responsibilities built into such advancements, may feel daunting at times.

PR roles and job titles are anything but stable, and may be categorized differently from company to company. The following sections of this chapter highlight the professional roles that are available. Keep in mind that certain skills (such as writing and critical, creative thinking) will always be relevant and valued by those looking to hire a PR professional. Presented with each of the following roles is a discussion of its underlying characteristics, responsibilities, and duties. Also included is a sample job posting for each role, with a job description that indicates the responsibilities the position entails and the qualities, skills, and experience the hiring manager for the position is looking for.

Intern (Pre–Entry Level)

The position of **intern** is the most common position offered to those beginning their careers as PR professionals. Most internships focus on the technical aspects of public

TABLE 13.2

Types of Roles for PR Professionals by Industry

Industry	Roles
Corporate	Corporate communication, internal communication, employee communication, marketing communication, promotions, social and influencer relations
Nonprofit	Public information, community relations, advocacy relations
Entertainment	Publicity, media relations
Government and politics	Public affairs, lobbying, media relations
Education	Media relations, public relations, donor relations, alumni relations
Sports and athletics	Sports information, media relations
Social media	Influencer relations, community management, social media coordination, social media strategy, social media management

CAREERS

The job market and roles in public relations are growing and evolving along with the changes happening in the industry themselves. You could be working in a position that has yet to be offered or created, which brings forth numerous opportunities to be part of the industry. However, in a field that is constantly in flux and rapidly shifting, this means the skills, experiences, and expectations for those working in public relations must be adaptive as well. Before venturing out in a career in public relations, you want to make sure you note the following things:

KNOW WHAT IT MEANS TO WORK IN PR

Public relations offers a constant change of pace, depending on where you are working. No two days are the same, which allows you to do multiple things for different accounts at one time. Do your research and see where you want to work, what you want to do, and where you see yourself having the most impact.

PICTURE WHERE YOU WOULD LIKE TO SEE YOURSELF WORKING

Do you see yourself working in a cubicle focusing on responding in real time to customer inquiries in a matter of seconds for one primary brand? Do you see yourself working at an agency where you may be working on a variety of different projects, brands, and clients? Or do you see yourself taking the entrepreneurship route where you are your own boss and company?

DO YOUR RESEARCH

The best way to get an idea of what it is like to work at an agency, company, brand, or on your own is to reach out to a professional who is doing that job. Ask them how they got to where they are, and what are the benefits and challenges of their work. Use this opportunity to get an idea of what it may be like for you. See if you can shadow someone to get an idea of their day-to-day activities.

GET AS MUCH EXPERIENCE AS POSSIBLE

This is a field where experience matters. Find internships (PRSA, MEOjobs, Twitter, Indeed, etc.) and see where you can go that could help you improve your writing, creative, research, and content creation skills. Not all experience is created equally, so make sure each internship and experience has a direct connection to your professional goals.

BUILD YOUR PORTFOLIO AND PERSONAL BRAND

It is about not only what you know, but who knows you. Invest not only in your skills, but in building networks and communities. Determine what separates you from others, based on your own experience and contributions.

relations—that is, assisting the team in efforts of creating content, writing reports, doing research, pitching to the media using Cision or Meltwater, creating media and influencer lists for campaigns and clients, and supporting team efforts. Most of the time, interns are not brought into a situation for strategic or managerial assistance, but this may depend on the internship in question.

Job Posting: Intern (Pre–Entry Level)

Public Relations Intern, Corporate & Public Affairs

Edelman Seattle

Edelman Seattle is looking for an intern to support our corporate team. Edelman internships are 3- to 6-month paid internships open to recent graduates, and designed to propel your career in public relations and digital marketing in the ever-changing arena of communications. A qualifying candidate must be able to work effectively with a variety of account service staff within a specific set of accounts, and help implement and monitor projects under the direction of a supervisor. The intern will work closely with, and support the needs of, the account teams.

Responsibilities

- Build and maintain an in-depth understanding of clients' business and industry trends

- Participate in brainstorms when invited by supervisor

- Identify and analyze media coverage across print, broadcast, and online resources

- Support media relations efforts by developing media lists, drafting pitches and long-form content, creating coverage reports, and pitching media under the direction of supervisor

- Support client announcements and launches to possibly include, but not be limited to, event planning, media relations, and community and stakeholder engagement

- Use social media as tools to monitor industry trends, report on PR results, and identify industry influencers

- Conduct and compile research for new business opportunities, clients, etc.

- Understand the tools used to support research and media list development (Cision, Factiva, Critical Mention, etc.)

- Build and maintain an in-depth understanding of the principles of PR

Qulifications

- Intern candidates must have interest in the PR field and possess good interpersonal and communication skills and the ability to work effectively with others.

Other Qualifications

- You must have completed a bachelor's degree in communications, journalism, or a related field; maintain an understanding of AP style; have strong organizational and time management skills and ability to adapt to new conditions, assignments, and deadlines; a keen eye for detail; solid knowledge of Microsoft Office Suite and superior verbal and written communication skills; and strong writing skills with willingness to grow.

About Our Internship Program

- We have 1–2 interns for each practice area at any given time. The duration of the internship is a minimum of 3 months and a maximum of 6 months. Interns are paid $15 per hour, plus overtime when approved by management. Most of our interns are postgraduates and work a full-time schedule (Mon–Fri, 8:30 a.m.–5:00 p.m.)

Source: Adapted from LinkedIn. (2020). PR intern, corporate & public affairs: Edelman. Retrieved from https://www.linkedin.com/jobs/view/1762415075/?alternateChannel=search

Account Executive (Entry to Senior Level)

The first entry-level position for those with bachelor's degrees is typically as an **account executive**. This role has more responsibilities than an internship does, and requires that candidates can take on both technical and managerial responsibilities for a brand or agency. In addition, account executives have the opportunity to have their own accounts and to work with specific clients as the liaison between the agency and client. There are content and writing responsibilities, but the focus is more on delivering strategic insights, pitching stories to media, and executing message strategies for the client.

Job Posting: Senior Account Executive—Media Manager (Senior Level)

Senior Account Executive

Golin Washington D.C.

Golin Washington D.C. is looking for someone who is a creative problem-solver, loves to write, and has a passion for digging into our clients' business to really understand and build strong media strategies.

In the role of Media Manager, you will work across multiple industries, including Fortune 500 companies, renowned nonprofits, and leading health care organizations. You will have direct client contact and work with a strong leadership team to deliver thoughtful and creative results for our clients.

What You'll Do

- Hold and set a high bar for smart and sound ideas, the flawless execution of press releases, and the thoughtful development of media strategies
- Develop targeted media lists and pitch appropriate media for clients
- Help craft and execute messaging specific to client needs
- Help develop and deliver client presentations
- Stay on top of industry best practice and client and competitor brand activity; ensure that Golin delivers game-changing ideas and solutions

What You Have

- At least 3 years of PR agency experience with growing responsibilities

- Excellent communication skills (written, verbal, and presentation)
- Proven ability to develop work that is client-ready with minimal oversight
- Experience developing media strategy as well as building targeted media lists and pitching a variety of media
- Solid understanding of client business, ability to provide agency with perspective and identify opportunities
- Ability to understand complex pieces of information and distill it into a clear and thoughtful press release
- Collaborative spirit, results-driven focus, capacity to manage multiple priorities and meet deadlines
- Excellent organizational and planning skills; ability to work quickly under pressure
- Experience in B2B, transportation issues a plus

Who You Are

- Creative
- Thoughtful
- Problem-solver
- Detail-oriented
- Collaborative

Source: Adapted from Monster. (n.d.). Senior account executive—Media relations: GolinHarris. Retrieved from https://job-openings.monster.com/senior-account-executive-%E2%80%93-media-relations-washington-dc-us-golinharris/5cd695af-b305-4bc0-b4f7-d2cffd976246

PR Coordinator (Entry Level)

A **PR coordinator** is most often housed within a brand and is responsible for supporting the activities of team members within the PR department. Most of the time, the work of the PR coordinator is to help amplify efforts to tell a brand's story, to coordinate measures to enhance opportunities and relationships within the community for the brand, and to help create and execute various communications for a brand. The list of

---

Job Posting: PR Coordinator (Entry Level)

PR Coordinator

Denny's

The Coordinator of Public Relations and Corporate Communications supports the activities of the following functions: Brand Public Relations, Internal Communications, and Corporate Social Responsibility (CSR). This role requires work with cross-functional stakeholders, franchisees, and agency partners to accomplish set goals and objectives. The PR Coordinator supports the telling of the Denny's story, protects and enhances the brand's reputation, and communicates internal activities. This position demands an individual who works effectively and efficiently in stressful situations that may require immediate action, and who can keep up with aggressive work demands and deadlines.

Essential Functions (Key Responsibilities)

- Actively collaborate with internal stakeholders and agency partners to enhance storytelling
- Mange the Mobile Relief Diner program from location selection to execution to final report
- Initiate, collaborate on, and issue internal communications
- Coordinate and execute annual No Kid Hungry partnership
- Develop and edit a wide range of content, including news releases, presentations, internal communications, media backgrounders, etc.
- Provide analysis of program success and results against program objectives
- Actively manage program budgets
- Have excellent project management skills, ability to manage multiple projects simultaneously
- Coordinate campaign assets including imagery, press materials, launch dates
- Assist in preparation of PR and CSR event launches

Education and Experience Requirements

- Bachelor's degree required, preferably in business, communications, public relations, or a related field.
- Should have 1–3 years of experience in communications, public relations, or related field; a constant sense of urgency tempered with a calm driving purpose

Required Knowledge and Skills

- Proficient in Microsoft Office (Excel, Word, PowerPoint)
- Strong communications skills, including excellent speaking, writing, and editing abilities
- Strong interpersonal skills; amicable yet persistent
- Passion for all things PR; appetite to learn new skills, keep up with trends
- Highly organized with attention to detail while working on multiple projects under tight deadlines
- Intellectually rigorous, with critical and creative thinking skills
- Works well with multiple internal and external teams
- Enthusiastic, collaborative, entrepreneurial; go-getter attitude no matter the size of project
- Graphic/visual design and video/multimedia production experience a plus

---

Source: Adapted from HelpWanted.com. (2019). Public relations coordinator—Spartanburg: Denny's Restaurant. Retrieved from https://www.helpwanted.com/6f209de8f0204-Public-Relations-Coordinator-Spartanburg-job-listingswashington-dc-us-golinharris/5cd695af-b305-4bc0-b4f7-d2cffd976246

the responsibilities of PR coordinators is long—they are writers, researchers, strategists, managers, and event planners, to name a few of their duties. This is also an entry-level position that is usually given to new graduates with a PR degree.

Account Specialist (Mid-Level)

An **account specialist** is assigned to a specific account or client for a specific reason. This individual specializes in specific PR functions (e.g., social media, crisis communication, or graphic design) or has expertise in the industry or area in which the client resides (e.g., labor unions or public diplomacy). The account specialist job tends to be a mid-level role held by someone with specialized experience and knowledge.

Job Description: Account Specialist (Mid-Level)

Account Specialist, Marketing and Public Relations

K Strategies Group

K Strategies is an award-winning marketing and public relations agency with a passion for generating creative ideas, engaging audiences, and building strong campaigns to help our clients achieve success. We value strategic thinkers, who work hard and bring results.

We're looking for a dynamic team player with marketing, public relations, and community engagement experience to join our team! You will be responsible for the strategy, tactical execution, and management as well as be the main point of contact for a variety of public engagement and marketing projects.

Candidates must demonstrate independent judgment, personal organization, and excellent communication skills and manage multiple projects. Specific requirements may include:

- Define, clarify, and create project documentation including scope, strategy, schedules, status reports, dynamic public involvement and community campaigns (both digital and print), and other documents as necessary.

- Help coordinate and lead regularly scheduled client meetings to identify required actions to achieve timely completion as well as documenting all meetings and communication.

- Write for a variety of content, including PR plans, communications materials, social media and website content, press releases, speaking points, and program reports.

- Possess strong media relations and story pitching experience.

- Conduct stakeholder engagement and outreach in target communities.

- Help develop and manage event coordination for public meetings and outreach events.

- Review all client deliverables to ensure high-quality, professional outputs that meet client expectations.

- Help manage and monitor project budgets.

- Be an entrepreneur by constantly looking for new ways to improve our team and company, along with strategies and ideas for our clients.

Additional requirements:

- 1–5 years of experience in managing public or community relations projects, transportation experience is a plus; salary will be based on experience

- Bachelor's degree in communications, public relations, marketing, or related field

- Excellent writing skills using AP style

- Experience using InDesign software is a plus

- Ability to multitask and set priorities with tight timelines and high client expectations

- Bilingual (English and Spanish) is a plus

Source: Adapted from LinkedIn. (n.d.-d). Marketing and public relations account specialist: K Strategies Group. Retrieved from https://www.linkedin.com/jobs/view/marketing-and-public-relations-account-specialist-at-k-strategies-group-1331993788/

Account Director (Advanced Level)

After several years of experience managing and working with different clients and different accounts, an advanced role that we can take on is that of **account director**. This leadership position focuses on coordinating efforts for the client, managing the team, and addressing the overall needs and expectations of the campaign and all parties involved. The account director oversees managerial and strategic responsibilities in public relations.

Job Listing: Account Director (Advanced Level)

Account Director

SutherlandGold

SutherlandGold is a PR agency specializing in the tech industry where ambitious creatives hit go. We're a bicoastal (NY/SF), full-service agency with clients who are leaders in security, fintech, AI, robotics, consumer tech, and SaaS. We're dedicated to the art of storytelling and helping companies own their narratives to inspire action in their target audiences. We work with market leaders and soon-to-be change makers to develop positioning and establish their thought leadership in their field.

We are looking for an Account Director with 8+ years of PR experience. As a member of our leadership team, this individual must be a visionary creative type with experience growing teams and satisfying clients. In this role you will oversee the development of high-level strategy with clients to ensure the team is successful with media strategies. Account Directors are involved in new business development and serve as mentors and managers.

Core Responsibilities

- Act as a primary client contact; foster the client-agency relationship and add value for brands.
- Take charge in leadership, management, and deliverables for clients.
- Develop and implement strategic PR programs to build clients' brands; map all strategies, programs, and plans to client's goals with measurable metrics for success.
- Run client launches and news announcements with support from team and media experts.
- Identify trend stories, executive features, and client/product spotlights; land stories

individually; direct teams in their pitching to achieve results.

- Make smart recommendations to clients for how to insert executives, products, and points of view into trending stories and themes.
- Think creatively about how digital marketing can support media relations (social, content, events) and put ideas into action.
- Participate in new business including crafting proposals/decks and attending presentations.
- Oversee the growth and professional development of direct reports; draft and deliver performance reviews, conduct regular meetings to assess progress, and elevate performance issues to management team as needed.
- Part of Leadership Team; participate in agency planning discussions on staffing, hiring, and overall growth plans.

Qualifications

- Bachelor's degree
- 8–10 years of experience in public relations agency or a similar position
- Solid overall understanding of technology industry
- Deep relationships with specific category of higher-level media (business, technology, or consumer) that result in significant coverage for client
- Excellent organizational and planning skills
- Exceptional writing capabilities
- Results-driven and self-motivated with a positive and professional approach to management

Source: Adapted from Peersight. (n.d.). Public relations account director at SutherlandGold Communications. Retrieved from https://www.peersight.com/job/sutherlandgold-communications-public-relations-account-director-in-san-francisco-ca

Job Posting: Policy Communication Manager

Policy Communication Manager

Twitter

The Twitter Policy Communications team focuses on storytelling around public policy issues that touch the critical intersection of technology, public policy, media, and governance. These communications issues range from freedom of expression to the health of online public conversations and internet safety, to data privacy and election integrity.

The Policy Communications team works closely with the Public Policy team to showcase the role of Twitter in government and elections, including civic participation, digital diplomacy, and e-governance. The Policy Communications team also tells the stories of how our #TwitterforGood efforts support NGOs in the areas of digital inclusion, freedom of expression, online safety and security, equality, women and minorities in tech, and emergency services/disaster mitigation and recovery.

What You Need

- Minimum of 3–4+ years' experience in communications/public relations. In-house, technology communications preferred.

- Strong media relations skills and experience working with a public relations/communications agency desired.

- Motivated to thrive in a fast-paced, pressurized environment, and to meet deadlines consistently.

- Ability to distil complex, technical information into simple and easy-to-understand language.

- Good project management and organizational skills.

- Knowledge of the EMEA political landscape desirable.

- Strong writing and editing skills.

- A global outlook and an ability to work with different cultures, perspectives, and attitudes.

- A compassionate and empathetic approach to work and a strong team player.

- Flexibility, amiability, and willingness to learn and be challenged.

Source: Adapted from LinkedIn. (n.d.-f). Policy communications manager, EMEA: Twitter. Retrieved from https://www.linkedin.com/jobs/view/policy-communications-manager-emea-at-twitter-1154246337/?originalSubdomain=ie

Communication Manager (Entry to Senior Level)

The overall focus of the **communication manager** is to listen, coordinate, and engage the various channels and communities for a particular organization. This role is an integrated role for a PR professional. That is, the person in this role is responsible not only for PR efforts, but for other associated discipline responsibilities, such as advertising, internal communication, and social media.

Media Relations Specialist/Publicist (Entry to Senior Level)

The overall focus of a **media relations specialist/publicist** is to generate coverage in the media for clients across various channels and audiences, and to coordinate proactive relationships with the media (traditional, social, and emerging). This PR role puts us on the front line of working with the media and audiences for news stories, features, and even crises communications, all on a 24/7 media cycle.

Job Posting: Media Relations Associate

Media Relations Associate

NewYork–Presbyterian Hospital

Step into New York's #1-ranked hospital and feel the pride of building on our reputation as a world-class organization. At NewYork-Presbyterian's nationally renowned campuses, your work will strengthen our relations with the public and media outlets throughout the country. It's the kind of career that's essential to our continued advancement in improving people's lives. Find out how you can Make It Possible.

Thrive in this role as you help coordinate and oversee media/public relations activities such as communications outreach planning, medical meetings, crises and press conferences responding to media queries. Focus on thought leadership strategy and outcomes. Identify platforms and opportunities at media and medical conferences. Collaborate with medical staff and service line administrators to identify priority areas for outreach. Conduct research to determine which outlets to target and develop pitches accordingly. Write press releases, tip sheets, expert alerts, social media content, and other materials that promote our organization. Serve as a field producer for local and national news crews filming at our medical center.

Supervise freelancers and support staff. Report on the outcomes of media/public relations activities, and participate in performance improvement initiatives.

This is a full-time position in a 24/7 media operation with evening, weekend, and on-call rotations required.

Preferred Criteria

- Health care policy experience
- At least 3–5 years of experience in media pitching/public relations/press releases
- Experience in a hospital/health care environment
- Experience integrating multimedia, social media, and online media strategies

Required Criteria

- College degree in English, journalism, communications, and/or related fields
- Excellent writing/editing

Source: Adapted from LinkedIn. (n.d.-e). Media relations associate: NewYork-Presbyterian Hospital. Retrieved from https://www.linkedin.com/jobs/view/media-relations-associate-at-new-york-presbyterian-hospital-1157717589/?trk=jobs_job_title&originalSubdomain=qa

Copywriter (Entry Level)

As mentioned previously, one of the most important skills for PR professionals to have is writing, and there are designated writing jobs in PR firms, agencies, and corporations. Many of these positions are filled by English majors and graduates, but for the most part, PR professionals are able to bring forth our creative and strategic writing to these positions. **Copywriters** have to be skilled in writing in different formats, media, and contexts. They must be able to write in different brand voices for targeted audiences. Expertise in AP style and format and the ability to edit, revise, and create content within time requirements are some of the skills that are essential for copywriters.

New and Emerging Roles and Job Titles

Within public relations, new roles based on new tools, practices, and ongoing changes in the industry emerge constantly. Some of these roles are for one person, but if an

Job Posting: Copywriter

Copywriter

VaynerMedia

The Copywriter works with designers to own content calendars and campaign execution for a set of brands. At VaynerMedia, we're lucky that everyone within our walls thinks strategically, shares a passion for emerging technology, and understands the world of big campaigns and content. Our copywriters serve a slightly different role than more traditional "digital creative types," but thankfully we'll never use the term "digital ninja."

Who are you?

You're an ultimate team player who will create value in any situation. You understand creative problem solving and have a passion for storytelling on every platform. You're an adaptable idea person who understands that good ideas can come from anywhere. You're highly observant and write because you love to. You can execute quickly and manage your time well. You're aware of your strengths *and* your weaknesses. You're cool in the face of a challenge. You'll be working primarily within the digital realm, so the portfolio you submit should reflect this; however, we love seeing your overall solutions and ideas throughout your book.

The task at hand:

- Own a range of creative work from content calendars to campaigns

- Work with a designer within a dynamic team structure with several creative leads, helping to support and deliver on our core product and brand-specific campaigns

- Organize and help direct content photo shoots with our in-house studio

- Care more about concepting, writing, developing, and putting the team in the best position to present our ideas than you do about getting credit for the work

- Be as much of a friendly mentor as a proficient doer when working within our dynamic brand team structure

The ideal candidate has:

- A bachelor's degree, or entrepreneurial street creds, and 1–3 years of experience copywriting, developing, and creating for digital/social media

- Experience or interest in finance, or past work on a financial brand

- Strong conceptual/brainstorming skills

- Strategic thinking skills and a passion for ideating focused campaigns

- The ability to follow direction and take constructive criticism

- An aptitude for time management, organization, and communication

- Strong presentation skills and the desire to present work to the client

- A talent for wearing multiple brand hats and switching easily among brand voices

- A passion for storytelling, a mastery of grammar and the English language, and the ability to tailor your writing to tell that story on a variety of platforms

- The ability to effectively collaborate with various teams, providing the most useful guidance in an enthusiastic and inspiring manner

- A mastery of industry best practices and the platforms we love, as well as be willing to learn and articulate the unique VaynerMedia point of view on each

- A sparkling personality that will mesh well with the existing VaynerMedia family and a smile on their face a majority of the time

- A basic understanding of UI/UX and an interest in the big social media platforms and their abilities/limitations

- Experience working with designers, developers, and team-focused creative process

- An obsession with sports, music, food, comedy, [fill in the blank]—we love people who can bring their own interests into the mix

Source: Adapted from Gary's Guide. (2019). Copywriter: VaynerMedia. Retrieved from https://www.garysguide.com/jobs/x7cz51c/Copywriter-at-Vayner-Media-Singapore

agency is small or just starting up, these roles may be add-ons to other duties that a PR professional must embrace. Among these roles are content creator, social media community manager, influencer relations specialist, and research and social media analyst.

Content Creator (Entry to Senior Level)

Content creators focus on more than writing: They tie in other pieces of content, such as visual, audio, and textual content, to bring forth a cohesive and transmedia experience for a brand. These professionals must be skilled across a variety of different programs, platforms, media, and tools to produce the best content for their clients.

Job Posting: Content Creator

Content Creator

Uber

At Uber, we ignite opportunity by setting the world in motion. We take on big problems to help drivers, riders, delivery partners, and eaters get moving in more than 600 cities around the world. We welcome people from all backgrounds who seek the opportunity to help build a future where everyone and everything can move independently. If you have curiosity, passion, and a collaborative spirit, work with us, and let's move the world forward, together.

About the Role

As a Content Coordinator, you'll work with team members across our organization to write and edit help articles, canned responses, and internal knowledge base articles. Content Coordinators work across lines of business and product teams. You may be a good fit if you enjoy writing clear and engaging content, are able to distill broad concepts into concrete steps, and enjoy project management/stakeholder management. Uber does not provide visa sponsorship and/or relocation support for this role.

What You'll Do

- Write and edit support copy across multiple channels including external help center,

saved responses, and internal knowledge base

- Effectively manage and prioritize steady stream of content requests from multiple departments with short, frequently changing timelines

- Be assigned to 1–2 lines of business and/or project managers to develop subject matter knowledge; work closely with project managers to develop content for product launches, policy updates

- Learn and master multiple knowledge base and content management tools

- Assist with ongoing large-scale content audits to ensure adherence to tone and style guidelines

- Work cross-functionally to ensure all content adheres to legal, brand, and support tone/voice guidelines

- Proactively identify opportunities to improve workflow and processes

What You'll Need

- Candidates must submit a writing sample to be considered for this role.

- Exceptional written and verbal communication skills

- Detail orientation and excellent prioritization skills

(Continued)

- Excellent interpersonal skills and ability to establish trust with partners
- Organized, self-driven, and comfortable handling a high volume of content requests/caseloads
- Optimistic leadership skills, an enthusiastic attitude, and passionate about making every support interaction a chance to impact our riders and driver partners in a positive way

Bonus Points If You Have

- Familiarity with Confluence or other enterprise content management systems (CMS)
- Experience writing or editing copy, or developing support content
- Experience creating flowcharts and process maps with tool such as LucidChart

Job Posting: Community Manager

Community Manager

McCann

The Role

We are looking for a Community Manager to join our team here in NYC. This person will be responsible for managing day-to-day social media activity across all platforms (Facebook, Twitter, Instagram, Snapchat, and any new platforms to market). This person will ensure ongoing community engagement and growth.

The Team

The McCann NY Strategy department is a collective of 45 brave, nimble, and smart individuals whose experience is as varied as their strategic approach. Our goal is to create work that allows brands to play a meaningful role in consumers' lives.

What You Will Do

- Build and maintain all social media communities through active interaction and become an advocate for the company in social media spaces
- Own, develop, and implement the social content calendar, working in collaboration with the creative teams
- Monitor, listen, and respond to users on a daily basis, and discover content and brand opportunities through social listening

- Plan, curate, and create content so sustain community growth and fan engagement
- Set and deliver on tangible social KPIs
- Track the effectiveness and success of content using proper assessment tools, in support of the reporting process
- Activate super-fan and surprise-and-delight strategies
- Explore, identify, and stay on the pulse of new social developments and opportunities/channels/innovations/competitors in order to proactively direct current and future opportunities

Who You Will Be

- 2+ years related experience required
- Experience managing digital content for a major consumer brand or media company preferred
- Strong working knowledge of and experience with various social media marketing technologies, such as social monitoring and publishing/content management system platforms
- Experience growing massive social communities and maintaining content calendars
- Bachelor's degree in related field required

Social Media Community Manager (Entry to Senior Level)

The role of the social media community manager is sometimes confused with the role of social media manager. These are two distinct yet related roles. Some key differences: A **social media manager** focuses on being the brand on social media, while a social media community manager focuses on advocating for the brand on social media. The main difference is that the social media manager is the brand—the one who creates content, uses the brand's voice, and answers questions as the brand.

Influencer Relations Specialist (Entry to Senior Level)

Everyone wants to engage with influencers for client accounts, campaigns, and endorsement deals. But there can be some confusion about the roles and expectations for **influencer relations** and the part of the organization that it fits into. However, brands such as Adobe and Whole Foods are creating specific roles for research influencers who are responsible for formulating relationships, designing media strategies, and reporting campaign initiatives for the client among audiences. This role requires PR expertise, but must also integrate social and digital chops, audience insights, media relations, analytics, and marketing campaign measures. This experience can lead to a director's role in influencer marketing, as we are seeing this role emerge at brands such as Adobe, L'Oréal, and other corporations.

Job Posting, Executive Leader and Consumer PR Specialist

Executive Leader and Consumer PR Specialist for Social and Influencer Marketing

Whole Foods Market

Whole Foods Market is seeking a charismatic leader who can work autonomously to integrate, invigorate, and inspire a team of PR, social media, and influencer marketing professionals. This individual will lead the team in designing and implementing consumer PR/social/influencer strategies to boost cultural engagement and cultivate brand love. They will demonstrate deep, exceptional knowledge of trends in each vertical market and be able to "connect the dots" across channels, customers, partners, and programs to identify interdependencies and long-term growth opportunities. In addition to setting cross-channel objectives, developing integrated tactics, and creating powerful messages, storylines, and events, this individual will coalesce a team of social media, influencer, and PR experts to develop and pitch big,

hairy, audacious, measurable ideas that support and take action against the set Annual Strategic Plan.

The ideal candidate will be an innovative, enthusiastic, magnetic individual who is as much a learner as a leader. With a minimum of 12+ years of experience in the consumer PR, social, and influencer marketing functions, the candidate will have a proven track record of galvanizing diverse subject matter experts, finding culture-shifting customer-connection opportunities, troubleshooting quickly and effectively through roadblocks, and focusing on the big picture while balancing daily challenges and opportunities. This person will be a self-starter, a big thinker, and a compelling storyteller who is energetic in spirit, poised in delivery, and relentlessly positive under pressure. This position will report to the VP of Brand and is based in Austin, TX.

(Continued)

(Continued)

Responsibilities	Must Have/Be
• Develop an integrated PR, social, and influencer strategy to align with our annual objectives, strengthen the brand, drive our business, and maximize cultural impact.	• BA/BS degree and 10+ years relevant experience *or* equivalent combination of education and relevant experience
• Collaborate closely with stakeholders across the organization to vision, align on, implement, and measure success of priority tactics.	• Advanced knowledge and understanding of social media platforms, influencer communities, and PR platforms
• Develop a construct for continuous improvement and constant innovation across the social/influencer and PR teams.	• Charismatic people-leader and generous mentor with experience integrating cross-functional teams
• Break down silos (and siloed thinking) to integrate, support, and strategically up-level a team of skilled subject matter experts.	

Source: Adapted from LinkedIn. (n.d.-c). Executive leader, consumer PR, social & influencer marketing: Whole Foods Market. Retrieved from https://www.linkedin.com/jobs/view/executive-leader-consumer-pr-social-influencer-marketing-at-whole-foods-market-1330582828/

Research and Social Media Analyst (Entry to Senior Level)

In public relations, we work with data and do math. Not only do we conduct research, but we embrace it wholeheartedly and integrate it into our media strategies, audience insights, and campaigns. Without data, we would not be able to formulate clear, real-time, creative, and comprehensive strategies for the clients we work with. To succeed in an **analyst** position, we need knowledge in certain programs, tools, and services. We need to know how to collect data, of course—but we must also know how to evaluate it and use those insights in creative and strategic applications. The strategic applications include running campaigns, applying communication audits, or identifying challenges and risks associated with a crisis communications plan.

Job Posting: Analyst for Digital and Social Media

Analyst for Digital and Social Media

Weber Shandwick

What will you be doing?

As an Analyst, you'll lay the groundwork and contribute to the day-to-day analytics needs of our clients and, depending on your experience, either deliver insights independently or in tandem with the Analytics Manager across:

• Social listening

• Audience profiling and influencers identification

• Analyzing data sets to extract key findings

• Implementing measurement and evaluation frameworks

- Performance monitoring
- Audience segmentation
- Campaign and monthly reporting
- Website reporting
- Understanding of media channel landscapes

Who are you?

- We are looking for both entry-level and analysts with a little experience, keen to work in the media, digital, and/or social domain. We know there is no unicorn (and if you are one please get in touch ASAP) but we hope your experience fulfills at least some of the below:

- Good knowledge of Excel and PowerPoint
- Analytical and numerate with the ability to learn fast
- Problem-solving mentality
- Experience with either reporting, social media monitoring, or digital tools
- Good understanding of business KPIs
- An appetite for challenge, innovation, and learning new skills
- Ability to work both independently and within a team
- Someone who enjoys a fast-paced environment
- Some basic coding skills in SQL, R, or Python (optional but a good bonus)

Source: Adapted from LinkedIn. (n.d.-a). Analyst (digital/social): Weber Shandwick. Retrieved from https://www.linkedin.com/jobs/view/analyst-digital-social-at-weber-shandwick-1645037027/?originalSubdomain=uk

How Do We Decide Where to Work?

One of the major decisions that we make as we enter the field of public relations is: Where do we want to work? PR agencies operate somewhat differently compared to other corporate settings. At corporations, things are structured, formal, and tied to regulations, especially if the corporation is a publicly traded company. PR agencies, on the other hand, have their own business practices and are considered to be external to the client company. This gives PR professionals the opportunity to gain experience working in different fields and areas and with a diverse listing of clients. This is quite different from working at a company that operates in only select markets in the industry. While the options for how and where to apply ourselves are more diverse and open than ever, we must begin by understanding the expectations that will be placed on us as new employees. We need to think about our potential roles and responsibilities, and to what extent the overall culture of a given workplace will benefit us (or not).

Many professionals in public relations today have either (1) majored in public relations in college through an established program, (2) worked in a related area such as journalism or communication and made the move to public relations, or (3) come in from a completely different field (e.g., English or graphic design) and made a big jump over to public relations for the opportunity to expand their professional growth. Universities across the world have established PR programs, and the number continues to rise each year.

As discussed in the previous section on careers and job titles, there are some new skills that we need to be aware of. Table 13.3 outlines these skills and how to get them.

Before deciding what area of public relations you want to work in, and where you may want to work, it's important to explore several matters about future employers.

New Skills for PR Professionals and How to Get Them

Skill	How to Obtain It
Writing in multiple channels	Freelance, guest blog, guest contributors
Research (traditional and social)	Certifications (Google Analytics, Facebook Blueprint, HubSpot, Talkwalker, SEMrush, and Brandwatch)
Creativity	Attend conferences, events, and sessions outside of public relations
Visual or video	Adobe Education Exchange, YouTube, books (e.g., *Vlog Like a Boss* by Amy Schmittauer), follow creators and tutorials, host virtual summits and conferences (Zoom, Microsoft Teams, etc.), record vlogs and tutorials (Adobe Premiere or Adobe Premiere Rush)
Social media	Certifications (Hootsuite, HubSpot, Stukent, Facebook Blueprint), freelance and consult, webinars, digital workshops
Strategic planning	Class clients, agency experience, internships
Diversity	Trainings, webinars, diverse experiences working with multiple teams from different backgrounds
Integrated business	Courses in business, business certifications, marketing certifications

Understand work environments and cultures.

You want to be in an environment where you can do your best work and have the opportunity to learn, grow, and contribute to the greater good for your clients. Toxic environments—for example, workplaces that foster unhealthy competition, or where coworkers steal each other's work—are not places you want to be. A better environment is one that gives you access to mentorship and education. Learning does not stop after classes are over or we walk offstage at graduation. In fact, a commitment to lifelong learning is essential in our field, which changes and evolves every day. Find out how much of an investment your prospective employer makes in workshop trainings, conferences, certifications, and other professional development opportunities.

Explore differences in salaries.

If you are motivated by money (cue Tom Cruise in *Jerry Maguire*: "Show me the money!"), then listen up. According to Indeed (2020), a PR intern might make an average of $33,651 per year while a director of marketing might earn $93,330. Also, it's important to know that salaries vary according to your geographic location. In New York City, you would likely make more money than you would in Boston, but you would also pay for a higher cost of living. Salaries also vary according to experience levels. The more leadership, managerial, and strategic duties you have under your belt, the more money you are going to get. If you work outside of public relations, the industry you choose matters, as well as your area of focus and specialization.

Be aware of organizational structures—and where public relations happens.

While public relations as an area of focus has matured, there are still some subtle differences in its applications across businesses and industries. If you plan to apply for a position, find out what skills you will need for that specific organization. For example, if you apply to an organization such as General Motors, and the PR department is part of marketing, then you will be reporting to the chief marketing officer (CMO). In that case, you'll need to tie your work and experience to marketing's goals, objectives, language, and style of content creation. The same applies in other fields as well. In a journalism setting, a social media professional needs to understand the writing, reporting, and research requirements and also know the importance of deadlines. The content we produce in a journalism setting must follow the structure, format, and style of the particular publication.

The PR field is filled with opportunities. There is no right or wrong way to approach your work experience trajectory. It all comes down to where you want to be, whom you want to work with, and where your professional goals take you in each part of your journey.

Consider large agencies.

One of the more popular routes that students take, after graduating from a four-year program, is to go to New York City, Chicago, or another large city to work for a large agency and gain experience. These agencies have some of the biggest clients on record and offer numerous services and areas of expertise. Working for such employers can give you a range of experience with clients and even areas of specialization. Examples of large PR agencies include Edelman, Golin, FleishmanHillard, and Ketchum. However, some traditionally founded advertising agencies now offer PR services, so this is another trend to explore for potential work. Ogilvy, Droga5, Wieden+Kennedy, and R/GA all offer some PR services for their clients.

Look into boutique agencies.

Boutique agencies specialize either in one aspect of public relations (e.g., media relations) or in a particular industry (e.g., public affairs or crisis communication). Compared with larger agencies, these smaller agencies can offer you a more specialized focus and level of expertise for handling specific tasks, channels, and strategies.

Learn about brands and corporations.

Brands can serve as their own social media outlets, telling their own stories of success with clients and campaigns. Most of these brands use their blogs to share case studies on what has and has not worked. Among these brands are Target, Airbnb, Papa John's, and Facebook, to name a few. Many times, brands focus on tools that provide services, training, and education for other organizations and individuals.

PR teams that work within large organizations create content and stories for internal and external audiences, monitor online conversations about their organizations, and proactively address customer concerns through their PR and social media practices. Adidas, Twitter, Tesla, and General Motors are just a few examples of brands that have their own internal teams of PR professionals. However, in these cases, the in-house professionals also work with outside agency professionals who are brought in to handle certain tactical and strategic elements for a brand. For example, General Motors might hire Weber Shandwick to focus on corporate account strategies for its corporate brand, but bring on FleishmanHillard to work specifically on creative strategies and message design for Chevy.

Check out nonprofit organizations.

Nonprofits of course employ PR professionals, but the resources at these organizations are not as plentiful as they are at corporate institutions. Those who work in the nonprofit sector take on multiple responsibilities, and in some cases, they do it all. Knowing how to fundraise, how to evoke powerful emotion, and how to persuade audiences to take action are some of the qualities we need to work in this industry.

Consider politics, sports, and entertainment.

Each of these specializations is very competitive, time-intensive, and ever-changing. Politics, sports, and entertainment professionals have to be skilled media relations strategists, planners, crisis managers, and innovators in the field. They have to be both **generalists** (professionals who know all aspects of public relations) and **specialists** (experts in a particular area of public relations or in the field). All three of these specializations are discussed in Chapter 14.

Think about small businesses.

Small businesses are a vibrant part of our economy, and a key group that needs strong PR efforts to promote their products and services.

Explore freelance or consultancy options.

Being a **freelancer** is one of the more popular avenues for working in public relations because this role gives us the flexibility and the independence to choose our clients and projects. Freelancers tend to focus on certain types of projects and particular areas within social media such as social media writing, content creation, videography, and **social media strategy**.

A **consultant** typically works with clients to share their ideas, but may not necessarily produce or execute the content proposed. Consultants usually need to have worked as a PR professional for several years (or, in some cases and in certain specializations in public relations, decades) to solidify their credibility to be hired. As a consultant, you are able to choose your own clients, set your rates (based on the level of experience and time you give to a project), and choose your areas of specialization. Melissa Agnes, an international consultant, specializes in crisis communication trainings for brands and nonprofit organizations. In addition, Dorothéa Bozicolona-Volpe, an entrepreneur with her own business called Social Espionage, focuses on influencer marketing based on her years of experience working with brands such as L'Oréal and Ryan Seacrest. Both professionals built their reputation through years of experience, projects, and presentations to provide them with a global reputation as highly sought-after consultants in the field.

Explore the entrepreneurial option.

Start-ups are the fastest-growing employers in need of PR professionals. It's one thing to develop a new product, service, or idea, but it's another to promote it and tell its story to key audiences. Some entrepreneurs have gravitated to social media to tell their own stories for their brands, as has Hi-Five Doughnuts in Louisville, Kentucky, which has also integrated public relations into its strategic plans for being featured in targeted food and travel publications and media outlets. This is an example of how a small business can establish a strong presence in a visual, yet strategic, manner. All of the visual cues (highlights, branding, etc.) are present and accounted for, and there is a strong alignment with

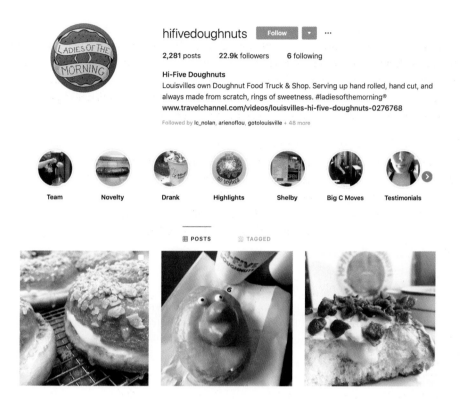

the purpose of the business. In public relations, consistency in presentation in messaging, voice, and visuals is a key element in making sure clients are effective in their engagement with their key publics. Content and presentation are just part of the puzzle here for successful efforts in PR message strategies and creative execution initiatives—there has to be engagement and dialogue between our clients (in this case, a small doughnut shop) and their publics. If publics have all of these elements, they are more likely to engage and do business with our clients. All of these factors help build a mutually beneficial relationship.

What Are Best Practices for Building a Career in Public Relations?

Going to school and studying public relations is just the beginning of building a career. To succeed in the field requires that you work continuously to build your career, reputation, and personal brand as a PR professional. The following are some best practices for how to accomplish this.

1. **Know the benefits and challenges of working in public relations.** There are many benefits to working in public relations, yet there are also several challenges that need to be addressed and accounted for. Public relations offers a constant change of pace, depending on where you are working. No one day is the same, which allows you to do multiple things for different accounts at one time. Also, because our field is constantly changing, you will never be "bored." Keep in mind that ours is a competitive industry where time, resources, and client work

are constantly being fought over. In some circumstances, it's fair to compare the PR world with the show *Game of Thrones*. Everyone wants to be on the "Iron Throne" of public relations, which makes ours a fast-paced and competitive market. In addition, our work is sometimes overlooked or overshadowed by other fields, such as marketing and advertising. But remember that public relations is much more—it is a growing strategic, systematic, and vibrant field that has connections with many other disciplines.

2. **Start small and work your way up in public relations.** Landing a big, high-paying job does not happen overnight. Take the time to hone your skills and make sure you are learning and growing as a professional. Keep in mind that such things take time, and that it's best to work at gaining experience, establishing relationships, and continuing to grow. Moving forward is the most important strategy.

3. **It's not only about what you know, but also about whom you know (and who knows you).** For some positions in public relations, it's all about who knows you. Invest not only in your skills, but in building networks and communities as well. Speak at local events, volunteer at professional functions, be a guest on a blog or webinar, or write content to share with various communities to develop your thought leadership. Remember to keep building on your personal brand—your reputation.

Having a single job in public relations may not be enough. Whether you are a PR manager or leading a team, consider having another job on the side, or a "side hustle." This means you might start a consulting business, invest in a start-up, take on videography or photography projects, or give paid presentations at speaking engagements, conferences, and functions. It's about taking the time to create engagement not only for your personal brand, but also for your community.

4. **Social media is a significant skill. Embrace it.** Social media is an integrated part of what PR professionals are responsible for today. Almost every job requires social media skills. Understanding the how, the why, and the impact that social media has on messaging, content creation, storytelling, and relationship management is key.

5. **Picture where you'd like to see yourself working.** Do you see yourself working in a cubicle, responding in real time to customer inquiries in a matter of seconds for one primary brand? Do you see yourself working at an agency where you have a variety of different projects, brands, and clients? Or do you see yourself taking the entrepreneurial route, where you are your own boss and company?

SUMMARY

The PR field is constantly changing. Our job titles and roles will continue evolving, layering in new features, responsibilities, and skills that we need to embrace to succeed in our work with clients and audiences inside and outside of our organizations or agencies. As we enter the field of public relations, it's important to know what's expected of us: We need to have traditional PR skills (research, writing, etc.), we need to be creative, and we need to keep learning new things (social media, entrepreneurship, data analysis, etc.) to become marketable candidates for future positions. The rule is this: If you're entering the PR field, don't be like everyone else; don't be a "cookie-cutter" professional. Succeeding in public relations is about owning your own story and brand, committing to lifelong learning and experience, and building the unique contributions you can offer to the field.

GAME CHANGER

Dave Remund, APR, Fellow PRSA, Executive Director of Drake University Communications and Marketing

Courtesy of Dave Remund

How did you get your start in public relations?

My first full-time position was with a statewide banking association. Our team was small, and I had an active hand in everything from member communications and media relations to product marketing and government relations. The diversity of that role, plus the opportunity to actively manage programs on my own, helped me transition to agency work within a year, and then to my first corporate management role several years later.

What is your favorite part of working in public relations?

Every day is different. There are so many challenges, and the challenges are constantly changing. I enjoy keeping a pulse on issues, collaborating to find solutions, and helping people and organizations adapt. The work is demanding yet also incredibly gratifying.

What is the most challenging part of working in public relations?

Being in the middle. You are always in the middle of some problem or opportunity; you are also often in the middle of a difference of opinions. That's why having a strong set of values is so important. That ethical core is what helps you stay the course, personally and professionally.

Who do you think are the biggest game changers for the PR industry?

Those who must fight for their opinions and concerns to be heard. Social and digital media have somewhat leveled the playing field. But it's still an uphill battle for many marginalized communities and causes. It takes persistence, vision, and innovation to break through the clutter and truly engage people's hearts and minds.

What are some things you wish you knew when you were starting out in public relations?

There are several things I wish I had known: how stressful this profession can be, how dramatically technology can influence communication, and how family and friends never seem to fully understand what PR practitioners do for a living!

David Remund serves as the chief communications and marketing officer for his alma mater, Drake University. Prior to this administrative appointment, Remund taught full-time within the School of Journalism and Mass Communication at Drake, and later for the University of Oregon. He has also made educational exchanges to Asia, Europe, and South America.

Before entering the academy, Remund designed and managed corporate-wide strategic communications programs for Bank of America, Principal Financial Group, and multiple divisions of Wells Fargo & Company. He had also worked for two regional agencies, most recently as a director of strategic planning for clients ranging in size from start-up to Fortune 250.

Remund has served as a Legacy Scholar with the Arthur W. Page Center for Integrity in Public Communication and as a fellow of the Plank Center for Leadership in Public Relations. He earned his doctorate from the University of North Carolina at Chapel Hill in 2011, and has been nationally accredited by the Public Relations Society of America (PRSA) since 2003. In 2015, PRSA named Remund to its prestigious College of Fellows.

CASE STUDY

Jimmy Fallon and Jake Sirianni: Using Performance and Parody to Get an Internship

NBCUniversal/Getty Images

As a communication student at Washington State University, Jake Sirianni wanted to land an internship with *The Tonight Show Starring Jimmy Fallon*, and wanted to do something to get Fallon's attention and perhaps be offered a position. With the use of Adobe products and editing skills, Jake was able to re-create a popular segment from the show (originally featuring *Harry Potter* actor Daniel Radcliffe) to persuade the *Tonight Show* host to hire him on for an internship. As a result of his efforts going viral and becoming a top trending story worldwide, Jake was able to get the internship he wanted.

Why did this case generate buzz?

- Jake's parody took a current, timely, and creative approach to getting the attention of someone who perhaps gets millions of internship requests and submissions and allowed him to stand out from the crowd.

- It was a creative new way of tying in interest, passion, skills, and a unique take on understanding the client he was trying to persuade to hire him.

- The video was entertaining and shareable. After it went viral, Fallon announced on his show he would bring Jake on as an intern.

What are the ethical and legal issues?

- As with all entertainment segments, there might be issues pertaining to copyright that could have been addressed here for Jake.

- If people did not like the content, it could have caused a backlash. While this situation did not happen, it could have.

What are some takeaways from this case?

- Jake embraced new skills to separate his story, skill set, and voice from other internship seekers. These are skills and ideas not previously emphasized (or even encouraged!) in most academic situations.

- Jake thought outside of the box. This took time, investment, and strategic thinking. These are the types of things brands, agencies, and professionals look for in applicants for positions. If Jake submitted just a regular résumé and cover letter, he would not have gotten the job. Instead, he took a creative risk, and it paid off.

APR EXAM

- Leadership and organizational skills

- Understanding the PR function

KEY TERMS

Account director 275

Account executive 272

Account specialist 274

Analyst 282

Communication manager 276

Consultant 286

Content creator 279

Copywriter 277

Freelancer 286

Generalist 286

Influencer relations 281

Intern 269

Internship 266

Media relations specialist/publicist 276

PR coordinator 273

Social media manager 281

Social media strategist 286

Specialist 286

DISCUSSION QUESTIONS

1. What are the different industries in which you can work in public relations? What are some similarities and differences in the roles?

2. Identify the difference between an account executive and an account specialist.

3. Name three new skills that professionals need to have to work in public relations.

4. What are the key things to note when applying for a PR position?

ACTIVITIES

Building Your Portfolio

Digital portfolio. When you are applying for your first job or internship, you need to create a digital portfolio to showcase your work. Outline the components you will want to have on hand for this digital portfolio:
- Mission and vision statement
- Résumé (infographic)
- Brand kit (your logo, etc.)
- Work samples (media kits, influencer work, etc.)
- Creative works (video and design)
- Social media
- Internship and fellowship experiences

Once you have created this list, explore the best sites for where you can host these materials and brand your digital portfolio.

Sites to explore to host your digital portfolio include WordPress and Squarespace.

Building Your Brand

Reviewing your skill set. This chapter covered various roles PR professionals can take on, along with some sample job ads. Look at the lists of sought-after skills and experiences, and ask yourself the following questions:
- What position do I want to take on for an internship or job after graduation?
- What skills and experiences do I have now that would make me a qualified applicant?
- What are skills and experiences I need to have?
- List three tasks you will take on to address the missing skills and experiences you need for your desired position.

SPECIALIZATIONS

....

Introduction

As you have explored this book, you've learned about the integrated nature of public relations, its creative innovations, and its evidence-based practices. We have discussed the core areas within public relations that need to be emphasized (e.g., diversity and inclusion, ethics, measurement, and research) and the steps to take to implement and execute a strategic plan. Many industries have embraced public relations, showing the power of PR work and the necessity for it across different sectors. No one industry or specialization dominates public relations, but each area shows the field in a different light and works with a different set of audiences. PR efforts are foundational to how all organizations, clients, and brands communicate and build relationships and communities, on- and offline.

At its core, public relations is an applied field of practice, meaning that the focus is not only on exploring why and how we build and maintain relationships, theoretically speaking, but also on how we actually do this in the real world. Career-wise, public relations offers a range of roles and at the same time provides professionals with opportunities to move into specialized areas. In this chapter, we will cover some of the areas of specialization; each section gives an overview of the specialization, identifies its primary focus, and highlights case studies and examples of professionals at work in these areas. Best practices and expectations are noted in each section as well. What follows is just a snapshot of the emerging, established, and innovative areas within our field. Each specialization could fill its own book! Included in this chapter is coverage of the following:

- Reputation management
- Crisis communication
- Influencer marketing
- Global public relations

- Social media public relations
- Entertainment and sports public relations
- Nonprofit public relations
- Politics public relations

Reputation Management: What Is It? How Is It Done?

One area that continues to grow as an area of expertise for PR professionals is **reputation management**. A **reputation** can take decades to build, but be damaged in mere seconds. The duties of a reputation manager typically include these:

- Conducting risk assessments on clients' reputations within their own industries, as well as on previous behavior, financial standings, and other factors
- Listening to and monitoring social media traffic, review sites, mentions, and overall tone and messages from audience members
- Engaging in content creation to help amplify a brand to audiences, whether in good or in challenging times
- Performing content removal (following or during a crisis)
- Engaging with key media professionals, such as trade publications, media outlets, and influencers
- Repairing a reputation in a time of crisis (Spilka, 2019)

The Focus of Reputation Management

In some circles, reputation management falls under public relations, but others argue that it is a separate and different area entirely (Reputation X, 2019). Reputation X, a consulting firm for reputation management practices, discusses how public relations is different from reputation management by outlining the following components:

1. Reputation management is focused on working behind the scenes, whereas public relations is more focused on working on the front lines.

2. Reputation management is specialized and integrated, whereas public relations is broader in nature.

3. Reputation management is focused on preserving the overall image of a brand, whereas public relations deals with the essence of the brand.

Examples of Reputation Management

Celebrities experience reputation crises that require them to restore how their audiences perceive their brand. Time to call a reputation manager.

Tiger Woods

Tiger Woods, who has enjoyed a resurgence of his brand's value and gained endorsements after winning the 2019 Masters Tournament, had earlier challenges in his personal life with cheating allegations and arrest records, which required the help of a reputation manager.

Nike

Nike, a major player in the sports and athletic apparel business, has also experienced a corporate reputation crisis. The brand is known for campaigns featuring athletes Colin Kaepernick and Serena Williams, and for leading the charge for equal pay for the U.S. women's national soccer team in 2019. However, in 2018, Nike's leaders found themselves at a crossroads in terms of how consumers perceived the brand. Why? Nike had been facing a lawsuit for gender bias and equal pay issues within the corporation (Blumberg, 2019). Ex-employees of Nike publicized this issue, causing audiences to take notice of the contrary information and shift their perceptions of Nike and the company's PR efforts. When there is a discrepancy, reputation dissonance occurs. If a brand boasts shining attributes for others to praise, but the brand's behaviors do not reflect these attributes, there is cause for concern. As a result, audiences get confused about which perspectives to believe, and discussion and clarification is the only thing that can help.

The evolution of digital media and platforms has provided an opportunity for organizations to define their identities and measure their reputation messages on a global scale. Tools that show how brands are being defined by others online, such as Reputation.com and BrandYourself, present new challenges for professionals who know that the power of identity and the value of reputation messaging are critical pieces of any effective communications strategy.

Reputation messages can include content that expresses audience impressions and attitudes toward an organization. Reputation messages can be found in the news media, in user-generated media, in trade journals, and in government publications, among other places. Reputations are built over time by constructing a solid foundation of values, ethical practices, and a sound mission statement that is carried out by those involved with the organization. Further, a strong reputation can increase media exposure (Jackson, 2004) and provide other advantages such as maintaining long-term customers who may grant a reprieve in a crisis situation (Fombrun & Rindova, 2000).

Best Practices for Working in Reputation Management

1. **Remember: Actions can speak louder than words**. In a time where authenticity and trust are needed more than ever, it's crucial to be aware of what you're saying—but also aware of what you're doing. Everything has to be aligned for a reputation to be rock solid.

2. **Never assume you are invincible, even if you have a strong reputation**. *Under Siege 2*, starring Steven Seagal, has a great line in it: "Assumptions are the mother of all #$W@%^" (you get the point). Essentially, if you "assume" that nothing can touch or hurt you, you're putting yourself at risk. Reputations are our most priceless possessions, as well as those of our clients.

3. **Know the importance of your character and reputation**. Sometimes people's **character** is forgotten in light of their reputation or celebrity status. However, as the famous basketball coach John Wooden has been quoted as stating: "Be more

SPECIALIZATIONS

There are many industries that have embraced public relations in their fields, showing the power and need for public relations efforts across different sectors. No one industry or specialization dominates public relations, but each area shows the field in a different light and audience. Public relations is a core part of how all organizations, individuals, and brands communicate and foster relationships to build communities across all sorts of boundaries, physically and digitally.

REPUTATION MANAGEMENT

1

- Conduct risk analysis for their clients on their industry, previous behaviors, financial standings, perceptions in the industry, etc.
- Listen and monitor for social media traffic, review sites, mentions, and overall tone from audience members
- Create content to help amplify brand to audiences in good and challenging times
- Remove content (in light of being in a crisis)

CRISIS COMMUNICATION

2

- Craft effective crisis messages, strategies, and statements for client
- Evaluate media coverage before, during, and after a crisis
- Prepare teams and identify early warning signs for potential crises and risks
- Provide media training for senior leadership and spokespeople
- Prepare for crises through trainings and workshops

INFLUENCER MARKETING

3

- Research, identify, and engage influencers
- Evaluate influencer performance and analysis of impact
- Coordinate partnerships with brands and influencers
- Identify costs and budgeting for influencers
- Create events, experiences, and opportunities for brands and influencers

INFOGRAPHIC 14

How We Specialize

GLOBAL PUBLIC RELATIONS

4

- Understand the culture, history, communities, and public relations practices in each country
- Communicate in different languages and formats to engage with audiences
- Implement strategies through media channels to reach targeted audiences

SOCIAL MEDIA & VIDEOGRAPHY

5

- Include multiple roles (paid media, content strategists, creator, customer service representative, PR, and more!)
- Create, brainstorm, and evaluate content
- Coordinate with influencers and creators on social media
- Tell stories through various formats
- Engage in planning steps to create best content for designated platform
- Emphasize storytelling aspects in content to spark emotion and response

ENTERTAINMENT AND SPORTS

- Pitch for their client to be on a cover or feature in a magazine
- Formulate partnerships with endorsement deals and media coverage
- Work with videographers, creators, and social media professionals
- Coordinate efforts for photo shoots, media interviews, exclusives, and partnerships
- Document and showcase the content for the celebrity across social channels
- Write content (press releases, media kits, blog posts and updates, etc.) to be shared across channels
- Conduct media training for interviews, media tours, and premieres

concerned with your character than your reputation, because your character is *what you really are*, while your reputation is merely *what others think you are*."

Crisis Communication: What Is It? How Is It Done?

If you want to have a guaranteed job in the PR field, then crisis communication is a good choice of specialization. There is always a crisis happening, and when you think you've seen it all, just wait. Something new, outrageous, and devastating for a brand, organization, or individual is just around the corner, ready to hurt a brand financially and emotionally, ready to ruin the brand's reputation. Reputation management and crisis communication in public relations usually go hand in hand because professionals in both specialty areas operate with the same scope and objectives: to protect a brand's image, character, and standing in the eyes of the brand's audiences.

The Focus of Crisis Communication

While the day-to-day experience of the professionals behind an organization or brand is generally positive, there are also negatively charged events and stories that distort daily activities and cause financial, emotional, and even personal harm to those involved.

These situations are conceptualized as crises. **Crises** come in various forms and can happen at any time. In other words, crises are significant, disruptive events that often feature a rapid onset (Coombs, 2013). Crises have been defined as events that either cause harm to or have the potential to harm an individual or organization. Whether the harm produces physical, emotional, or environmental damage to those involved in the crisis, or damage to the corporate reputation or financial standing of an organization, the type and scale of harm is different in each situation. To have a full understanding of a crisis, we must identify the precipitating event and learn what happened between that trigger point and the moments that stakeholders perceived a crisis. We need to know not only what happened, but also how and why it happened, and how long it took.

There are many roles that PR professionals take on in crisis communication, which requires us to design, create, and execute messages effectively. Coombs (2013) described seven crisis communication message strategies:

1. **Attack the accuser**. The crisis manager confronts the person or group claiming something is wrong with the organization.

2. **Denial**. The crisis manager asserts that there is no crisis.

3. **Excuse**. The crisis manager minimizes organizational responsibility by denying intent to do harm and/or claiming inability to control the events that triggered the crisis.

4. **Justification**. The crisis manager minimizes the perceived damage caused by the crisis.

5. **Ingratiation**. The crisis manager praises stakeholders for their action.

6. **Corrective action**. The crisis manager offers money or other gifts to victims.

7. **Full apology**. The crisis manager indicates that the organization takes full responsibility for the crisis and asks stakeholders for forgiveness.

Types of Crises

Victim	Accidental	Preventable
Natural disasters: Acts of nature occur such as tornadoes or earthquakes. *Rumors*: False and damaging information is being circulated about your organization. *Workplace violence*: A former or current employee attacks current employees onsite. *Product tampering/malevolence*: An external agent causes damage to the organization.	*Challenges*: A stakeholder claims that the organization is operating in an inappropriate manner. *Technical error accidents*: Equipment or technology failure causes an industrial accident. *Technical error product harm*: Equipment or technology failure causes a product to be defective or potentially harmful.	*Human-error accidents*: An industrial accident is caused by human error. *Human-error product harm*: A product is defective or potentially harmful because of human error. *Organizational misdeed*: Management actions put stakeholders at risk and/or violate the law.

Professor Timothy Coombs (2013) at Texas A&M University discusses how a **social media crisis** is different from other crises by highlighting the fact that a social media crisis happens on social media or on a particular platform, rapidly spreads from person to person, and spreads virally to become a news story. Coombs also describes various types of crises based on attribution of responsibility to those involved (e.g., brands, PR professionals, and senior leaders, to name a few). As illustrated in Table 14.1, victim crises have minimal crisis responsibilities; that is, those who are impacted by the crisis have little to no responsibility for what happened during the crisis. Accidental crises also have minimal levels of responsibility; some blame is attributed to the parties in question, but not as much as in preventable crises. Preventable crises have the highest level of responsibility and are most often talked about because they could have been prevented, and they cause the most outrage because the early warning signs that pointed to these events could have been addressed.

Examples of Crisis Communication

It is important to note that crises are not created equally. They can strike anytime, take different forms, and create different situations. Examples include natural disasters (e.g., earthquakes, floods, and hurricanes), workplace or school violence (e.g., the Parkland, Florida, school shooting), corporate incidents (e.g., Papa John's), scandals (e.g., Harvey Weinstein and Kevin Spacey), and other crises that have been covered in crisis literature. Let's take a look at some of these cases to evaluate and discuss the effectiveness of crisis communication.

Boeing

Airplane manufacturer Boeing has faced serious challenges with its 737 MAX model. Two deadly crashes involved the 737 MAX, one in Indonesia in October 2018 and another in Ethiopia in March 2019, both of which sparked outrage and a media storm for the brand worldwide (Arenstein, 2019). Pilots quickly reported that Boeing's simulation trainings on 737s were extensive, yet optional, raising concerns that the crises could have been prevented (Arenstein, 2019). As a result, Boeing lost $3.38 billion for

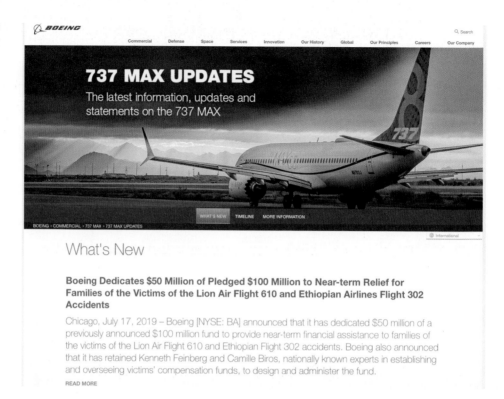

Boeing's dedicated page on news and updates for 737 MAX activities

Retrieved at https://www.boeing.com/commercial/737max/737-max-update.page#/timeline

the quarter on $15.7 billion in revenue, and has temporarily shut down production of the 737 MAX (Gregg, 2019). As Boeing's former CEO Dennis Muilenburg stated to investors, "This is a defining moment for Boeing, and we're committed to coming through this challenging time better and stronger as a company" (Gregg, 2019). The brand has since created a microsite dedicated to the 737 MAX for audiences to follow (boeing.com/737-max-updates). There, as part of its crisis communication efforts, Boeing provides news releases, updates, a timeline of events, and other points of information for customers and other audiences.

SoulCycle

The popular exercise and spin company SoulCycle faced backlash on several fronts in 2019 when it was faced with a number of high-profile crises. First, the company came out with its own on-demand bike to compete with the popular direct-to-consumer brand Peloton. It was revealed that the founder of Peloton had pitched the idea to SoulCycle before starting Peloton, but SoulCycle did not want to work with the founder. Second, SoulCycle has faced outrage and boycotts in response to the actions of Stephen Ross, founder of the parent company Equinox, who raised funds for President Donald Trump's reelection campaign (Ingraham, 2019). Celebrities and others went on social media, particularly Instagram, to state they were leaving SoulCycle and dropping their membership because Ross hosted a $250,000 Trump fundraiser (Hamblin, 2019). The brand has been dealing with mixed messages from SoulCycle franchise owners as well as the parent company itself. Organizations need a strong presence and consistent message that is shared and articulated across the board. If there are mixed messages, the result is confusion and possible escalation of the crisis.

To our Soul family,

At SoulCycle, we wake up every day committed to our community, and creating a safe space where all are welcome. We believe in diversity, inclusion, and equality. SoulCycle in no way endorses the political fundraising event being held later this week. SoulCycle has nothing to do with the event and does not support it. Consistent with our policies, no company profits are used to fund politicians. We're committed to all our riders and the communities we live in. Mr. Ross is a passive investor and is not involved in the management of SoulCycle. We'll always stay true to our values and committed to our community. We know who we are and we know what we believe in, and nothing will ever change that.

Melanie Whelan, Rider and CEO

Coach and Versace

The Coach and Versace companies came under fire because a T-shirt they promoted in China referred to Macau and Hong Kong as separate countries, rather than as Chinese colonies (Togoh, 2019). Donatella Versace, head of the Versace brand, released the following statement on the incident: "Never have I wanted to disrespect China's National Sovereignty and this is why I wanted to personally apologize for such inaccuracy and for any distress that it might have caused" (Togoh, 2019). What Versace did and what other fashion brands do to minimize damage is to act quickly, apologize, and take action to make sure the crisis is/was handled in an effective and transparent manner.

Best Practices for Working in Crisis Communication

Nearly all PR professionals will experience a crisis in their brand history or career, but how you handle the situation determines whether or not you will be able to recover. Don't worry—here are some best practices to keep in mind and use as a resource for your future efforts in crisis communication:

1. *Honesty is the best policy.* Telling the truth and not misleading people is a good practice in general. Taking responsibility for actions that led up to the crisis is crucial. It may hurt the business or reputation at first, but it is better than denying or, worse yet, lying about it.

2. *Never say "no comment."* What is the kiss of death to our credibility and honesty in public relations? Saying "no comment" to a reporter. "No comment" gives the impression that you are hiding something and may be guilty. If you do not yet have the information to respond to a question or crisis, clearly state you are gathering the information, and that you will provide an update at a scheduled time.

3. *Be accessible and available.* It's not the media we need to worry about during a crisis, but our online communities. If you have a digital or social media presence and

touchpoint for audience members to contact you, you must be present in that space (or spaces) to hear what they are saying, commenting on, and asking about. Monitor and listen with media tools such as Cision, Meltwater, Zignal Labs, and Salesforce. Use the data you gather to determine audiences' main concerns and the individuals who are driving the conversation.

4. *Train, educate, and train some more.* Crisis communication is all about planning and thinking ahead. This means we and our teams need education, constant training, and workshops on the latest cases and strategies to make everyone as prepared as possible to handle any situation. Simulations are a great way to discover who is prepared and how well, and where improvement is needed. All statements, plans, message strategies, and decision maps should be on hand before a crisis hits. Otherwise, you'll find yourself in complete and total chaos as you try to create these items in the midst of a crisis. No amount of coffee will help you handle this.

Influencer Marketing: What Is It? How Is It Done?

As explained in Chapter 9 on audiences and relationship management, influencers are a growing audience for brands, organizations, and PR agencies. Influencer marketing has become its own area of specialization within the disciplines of public relations, marketing, advertising, and communication. Many boutique agencies have formed teams dedicated to the arena of influencer marketing practices.

However, influencers come in many flavors, and their work is increasingly being tied into our PR practices. From attracting influencers who are niche in focus (micro influencers) to creating stories and content that resonates with audiences, influencer marketing has become its own scientific yet creative area within our field (Sheridan, 2019). There are many influencer campaigns to use as examples of what to do and what not to do.

Examples of Influencer Marketing

Let's look at a few companies and brands that are working with influencers in new and strategic ways. These examples show what is involved in influencer marketing and reflect the innovation of ideas generated by this specialized area.

Adidas

The famous global shoe company Adidas is no stranger to the use of influencers in campaign efforts. From presenting iconic sports figures, such as Billie Jean King at the U.S. Open, to growing an industry of creators with its "Here to Create" campaign, Adidas has added a new twist by empowering influencers not only to increase its brand awareness but to help themselves, too. In its new initiatives, Adidas has allowed influencers to sell their own products on the company's social media channels, particularly on Instagram, with the hope that influencers will reap the rewards of the partnership (Beer, 2019).

The U.S. Navy

Who says the armed forces can't use influencers? The U.S. Navy has done so in a way that pushes the envelope of what influencers can do for organizations, brands, and entities within industries. Influencer marketing has no boundaries and can be applied anywhere—as long as there is a strong rationale, purpose, and strategy behind it. The Navy launched a campaign called "Sailor VS," allowing three influencers who have a voice in the armed forces community to gain unprecedented access to experiences. They got to enjoy exclusive views of a Navy ship, experience what it's like to be a sailor, and interview and chat with key personnel as they documented, shared, and used their stories to engage their community (McAteer, 2019). This opened up conversations between the Navy and potential recruits, fans, and others who are curious to see what it is like to be part of the Navy's communities.

Microsoft

One of the biggest brands to use influencers to compete with other large brands, such as Amazon, is Microsoft. A person named Ninja, who was one of Amazon's biggest influencers for its Twitch brand, switched sides and signed exclusively with Microsoft (Tassi, 2019). This case shows that influencers are not just engaged individuals with large followings. They are business professionals looking for partnerships to benefit them both from a brand standpoint and from an innovative and futuristic perspective. Influencers want to invest their time, energy, and resources in relationships built on similar interests and values, and this shows a growing trend for PR professionals to note.

Samsung

The Samsung case is a lesson in what to do before you sign a deal or partner with influencers. Always, always look at what they have shared, posted, and commented on in the past. If what they share is controversial and goes against your brand, walk away. This is what Samsung should have done. Taylor Lorenz, former reporter for the *Atlantic* and now at the *New York Times*, raised some concerns over the racist comments and tweets that GirlWithNoJob (GWNJ) had shared on her account before the announcement of her partnership with Samsung (Schomer, 2019). Samsung had to address this openly after stories and comments arose in response to Lorenz's comments.

Best Practices for Working in Influencer Marketing

As we look to the future of influencer marketing, we need know and implement some best practices. This area of specialization is evolving and will likely become more mainstream. Understanding the fluidity of influencer marketing is the name of the game for staying on top of trends, issues, case studies, and resources.

1. *Research and data are your friends.* Get to know who has a natural tie to your brand and a vested interest in it. Among these people are the individuals to partner with. Investing in tools including Traackr, Zoomph, and Talkwalker will be helpful in connecting with audiences and future influencers. Despite the threats of losing key metrics such as "likes" on Instagram, influencer marketing is here to stay (Wong, 2019).

2. *Influencers must be authentic, trustworthy, and relevant to a brand.* Given the many case studies on fake influencers and events that promote unethical practices (e.g., the Fyre Festival), being true to yourself and being relevant to others are essential

GAME CHANGER
Albane Flamant, Talkwalker

How did you get your start in the industry?

That's a complicated one! I have a bit of a mixed background (a BS in communications, a BS in European and international law, and dual master's degrees in journalism and international relations) and worked throughout my studies in different public-oriented organizations.

When I finished my master's program, I was still working for a media website that specializes in labor questions in France and in Europe. It was a great job because I got to learn so much—I was in charge of the website, the social media channels, and the organization of the editorial board; I created infographics; I wrote articles and recorded interviews. . . .

I had a talk with one of my mentors, who encouraged me to go work in the private sector for a while to experience another type of work environment. I liked the idea and started looking for another job.

I had always been fascinated by the topic of online data and its handling—I actually wrote my law school thesis on the topic of the right to be forgotten in the then draft of the General Data Protection Regulation (GDPR). So when I stumbled on a job posting for Talkwalker while browsing job-hunting Facebook groups, I was instantly attracted.

The job posting was for a marketing position, but the skills required seemed very familiar: social media proficiency, blog writing, website management, and so on. I was very interested in the product—a social listening platform—and figured I would give it a shot.

My manager liked my enthusiasm and passion for social media, and I got the job! It's now been four years, and I am still with Talkwalker.

What is your favorite part of working in the industry?

I love the fact that there is always something new to learn. The social media/digital marketing field is constantly evolving, and it takes discipline to keep track of everything. However, I really enjoy seeing new technologies, new algorithms, or new workplace practices spring into life, and try to understand how

they will impact the business as a whole. I frequently get to interact with real experts in marketing and analytics who give me the best insights as to these new trends. These conversations are always the best part of my workday.

What is the most challenging part of working in your industry?

In marketing, there is just no single recipe for success. There are 10,000 things you can do to promote your brand. The difficult part is to remain focused on the ones that will truly help your organization reach its business goals. It's very easy to lose sight of your priorities when you're pressed for time. If you're not able to prioritize, you will drown, even if you work a full 24-hour day.

Who do you think are the biggest game changers for your industry?

It's hard to talk about digital marketing and social media without mentioning artificial intelligence. I see this technology as an incredible opportunity for marketers—just because it will get rid of a lot of manual work I do not enjoy in my day-to-day, which will give me more room to focus on more creative tasks. It's also amazing to see what machine learning can help us do—you can teach machines to read the content of images and videos, or to understand the sentiment expressed in a tweet, almost as well as a human.

Another big trend has definitely been the public pushback against the GAFA platforms to promote data privacy—it will be interesting to see if this translates into actual changes in behavior at all levels, from the tech giants like Google, Apple, Facebook, and Amazon all the way to individual marketing contributors.

What are some things you wish you knew when you were starting out in the industry?

I could talk about some regrets I have, such as not spending enough time learning how to code, or polishing my video taking and editing skills. Yet when

I look back, a big chunk of what I learned in school is no longer relevant to today's industry. The most important skills I learned were reaching further than my future career, such as how to critically analyze information and how to keep learning every step of the way. I only acquired some much-needed context as to the evolution of the industry—given its pace of evolution, you need some perspective to actually understand the real impact of algorithm changes or public opinion reversals.

I think the main things I wish I had known before starting out are linked to the more practical aspects of the life of digital marketers: time management, basics of accounting, what it takes to advocate for a team project or coordinate a project among international teams, and so on.

characteristics of today's influencers. As PR professionals, we need to evaluate these partnerships from strategic and creative viewpoints, and we need to make ethical choices.

3. *Influencers may need training.* Influencers may come armed with flashy media kits and branded videos, but do they have proper communication skills? Do they know crisis management protocols? Are they experienced in media relations? To ensure that they have these skills, we need to conduct workshops and provide training to prepare, educate, and support influencers. It's also important that we convey our expectations.

4. *Make it a win-win situation.* Influencers want established relationships with brands and organizations, relationships that ensure that everyone walks away a winner. Influencers gain experiences to share with their audiences, and brands gain audience exposure and awareness of their activities.

5. *Public relations is constantly evolving.* As we are experiencing a shift in media coverage—that is, a move from mainstream to niche communities—it's a great time to partner with influencers who can help us reach audiences who are invested in them and who trust their perspectives.

6. *Everyone has influence.* Sure, influencers can be great, but we should never put them on a pedestal. They are human beings, just like you and me. Any one of us can be influential if we're willing to take time to invest in our craft, determine the medium we want to create in, and strive to build a community in which we spark dialogue and interest.

Global Public Relations: What Is It? How Is It Done?

Public relations is a global profession. The numbers of professionals, organizations, businesses, and campaigns are growing around the world. To better understand our field, we must explore how public relations is practiced in regions and countries beyond the United States.

The Focus of Global Public Relations

Global public relations is practiced by organizations that include the Global Alliance for Public Relations and Communication Management, the Chartered Institute of Public

Relations, the Public Relations Society of America, the International Public Relations Association, and the Cannes Lions International Festival of Creativity, to name a few. International festivals and conversations give us opportunities to learn, grow, and understand the differences in how public relations is defined and practiced elsewhere. Gaining international awareness can lead us to new knowledge and even to innovative ideas that we can incorporate into our own practices and global learning community.

Examples of Global Public Relations

Of course, there are many global campaigns that we could focus on, but let's take a look at some mini cases. They showcase specific areas of innovation, strategy, and best practices in moving public relations into the next chapter in its professional history.

Burger King and Mexico City

What do you get when a burger brand sets out to connect with customers dealing with some of the world's worst traffic jams? An idea that is innovative and sparks the company to offer a new feature (Diaz, 2019). Burger King's leaders identified a need that their audience had: Drivers were hungry and stuck in traffic. To meet that need, the company created a new delivery system that allowed its drivers to hand-deliver orders to customers, beginning in Mexico City. The customers had a new experience with the brand, one that they were willing to share with their audiences.

Qantas

It is not every day that two CEOs meet together, but when one CEO is 10 years old, the event sparks some interest. Alex Jacquot wrote to Alan Joyce, CEO of the Australian airline company Qantas, to learn more about the business (Burns, 2019). Joyce responded with the letter on the following page, and invited Alex and his "deputy CEO" Wolf Stringer to a set of business meetings where they would gain an exclusive look at Qantas from a CEO's standpoint. This move sparked goodwill, positive press, and acknowledgments from all over the world for Qantas.

Amarula and #DontLetThemDisappear

As an author's side note, while I was in South Africa, one of the accounts I worked on was Amarula, and the brand continues its efforts in raising awareness about elephant protection efforts around the world to this day. The global cream liqueur company, which features the elephant as part of its brand logo and identity, is active in raising awareness about the impact of the ivory trade on elephant populations (Amarula, n.d.). Amarula has brought this message to airports around the world with the elephant campaign that places its message and large, three-dimensional elephant figures in most duty-free shops (Coleman, 2019).

Best Practices for Conducting Global Public Relations

When practicing public relations overseas and abroad, it is important to keep ethical and legal practices in mind and to note the following:

1. *Know that PR practices can vary from place to place.* What is considered unprofessional in one country may be perfectly okay in another. Explore the PR

19 February 2019

Dear Mr Jacquot,

Thank you for letting me know about your new airline. I had heard some rumours of another entrant in the market, so I appreciate you taking the time to write.

Firstly, I should say that I'm not typically in the business of giving advice to my competitors. Your newly-appointed Head of Legal might have something to say about that, too.

But I'm going to make an exception on this occasion, because I too was once a young boy who was so curious about flight and all its possibilities.

My number one tip for starting an airline is to put safety front and centre. And do everything you can to make travel as comfortable and affordable as possible for your passengers. That's been the Qantas way for almost 100 years, and it's worked for us.

Now, to your troubles thinking about sleep on 21-hour flights. This is something we are grappling with too, as we embark on *Project Sunrise* (which is our plan to fly passengers non-stop between the east coast of Australia and London).

To help with sleep, we're looking at different cabin designs that give people spaces to stretch out and exercise.

We want to think up as many ideas as possible to make the journey more comfortable for all.

For this reason, I would like to invite you to a Project Sunrise meeting between myself, as the CEO of Australia's oldest airline, and you, as the CEO of Australia's newest airline.

At this meeting we can compare notes on what it's like to run an airline. And I'd like to offer you a tour of our Operations Centre (where we keep an eye on every Qantas flight, wherever they are in the world).

Thank you, again, for your letter. I'll be in touch shortly about finding a time for our meeting.

Yours sincerely

Alan Joyce

Note: Typos and grammatical errors are intentional; they were part of the original version.

landscape of the countries you do business with to discover what is similar, but also what is different.

2. *Take time to learn, read, and connect with others.* Social media makes it easy for us to network, engage, and learn from each other, wherever we are on the planet. While it's easy for us to stay in our own circles and our own regions and home countries, the world is a big one, and we have to explore it.

3. *Invest in learning culture and language.* When you do business globally, it's important to take time and effort to learn and appreciate the cultures, communities, and languages of the people you work with. Sharing your dedication helps you to strengthen relationships with hosts and colleagues. You do not need to be fluent (this would be an extra and impressive bonus!), but showing them that you are learning and have mastered common phrases can go a long way in building goodwill.

4. *Go deeper to understand contexts.* Being a student of culture and community while practicing abroad is essential and will help you learn more about how public

relations functions in a given environment. For example, in South Africa, being aware of the importance of food during meetings and gatherings is critical. Food brings people together, especially because there was a time when food was not so readily available. Understanding symbols, historical events, and perceptions of the country by seeing it for yourself are a few things that will provide a greater education than any book can.

Social Media Public Relations: What Is It? How Is It Done?

PR professionals who specialize in social media are working in one of the fastest-growing and most in-demand areas of the field. As discussed throughout this book, social media is integrated into all aspects of our work, from research to audience analysis, to creative executions and activations.

The Focus of Social Media Public Relations

There are certain expectations that PR professionals need to know about as we enter the social media industry. First, we need to understand the ins and outs of social media platforms and commit to being students of the field. Platforms including Facebook and Twitter change their algorithms, features, terms of service, and expectations on a daily basis, so we need to be diligent in adapting and responding to these changes.

Second, we must understand the how and why of these platforms. How are the platforms and their communities connected, and how can a platform foster stronger relationships? It's crucial to first identify the state of the relationships among users on a social media platform. Some users are our biggest fans and will want to be on every platform we're on. While understanding the specifics of the tools is important, more important is learning people's behaviors and reasons why people use the tools in the first place. Each platform has a different function and overall purpose, as well as varying degrees of trustworthiness to consider. This is imperative given that we do a lot on social media. It's where we go to get news, create branding, promote clients, engage in customer service, share experiences, respond to crises, create and share stories, initiate calls to action to drive sales, manage reputations, and build on our established communities.

Third, we need to understand the different roles and skills that are necessary to specialize in social media. Writing, research, and creative execution are skills seen in marketing, public relations, and other communication disciplines. However, the rising expectations of the field as it matures have also allowed the expectations for young professionals entering the field to rise a bit higher. Of course, this depends on the industry, business, and even company or organization in focus. There is no real set "standard" for the expectations, roles, or even qualifications. Yet there are some fundamental skills, experiences, and qualifications that need to be taken into consideration.

Social Media Public Relations and Data

Data help us to tell and discover stories, and will of course be your friend when it comes to engaging with content and audiences on social media, depending on the platforms in question. You will be able to determine the time, frequency, responses, and views of your content. These data and insights will help you determine when it is appropriate to post content and share videos, and even how soon people expect a response to a customer comment on social media. In addition, analytics and data will help you determine, in the end, how well you (or your team) did in addressing the question, challenge, or content created for a campaign. Most of the links, updates, and conversations are archived online and can be collected either through the native measurement platforms available on the platform itself or through a third-party service.

Examples of Social Media Public Relations

Social media case studies highlight the power of storytelling, content creation, brand voice, and creative execution to generate real engagement from audiences. Let's look at campaigns for Disney+ and Popeyes® Louisiana Kitchen.

Disney+

One of the biggest trends in the social media space and technology sector has been the rise of streaming videos. Netflix, Hulu, Amazon, and other networks are jumping into this, providing access to various shows and movies for audiences to binge-watch and consume. Everyone wondered when Disney would enter the game with its products, and eventually, we witnessed the birth of Disney+. Disney+ features all of Disney's brands under its parent company umbrella, which includes Disney, Marvel, Star Wars, and National Geographic. During Disney's Expo event, the

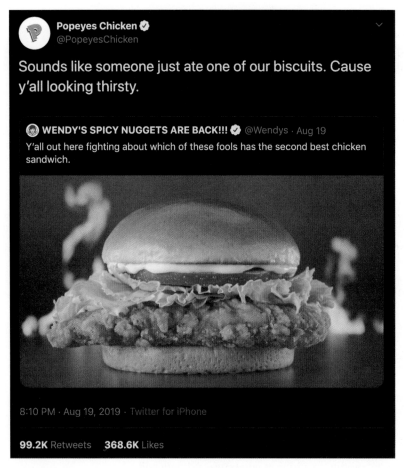

Popeyes' Twitter engagement related to the chicken sandwich release

Twitter/@PopeyesChicken

Popeyes Chicken ✓
@PopeyesChicken

Sounds like someone just ate one of our biscuits. Cause y'all looking thirsty.

WENDY'S SPICY NUGGETS ARE BACK!!! ✓ @Wendys · Aug 19
Y'all out here fighting about which of these fools has the second best chicken sandwich.

8:10 PM · Aug 19, 2019 · Twitter for iPhone

99.2K Retweets   **368.6K** Likes

company launched its Disney+ social media channels, creating a media storm. However, what made the launch even more powerful was the coordination of all of the accounts together to make the Disney+ announcement on Twitter. The planning and activation were central to the success of Disney's social media launch.

Popeyes

Who doesn't love a chicken sandwich? Okay, maybe the vegans and vegetarians among us. But generally, nothing brings people together like (1) a new chicken sandwich and (2) a Twitter battle royal among brands. This is what happened when Popeyes Louisiana Kitchen released its new chicken sandwich, which sparked a conversation on social media about which brand had the best chicken sandwich. Wendy's, Chick-fil-A, and others participated in the conversation, but the focus was mainly on Popeyes and its release. As *Adweek* pointed out, this campaign and launch made Popeyes a brand to watch on social media:

> While Popeyes' longtime, loyal fans—especially within the culture-defining collective of Black Twitter—deserve much of the credit for turning the brand's chicken sandwich launch into a viral phenomenon that has led to long lines and sold-out stores, the brand has also been positioning itself for just such a moment. (Griner, 2019)

As a result, Popeyes has garnered considerable earned media, press, and praise for how the company has engaged with audiences and driven them to take action. In addition, the brand is now being run by Global Chief Marketing Officer Fernando Machado, who also oversees Burger King, which was named Brand of the Year at the 2019 Cannes Lions International Festival of Creativity (Griner, 2019). A fresh perspective can spark innovation, raise a brand's image, engage audiences, and attract new ones.

In addition to garnering earned media coverage, Popeyes succeeded in catching the eye of the social media professional community. Matthew Kobach, who oversees the New York Stock Exchange's social media strategy, shared his take on the Popeyes success story through this venture. Kobach mentioned on his Twitter account (@mkobach) how Popeyes launched its new chicken sandwich, but not until Popeyes engaged with Chick-fil-A on Twitter did the story go viral on social media, generating so much traffic to Popeyes restaurants that they sold out of the sandwiches.

Best Practices for Social Media Public Relations

Working in social media and public relations allows us to be both creative and strategic, a perfect combination. Be sure to keep the following points in mind when working in this area of public relations.

1. *Take every opportunity to learn and grow your skill set.* Taking part in social media certifications and programs (such as Facebook Blueprint, Hootsuite, HubSpot, Google, and Brandwatch's certification programs) will add to your list of skills and expertise in the area.

2. *Invest in skills that others don't have yet.* Look at where professionals are working in social media and see what skills they highlight in their résumés and portfolios. If you see any areas that are missing, those are the skills you need to embrace and master. Videography, for example, is one of those skills (see the Game Changer feature for this specialization on page 310). In this industry, always invest in making yourself stand out from the crowd.

3. *Know that experience rules.* While others may say that they "know" social media, you must showcase your knowledge and experience as a social media practitioner. Volunteer, consult, and gain experience working in the field. Starting small with a few clients is a great way to begin your career in social media.

4. *Know the power of networking.* Networking is not only whom you know, but who knows you and what you can do. Establishing your personal brand is even more important in this specialization than in others. Understanding how to connect both virtually and in person is critical for making the connections and gaining the opportunities that will set you apart from the rest.

5. *Commit to being a forever student of the field.* Social media platforms and practices change not only daily but by the minute. So if you're thinking that learning stops when you finish this class and this book, I'm sorry to tell you: It's just beginning. In the social media industry, learning is an ongoing process. Staying on top of new trends, platforms, and best practices will give you another important skill, and that is the ability to educate. In this role, you become the most likely person to be called on to educate, train, and promote learning in your business, organization, or agency. Use this opportunity to be a resource for your fellow colleagues, and as a way to establish your own thought leadership. The best way to learn about a subject is to be able to teach others.

6. *Use your data.* As you engage in social media relations and campaigns, use data to gain insights on your audiences and their responses to your content and other communications. Data also allow you to evaluate your work and impact.

GAME CHANGER
Ty Rogers, Videographer

How did you get your start in the industry?

My first job in the industry was back in 2014–2015 with Indiana men's basketball. I was previously a college baseball coach (2014 and earlier) and started a side hobby in graphic design. The head basketball coach at the time—Tom Crean—got word of my work, aka "my hobby"—and wanted to hire me for this new position. Long story short, I completely changed my career and jumped in with both feet. My job title at Indiana was graphic designer, and my role was to help with recruiting and social media. This was how I got my start in this industry.

What is your favorite part of working in the industry?

Two things come to mind when people ask me what's my favorite part of being in this "creative world." My absolute favorite part is working with the athletes—whether college or professional, interacting and working with them is hands-down my favorite part of the job. The athletes are what drives my content, and the hands-on experience of getting to work with them up close has provided some of my greatest moments personally. The relationships you get to build with them have as well. A weeklong vacation to Cancun with Cam Newton (for example) is the best moment of my career by far (and I've had a few good moments). I am blessed to say I get to do what I love every single day, and working with these superstars is a big reason why it makes me feel that way. I would say the next thing that comes to mind is getting to meet or know others in the industry who get to do what we do every day. It's a smaller industry— but there are so many other talented individuals out there who inspire me. The relationships and connections you build in this industry are so important, and I'm thankful for all of them. I wouldn't be where I am today without them.

What is the most challenging part of working in your industry?

I'm a full-time freelancer. The most challenging part for me is doing my best to not get behind in my work—but at the same time looking ahead three to four weeks and trying to schedule future work with other brands. For me, nearly half my time spent is on the job site filming or photographing, and the other half is back home at my office editing the project until completion. Balancing all of that—and multiple projects at the same time—while trying to stay ahead with my schedule has been a learning curve, but so far it's gone pretty well. I say this is the most challenging because I like to take on a lot of work, and in most cases that requires being onsite for multiple projects and then getting back home and having several things to complete with a deadline. It's a game of balance and organization for sure, and it took me a few weeks to get it down. Now I have a better idea of how many jobs I can take on and can better determine whether I can schedule more or have to turn some down.

Who do you think are the biggest game changers for your industry?

This could go several ways, but I'm going to go in a different direction to answer this one. I'd say one of the biggest game changers in our industry is the person we directly work with or directly report to. For me, most of my jobs in the past four years have been working directly for college teams. I can't say enough about the people I've worked for and how they've helped me. They provide me access to things I wouldn't have otherwise. They've pushed to get me paid better. They've been there for me if I was struggling with something. They've also gone out of their way to help me get jobs. Dave Bradley (Duke basketball) has helped my career so much, and I'm thankful for him and everything he's done for me.

What are some things you wish you knew when you were starting out in the industry?

I wish I had a better idea how much jobs in this industry pay (ha!). It might scare some people early on, but if you stick with it, you'll eventually find some opportunities that can pay well enough for you. I just hope that someday the schools and/or teams can see that the people in this industry deserve better pay than what is the norm right now. I think it's heading in that direction. The ones who pay best somewhat control this, and as those salaries go up, so will the rest. We have the ability to drive a team's brand, and that shouldn't be taken without much care. It's much better than when I first started out. The amount of new jobs opening up in this industry and improved salaries—it's heading in the right direction.

I also wish I knew I was once again going to change my career! From graphic design to now being a content creator with a camera (video/photo), my career has changed again (since working for Duke). While remaining in the same industry, my day-to-day workflow has completely changed. I'm now hands-on with a camera and creating my own content. I have now been doing this for three years and love every bit of it. I really believe this is what I'm supposed to do and am grateful that each turn in my life has been for the better. One passion has turned into another and has led me to where I am today.

Entertainment and Sports Public Relations: What Is It? How Is It Done?

Many students want to go into the entertainment industry for the glitz and glamour. Hosting an amazing gala to raise awareness about a specific cause or attending an awards ceremony for A-list actors where you take pictures and work the red carpet sounds like fun.

The Focus of Entertainment Public Relations

Yes, entertainment public relations can be glitzy and glamorous, but there is much more to it. In entertainment public relations, professionals are responsible for all of the following:

- Pitching for their client to be on the cover of or featured in a magazine

- Formulating partnerships with endorsement deals and media coverage

- Coordinating efforts for photo shoots, media interviews, exclusives, and partnerships

- Documenting and showcasing content for their client across social channels

- Writing content (press releases, media kits, blog posts and updates, etc.) to be shared across channels

- Conducting media training for interviews, media tours, and premieres

- Preparing for crisis situations when needed

Many different titles and jobs describe entertainment public relations. One of the primary goals is to generate press and media coverage for a client, which means fulfilling the role of a **publicist**. A publicist generates awareness and coverage for a client specifically by working with the media, which is sometimes classified as being in media relations. These roles are quite prominent among those who work in the entertainment sector.

Examples of Entertainment Public Relations

Entertainment case studies can teach us about this area of public relations, offering further insights into personal branding and other efforts. It is not always the big movie studios that have the most innovative campaigns. Often the best ideas come from those who are unique in the field and have a vision that changes the game for others.

Lil Nas X and Billy Ray Cyrus

One of the biggest campaigns and musical hits during the summer of 2019 was "Old Town Road" by the musician Lil Nas X. Lil Nas X, who is a gay African American, had some difficulties getting his song out in the country music scene, but that changed when he was able to partner with Billy Ray Cyrus on a remix of the song. This pairing of musicians made a huge impact and brought about a cultural shift in the entertainment industry. As a result, the song became the most successful on Billboard's top hits list, topping the list at number one for 19 weeks straight and setting a new record (Lipshutz, 2019).

Ryan Reynolds on Twitter
Twitter/@VancityReynolds

The Rock

We all know who Dwayne "The Rock" Johnson is, and that's because of the awesomeness of his personal brand. He is someone to evaluate and learn from for his expertise in marketing, promoting, and managing a personal brand on social media. Johnson is now the highest-paid actor in Hollywood, and much of this is thanks to his strategic and innovative use of his own social media channels to engage with fans, share his personal perspectives on life, and showcase his personality for the world to see (Robehmed, 2018).

Ryan Reynolds

Ryan Reynolds, famous for his roles in movies such as *Deadpool*, has risen in the entertainment sphere for his innovative and creative work in marketing, public relations, and social media. Reynolds has practiced these innovative techniques not only for his own brand as an actor, but in his work for his gin company, Aviation. As discussed in this book, his responsive commercial featuring Monica Ruiz (the "Peloton wife") with Aviation Gin has become the new "Oreo blackout tweet" in responsive creative content strategies. Plus, he is an actor who engages with his fans, including following this textbook author (#authorgoals). The Peloton commercial went viral, but Reynolds has since gained traction for his creative work with his team with his campaigns, making him a must-follow in the entertainment and social media space for public relations.

Lizzo

One popular musician who has made her own path by taking ownership of her brand, story, and direction in the entertainment industry is Lizzo. Lizzo, who has been labeled as an empowered singer, is praised for raising awareness of self-love and body image standards. She has boosted her career by separating herself from others in the industry (Pike, 2019). In addition to her success as a musician, Lizzo is an advocate for the rights of individuals who identify as lesbian, gay, bisexual, transgender, and queer/questioning (LGBTQ+), and she uses star status to empower the community (Setoodeh, 2019).

The Focus of Sports Public Relations

The integration of sports and public relations creates a natural setting for innovation. Some of the best storytelling and most creative work is coming from the sports industry, at both collegiate and professional levels. Data analytics play a huge part in combining these fields together to create new messaging, gather new insights, and produce more data-driven initiatives through evidence-based practices.

In particular, professionals in the sports PR industry are very forward-thinking in their use of social media. Social media has transformed not only how fans and other audiences get information, but also how they consume information and share and create stories about their favorite sports teams. For the teams, it's changed how they recruit and engage with fans.

Examples of Sports Public Relations

Sports teams, organizations, and individual athletes have all contributed to creating a strong PR presence in the industry. Here are some ways that brands and teams are changing the PR game in the sports industry.

Adidas and the *Change in Play* Show

Adidas has launched a show featuring a group of all-star female athletes who share their stories and experiences, even their struggles, in the sports industry. The new show, called *Change in Play*, will feature Women's National Basketball Association All-Star Chiney Ogwumike, Olympic hockey gold medalist Kendall Coyne Schofield, Olympic volleyball bronze medalist Rachael Adams, Ultimate Fighting Championship fighter Paige VanZant, and National Football League agent Nicole Lynn (Adidas, 2019). Female athletes (e.g., the U.S. women's national soccer team) are affected by unequal pay and by challenges, including abuse, that have brought crises to specific sports (e.g., USA Gymnastics). Adidas launched this initiative to raise awareness of these stories for future generations of female athletes.

Gritty of the NHL's Philadelphia Flyers
Len Redkoles / Getty Images

Gritty, the Mascot

People love sports team mascots for their enthusiasm, appearance, personality, and ties to teams and communities. However, Gritty, the mascot for the National Hockey League's Philadelphia Flyers, takes the cake for being adored despite his personality and appearance, which differ from those of other mascots. The media campaign for Gritty was not successful at first, when he was introduced to the team and then announced to the public. Fans were not pleased with the new mascot, but when their rivals, the Pittsburgh Penguins, made a negative comment about Gritty, Flyers fans came together to support him (Fleming, 2018). The Gritty campaign has been huge as far as exposure and engagement goes, reaching nearly 70 million people on TV and earning about $151 million in earned media coverage (Fleming, 2018). Gritty has gone from being an initially unloved mascot to becoming a sports cultural icon. In fact, Gritty will make his official debut in the *NHL 20* video game, signaling his status to the sports community (NBC Sports Philadelphia Staff, 2019). Sometimes being different and separating yourself from the crowd pays off big. It is a risk, but well worth it, especially in the case of Gritty.

Donovan Mitchell and Spider-Man

Sports and entertainment come together really well, as is evident in the brand partnership between Utah Jazz basketball player Donovan Mitchell and Spider-Man, who is played by Tom Holland. Mitchell, a former basketball player for the University of Louisville, gained the nickname "Spida," which is defined as "a basketball species usually found above the rim; equipped with superhuman sense, shot-slinging abilities and unrivaled bounce" (West, 2018). When the film *Spider-Man: Far From Home* was being marketed and about to be released, Marvel decided to reach out to Mitchell to make a commercial for the film. In the commercial, Holland gets Mitchell's newly designed shoes from Adidas, and Mitchell gets the Spider-Man suit (Tobin, 2019). It was a nice crossover between two brands that are well established and known in their industries, but it also served as an opportunity for both parties to reach new audiences. The campaign was integrated and aligned, making it successful.

Best Practices for Entertainment and Sports Public Relations

Some best practices to keep in mind when working in entertainment or sports public relations include the following.

1. *Make connections.* As we've discussed, specialized public relations is not only about what you know, but about who knows your work. Your connections and networks can get you in the door for many opportunities, but you have to have a level of expertise and experience in the field. Gain as much experience as you can volunteering, going to games, helping out with internships, and investing in your future at conferences and networking sessions. Subscribing to resources like Front Office Sports or following the Twitter hashtags #SMSports and #Sports-Biz will allow you to start networking with professionals in the sports industry immediately. The same goes for entertainment. This is a universal best practice to keep in mind.

2. *Expect to wear many hats.* Working in entertainment and sports public relations requires you to be a content creator, storyteller, manager, event planner, spokesperson, writer, customer service representative on social, reputation manager, data analyst, creative director, and much more. Be prepared to use all of the experiences, skills, and class work you have collected and immediately be able to apply it.

3. *Know that it's not all fun and games.* Doing public relations in the entertainment and sports industries is a lot of work. *A lot.* Expect to work at all hours and be adaptive to changes, news, and evolving trends. Thinking and creating on your feet is going to be a valuable skill along with working with limited resources.

4. *Love your data. Tell stories.* As noted in the social media section of this chapter, data and the insights data provide can help us come up with fresh ideas in response

GAME CHANGER

Amir Zonozi, President of Zoomph

Courtesy of Amir Zonozi

How did you get your start in the industry?

Honestly, it all started with AIM buddy lists and away messages—I was hooked on creating witty messages, and the engagement that generated was all I needed to get hooked. Pretty soon I was freelancing with friends and then with small businesses before social media was really a thing, and one thing led to another and I found myself with one of the most innovative teams I have ever been on, and that team had created Zoomph.

What is your favorite part of working in the industry?

My favorite part about working in this industry is meeting new people, and bonds that are created even before meeting in person. I can't tell you how many people I have met first online, then in person.

What is the most challenging part of working in your industry?

The most challenging aspect of our industry is also the most thrilling—it is always changing. What works today will certainly not work tomorrow—it's a constant state of evolution.

Who do you think are the biggest game changers for your industry?

There are so many aspects to this question, it's hard for me to answer, but some people I have recently appreciated are Jon Becher at the San Jose Sharks, Al Guido of the San Francisco 49ers, Jess Smith of the New York Yankees, Adam White of Front Office Sports, Will Yoder of Instagram, Shelley Pisarra of Wasserman, TJ Adeshola of Twitter Sports, and Paul Greenberg of 56 Group.

What are some things you wish you knew when you were starting out in the industry?

I wish I knew that you will never be ready for what you are preparing for, and you must chase after what you want. Comfort is the enemy of greatness.

Amir Zonozi is Zoomph's resident drone crasher, YouTuber, co-founder, and chief strategy officer. Amir leads Zoomph's overall client solutions, data, and partnership strategy for the Fortune 100 brands, esports, teams, leagues, and agencies that Zoomph works with globally across Facebook, Instagram, Twitter, YouTube, and Twitch.

You can find him here:

> *www.twitter.com/zonozi*
> *www.youtube.com/azonozi*
> *www.instagram.com/zonozi*
> *www.zoomph.com*

to audience needs. Invest in the knowledge, experience, and tools that will help you collect, analyze, and report insights that you can use for stories, features, and brainstorming sessions.

5. *Work hard. Win easy.* This is a personal motto that I had as a student-athlete competing for the University of Florida and the University of Southern California in track and field. Entertainment and sports public relations is fast-paced and exciting, but a ton of work. You will have long hours, long trips, and many responsibilities. However, if you put in the time, resources, and energy to invest in your future, you will be successful for the long run.

Nonprofit Public Relations: What Is It? How Is It Done?

Nonprofit public relations is a large specialization within our field. There is a natural connection between nonprofits and the use of public relations to accomplish many of their goals.

The Focus of Nonprofit Public Relations

Among the PR goals for nonprofits are the following:

- Community engagement and support
- Education
- Support for underrepresented audiences
- Raising awareness of issues and challenges facing society
- Brand building and reputation management
- Program recruitment
- Fundraising

Many great nonprofits have done significant work in addressing the needs and challenges facing society. Ultimately, when we do public relations for a nonprofit, we must make sure that the messages and content that we distribute on our channels must tie back to what is set out in our communication plan. Nonprofits such as GivingTuesday and Metro United Way do a great job in telling their stories and supporting their communities through stories. They also make sure their fundraising messages are integrated across channels, audiences, brands, and industries, which is central to raising awareness about their organizations' efforts. We must tell the story of what our nonprofit is doing for the community and document its impact. These practices provide opportunities for relationships and evidence of success, and build trust by creating transparency.

Examples of Nonprofit Public Relations

Several nonprofits stand out for using social media strategically and creatively in various situations to gain traction for their causes.

GivingTuesday

GivingTuesday (GivingTuesday.org) is the day when audiences can donate to charities following Black Friday after the Thanksgiving holiday. The goal of the event is to "inspire millions of people across the globe to show up and give back to causes and issues that matter to them" (GivingTuesday, n.d.).

Red Nose Day

Red Nose Day has been celebrated to support the reduction of childhood poverty across the globe (Red Nose Day, n.d.). Poverty levels over the past 20 years have decreased worldwide, but there are always people in need of help. The red "nose" symbolizes the need for the world to come together to "share a laugh and give the world something to smile about" (Red Nose Day, n.d.). Celebrities including Elizabeth Banks (*Pitch Perfect*),

Mandy Moore (*This Is Us*), and others have supported the effort across their own social media channels to spark awareness about this nonprofit and childhood poverty (Red Nose Day, 2018).

Game of Thrones and the American Red Cross

Sometimes you find an example of partnership heaven. The partnership between *Game of Thrones* and the American Red Cross is one of those. For its last season, *Game of Thrones* partnered with the Red Cross to support a blood drive called "Bleed for the Throne," asking fans to donate their blood at various blood banks during the airing of the show's final season (American Red Cross, 2019).

"Bleed for the Throne" campaign
American Red Cross

Best Practices for Nonprofit Public Relations

Like all of the professionals who specialize in specific areas of public relations, those in nonprofit public relations need to keep some basic practices and guidelines in mind.

1. *Remember, money does not grow on trees.* Fundraising is a huge part of what makes nonprofits operate. Invest in workshops, classes, and sessions that will teach fundamental and innovative ways to engage audiences so that you can raise money for causes. Cases such as the fire at Notre-Dame cathedral and the Ice Bucket Challenge are good to study.

2. *Build partnerships and collaborations.* Influencers, brands, and other organizations should be on your mind when exploring how to boost awareness, share educational resources, tell stories, and reach new audiences.

3. *Be the best advocate and storyteller for your nonprofit.* To persuade others to take action, you first have to master the art of storytelling. Set your goals, be clear and creative, and share your narratives with your audiences in ways that bring the most engagement. To learn more, see the Game Changer feature with Chris Strub, which follows.

Politics Public Relations: What Is It? How Is It Done?

The political arena, which is in constant flux, appears in the spotlight during campaigns and initiatives brought forth by political parties, individual politicians, and others.

The Focus of Politics Public Relations

Political PR professionals have a range of responsibilities to oversee at the local, state, national, and even international level of practice. Some of the responsibilities include these:

- Managing public opinion on various issues pertaining to political parties, candidates, political figures, and others across various levels

- Creating and launching campaigns to frame the messages and promotion efforts of the potential bills to be presented to Congress (**Lobbyists**, those who work

GAME CHANGER
Chris Strub, Giving Day Guy

How did you get your start in the industry?

Graduating from college in 2007, my first "real job" was in the newspaper industry. I was a copy editor and page designer by trade, but as one of the youngest members of the *Press & Sun-Bulletin* newsroom in Binghamton, New York, my job quickly began to include digital responsibilities, like updating our website, managing our Facebook page, and handling the Twitter account. As the years ticked by, our newsroom's digital presence became increasingly important; we were told to ditch the name "newsroom" and instead use the phrase "Local Information Center." I was able to simultaneously learn from the many experienced journalists surrounding me, while getting a firsthand education in how to best use the digital tools at our disposal.

So in 2014, I made the most difficult decision of my career: I left the ad agency to embark on a 48-state solo road trip. My strategy was to create epic video and photo content around the United States, with hopes of becoming a social media star in the mold of a Casey Neistat. I completed the trip and ended up moving to Greenville, South Carolina, using social media to make valuable connections all along the way.

I called the trip, fittingly, "50 States, 100 Days," and this time, the hook caught on. Armed with the knowledge of the local news scene from my days at the *Press & Sun-Bulletin*, "50 States, 100 Days" was picked up by news outlets around the United States, including the *Montgomery Advertiser* (Alabama), the *Baltimore Sun* (Maryland), the *Missoulian* (Montana), the *Dickinson Press* (North Dakota), 6ABC Philadelphia, News 12 Long Island, *Newsday*, and many more. I managed my PR strategy alone on the road, sending emails and placing phone calls a day or two in advance of each visit, making certain to localize the pitch as best as possible.

Having a clever hook like "50 States, 100 Days" has led to dozens of incredible opportunities since the trip ended in August 2015. I self-published *50 States, 100 Days: The Book*, both as an eBook and as a paperback, and in July 2018, I partnered with Scofield Digital Storytelling out of Indianapolis to create *50 States, 100 Days: The Film*. We've embarked on a nationwide effort to screen *The Film* in all 50 states, debuting the project at Social Media Marketing

World 2019 in San Diego. I also partnered with the Salvation Army USA to create the "Fight for Good Tour," a 25-state, 38-day adventure in November and December 2017 that highlighted the work being done by the Salvation Army from coast to coast. That trip raised more than $6,200 for local chapters of the organization, and my vlogs were edited by NBCUniversal and hosted on Today.com.

What is your favorite part of working in the industry?

I'm blessed to work with nonprofits, so every day, I encounter stories of happiness and joy, resulting from the hard work being done by nonprofit leaders around the United States. For me, this represents a much different view of "the media" than I experienced at the *Press & Sun-Bulletin*, where in a more traditional sense, we lived by the phrase "if it bleeds, it leads." Our culture's perspective on the news is unfortunately traditionally shaded by bad news, especially in the last few years, but my various travels and online exchanges have only strengthened my belief that our country consists mainly of hardworking, compassionate, and kindhearted individuals.

There's no better example of this than the people I met during the "Fight for Good Tour" with the Salvation Army USA. Starting in Houston, weaving north to Minneapolis and Chicago, south to New Orleans and Jacksonville, and then back to the Northeast, including Baltimore, Philadelphia, and New York City, I encountered hundreds of the most wonderful individuals this country has to offer.

What is the most challenging part of working in your industry?

The most challenging part of working in this industry is also the most rewarding: remembering that the stories that you tell really, sincerely matter—and that the people behind those view counts are real people. I call my company "I Am Here, LLC" because I take such sincere joy in physically being around those who are doing the hard work, day after day.

I have been incredibly blessed to take part in a lot of the social media industry's top events, including The Social Shake-Up; the Midwest Digital Marketing

Conference in St. Louis, Missouri; various Social Media Day events, from Dayton, Ohio, to Denver, Colorado, to Wichita, Kansas, to Houston, Texas; Social Media Week Lima; and even Social Media Marketing World.

But even more rewarding for me than the event scene is visiting the nonprofits that are making our country a better, safer, and healthier place every day.

I can definitely see how, for many professionals out there reading this book, it may be challenging to feel sometimes like your work makes a difference. But when you get out in the field and meet the people to whom your message and your work really matters, that stress and uncertainty is quickly lifted.

Who do you think are the biggest game changers for your industry?

While my role as a road trip marketer, author, and speaker straddles the PR industry, I'm generally more familiar with the change makers in the social media space. There are countless individuals whose work I admire.

I greatly admire everyone who has the guts to create their own industry event. Creating a forum that brings people together is an invaluable skill, and there are some in our industry who have mastered this art over the years, like Mike Stelzner and Phil Mershon of *Social Media Examiner* (Social Media Marketing World); Perry Drake of the University of Missouri–St. Louis (Midwest Digital Marketing Conference); and Sophie Maerowitz, Justin Joffe, and the team at *PR News* (The Social Shake-Up). Without those three industry events, I would have missed the opportunity to connect with hundreds of other professionals

in my field. I'd offer similar credit to those who spearhead local social media events in their own communities, like Rebecca Councill (Houston); Sara Moore (Dayton, Ohio); Erin Cell (Denver, Colorado); Jen Cole, Julie Riley, and the committee in Wichita, Kansas; Jessika Phillips (Lima, Ohio); Lauren Davis (Rockford, Illinois); and Tyler Anderson (San Diego, California).

What are some things you wish you knew when you were starting out in the industry?

If I had a time machine, I'd tell myself not to *not* make mistakes, but to think strategically about the growth potential from those mistakes: What can I learn from this experience that I can adopt from and be better moving forward? Ultimately, you can't improve unless you are consciously willing to make what other people may view as mistakes—but the faster you can apply the learnings from those imperfect experiences and move forward, the better off you'll be.

Chris Strub is the "Giving Day Guy," partnering with giving days around the United States to create real-time social media content that boosts awareness and drives donations. As the CEO of I Am Here, LLC, Chris has authored 50 States, 100 Days: The Book *and* Fight for Good Tour: The Book *about his cross-country road-trip marketing experiences with some of the nation's largest nonprofits. Chris is a keynote speaker, course instructor,* Forbes *contributor, and livestreaming event host from Long Island, New York, and currently lives in Greenville, South Carolina. Follow Chris across social media channels @ ChrisStrub, and learn more about his work at www.teamstrub.com and www.givingdayguy.com.*

with Congress to get legislature and bills passed, are a particular specialization within the political and government arena.)

- Writing statements, coordinating interviews, media training, and hosting and organizing press ventures and conferences to announce news or updates on political and government activities

- Being the spokesperson for a particular branch of government to the public, and to other government agencies (There of course are those who operate and work in public affairs, which are designated for government organizations and military branches of government.)

- Creating persuasive messages that motivate audiences to take action for a bill, candidate, initiative, or effort to spark change

- Coordinating various campaign efforts during election years

- Working with other government agencies on various situations and efforts

Examples of Politics Public Relations

Among the many significant cases of political public relations are the following.

The 2016 Presidential Election: Donald Trump and Hillary Clinton

The 2016 U.S. presidential campaigns and the election itself present a number of take-aways and lessons. Both candidates, Donald Trump and Hillary Clinton, used their campaigns to share their stories and persuade audiences of the reasons that they were the best candidate, but each approached the effort in different ways. President Trump used social media to go directly to his audience group while bypassing the mainstream media. Secretary Clinton relied more on the mainstream media and partnered with celebrities such as Beyoncé and Jay-Z to coordinate fundraising efforts. The candidates used different strategies for how to engage, create content, and go to the location of their audience bases. As social media and other channels continue to evolve, so will the use and implementation of these efforts by politicians and the PR professionals supporting them.

United and Fort Wayne International Airport

In public affairs and government relations, it can take time to spark change for a greater need, especially for millennials and younger audiences moving to Fort Wayne, Indiana. This is what the Asher Group did for Fort Wayne International Airport, by partnering and working with United to provide a direct route to New York City (Asher, n.d.).

Pete Davidson and Dan Crenshaw *SNL* Skit

The entertainment industry and the political arena are intertwined sometimes. In fact, Presidents Ronald Reagan and Donald Trump each had their time in the media and under the entertainment spotlight before being elected to office. However, the popular show *Saturday Night Live*, which often features parody skits focused on political candidates, crossed a line of tastefulness with Pete Davidson's comments about congressional candidate Dan Crenshaw's war-related injury. As a result of the backlash it got from the media and audience members, *SNL* invited Crenshaw on the show for an on-air apology (Sims, 2018).

Best Practices for Politics Public Relations

For those who would like to go into political public relations or work in government relations, there are a few things to think about:

1. *Take initiative. Build experience.* To work in this industry, you have to be motivated to work and practice political and government relations. Volunteer at political functions, work on a campaign, coordinate efforts with public affairs groups, and get involved in student or professional groups to get some experience with the political spectrum.

2. *Interview and network with others in the field.* To see what it is really like to be part of the industry, talk with those who are already working in it. Understanding the experience, expectations, and job requirements for this particular industry is very important.

3. *Take time to understand other viewpoints.* For us to be aware of what our audiences are thinking, we have to first be aware of what people in general are thinking. Be open to hearing opinions that are different from your own, and learn how to have proactive and constructive discussions on issues and topics. In the end, you may find that people have more in common than you think.

SUMMARY

Congrats! You have finished the longest chapter of this entire book! #GiveYourselfAMedal.

There are many different areas of public relations, which is exciting to see because it means our field is growing. Each of these areas can offer internships and entry-level jobs to those who are new to the field, the potential for learning and

advancement, and mentors who can help you achieve your professional goals. While the specializations featured in this chapter do not cover all of the areas that you might want to explore and work in as a PR professional, they do provide a window into the many possibilities—the exciting possibilities!— of the field.

APR EXAM

- Crisis communication and management
- Entertainment public relations
- Politics
- Reputation management
- Social media

KEY TERMS

Attack the accuser 296

Character 294

Corrective action 296

Crisis 296

Denial 296

Excuse 296

Full apology 296

Ingratiation 296

Justification 296

Lobbyist 317

Publicist 311

Reputation 293

Reputation management 293

Social media crisis 297

DISCUSSION QUESTIONS

1. What are the differences between reputation management and crisis communication?

2. Identify the seven message strategies that are used in crisis situations.

3. Along with authenticity, what are two other characteristics influencers need to have?

4. Identify three best practices for working in the entertainment, sports, and data industries.

5. What is the name of the role that is designated to focus on generating media coverage for a client?

ACTIVITIES

Building Your Portfolio

Interview a professional in your designated specialization. Pick a specialized area in public relations you wish to go into, and research individuals with whom you would want to chat about

their experiences. Reach out to them via email or social media (e.g., Twitter and/or LinkedIn), and see if you can ask them a few questions about their story, how they came to the profession, and any recommendations they have for you. A bonus is if you are able to job shadow them to see their daily activities working in their position.

Building Your Brand

Pick a specialization. Of the specializations highlighted in this chapter, decide which one you would want to pursue and discuss why. Identify the skills and experiences you have built up so far in your studies that would make you successful in this area. Outline three steps you will take to further your experience, knowledge, and skills so you can gain an internship or job in this area after graduation.

SUMMARY

Chapter 15
The Future

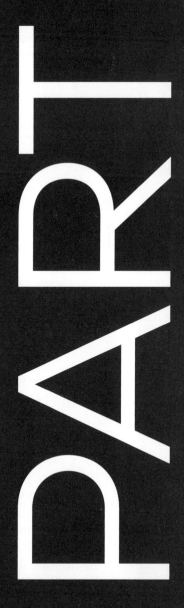

THE FUTURE

··

LEARNING **OBJECTIVES**

- Evaluate public relations as an industry and consider future opportunities and specializations.

- Plan future steps to learn more about public relations and to carry out creative, sustainable, and evidence-based practices.

- Learn best practices for working and moving forward in the field.

Introduction

Great job! You have completed your reading of this book, are finishing up your course, and are ready to dazzle. You are equipped with all of the tools and insights you need to be successful. You have officially graduated as an expert in public relations. Let's do it.

Hold on a sec. As Lee Corso from *College GameDay* says: *Not so fast!*

While we've covered a lot of the fundamentals of public relations in this book, I don't think we're there yet, at least not at expert level. There is still plenty of experience to gain. There's still so much to learn, observe, and talk about, and there always will be, given the changing nature of our work and our enthusiastic commitment to it. And here's the thing: This is a great moment to enter the field. We are beginning a new era that will bring new applications, evidence-based practices, and powerful opportunities for innovation.

Where Are We Headed? What Are the Opportunities and Obstacles?

We have more resources and opportunities than ever to tell our best stories—and to tell them to a worldwide audience. Thanks to digital and social channels, we can do so with the touch of a button or the swipe of a screen. We have thousands of case studies to choose from to gather best practices *and* learn from mistakes. Simply put, we are positioned to do our best work.

Of course, like pretty much all industries, public relations has a ways to go to address its challenges. For example, we need to better integrate business acumen into our practices and fine-tune our measurement methods, expectations of roles, and metrics. In our day-to-day work, facing obstacles such as the shifting of the rules

Congrats! You have made it to the end of the textbook!

iStock.com/PeopleImages

that govern what we do (e.g., new privacy regulations, such as the California Consumer Privacy Act of 2020) can feel overwhelming at times. As we embrace the constant change happening in our industry, we may sometimes want to hit the pause button to catch our breath. And yes, we can do better. As they say, Rome was not built in a day. As future practitioners and scholars, we can tackle these problems together by taking things one day at a time and taking small measures each day to address our challenges proactively. In fact, to make public relations the best industry it can be will require each and every one of you to enter the workplace with a can-do, collaborative spirit—and a desire to advance your careers, organizational and specialty roles, and work with clients, as well as the profession itself.

As we venture forth, let's be aware of the potential roadblocks ahead. While most other textbooks avoid giving an honest, upfront view of what to expect in our field, I think it's important to do so. First, to quote Rihanna, you'll need to work, work, work, work, *work*. Public relations is an extremely competitive and demanding field, meaning that there will be people who mentor and support your success, and there will be others who see you as a threat and may even undermine your work. That said, while public relations is not a hunky-dory skip down the yellow brick road, it is also not a cutthroat *Survivor*-type situation, where everyone is out to get each other. As you advance in the field, you will also encounter the constraints presented by the gatekeepers of traditional schools and practices of thought. Getting past these constraints requires you to be confident in what you have to offer to the field as far as diverse perspectives, experiences, and ideas go. You are on the right side of history here. The traditional approaches and gatekeepers of the field are trying their best to stay relevant, but the world is moving forward—and we have to join in on this journey and welcome these changes.

Public relations as a field and profession needs more of us to be willing to test the boundaries, ideologies, and schools of thought that limit us. Over the last several decades, there has been a narrow view, held by only a few academic schools of thought, of how we should practice our craft. Some established programs in higher education want to continue ingraining their leadership and viewpoints in today's and future generations. To do so, they assert their influence through research, practice, alumni, and other channels to maintain authority. However, to truly advance, we need more diverse experiences, perspectives, schools of thought, and representations of ideas to move our field toward the future. For example, more companies and agencies are going out to network and establish partnerships with schools, programs, and professionals new to the field. Recruiters are no longer just heading to the large cities or legacy PR programs for talent: They are going elsewhere, to places they have not been, to invite people with new ideas and enthusiasm. PR talent can come from anywhere.

What Have We Learned So Far?

We have discussed a lot of the ideas, aspects, and practices of public relations over the course of this book. Hopefully the argument that public relations is more than hosting parties, dodging paparazzi, and handling other people's PR nightmares has resonated with you.

Case Studies Review: Boeing, KFC, and Varsity Blues

During our exploration of public relations, we have also looked at a number of modern-day case studies, such as the Boeing crisis of 2018–2019, KFC's fresh efforts to boost its brand, and the college admissions crisis. Arby's is another interesting case.

Boeing

Besides tragic loss of life from two separate 737 MAX crashes—with a death toll of 346 passengers, according to Business Insider (Slotnick, 2020)—the Boeing case offers a lesson in what needs to be done in a crisis situation. In this context, PR professionals had to handle employee relations, government relations, and partnership deals with other airlines to connect with audiences and manage the negative impact of the crisis on the brand's reputation (Kitterman, 2019).

KFC

Another case we have studied is KFC. The company set out to strengthen its established brand voice and traditions, but also to be innovative in its latest campaigns to engage audiences on a new level, even turning Colonel Sanders into a sexy digital avatar (Fleming, 2019).

College Admissions Crisis

The college admissions crisis, affecting the University of Southern California and other prestigious colleges and universities, showed the world the nature of unethical practices at all levels of an organization, and the totally unethical relationships and practices the organizations involved had built with audiences. This case of "Varsity Blues" demonstrates the need for transparency, oversight, and training, as well as the crucial role of PR work, at every stage of a crisis (Kitterman, 2019).

Arby's

Arby's, the "We Have the Meats" brand, got into the conversation around "meatless" products with its competitors KFC, McDonald's, and Burger King by announcing the "marrot," a "meat-based" carrot product (Entis, 2019). While some may think this is a joke, Arby's conducted a playful media blitz featuring the marrot, which is made from turkey breast meat, to show that, like its competitors, Arby's can interject itself into the conversations among key publics and frame its brand in a different light (Valinsky, 2019).

The list of relevant and timely cases goes on and on—and there will be many more cases to discuss in the future. Public relations as a field is never boring, and when you think you have seen it all, wait. You will see something (e.g., a "marrot") that you never would have expected.

Coverage Review: From an Introduction to Career Options

The purpose of this book is to open doors for you to an evolving field of practice. Let's do a quick recap of what we covered in previous chapters. In the first part of the book, "Foundations" (Chapters 1–7), we began with a discussion of the current state of public relations. In Chapter 1, we looked at the rising expectations placed on PR professionals, and what it takes to be successful in the industry. We talked about what *is* public relations—and what *is not* public relations. You considered the different perceptions of our work, both in and outside of the field, and learned how we collaborate with related disciplines such as advertising, marketing, and journalism. In other words, Chapter 1 presented how public relations can be a centralized profession that is associated with other disciplines.

Chapter 2 focused on the history, contexts, and evolution of practices in our field. We learned how public relations started and which key people helped shape the field into what it is today. It's important to recognize the founders of our field, such as Ivy Lee and Edward Bernays, but to also look toward the individuals who are or will be at the forefront of the future of the profession, such as those who are changing the field at this very moment. #MaybeThat'sYou! To understand where we're going, we need a balanced perspective of what has been done, what's happening now, and what forward-thinking steps will lead to further transformation in our field.

In other PR textbooks, ethics and the law are usually tagalongs to other chapters, or appear in appendices at the end of the book. That is not the case here. Because ethical and lawful practice is essential to our work, our chapter on ethics and the law, Chapter 3, appears at the beginning of this book, inviting you to build a solid foundation for ethical practice and familiarize yourself with some of the legal challenges you may encounter. Challenges associated with ethics and the law are ongoing in the industry, and while change will not happen overnight, we can all come together to address these problems and make our work and work lives all the better.

Chapter 4 offered a thorough overview of the issues of diversity and inclusion in public relations. This chapter discussed some of the main issues in the areas of diversity and inclusion that need to be taken into consideration and acknowledged in our day-to-day practices. We are getting better in representing all aspects of diversity and inclusion in our internal and external efforts. We are making a good effort to be more inclusive, but we need to better integrate this fundamental practice into all aspects of our field.

Chapters 5 and 7 focused on two essential skills that will always be universally required of PR professionals: (1) research and evidence-based practices and (2) writing. Chapter 5 discussed the core principles of research in public relations including the newest methods we use to gather research, create and discuss insights, and apply these insights to actionable strategies. Chapter 7 focused on the essential principles for writing effective PR assets and covered the most common genres of PR writing, such as news releases, press releases, media kits, brochures, websites, blogs, and social media.

Branding, covered in Chapter 6, is an area of essential practice for all PR professionals, whether we are branding our clients or ourselves (personal branding). Branding involves more than just stating what you stand for. It's also about understanding the components that make up a brand, knowing how to manage a brand for a client, and homing in on the steps you need to take to position yourself in the industry so that you stand out from others.

The second part of the book, "Applications" (Chapters 8–14), presented the ways in which public relations is applied and integrated in real-world circumstances.

Chapter 8 on strategic campaigns focused on the planning framework for PR campaigns and ideation, a main focus of the work that we do. As this chapter discussed, we use many different formats and models to create and carry out our PR campaigns, but adapting the framework of a strategic plan for public relations can add specific, helpful details that are missing from most PR campaigns.

Audiences and relationship management were the primary focus of Chapter 9. Relationship management is a core part of what makes public relations the field and profession that it is. This chapter focused on the key publics that are important to formulate a relationship with, as well as the traditional publics—and the emerging ones—that are prevalent in modern PR practices.

To make a positive impact for your client or organization, you must have strong content that you then execute in a strategic and creative manner. This is the focus of Chapter 10, where we defined and discussed content creation, content curation, content amplification, and content strategy. These principles are part of our social media practices, but they are also linked together, strategically, within all PR practices. This chapter also blended the importance of writing and visual content creation, outlining the various pieces of content that we are responsible for. Best practices were highlighted for each of these different areas, and you were introduced to new forms to be aware of.

Chapter 11 addressed a much-needed area of focus, as pointed out by the Commission on Public Relations Education. Management and business acumen are areas that focus on the integration of business and leadership concepts into PR practices. This chapter went over the details associated with these concepts, and covered how they can be tied into our current models and approaches.

As they say, if you can't measure it, then don't do it. Chapter 12 focused on the importance of measurement and evaluation in relation to our PR efforts, including running strategic campaigns and meeting our clients' goals. Further, we can use measurement and evaluation to show and prove the value of our efforts. These data and metrics help us align with management's objectives and validate our team's efforts for clients and senior management.

One of the most popular questions raised about working in public relations is: What, exactly, are some of the best roles and jobs to take on in the industry? Chapter 13 discussed the different careers and positions that are available, including both time-tested and emerging roles, along with the skills, experiences, and expertise that we need to succeed in the field.

Last but not least, Chapter 14 introduced us to various areas of specialization that exist within public relations. This chapter highlighted what to expect in each specialty area in terms of best practices, case studies, and the different roles and skills required to excel. This chapter was filled with additional stories and perspectives from various Game Changer features, ranging from professionals working in videography to sports and entertainment to influencer marketing. The possibilities are endless for future specializations within the field thanks to its constant evolution and related adaptations taking place as we speak.

Who Are These Fine New Professionals? Meet Candice, Abbie, Michael, and Megan

As we've discussed, there are many talented established professionals and game changers in the field of public relations. Yet sometimes the best ideas and advice come from new professionals who are just entering the profession. Following are the stories of four newly minted graduates who have launched their PR careers and would like to share their best practices and tips to keep in mind when entering the industry and field.

Candice Champlin, a senior at the University of Louisville, first started her undergraduate career majoring in veterinary sciences and equine business. However, she switched her major and has since worked with brands including the Kentucky Derby, Facebook, Breeders' Cup, and Adobe during her undergraduate studies. Her advice is to network and to prioritize establishing relationships that will help you grow your own brand in the PR field.

Candice Champlin
Courtesy of Candice Champlin

Every student reading this, please, I ask of you one thing: Go to class each day and prioritize building relationships with your professors first, and peers second. Yes, friendships are vital to our human spirit, but while you're in school, maximize your time with the professionals in front of you. They are lending their time so that you may learn. Sit in the front row. Make eye contact. Stand out. It is a privilege to be taught by these willing mentors who want you to learn; don't spend your time sitting in the back. Always seek additional opportunities; ask all your questions, even if they seem silly. These habits can only lead to growth before blossoming into success. Be consistent, be reliable. As Mark Schaefer says, "Passion is common, but endurance is rare." Beginnings aren't impressive, but completing your future goals is. When one checkpoint is finished, already be on the way to your next milestone. That is something to take pride in. Most importantly, whether you are in social media, marketing, or underwater basket-weaving, remember that there is something to learn from everyone. Find the patience to truly listen from the wonderful world around you. Networking is everywhere, and it is constant—don't miss out!

Candice was born and raised in Louisville, Kentucky. After spending over a decade in the veterinary industry, she discovered the power of storytelling through social media for improving the relationship between clinician and client. Today she teaches those same concepts to business owners and individuals at an international level through her company Red Rein Media, LLC. When not working, she can be found beside her Great Dane, her horses, or her many fish tanks.

Abbie Chambers
Courtesy of Abbie Chambers

Abbie Chambers, a recent graduate working in public relations and social media with Hyland Insurance, is building her career by gaining experience at local and global events including the Kentucky Derby, Unbridled Eve, and other happenings in Louisville. Abbie discusses the need to gain experience through volunteer efforts and making sure to build strong connections online as well as offline in the industry.

Throughout my time at the University of Louisville, I was fortunate enough to work with brands both locally and nationally. My education and the connections that I have made have allowed me to get involved in my city in ways I would've never imagined, like working with the Kentucky Derby, during one of the most controversial sports calls in Churchill Downs history in 2019 (talk about crisis), and working other major events and brands around town such as Unbridled Eve, Papa John's, and Heaven Hill Brands.

My best advice for any student in the realm of public relations is to stay connected. Public relations and all of its different aspects are ever-evolving, so push yourself out of your comfort zone and make it a priority to go to networking events so that you can keep learning. One way you can do this as a student is to reach out to the speakers that your professors bring in. They are there to help—they wouldn't be volunteering their time to speak to your class if they weren't—so, don't be afraid! Send them a message, ask to meet up for coffee (or meet virtually, if they aren't local), talk about their experiences, share your goals, and work to build a genuine relationship with them. Another very important tip that I recommend is to always show your gratitude. There's a reason you reached out to these people—you admire them! Show your gratitude for their time by doing your research on them and their work, follow them on social media, and learn as much as you can about them before you meet. This will show that you are genuine, thankful, and appreciative of their knowledge and time. There is enough room at the table for everyone, so don't be intimidated—you got this!

Abbie Chambers attended the University of Louisville, where she earned her bachelor's degree in communication in 2018. Throughout her time at the University of Louisville, she was able to work with brands both locally, with the Louisville City Football Club and the Louisville Bats, and nationally, with Cinnabon. Her education, mentors, and the connections that she has made have allowed her to get involved in the city in many ways she would've never imagined. Since graduating, she has been able to work with Churchill Downs (covering events like the Kentucky Derby 145), the Forecastle Festival, Heaven Hill Brands, Facebook Blueprint, and Papa John's, as well as to cover other events throughout the city. Abbie's goal is to be the "go-to girl" when it comes to covering events in Louisville. She has combined her love for the city and her passion for social media marketing to help raise awareness on all that Louisville has to offer.

Michael Jester, a nontraditional student who came back to college after working for several years, discusses the importance of understanding what skills and experiences are needed in the field, while also noting key skills employers are looking for in their candidates.

Social media is the catch-all of modern communication. It's public relations, marketing, entertainment, and educational. As you make your way through college and prepare for "the real world," don't let the experience pass you by while you sit on the sidelines! Take every opportunity you can grab ahold of through internships, freelance work, and other professional experiences that revolve around social media and the specialty you are interested in. Also, talk to your professors! They're thought leaders in the arena you are trying to enter and are not only experts in their fields, but also usually well connected to those communities and know who might be looking for an excited, talented student hungry for real-world experience. Once you make that leap to your first (or next) job, continue to feed that hunger for growth. Be the best you can be at what you do, and make sure the people who make the decisions know your name, that you are a hard worker, and that you want to continue to grow and learn to help the company as a whole. The squeaky wheel gets the grease, they say, so stay squeaking—and good luck!

Michael Jester
Courtesy of Michael Jester

Michael Jester is a copywriter and social media manager based in Louisville, whose career has taken him from composing tweets for local businesses to composing Instagram Stories for international events like the Kentucky Derby. He is a graduate of the University of Louisville and counts Dr. Freberg as one of his favorite professors!

Megan Richardson, a recent college graduate now working at Norton Healthcare as a social media specialist and online reputation manager, believes in taking every opportunity to invest in the professional relationships you can make in the industry as well as in your community.

Take advantage of every opportunity given to you. When given class projects, invest in them and take the time to learn from them because you never know when an issue or problem could be resolved from that experience. You also want to take advantage of talking to professors in the field you want to go in. They can give you advice, help you make connections, or even help you find internship opportunities. Networking is key when in college. These connections can be carried along after college and may give you an opportunity for a job. Networking can also help you grow and keep up with trends in the industry. Enjoy every moment!

Megan Richardson
Courtesy of Megan Richardson

Megan Richardson is a University of Louisville graduate with a degree in communication who excels and works hard as a social media specialist at Norton Healthcare. She is an expert in strategically managing profiles on social media platforms like Facebook, Twitter, LinkedIn, and Instagram, and has been successful in expanding online presence through personalized interactions with target audiences. Connect with Megan on social at @megan_macr.

REINVENTION AND THE FUTURE

In moving forward as a profession, there are still some practices that will never go out of style and will still be important to embrace when entering the next chapter in your career as a rising professional.

ALWAYS PAY IT FORWARD AND BE AWARE OF HOW CHANGE IS VIEWED BY THE PROFESSION

In order for the field to grow, mentorship should be at the heart of what we do. No one is successful purely on their own. We all have mentors and people that have helped us along the way in our journey.

ALWAYS BE MINDFUL OF BALANCE

It is very tempting to get wrapped up in all aspects of public relations. We are in an on-demand economy, where everyone expects a notification or response immediately in real time. But as we have learned over the years, this does not make up for a healthy lifestyle. In order to avoid burnout, you have to have balance in your perspectives and life.

LEARNING DOES NOT STOP AFTER YOU LEAVE THIS CLASS

Continue to study and search for new information. Uncover ideas from other fields and discuss how they can be possibly incorporated in public relations. Seek out mentors in the field so you can learn from their experiences. Set forth goals that will help you continue your educational practices; we are all students in public relations. No one is an expert and we can all learn from each other.

DON'T BE SURPRISED THAT THE FIELD WILL CONTINUE TO CHANGE

Public relations is not going to sit idly while other fields advance with the new challenges and opportunities we're seeing with the evolution of technology platforms. in fact, not only should we be aware of these changes, we should be the ones sparking the changes.

GO TO AN AREA OF PUBLIC RELATIONS WHERE NO ONE ELSE IS

As you go forward, do an audit of the skills and areas of expertise each industry has to offer. It is important to invest in the skills, experiences, and areas in PR no one else is going into to offer something unique and different.

What Are Best Practices for Advancing Your Future?

As you embark on your new careers as future PR professionals, I feel it is appropriate to share with you some words of advice and experience as you venture out into the industry with your new talents and skills. There are certain things that you can't learn in textbooks that will help you as you start your careers. I hope these words of wisdom provide you with some reassurance as well as some awareness of what to expect. These points are meant to address everything you may want to know about public relations, but are afraid to ask about.

1. *Embrace change and make an impact.* Mentorship should be at the heart of every-thing we do. No one is successful purely on his or her own. We all have mentors, friends, family, professors, colleagues, and others who have helped us along in our journey, and we can learn from each other. We can, and should, do our best to lift each other up by taking moments to say a kind word or offer support and guidance. But be aware: Unfortunately there are people who want to hold others down, likely because they are afraid of change and want to maintain the status quo. As unfair as it is, you may encounter this from people in powerful positions, people who may be wary that you offer a different perspective or come from a different background. We should never be afraid to raise questions and ideas that are distinct, forward-thinking, or even potentially revolutionary. If you see people coming forward with innovative ideas and perspectives that can make a positive difference in our field, please support them. Take them out for coffee and learn their story. Share your wisdom or years of experience with newer professionals so they do not enter the field misguided or blindfolded. For all of us to grow, we have to support each other. Otherwise, we are on the path to self-destruction as a profession. The point here is not to scare you. Some backlash happens in any field when a new generation enters the workplace with fresh ideas and motivation to spark change. At the end of the day, be that spark.

2. *Strive for balance.* It is very tempting to get wrapped up in all aspects of public relations. In this field, we are constantly on the go, working with clients, strategiz-ing new ideas, and integrating research into our campaign strategies. We are in an on-demand economy, where everyone expects a notification or response imme-diately, in real time. But as we have learned over the years, this does not make for a healthy lifestyle. To avoid burnout, you *must* have balance in your life. Be focused on your work, but make sure you take time to enjoy life and what it has to offer. When you are evaluating internships and jobs, look for how the people in the workplace integrate balance in their work and personal lives. If you're working for an agency that prides itself on working 24/7, this may not be the place for you. Having balance in your life will make you able to do the best work you possibly can. Make sure to take up hobbies and activities that restore and energize you. We all have the same hours in the day, but we also have the power and choice to set our own expectations and standards.

3. *Know that learning does not stop after you leave school.* Over the years, this is something that I've shared with my students as they venture out in public rela-tions. Many say, "I'm so glad I'll be getting a job—and I'll never have to do homework again." I respond with this: You are a lifelong learner. We are all

lifelong learners. Learning does not stop when you leave class and graduate. In fact, it is just the beginning. Ours is a field that is constantly changing and evolving, and if you stop taking the time to learn, you will quickly discover that your skills, expertise, and knowledge will soon become dated. Treat learning like you would reading about or working on a hobby, or practicing a musical instrument or sport. Spend time every day to gain knowledge and grow and hone your craft. *Be a student of the field.*

4. *Study. Prepare. Do your homework.* It's important to stay on top of what's happening in the industry, and on what you need to know to do your job well. Because our field is in constant flux, there is always something you don't know yet. Platforms change rapidly each and every day, as do the best practices that we follow when we carry out our PR efforts. If we assume we know everything that needs to be known, we are only taking a tiny slice of the enormous possibilities of the field. Look and search for new information. Explore new, diverse ideas from other fields and discuss how they possibly can be incorporated into public relations. Seek out mentors in the field so you can learn from their experiences. Set forth goals that will help you continue your education. We are all students in public relations. No one is an expert, and we can all learn from each other.

5. *Get comfortable with change. Advance with technology.* Back in the day, when I was at the University of Florida studying public relations, we were talking about these new things called *blogs*. We may laugh about that now, but at the time, blogs were absolutely revolutionary for our work in public relations. Fast-forward to today, and we're talking about augmented reality, mixed reality, artificial intelligence, and many more exciting developments that have a direct impact on how we communicate, engage, and formulate strategic relationships with our audiences. This is the nature of our field. Public relations is not going to sit idly by while other fields advance with the opportunities that come with the evolution of technology platforms. Not only should we be aware of these changes; we should be the ones sparking the changes.

6. *Enter an area of public relations that is underpopulated.* You may be questioning why I'm telling you this as you are finishing this textbook. But I mean it: To be relevant, to stand out in the industry, and to push it forward, sometimes you have to go where others are not willing to go. As you consider your future path, do an audit of the skills and areas of expertise that various parts of the industry have to offer, and even look further to PR practices within other industries. Doing so provides you with invaluable insights that you can apply as you do your own audit of the field, and of your own aptitudes, to see where you fit the best. If you discover you have certain abilities and skills that are not only practiced in the industry but extremely valuable because of the scarcity of the skills and experiences, you will be marketable. Not only that, but there will be people who will want you to join their team and be able to teach fellow colleagues what you know. Being different and bringing forth outside-of-the-box thinking is the name of the game.

7. *Take a stance. Be a leader.* My advice to you all is simply this: If you see the field going in a direction that you feel is not where it should be going, do not be afraid to raise your hand and say we need to evaluate where we're going as a profession. In my own career, I've tried my best to showcase different ideas and perspectives that can help PR professionals to move forward. Some of these ideas have been embraced, and some have crashed and burned because the idea requires that "change" will have to happen. This sometimes happens in our field, but do not be discouraged. Feel empowered to stand up with your ideas. What is the worst thing that can happen? Do not let anyone tell you that you can't do something. Embrace what others say and use it as motivation. This was something I learned as a track and field athlete in high school and college. What better way to respond to these comments than to say "Watch me"?

8. *Don't worry about getting bored. It will never happen.* As we've learned throughout this book, the places where a degree in public relations can take you are limitless. Each day is different, and we're a very fortunate group to have the opportunity to learn new skills that test our abilities and to apply and integrate them into our practices. There's no better time to be in public relations, and no better time to explore its possibilities. We are going places.

9. *Have fun. Be creative.* Our profession is a fun one. It allows us to impact other people's lives and to create positive change. Whether we practice this in our own companies or brands, through agencies, or through networking and reaching out to new audiences for our clients, public relations is a field in which we can embrace our personal creativity and be celebrated for it. Think of it. Your creative ideas can be used to do good in the real world, on a global stage. I may be a little biased, but my career in public relations is a rewarding one, and one that I would not exchange for any other out there.

SUMMARY

Now that I have been able to pass along my words of wisdom from the years that I've been teaching and working in public relations, as well as to embrace my inner Obi-Wan Kenobi for you all, I wish you the best of luck. This is just the beginning of your journey and adventure in public relations. If your college or university offers majors and minors in public relations, I hope you will consider applying for them. If your program offers other courses in public relations, I hope that you take advantage of them with the same enthusiasm as you brought to this course.

Rest assured, there'll always be people out there who will be with you and help you along the way in your PR journey. As you begin your career, you can always reach out to those of us who want to serve and mentor your generation of PR professionals. We're out there willing to help in any way we can. You are the future of our field, and we are here to make sure you achieve your dreams, make the impact you want to make, and advance public relations toward a modern future, toward its next chapter.

I look forward to working together. Let's go out and discover what we can do for the future of public relations.

May the PR force be with you all. —*Star Wars*

May the job and internship odds be ever in your favor. —*The Hunger Games*

I drink coffee, and I know PR things. —Tyrion from *Game of Thrones*

Go! Fight! Win—and email/tweet/Insta when you get done. I enjoy our visits. —Edna Mode from *The Incredibles*

GAME CHANGER

Brian Solis, Digital Anthropologist, Author, and Keynote Speaker

Courtesy Brian Solis

How did you get your start in the industry?

The truth is I didn't set out to get involved in the communications or marketing industry. It's something I fell into.

Early in my career, I was a database architect and tech geek living in Los Angeles. That was a very difficult place to be, considering it was the early '90s and there weren't a lot of technologies there yet. So I took the only job available to me at the time, database manager at a technology-centered advertising and PR agency. At that time, in the early '90s, tech was really about business-to-business and enterprise audiences. As a database architect for a small firm, I found it easy to hear conversations on topics from ad strategy to creative to media buying and communications strategies. I used to add my voice to conversations, even when it wasn't sought. However, as a technologist, I felt I had something to say to help the teams be more compelling and thoughtful in their work considering I was in their audience.

After months and months of offering my opinion, one day the president of the agency playfully quipped, "If you think you can do better, why don't you try it?" He offered me a few small clients on the communications side and opportunities to add insights to creative and media on the advertising side.

And that was the beginning of many years of trying to invent my way through marketing.

And by *invent* I mean that I had no marketing background. So, instead of learning classical marketing approaches, I thought the best way to be successful was to start with the end in mind. Which, in this case, was how do I reach (tech) people like me? How to build bridges between the technologies I represent, the value propositions they offer, and the points and opportunities of the people I'm trying to reach? Where do they go for direction, and whom do they trust?

I was able to find answers that weren't in the textbooks or (commercial) marketing books at the time. To me, my marketing approach meant making markets by bringing human-centered solutions across the board.

What is your favorite part of working in the industry?

At that time, my favorite part was about invention and having to prove myself and earn the respect and support of clients and industry influencers who had no idea who this person was and where he came from. And why a technologist would become a marketer. Those drivers really inspired me to push harder and harder over the years.

What really motivated me was invention and the need to invent or create markets that didn't exist. You had two types of technology solutions at that time. One was creating an entirely new market. The other was automating or iterating based on the previous generation's technology. I focused solely on market creation and growth. And that's where I believe my calling came to light—creating markets.

When you have to create markets and drive growth for companies that are paving the way for the future, you too have to find new ways to help—and never with enough resources/budget or understanding.

And that's what led to a lot of innovations that I was part of in many, many stages of my career.

Lastly what I think drove me was a counterintuitive approach—sharing everything I was trying and learning—in the early days of the consumer internet. Without seeking to, I built for an audience of peers and those looking to approach marketing and growth differently.

What is the most challenging part of working in your industry?

At the time, none of this was popular or understood or even validated other than through my own case studies and experiences. And it's not like there was a demand for those types of services. Not only did I have to create but I also had to *sell* to audiences that were unaware of what was available to them.

And this is where the story becomes very personal. When you invent new ways of approaching goals, you can't always bring that into a legacy organization. I had to create my own start-ups dedicated to the practice of these techniques and experimentation with new ideas. So I was inventing on all fronts and growing on all fronts.

What are some things you wish you knew when you were starting out in the industry?

In some ways, I was lucky enough to not know what I was getting myself into. That's what allowed me to create what I hope are ideas and approaches that the industry can still benefit from today.

I wish I knew, though, how difficult it is to change mindsets. A lot of what I was doing then was effective, but it was only as effective once people believed they could benefit from the work.

And in many ways that is still what I deal with today, changing mindsets and helping people see new ways, even though they challenge convention. It is how we change the world.

Another important thing: how to be more competent in blazing new trails and not constantly overthinking or second-guessing the things I was doing. I remember it being a lonely space. That's why I surrounded myself with entrepreneurs and investors who formed a support group of sorts.

And that helped me go to bed every night feeling like I was working on something important and wake up the next morning with the strength to get through the day. I would love to have known more about life and development skills that would have helped strengthen my belief system and help me be more assertive at that time.

In fact, I moved away from marketing because of the amount of effort it took to convince executives to believe in new possibilities and to trust that the innovation around growth was worth the effort.

So I shifted gears to go after the C-suite. The same problems were affecting the transformation of businesses.

If I was going to expend so much energy, I wanted to have greater impact.

Who do you think are the biggest game changers for your industry?

I remember the time in the early 2000s that blogging started to become influential. If you shared something that was helpful and thoughtful, you would spark a very big and meaningful conversation. During those early years of blogging and the rise of social media, the impact of my work became increasingly exponential. In that time I was lucky enough to meet Geoff Livingston, who asked me to help him with the launch of his book *Now Is Gone*.

Shortly afterward, I was asked to co-author a book with another industry pioneer, Deirdre K. Breakenridge, *Putting the Public Back in Public Relations: How Social Media Is Reinventing the Aging Business of PR*.

Both experiences allowed my ideas to reach new audiences, which led to greater impact.

Brian Solis is a world-renowned independent digital analyst, anthropologist, and futurist. He is also an award-winning author, prominent blogger/writer, and global keynote speaker.

Solis has studied and influenced the effects of emerging technology on business, marketing, and culture. His research, talks, and books help executives, and also everyday people, better understand the relationship between the evolution of technology and its impact on business and society and also the role we each play in it. As a result of his work, Solis helps leading brands, celebrities, and start-ups develop new digital transformation, culture 2.0, and innovation strategies that enable businesses to adapt to new connected markets from the inside out.

CASE STUDY

A University of Tennessee Fan and His T-Shirt:
A Lesson in Going for It

Student-designed UT Vols shirt being sold by the University of Tennessee

Knox News

The power of a story capturing the world by storm came from a single post from an elementary school teacher. Laura Snyder, who teaches fourth grade at Altamonte Elementary School in Florida, shared a picture of one of her students wearing his own designed T-shirt supporting the University of Tennessee on College Colors Day (Abrahamson, 2019). In 2019, Snyder wrote on her Facebook page:

Last week, my elementary school participated in college colors day. When I told my students about this day a week before, this particular child came to me and told me that he wanted to wear a University of Tennessee shirt, but he didn't have one. We discussed that he could wear an orange shirt to show his spirit. He told me every day leading up to it that he had an orange shirt that he was going to wear. So when the day finally arrived, he was SO EXCITED to show me his shirt. I was impressed that he took it one step further to make his own label. After lunch, he came back to my room, put his head on his desk and was crying. Some girls at the lunch table next to his (who didn't even participate in college colors day) had made fun of his sign that he had attached to his shirt. He was DEVASTATED. I know kids can be cruel, I am aware that it's not the fanciest sign, BUT this kid used the resources he had available to him to participate in a spirit day (one that I celebrated all week: Go Noles)! I plan to get him a University of Tennessee shirt, but was wondering if anyone has any connections to the University of Tennessee. I wanted to make it a little extra special for him. If anyone has any contacts that they'd be willing to share, please let me know. Thanks!

Once Synder posted this update, it spread like wildfire on social media, where audiences were sharing the story and supporting the boy and his T-shirt design, and even major outlets like the *New York Times*, the *Today* show, ESPN, and *College GameDay* covered the story for everyone to hear about.

As a result of the viral nature of this story, the University of Tennessee not only re-created the T-shirt to sell and support efforts against bullying, but offered the student a scholarship to attend the school for four years (Klein, 2019).

Why did this case generate buzz?

- This case sparked a lot of discussion related to the nature of the story. The boy that designed the University of Tennessee shirt was bullied by other classmates for his homemade designs, but this was then shared on social media, and the results were positive and outpouring to the student in question—media coverage, donations to support efforts to combat bullying, and even financial incentives to support the student's future studies at the University of Tennessee.

- The University of Tennessee listened and wanted to make sure the teacher and student knew their support was appreciated by going the extra effort in fostering this new relationship. The university went beyond what was expected in many cases, which raised its own brand presence and positive mentions in the media and community as well.

What are the ethical and legal issues?

- Since the student in question is a minor, there are concerns related to privacy and others who will try to capitalize on the situation for unethical and illegal means.

- The University of Tennessee had to make sure it was very transparent in making sure it was not profiting from the boy's design, but supporting efforts to combat bullying. This could have been an ethical issue if the university was portrayed as trying to take advantage of a story like this.

- This also brings forward the potential for others to try to do something like this in the future. The University of Tennessee will need to of course have a protocol and policy in place in case certain cases come forward, and determine the most ethical way to handle these situations.

What are some takeaways from this case?

- Taking one simple action to change the life of one person can empower a brand, company, and community.

- The University of Tennessee did not have to do anything from this case, but it did and went beyond what was expected. There was an emotional tie and reason for the university to engage and interact with its young fan in Florida, and as a result, the university built up goodwill for its efforts on a global stage.

- It does not take a multimillion-dollar campaign to make a difference in someone's life or a community's. All it takes is kindness, empathy, and doing the right thing. This is what all PR professionals need to strive for in our work—to make an impact and difference in the lives of others.

DISCUSSION QUESTIONS

1. What have been the biggest takeaways from the book? What areas do you feel you want to learn more about in future classes and sequences in public relations?

2. Where do you see the future of public relations going? Highlight two trends you feel PR professionals need to invest in and why.

3. What are your next moves in the PR field? Explain the next steps you will take in your PR journey.

ACTIVITIES

Building Your Portfolio

Creating your digital media kit and portfolio. Now that you have completed the various assignments and exercises in this book, it is time to put everything together in a complete digital and offline copy. You will be asked to create a digital portfolio (using a free website host platform such as Wix, Squarespace, or WordPress) to upload your materials. Create a bio page highlighting your background, goals and objectives for working in public relations, social media profile pages, and ways to get in contact with you. Upload your top five assignments from this book you feel showcase your insights, expertise, and experiences so far.

Building Your Brand

Personal video take on future of public relations. Create a one- to two-minute video of yourself talking about your biggest takeaways from public relations. Highlight areas you are interested in and steps you will be taking to further your education, training, and understanding of the field. Edit this video in Adobe Premiere Rush, Adobe Premiere, or Final Cut Pro to be uploaded on YouTube (for personal branding purposes).

GLOSSARY

Account director: This leadership position focuses on coordinating efforts for the client, managing the team, and addressing the overall needs and expectations of the campaign and all parties involved; a professional who oversees managerial and strategic responsibilities in public relations.

Account executive: The first entry-level position for those with bachelor's degrees; professionals in this role have more responsibilities than interns, and are required to take on both technical and managerial responsibilities for a brand or agency.

Account specialist: A PR specialist who is assigned to a specific account or client for a specific reason.

Activities: The strategies and tactics portion of a campaign plan; the content and messages we will create and disseminate out to our audiences.

Advertising: The persuasive form of paid media content to create an emotional connection with an audience member.

Advertising value equivalents: Also known as AVEs; first implemented by advertising firms in the 1940s with the overall purpose of evaluating the effectiveness of message exposure.

Advocacy program: A partnership with those who are strong supporters of a brand in a professional capacity.

Alignment balance: Having a consistent, authentic, and true representation of who you are in various circles and communities.

Ambassador program: A program focused on audiences of loyal supporters outside of the company who have a strong affinity for the company.

Ambassadors: Employees who leverage their own loyalty as a currency; these individuals are engaged, transparent, and willing to share their stories and insights with communities both on- and offline.

Analysis: Determines what happened in the past and what we can learn from that experience.

Analyst: A professional who conducts research to be integrated and applied into media strategies, audience insights, and campaigns.

Analytics: An integrated approach for collecting data, interpreting data patterns, and applying data insights into actionable strategies.

Attack the accuser: In crisis management, to confront the person or group claiming something is wrong with an organization.

Audience segmentation: The process of categorizing people into groups based on specific criteria, which can be broad in nature, organizing audiences based on demographics and population data, or narrowly focused (niche), organizing audiences according to specific categories such as industries, interests, or visual drive.

Audio content: Spoken and recorded content.

B2B: Business-to-business practices and audiences.

B2C: Business-to-consumer practices and audiences.

Backgrounder: An overview of the key players involved in a PR campaign.

Behavioral segmentation: Analyzing the actual behavior and actions individuals take; going beyond psychographics to consider how an audience has behaved or acted in relation to a client or brand.

Blog: A "traditional" piece of digital content that provides (along with other long-form content) the means to share updates, insights, reflections, and news related to a company, professional, or individual.

Branding: The strategic promotion of a product, company, or person through various visual, written, and design capabilities; beyond visual messaging and storytelling, it requires a commitment to showing key audiences that we and our clients are different from our competitors.

Budget: Collection and analysis of resources that show how much these items cost in a campaign.

Business acumen: Understanding of business principles such as accounting, finance, marketing, and sales.

Calendar: An overview of the length and timing of items happening before, during, and after a campaign.

Celebrity influencer: An influencer who is prominent based on work in other fields (movies, sports, politics, etc.).

Character: What you really are (while your reputation is merely what others think you are).

Chief diversity and inclusion officer: The professional in the C-suite who oversees the internal and external diversity and inclusion efforts in campaigns, communication, policy, and marketing initiatives.

Client overview: A brief section of a PR plan introducing our clients and where they stand presently before a campaign.

Code of ethics: A set of guidelines and principles for proper conduct to follow.

Communication channel segmentation: Audience engagement and interaction across various channels (media, individuals, communities, devices, platforms, influencers/advocates/creators, sources, etc.).

Communication manager: A professional whose overall focus is to listen, coordinate, and engage the various channels and communities for a particular organization.

Consultant: A professional who works with clients to share their ideas, but may not necessarily produce or execute the content proposed; allows for choosing your own clients, setting your rates, and choosing your areas of specialization.

Content amplification: The distribution of content and messaging to audience feeds and accounts.

Content creation: The development of original materials made up of relevant information, stories, and other pieces not previously produced.

Content creator: A professional who focuses not only on writing but on tying in other pieces of content, such as visual, audio, and textual content, to bring forth a cohesive and transmedia experience for a brand.

Content curation: The search for relevant articles, resources, and materials that others (fans, customers, brands, media personalities, influencers, creators, etc.) have composed.

Content execution: A focus on how and where we'll deliver our materials to our audiences.

Content ideation: Having a great idea, or great ideation, that allows us to see the big picture of our writing situation and to strategize how to bring our concept to life.

Content marketing: The process of promoting our content to audiences, giving brands and audiences new ways to make connections, start dialogues, and reinforce perceptions.

Content strategy: Looking at how and why we create and manage our materials, as well as how to update them for future use.

Copywriter: A professional who is skilled in writing in different formats, media, and contexts.

Core problem statement: A one-sentence statement summarizing the big issue that needs to be addressed in a strategic campaign.

Corporate social responsibility: Tying together the social, environmental, and financial efforts to support specific campaigns and causes aligned with a brand.

Corrective action: In crisis management, the offer of money or other gifts to victims of a crisis.

Creative content: Innovative and unique approaches to crafting stories and strategic messages into consumable content that is relevant and sparks entertaining interest for the key public.

Creative writing: Creative messaging that goes beyond the simple transmission of information to engage and entertain, an important element for PR professionals.

Creator: A member of a subset of influencers who create for brands original content in their own voices, and who view their creativity as the most important part of their contribution to a brand.

Crisis: A significant, disruptive event that often features a rapid onset.

C-suite: All senior-level officials for a corporation based on different departments and responsibilities.

Deception: Occurs when someone makes a false or misleading statement to persuade audiences.

Defamation: Any false statement about a person or organization that creates public hatred, contempt, or ridicule, or that inflicts injury on a reputation.

Demographics: Population data points such as age, gender, income, education, and race.

Denial: In crisis management, asserting that there is no crisis.

Digital media: All channels and outlets that are online, including discussion board forums, blogs, social media, and other aspects of the World Wide Web.

Diversity: Made up of several components, such as race, ethnicity, gender, sexuality, culture, and political thought.

Diversity head: A professional who oversees the programming, planning, policymaking, and advocacy efforts to be inclusive in and outside of an organization.

Earned media: Media channels and content gained by word-of-mouth communications and relationships; part of the PESO model.

Employee advocacy program: A program that is designed to incentivize and encourage employees to tell their stories, perspectives, and views to external as well as internal audiences.

Employee relations: Engaging in PR practices not with outside clients but with employees, staff, and others who work inside our organization or brand; also known as internal relations.

Engagement: The interaction of an audience member or public with a client or community.

Entrepreneurship: The pursuit of opportunity beyond resources controlled.

Environmental scan: An overview of the factors that are happening outside of our clients' internal environment that can impact their work; also known as an external scan.

Ethics: How one should behave based on values and what is right or wrong.

Evergreen content: Content that is relevant and sustainable for a long period of time.

Evidence-based practices (EBPs): Research that is bottom-up and begins and ends with the client, moving well beyond a one-size-fits-all model and encompassing clients' unique experience with their presenting problems.

Excuse: In crisis management, denying intent to do harm and/or claiming inability to control the events that triggered the crisis, minimizing organizational responsibility.

Exposure: How many people were able to see a message.

Feature story: A long-form piece of content in which the writer tells a story using the tools of narrative writing, such as dialogue, detail, and creativity.

Fieldwork: Work including observation and enthography studies that we do in the real world, in the natural environment and in various settings such as communities and corporations, and that takes a lot of time.

Flywheel: HubSpot's new approach to the marketing funnel that has three main objectives: to attract, engage, and delight.

Formal research: Research that can be published since it went through the rigorous process of data analysis and recruiting.

Freelancer: A professional who takes advantage of having his or her own clients and focusing on specific projects and clients.

Full apology: Indication by the crisis manager that the organization takes full responsibility for the crisis and asks stakeholders for forgiveness.

Generalist: A professional who knows and has experience in all aspects of public relations.

Impact: High-level objectives that contribute to social media protocols and actions, and to the well-being of the entire organization; objectives that reflect brand reputation, changes in policies, or improved business practices.

Impressions: Interactions between a piece of content and an audience member.

Impressions value: How much the exposure would cost you if you had to pay for this coverage.

Inclusion: The bringing together of people with different experiences, perspectives, backgrounds, and ideas to make sure each group is representative of its audiences and the public at large.

Influencer: Someone who has built an audience, naturally and over time, and who is viewed as an authority on a certain subject, practice, or perspective in online spaces; with the trust of a community, this person can share content that persuades an audience to take a specific action.

Influencer relations: A role that requires PR expertise, but must also integrate social and digital chops, audience insights, media relations, analytics, and marketing campaign measures.

Infographic: An illustration used to present data (research), share knowledge (information), and capture attention (visual experiences).

Informal research: Research that is done on a whim.

Information processing: Characterizes audience members who prefer to wait for information to come to them.

Information seeking: Characterizes audience members who want to understand and fix a problem.

Ingratiation: In crisis management, praising stakeholders for their action.

Inputs: Who our target audience is, what the current situation is, and what resources are available to understand them.

Intern: The most common position offered to those beginning their careers as PR professionals.

Internships: Positions, offered for class credit or no credit, that boost our experience levels and our résumés.

Justification: In crisis management, minimization of the perceived damage caused by the crisis.

Libel: Printed falsehood.

Listening: Uncovering emerging trends, opportunities, activities, and issues that could impact an organization either positively or negatively.

Lobbyist: A professional who works with Congress to get bills passed; a particular specialization within the political and government arena.

Long-form content: Content that is long in length and time.

Management by objectives: Ensuring that the objectives of our strategic plan are simple, understandable, and connected with measurable achievements.

Manager: A professional who oversees management and strategy components of public relations.

Marketing: The field that promotes and engages in business practices to motivate audiences to make a purchase of a product or service; oversees efforts in public relations, advertising, and related disciplines.

Measurement and evaluation: The systematic assessment of PR initiatives; determining whether PR professionals and clients have been held accountable for efforts in a campaign.

Media: The means (visual, audio, written, or all of the above) to broadcast information to the masses.

Media kit: A collection of premade promotional and informational materials that cover a brand, person, or cause that is targeted for distribution to media professionals.

Media relations specialist/publicist: A professional whose overall focus is to generate coverage in the media for clients across various channels and audiences, and to coordinate proactive relationships with the media (traditional, social, and emerging).

Mega influencer: An influencer who has a prominent status on social media and a broad appeal that puts him or her on track to reach celebrity status; an individual who shapes culture and industries and makes a direct impact on the community by driving sales of products and services.

Message strategy: Highlights the key points that we want to communicate.

Micro influencer: An influencer who has generated significant attention over the past few years because of an ability to cultivate strong communities around particular interests.

Mixed-methods research: The combination of qualitative and quantitative methods.

Monitoring: The systematic process of analyzing and reporting online insights and conversations on a brand's reputation, position, and community, and the opinions of key audience members.

Nano influencer: An influencer with few followers, and with audiences even smaller than those of micro influencers.

News release: Publishing content that focuses on hard news, such as breaking news and announcements.

Objectives: Statements on what we want to accomplish in our campaign.

Opportunity: The idea that a product or service being offered is unique in a variety of ways; perhaps it represents an innovative product, a newer or cheaper version of a product, the targeting of a new audience with a product, or the use of a new business model.

Outcomes: How well the audience receives our messages; the extent to which audience members changed their views or attitudes.

Outputs: The specific measures that we are able to collect and evaluate, including likes, comments, reach, impressions, and engagement.

Outtakes: The reactions and behaviors that occur as a result of our messages, content, and actions; the likeliness that others recall our content and share it with others.

Owned media: Media channels and content that are owned by the client or individual; part of the PESO model.

Paid media: Media channels and content that are paid for by the client or individual; part of the PESO model.

Persona: The reflection of a customer who typifies the audience we are trying to reach; creating a persona allows us to illustrate the unique characteristics that separate one audience from another and help us better understand the motivating factors and influences that drive a particular audience to engage with, act upon, or respond to certain messages and campaigns.

Personal brand: A collection of a person's various attributes, expertise traits, personality characteristics, and insights that take place both on- and offline.

Persuasive writing: Creating stories, content, and messages that resonate with audiences at an emotional, logical, and practical level, motivating them to take an action or to think differently.

PESO: A model that focuses on paid, earned, shared, and owned media.

Pitch: A short memo, message, or statement outlining clearly what you are trying to accomplish and what you are able to provide in a win-win situation.

PR campaign: A systematic, thorough, and aligned (presented in a consistent and branded fashion) document that outlines from start to finish what an individual, organization, or brand wants to accomplish.

PR coordinator: A professional who is most often housed within a brand and is responsible for supporting the activities of team members within the PR department.

Press agentry and publicity model: A PR model that is characterized by one-way communication from a sender to a receiver with the goal of getting the receiving audience's attention, whether positive or negative.

Press release: Publishing content that focuses on soft news, such as news of partnerships and event coverage.

Primary audiences: The audiences you want to target directly and that have a meaningful relationship and connection to the client.

Primary messages: The key ideas that we need to articulate.

Primary research: Original research, conducted by an individual or team, that has not been published or presented previously.

Psychographics: Lifestyle characteristics such as opinions, attitudes, and behaviors.

Public information model: A PR model focused on providing information to the public from the company's perspective.

Public relations: The strategic communication process that builds mutually beneficial relationships between organizations and their publics.

Publicist: A professional working on generating coverage and media press for a client.

Publics: Individuals who have a clear relationship with the client and will be the primary targets for the message strategies being implemented in a PR campaign.

Puffery: An exaggerated statement (e.g., "This is the best brand ever" or "This is the greatest and best event you could ever go to").

Pursuit: The specific focus and dedication needed to accomplish a set goal for the launch of a new product or service.

Qualitative research: Research that involves exploring how and why things are occurring; addressing questions of quality and characteristics; or exploring what is happening in detail on a one-to-one, or one-to-many, basis.

Quantitative research: Research that addresses questions of "what" or "how many" and is usually evaluated using formal statistical methods, and that allows us to focus on objective measures to predict how certain concepts and variables will act in a controlled setting (like a lab).

RACE: A campaign strategy focusing on research, action, communication, and evaluation.

Real-time writing: A new way of defining the writing that emerges online when timing is of the essence, which requires PR professionals to think on their feet.

Relationship management: A strategy that allows us to focus on our connections with audiences, especially on the strategic communications between our client organizations and their key publics, guiding the choices we make whether we're conducting research, seeking new opportunities for business, or carrying out campaigns.

Reliability: The ability to replicate the results of our research.

Reputation: A collection of perceptions about you or your brand from all stakeholders.

Reputation management: Working on a reputation behind the scenes, rather than on the front lines.

Research: The systematic gathering of information conducted in a scientific and objective manner to help answer questions.

Resources: The constraints that must be evaluated as we consider a possible new venture; they can be social, financial, emotional, and/or time-based, and sometimes are out of our control but in control of others involved.

ROPE: A campaign strategy focusing on research, objectives, planning, and evaluation.

Scientific method: A method of research in which we identify a problem, gather relevant data, form a hypothesis, and then test that hypothesis empirically.

Secondary audiences: Audiences who are supportive and potentially viewed as influencers by the primary audience members.

Secondary messages: The points of evidence that support our primary messages.

Secondary research: The collection and summary of already-published materials, such as reports, articles, communication audits, news reports, and academic articles, that have been reviewed by experts to evaluate quality and identify new insights presented.

Sentiment: How people feel about content—positive, negative, or neutral.

Sentiment analysis: An evaluation of the overall tone of a message as positive, negative, or neutral.

Shared media: Media channels and content that are shared with others; part of the PESO model.

Short-form content: Content that is short in nature.

Situational analysis: A section of the strategic plan for a PR campaign in which we combine the findings of our background research to create a clear overall picture of what is going on for our individual client or our client's organization.

Situational theory of publics: A theory that focuses on organizing audiences based on specific characteristics and attributes.

Slander: Spoken falsehood.

Slow-form content: Content that takes a long time to create but has a long shelf life.

SMART criteria: Specific, measurable, achievable, realistic, and time-specific—important characteristics of a strategic PR plan.

Social capital: Endorsements based on expertise and validation in the community, for an individual in various subject areas, that are key for creating and strategizing how to establish a personal brand, as well as how to market and promote it on- and offline.

Social media: A collection of platforms to engage and interact with, create, and distribute information.

Social media crisis: A crisis that happens on social media or on a particular platform, rapidly spreads from person to person, and spreads virally to become a news story.

Social media manager: A professional who focuses on being the brand on social media.

Social media strategist: A role that ties research and creativity into activating initiatives online for a brand and client; this professional is in charge of managing the messaging, creative assets, audiences, planning, and execution of campaign efforts in social media.

Social proof: Evidence documented online by others validating your brand by showcasing your level of expertise (testimonials, endorsements, quotes, work samples, etc.).

Social selling: Selling practices conducted through social media platforms.

Specialist: An expert in a particular area of public relations or in the field.

Stakeholders: Those who have an invested stake (financially and emotionally) with the client.

Storytelling: Writing the story for a brand as intertwined with the brand purpose, messaging, and essence that can be shared and distributed across different platforms.

Strategic implication: The component of SWOT analysis in which we look at the "so what" factor, which helps us figure out how to move our clients forward, outlining the main challenge and opportunity that needs to be addressed.

Strategic plan: A plan for conducting a PR campaign that must include background, situational analysis, goals, objectives, strategies, tactics, evaluation, and recommendations.

Strategies: How we are going to accomplish our set goals and objectives.

Tactics: The nuts of bolts of a campaign, focused on the tools of communication.

Tea accounts: Accounts inspired by the word *tea*, which is slang for juicy information, similar to online gossip magazines (e.g., networks of Instagram pages, YouTube channels, Twitter handles, and Facebook groups).

Technician: A professional who focuses on producing tactical components in public relations.

Two-way asymmetrical communication model: A PR model that focuses on two-way lines of communication, allowing both sender and receiver to participate in a conversation; the asymmetrical aspect refers to the fact that the receivers are not equal participants in the conversation.

Two-way symmetrical communication model: A PR model that presents a level playing field, making it the "ideal situation" for public relations; a negotiation with the audience with the goal of reaching a cooperative, win-win outcome.

Validity: Whether a measure does what it is advertised to do.

Vanity metrics: Measures that look good but do not really show anything other than high numbers (follower count, impressions, etc.).

Visual content: Images, videos, and illustrations, for example.

Website: A designated online space with a URL and domain name that is attached to a person, organization, or business.

REFERENCES

CHAPTER 1

Andriof, J., & Waddock, S. (2002). Unfolding stakeholder engagement. In J. Andriof, S. Waddock, B. Husted, & S. S. Rahman (Eds.), *Unfolding stakeholder thinking: Theory, responsibility and engagement* (pp. 19–42). Sheffield, UK: Greenleaf.

Argenti, P. A. (1996). Corporate communication as a discipline: Toward a definition. *Management Communication Quarterly, 10*(1), 73–97.

Associated Press. (2018, August 27). Town of Mayo temporarily chjanges its name to "Miracle Whip." *New York Post.* Retrieved from https://nypost.com/2018/08/27/town-of-mayo-temporarily-changes-its-name-to-miracle-whip/

Avidar, R. (2017). Public relations and social businesses: The importance of enhancing engagement. *Public Relations Review, 43*(5), 955–962. doi:https://doi.org/10.1016/j.pubrev.2017.03.015

Brass, D. J., Butterfield, K. D., & Skaggs, B. C. (1998). Relationships and unethical behavior: A social network perspective. *Academy of Management Review, 23*(1), 14–31.

Broom, G. M., & Dozier, D. M. (1983). An overview: Evaluation research in public relations. *Public Relations Quarterly, 28*(3), 5–8.

Cacioppo, J. T., & Freberg, L. A. (2019). *Discovering psychology: The science of mind* (3rd ed.). Boston, MA: Cengage.

Clarkson, S. (1995). A stakeholder framework for analyzing and evaluating corporate social performance. *Academy of Management Review, 20*, 65–91.

Commission on Public Relations Education. (2018, April). *Fast forward: The 2017 report on undergraduate public relations education.* Retrieved from http://www.commissionpred.org/

Cutlip, S. M., & Center, A. H. (1971). *Effective public relations.* Englewood Cliffs, NJ: Prentice Hall.

Dhanesh, G. S. (2017). Putting engagement in its PRoper place: State of the field, definition and model of engagement in public relations. *Public Relations Review, 43*(5), 925–933. doi:https://doi.org/10.1016/j.pubrev.2017.04.001

Dietrich, G. (2020, February 6). PESO Model 2.0: A new masterclass to help you in 2020 and beyond. *SpinSucks.* Retrieved from https://spinsucks.com/communication/peso-model-masterclass/

Freeman R. E. (1984). *Stakeholder management: Framework and philosophy.* Mansfield, MA: Pitman.

Gregory, A., & Halff, G. (2017). Understanding public relations in the "sharing economy." *Public Relations Review, 43*(1), 4–13. doi:https://doi.org/10.1016/j.pubrev.2016.10.008

Grung, J. E., & Repper, F. C. (1992). Strategic management, publics, and issues. In J. E. Grunig (Ed.), *Excellence in public relations and communication management* (pp. 117–158). Hillsdale, NJ: Lawrence Erlbaum.

Heath, R. L. (2000). A rhetorical perspective on the values of public relations: Crossroads and pathways toward concurrence. *Journal of Public Relations Research, 12*(1), 69–91.

Hillman, A. J., & Keim, G. D. (2001). Shareholder value, stakeholder management, and social issues: What's the bottom line? *Strategic Management Journal, 22*(2), 125–139. doi:10.1002/1097-0266

Laplume, A. O., Sonpar, K., & Litz, R. A. (2008). Stakeholder theory: Reviewing a theory that moves us. *Journal of Management, 34*(6), 1152–1189.

Myers, C. (2018). Public relations or "grassroots lobbying"? How lobbying laws are re-defining PR practice. *Public Relations Review, 44*(1), 11–21. doi:https://doi.org/10.1016/j.pubrev.2017.11.006

Public Relations Society of America. (2020). *About public relations.* Retrieved from https://www.prsa.org/all-about-pr/

Schneider, M. (2018, September 19). Report: PR pros outnumber journalists by a 6-to-1 ratio. *PR Daily.* Retrieved from https://www.prdaily.com/report-pr-pros-outnumber-journalists-by-a-6-to-1-ratio/

Sha, B.-L. (2011). Accredited vs. non-accredited: The polarization of practitioners in the public relations profession. *Public Relations Review, 37*(2), 121–128. doi:https://doi.org/10.1016/j.pubrev.2011.02.003

Supa, D. W. (2016). Do you see what I see? An examination of perceptions between advertising and public relations professionals. *Public Relations Review, 42*(3), 408–417. doi:https://doi.org/10.1016/j.pubrev.2016.02.007

Tannahill, J. (2015, September 18). Different definitions of public relations. *Everything PR.* Retrieved from http://everything-pr.com/public-relations-definition/59142/

Tkalac Verčič, A., Lalić, D., & Vujičić, D. (2017). Journalists and public relations practitioners: Comparing two countries. *Public Relations Review, 43*(3), 527–536. doi:https://doi.org/10.1016/j.pubrev.2017.04.006

Valentini, C. (2015). Is using social media "good" for the public relations profession? A critical reflection. *Public Relations Review, 41*(2), 170–177. doi:https://doi.org/10.1016/j.pubrev.2014.11.009

Verčič, D., van Ruler, B., Bütschi, G., & Flodin, B. (2001). On the definition of public relations: A European view. *Public Relations Review, 27*(4), 373–387. doi:https://doi.org/10.1016/S0363-8111(01)00095-9

Wright, D. K. (2018, January 3). What lies ahead for public relations in 2018? *PRsay* (blog). Retrieved from http://prsay.prsa.org/2018/01/03/what-lies-ahead-for-public-relations-in-2018/

CHAPTER 2

Ajzen, I. (1991). The theory of planned behavior. *Organizational Behavior and Human Decision Processes, 50*(2), 179–211.

Ajzen, I. (2001). Nature and operation of attitudes. *Annual Review of Psychology, 52*, 27–58.

Arenstein, S. (2018, April 18). How Southwest communicated news and empathy in the aftermath of Flight 1380. *PR Newswire*. Retrieved from https://www.prnewsonline.com/how-southwest-communicated-news-and-empathy-in-the-aftermath-of-flight-1380/

Arthur W. Page Center. (n.d.-a). *Arthur W. Page*. Retrieved from https://bellisario.psu.edu/page-center/about/arthur-w-page

Arthur W. Page Center. (n.d.-b). *Ethics & the public relations models: Press agentry model*. Retrieved from https://pagecentertraining.psu.edu/public-relations-ethics/core-ethical-principles/lesson-2-sample-title/ethics-the-public-relations-models-press-agentry-model/

Arthur W. Page Society. (n.d.). *The Page Principles*. Retrieved from https://page.org/site/the-page-principles

Bernays, E. (1928). *Propaganda*. New York, NY: H. Liveright.

Blevins, J. L. (2016). Social media mobbing diminishes the quality of public discourse. *The Cincinnati Project*. Retrieved from http://thecincyproject.org/2016/08/28/social-media-mobbing-diminishes-the-quality-of-public-discourse/

Boies, J. (2012, October 15). How Red Bull Stratos successfully soared across social media. *Salesforce* (blog). Retrieved from https://www.salesforce.com/blog/2012/10/how-red-bull-stratos-successfully-soared-across-social-media.html

Bromwich, J. E., & Maheshwari, S. (2019, February 3). Meet the creator of the egg that broke Instagram. *New York Times*. Retrieved from https://www.nytimes.com/2019/02/03/style/world-record-egg-instagram.html

Burson Cohn & Wolfe. (n.d.). *Celebrating Harold Burson*. Retrieved from http://www.haroldburson.com/about.html

Cain, Á. (2019, January 14). Gillette is facing backlash for its #MeToo-inspired commercial that criticizes men—and it's not the first time men rioted after being told to act a certain way. *Business Insider*. Retrieved from https://www.businessinsider.com/gillette-faces-backlash-metoo-commercial-2019-1

Colleary, E. (2012, July 19). How bacon and eggs became the American breakfast. *American Table*. Retrieved from http://www.americantable.org/2012/07/how-bacon-and-eggs-became-the-american-breakfast/

Davenport, C. (2018, February 26). After 2016 rocket explosion, Elon Musk's SpaceX looked seriously at sabotage. *Washington Post*. Retrieved from https://www.washingtonpost.com/news/the-switch/wp/2018/02/26/after-2016-rocket-explosion-elon-musks-spacex-looked-seriously-at-sabotage/?utm_term=.e951efc3d305

Deephouse, D. L. (2000). Media reputation as a strategic resource: An integration of mass communication and resource-based theories. *Journal of Management, 26*(6), 1091–1112.

Edelman. (n.d.). *Richard Edelman: CEO*. Retrieved from https://www.edelman.com/people/richard-edelman

Fishbein, M., & Ajzen, I. (2010). *Predicting and changing behavior: The reasoned action approach*. New York, NY: Taylor & Francis Group.

Freberg, K. (2016). Social media. In C. Carroll (Ed.), *The SAGE encyclopedia for corporate reputation* (pp. 773–777). Thousand Oaks, CA: SAGE Publications.

Grunig, J. E., & Hunt, T. (1984). *Managing public relations*. New York, NY: Holt, Rinehart & Winston.

Hallahan, K. (2002). Ivy Lee and the Rockefellers' response to the 1913–1914 Colorado coal strike. *Journal of Public Relations Research, 14*(4), 265–315. https://doi.org/10.1207/S1532754XJPRR1404_1

Hearn, I. (2019, January 21). What Gillette's controversial ad teaches marketers about "woke advertising." *IMPACT*. Retrieved from https://www.impactbnd.com/blog/what-gillettes-new-ad-teaches-marketers-about-woke-advertising

Henderson, C. (2019, October 9). George W. Bush responds to Ellen DeGeneres' defense of friendship. *USA Today*. Retrieved from https://www.msn.com/en-us/news/us/george-w-bush-responds-to-ellen-degeneres-defense-of-friendship/ar-AAIrc0t?li=AA54y7

Kennedy, M. (2019, October 15). Back from China, LeBron James speaks out on NBA controversy. *NPR*. Retrieved from https://www.npr.org/2019/10/15/770305688/back-from-china-lebron-james-speaks-out-on-nba-controversy

Kerpen, D. (2019, January 17). 3 Reasons the new Gillette commercial is an absolute winner. *Inc*. Retrieved from https://www.inc.com/dave-kerpen/3-reasons-new-gillette-commercial-is-an-absolute-winner.html

Ketchum. (2017, November 28). Ketchum appoints Barri Rafferty chief executive officer, Rob Flaherty continues as chairman. *PR Newswire*. Retrieved from https://www.prnewswire.com/news-releases/ketchum-appoints-barri-rafferty-chief-executive-officer-rob-flaherty-continues-as-chairman-300562594.html

McCluskey, M. (2019, January 16). Gillette makes waves with controversial new ad highlighting "toxic masculinity." *Time*. Retrieved from http://time.com/5503156/gillette-razors-toxic-masculinity/

Museum of Public Relations. (2017, June 20). Crisis management: The historic relationship between Ivy Lee & John D. Rockefeller. Retrieved from http://www.prmuseum.org/blog/2017/6/20/crisis-management-the-historic-relationship-between-ivy-lee-john-d-rockefeller

Museum of Public Relations. (n.d.). *Public relations through the ages: A timeline of social movements, technology milestones, and the rise of the profession*. Retrieved from http://www.prmuseum.org/pr-timeline/

Plank Center for Leadership in Public Relations. (n.d.-a). *Betsy Plank—First Lady of public relations*. Retrieved from http://plankcenter.ua.edu/about/betsy-plank/

Plank Center for Leadership in Public Relations. (n.d.-b). *Betsy Plank Day*. Retrieved from http://plankcenter.ua.edu/betsyday/

Public Broadcasting Service. (n.d.). The Ludlow massacre. *American Experience*. Retrieved from https://www.pbs.org/wgbh/americanexperience/features/rockefellers-ludlow/

Public Relations Society of America. (2020). *About public relations*. Retrieved from https://www.prsa.org/all-about-pr/

Southwest Airlines Flight 1380 Statement #2—Issued 3:00 p.m. CT. (2018, April 17). *Southwest Media*. Retrieved from https://www.swamedia.com/releases/southwest-airlines-confirms-accident-our-hearts-are-with-those-affected

Taylor, M., Kent, M. L. (2010). Anticipatory socialization in the use of social media in public relations: A content analysis of the PRSA's Public Relations Tactics. Public Relations Review, 36(3), 207-214.

Wadsworth, J. (2018, April 25). P.T. Barnum: How "the greatest showman" would survive in PR today. *Platform Magazine*. Retrieved from http://platformmagazine.org/2018/04/26/p-t-barnum-how-the-greatest-showman-would-survive-in-pr-today/

5W Public Relations. (2020, February 27). 5WPR survey reveals 38% of beer-drinking Americans wouldn't buy Corona now. *PR Newswire*. Retrieved from https://www.prnewswire.com/news-releases/5wpr-survey-reveals-38-of-beer-drinking-americans-wouldnt-buy-corona-now-301012225.html

Addady, M. (2016, April 11). Coca-Cola can't keep saying that Vitaminwater is healthy. *Fortune*. Retrieved from http://fortune.com/2016/04/11/coca-cola-vitaminwater/

Arthur W. Page Center. (n.d.-a). *About the center*. Retrieved from https://bellisario.psu.edu/page-center/about/about-the-center

Arthur W. Page Center. (n.d.-b). *The pillars of public relations ethics*. Retrieved from https://pagecentertraining.psu.edu/public-relations-ethics/core-ethical-principles/lesson-2-sample-title/the-pillars-of-public-relations-ethics/

Balkin, J. (2018, November 26). If Facebook is really at war, the only way to win is to put ethics first. *Washington Post*. Retrieved from https://www.washingtonpost.com/outlook/2018/11/26/if-facebook-is-really-war-only-way-win-is-put-ethics-first/?noredirect=on&utm_term=.095c4dd9b906

Baysinger, T. (2019, January 15). Rival Fyre Festival docs ignite words between filmmakers. *The Wrap*. Retrieved from https://www.thewrap.com/netflix-vs-hulu-competing-fyre-festival-documentaries-sets-off-war-of-words-between-two-filmmakers/

Booth, R. (2014, June 29). Facebook reveals news feed experiment to control emotions. *The Guardian*. Retrieved from https://www.theguardian.com/technology/2014/jun/29/facebook-users-emotions-news-feeds

Bowen, S. A. (2003). "I thought it would be more glamorous": Preconceptions and misconceptions among students in the public relations principles course. *Public Relations Review*, 29(2), 199–214. https://doi.org/10.1016/S0363-8111(03)00012-2

Bowen, S. (2007, October 30). *Ethics and public relations*. Institute for Public Relations. Retrieved from https://instituteforpr.org/ethics-and-public-relations/

Bowen, S. A. (2016). Clarifying ethics terms in public relations from A to V, authenticity to virtue: BledCom special issue of PR review sleeping (with the) media: Media relations. *Public Relations Review*, 42(4), 564–572. https://doi.org/10.1016/j.pubrev.2016.03.012

Bucksbaum, S. (2019, January 18). This is what Fyre Founder Billy McFarland's future looks like. *Refinery29*. Retrieved from https://www.refinery29.com/en-gb/2019/01/222052/is-billy-mcfarland-in-jail-fyre-organizer-2019

Commission on Public Relations Education. (2018, April). *Fast forward: The 2017 report on undergraduate public relations education*. Retrieved from http://www.commissionpred.org/

Conner, C. (2017, September 8). PR Infamy: UK's Bell Pottinger nearing closure after "worst ethical breach in history." *Forbes*. Retrieved from https://www.forbes.com/sites/cherylsnappconner/2017/09/08/pr-infamy-uks-bell-pottinger-agency-nearing-closure-after-worst-ethical-breach-in-history/

Frankel, S., Confessore, N., Kang, C., Rosenberg, M., & Nicas, J. (2018, November 14). Delay, deny and deflect: How Facebook's leaders fought through crisis. *New York Times*. Retrieved from https://www.nytimes.com/2018/11/14/technology/facebook-data-russia-election-racism.html

Hern, A. (2019, September 25). Revealed: How TikTok censors videos that do not please Beijing. *The Guardian*. Retrieved from https://www.theguardian.com/technology/2019/sep/25/revealed-how-tiktok-censors-videos-that-do-not-please-beijing

Izadi, E. (2017, September 13). "It's important to stand up to bullies": Rebel Wilson wins record amount in defamation case. *Washington Post*. Retrieved from https://www.washingtonpost.com/news/arts-and-entertainment/wp/2017/09/13/its-important-to-stand-up-to-bullies-rebel-wilson-wins-record-amount-in-defamation-case/

Keating, C. (2018, November 6). Fyre Festival founder apologizes from prison: "I've made many wrong and immature decisions." *People*. Retrieved from https://people.com/music/fyre-festival-founder-billy-mcfarland-prison-apology/

Kowitt, B. (2016, May 10). In reversal, the FDA says "healthy" can return to Kind bar packaging. *Fortune*. Retrieved from http://fortune.com/2016/05/10/kind-bar-healthy-fda/

Lee, B. (2017, May 1). Fyre Festival: A case study in social media MisUse. *Inc*. Retrieved from https://www.inc.com/ben-lee/how-social-media-built-up-fyre-festival-then-burned-it-to-the-ground.html

Leggett, T., & Palumbo, D. (2019, December 31). Carlos Ghosn: Four charts on the Nissan boss scandal. *BBC News*. Retrieved from https://www.bbc.com/news/business-46321097

Moore, T. (2018, July 13). Timeline of a crisis: Papa John's deletes founder from marketing. *PR Week*. Retrieved from https://www.prweek.com/article/1487792

Mounck, Y. (2020, February 28). What the dubious Corona poll reveals. *The Atlantic*. Retrieved from https://www.theatlantic.com/ideas/archive/2020/02/about-corona-poll/607240/

Neill, M. S. (2016). Accredited vs. non-accredited: How accreditation impacts perceptions and readiness to provide ethics counsel. *Public Relations Review*, 42(5), 856–866. https://doi.org/10.1016/j.pubrev.2016.08.002

Neill, M. S., & Weaver, N. (2017). Silent & unprepared: Most millennial practitioners have not embraced role as ethical conscience. *Public Relations Review*, 43(2), 337–344. https://doi.org/10.1016/j.pubrev.2017.01.002

Nissan Motor Corporation. (2018, December 10). Regarding violation of Japan Financial Instruments and Exchange Act involving Nissan. Retrieved from https://newsroom.nissan-global.com/releases/release-b80d5f605e170e28db6d451af70ecda1-181210-04-e?lang=en-US

Petit, S. (2017, May 1). Fyre Festival hit with $100 million lawsuit. *Entertainment Weekly*. Retrieved from https://ew.com/music/2017/05/01/fyre-festival-lawsuit/

Public Relations and Communications Association. (n.d.). Bell Pottinger case study. Retrieved from https://www.prca.org.uk/campaigns/ethics/bell-pottinger-case-study

Raab, P. (2018, July 20). Papa John's: An ethical dilemma for PR firms. *PRWeek*. Retrieved from https://www.prweek.com/article/1488452

Richards, K. (2018, October 9). Inside Papa John's transformation: How diversity and marketing leaders are changing the brand. *Adweek*. Retrieved from https://www.adweek.com/brand-marketing/inside-papa-johns-transformation-how-diversity-and-marketing-leaders-are-changing-the-brand/

Segal, D. (2018, February 4). How Bell Pottinger, P.R. firm for despots and rogues, met its end in South Africa. *New York Times*. Retrieved from https://www.nytimes.com/2018/02/04/business/bell-pottinger-guptas-zuma-south-africa.html

Shane, D. (2019, January 18). Japanese carmakers say Carlos Ghosn took $9 million in unauthorized payments. *CNN*. Retrieved from https://www.cnn.com/2019/01/18/business/carlos-ghosn-nissan-mitsubishi/index.html

Shiraki, M., & Tajitsu, N. (2019, January 29). Ghosn may have had questionable ethics, co-chair of external Nissan probe says. *Reuters*. Retrieved from https://uk.reuters.com/article/uk-nissan-ghosn/ghosn-may-have-had-questionable-ethics-co-chair-of-external-nissan-probe-says-idUKKCN1PE0HM?il=0

Truth in Advertising. (2012, July 3). Seeking the truth in food labels. Retrieved from https://www.truthinadvertising.org/always-read-the-label-food-label-deception/

CHAPTER 4

Adidas and Beyoncé announce iconic partnership. (2019, April 4). Retrieved from https://news.adidas.com/originals/adidas-and-beyonc--announce-iconic-partnership/s/68dc185b-d36a-4833-983d-774ecb6decb3

Amatulli, J. (2019, April 5). Reebok denies rumors that Beyoncé walked out of meeting over lack of diversity. *HuffPost*. Retrieved from https://www.huffpost.com/entry/reebok-beyonce-adidas-diversity-representation_n_5ca79253e4b0dca0330108c2

Bromwich, J. E., & Friedman, V. (2019, April 4). Beyoncé and Adidas team up to make shoes and money. *New York Times*. Retrieved from https://www.nytimes.com/2019/04/04/style/beyonce-adidas-collaboration.html

Chitkara, A. (2018, April 12). PR agencies need to be more diverse and inclusive. Here's how to start. *Harvard Business Review*. Retrieved from https://hbr.org/2018/04/pr-agencies-need-to-be-more-diverse-and-inclusive-heres-how-to-start

Clif Bar & Company. (2017, April 3). Equal pay. Retrieved from https://www.clifbar.com/press-room/press-releases/equal-pay

Commission on Public Relations Education. (2018, April). *Fast forward: The 2017 report on undergraduate public relations education*. Retrieved from http://www.commissionpred.org/

Duarte, J., Crawford, J., Stern, C., Haidt, J., Jussim, L., & Tetlock, P. (2015). Political diversity will improve social psychological science. *Behavioral and Brain Sciences*, 38, e130. doi: https://doi.org/10.1017/S0140525X14000430

Edelman. (2020). Department of Defense: Warrior Games. Retrieved from https://www.edelman.com/work/department-defense-warrior-games

Edwards, L. (2015). *Power, diversity and public relations*. London, UK: Routledge.

Fitzpatrick, A., & Law, T. (2019, February 4). These are the best Super Bowl 2019 commercials. *Time*. Retrieved from http://time.com/5515400/best-super-bowl-commercials-2019/

Florentine, S. (2019, February 19). Diversity and inclusion: 8 best practices for changing your culture. *CIO*. Retrieved from https://www.cio.com/article/3262704/diversity-and-inclusion-8-best-practices-for-changing-your-culture.html

Gassam, J. (2019, April 6). Why Beyoncé's new partnership with Adidas highlights an important diversity issue. *Forbes*. Retrieved from https://www.forbes.com/sites/janicegassam/2019/04/06/why-beyonces-new-partnership-with-adidas-highlights-an-important-diversity-issue/

Golin. (2020). Luna Bar: Equal Pay Day. Retrieved from https://golin.com/work/luna-bar-2018-equal-pay-day/

Guzior, B. (2019, April 3). $718K donation levels the field for soccer team. *BizWomen*. Retrieved from https://www.bizjournals.com/bizwomen/news/latest-news/2019/04/718k-donation-levels-the-playingfield-for-soccer.html

Holt, K. (2019, January 31). Gaming accessibility is the star of Microsoft's Super Bowl ad. *Engadget*. Retrieved from https://www.engadget.com/2019/01/31/microsoft-super-bowl-ad-xbox-adaptive-controller-accessibility/

Hunt, V., Yee, L., Prince, S., & Dixon-Fyle, S. (2018, January). Delivering through diversity. McKinsey Retrieved from https://www.mckinsey.com/business-functions/organization/our-insights/delivering-through-diversity

Ketchum. (2017, November 28). Ketchum appoints Barri Rafferty chief executive officer, Rob Flaherty continues as chairman. *PR Newswire*. Retrieved from https://www.prnewswire.com/news-releases/ketchum-appoints-barri-rafferty-chief-executive-officer-rob-flaherty-continues-as-chairman-300562594.html

King, N. (2019, February 15). Making the case for diversity in marketing and PR. *Forbes*. Retrieved from https://www.forbes.com/sites/forbescommunicationscouncil/2019/02/15/making-the-case-for-diversity-in-marketing-and-pr/

Kozuch, E. (2019, March 28). HRC releases annual Corporate Equality Index with 571 top U.S. companies earning perfect scores. *Human Rights Campaign*. Retrieved from https://www.hrc.org/blog/hrc-releases-corporate-equality-index-with-571-top-us-companies-earning-100/

Logan, N. (2017). Power, diversity and public relations: Theorizing a new paradigm for democratic public relations practice and scholarly analysis. *Public Relations Inquiry*, 6(3), 313–319. doi: https://doi.org/10.1177/2046147X17721945

NBA Media Ventures. (2020). Love Wins Pride Night: Atlanta Hawks. Retrieved from https://www.nba.com/hawks/pride

Phillips, K. W. (2014, October 1). How diversity makes us smarter. *Scientific American*. Retrieved from https://www.scientificamerican.com/article/how-diversity-makes-us-smarter/

PR Council. (2018, October 4). *Diversity talks: 2018 diversity and inclusion resource guide*. Retrieved from http://prcouncil.net/blog/diversity-talks-2018-diversity-inclusion-resource-guide/

Public Relations Society of America. (2020). Diversity and inclusion: Working toward a more diverse profession.

Retrieved from https://www.prsa.org/about/diversity-inclusion

Puritty, C., Strickland, L. R., Alia, E., Blonder, B., Klein, E., Kohl, M. T., . . . Gerber, L. R. (2017). Without inclusion, diversity initiatives may not be enough. *Science, 357*(6356), 1101–1102. https://doi.org/10.1126/science.aai9054

Science benefits from diversity. (2018, June 6). *Nature, 558*(5). doi: https://doi.org/10.1038/d41586-018-05326-3

Sesame Workshop. (2019, April 18). Sesame Workshop kicks off "Respect Brings Us Together" campaign. Retrieved from https://www.sesameworkshop.org/press-room/press-releases/sesame-workshop-kicks-respect-brings-us-together-campaign

Shah, A. (2018, January 18). Why the PR industry's diversity initiatives fail. *PRovoke*. Retrieved from https://www.provokemedia.com/long-reads/article/why-the-pr-industry's-diversity-initiatives-fail

Shorty Awards. (n.d.-a). True comes in all colors: The Atlanta Hawks' diversity and inclusion campaign. Retrieved from https://shortyawards.com/3rd-socialgood/true-comes-in-all-colors-the-atlanta-hawks-diversity-inclusion-campaign

Shorty Awards. (n.d.-b). Universal love. Retrieved from http://shortyawards.com/3rd-socialgood/universal-love-songs

Warren, T. (2019, January 31). Microsoft's Super Bowl ad is all about the Xbox Adaptive Controller. *The Verge*. Retrieved from https://www.theverge.com/2019/1/31/18205193/microsoft-super-bowl-2019-commercial

Warrior Games. (2020). History. Retrieved from https://dodwarriorgames.com/about/history/

Webby Awards. (2018). Hidden figures. Retrieved from https://www.webbyawards.com/winners/2018/advertising-media-pr/individual/augmented-reality/hidden-figures/

Weber Shandwick. (2020). Showing Uno's true colors. Retrieved from https://www.webershandwick.com/work/showing-unos-true-colors/

CHAPTER 5

Arenstein, S. (2019, February 5). Lessons for PR pros from Amazon's campaign to win over NY. *PR Newswire*. Retrieved from https://www.prnewsonline.com/Amazon-NY-PR

Daniels, C. (2019, May 10). Why mental health advocates are backing Burger King's Unhappy Meals. *Campaign US*. Retrieved from https://www.campaignlive.com/article/why-mental-health-advocates-backing-burger-kings-unhappy-meals/1584331?utm_source=website&utm_medium=social

Day One Staff. (2019, February 14). Update on plans for New York City headquarters. *Day One: The Amazon Blog*. Retrieved from https://blog.aboutamazon.com/company-news/update-on-plans-for-new-york-city-headquarters

Edelman. (2020, January 19). 2020 Edelman Trust Barometer. Retrieved from https://www.edelman.com/trustbarometer

Lee, L. (2019, May 14). Burger King launches "Real Meals" and faces backlash on Twitter. *Los Angeles Times*. Retrieved from https://www.latimes.com/food/la-fo-burger-king-unhappy-meals-mental-health-awareness-20190504-story.html

Lindenmann, W. K. (2006). *Public relations research for planning and evaluation*. Institute for Public Relations. Retrieved from https://instituteforpr.org/pr-research-for-planning-and-evaluation/

Michaelson, D., & Stacks, D. W. (2014). *A professional and practitioner's guide to public relations research, measurement and evaluation* (2nd ed.). New York, NY: Business Expert Press. Retrieved from https://www.businessexpertpress.com/oabooks/9781606499849.pdf

Shlonsky, A., & Gibbs, L. (2004). Will the real evidence-based practice please stand up? Teaching the process of evidence-based practice to the helping professions. *Brief Treatment and Crisis Intervention, 4*(2), 137–153.

Streitfeld, D. (2018, November 6). Was Amazon's headquarters contest a bait-and-switch? Critics say yes. *New York Times*. Retrieved from https://www.nytimes.com/2018/11/06/technology/amazon-hq2-long-island-city-virginia.html

CHAPTER 6

Arruda, W. (2019, March 12). Personal branding advice you must ignore. *Forbes*. Retrieved from https://www.forbes.com/sites/williamarruda/2019/03/12/personal-branding-advice-you-must-ignore/#492a6a50252f

Chan, G. (2018, November 8). 10 golden rules of personal branding. *Forbes*. Retrieved from https://www.forbes.com/sites/goldiechan/2018/11/08/10-golden-rules-personal-branding/

Falls, J. (2019, February 22). Are you ready for the content marketing separation? *Jason Falls* [Blog post]. Retrieved from https://jasonfalls.com/content-marketing-separation/

Ferrante, M. B. (2018, November 29). 5 things I learned from Reese Witherspoon's company Hello Sunshine. *Forbes*. Retrieved from https://www.forbes.com/sites/marybethferrante/2018/11/29/5-things-i-learned-from-reese-witherspoons-company-hello-sunshine/#1d5b6cc5760b

Heitner, D. (2018a, February 22). How college athletes can immediately begin building their brands. *Inc*. Retrieved from https://www.inc.com/darren-heitner/how-college-athletes-can-immediately-be-building-their-brands.html

Heitner, D. (2018b, June 18). New Orleans Saints QB Drew Brees makes significant investment in comfortable clothing brand UNTUCKit. *Forbes*. Retrieved from https://www.forbes.com/sites/darrenheitner/2018/06/18/new-orleans-saints-qb-drew-brees-acquires-material-stake-in-comfortable-clothing-brand-untuckit/

Horn, J. (2016, September 30). Brands of the Year 2016: Superwoman Singh. *Strategy*. Retrieved from http://strategyonline.ca/2016/09/30/brands-of-the-year-2016-superwoman-singh/

Kaludi, M. (2014, March 29). 6 personal branding mistakes that are holding you back. *BlogPress*. Retrieved from https://magazine3.com/demo/blogpress/focus-on-your-brand-experience-and-personal-word-of-mouth-marketing/

Lukovitz, K. (2019, April 3). Oreo recreates "Game of Thrones" opening using cookies. *MarketingDaily*. Retrieved from https://www.mediapost.com/publications/article/334063/oreo-recreates-game-of-thrones-opening-using-coo.html

Rahmaad, J. (2018, June 1). Council post: How to build your personal brand using PR. *Forbes*. Retrieved from https://www.forbes.com/sites/forbescoachescouncil/2018/06/01/how-to-build-your-personal-brand-using-pr/#3a8f38675a8d

Ross, L. (2017, November 2). 7 ways to PR your personal brand on a budget. *Duct Tape Marketing.* Retrieved from https://ducttapemarketing.com/personal-brand-budget/

Russo, H. (2018, May 16). Creating a winning brand in the NFL. *Platform Magazine.* Retrieved from http://platformmagazine.org/2018/05/16/creating-a-winning-brand-in-the-nfl/

Schaefer, M. (2017, March 14). The art and science of becoming "known." *Neuromarketing.* Retrieved from https://www.neurosciencemarketing.com/blog/articles/mark-schaefer-known.htm

Schomer, S. (2019, December 28). Lilly Singh conquered YouTube—Now she's taking on Hollywood. *Entrepreneur.* Retrieved from https://www.entrepreneur.com/article/328067

Solis, B. (2019). *Lifescale: How to live a more creative, productive, and happy life.* Hoboken, NJ: John Wiley & Sons.

Stukent. (2018, August 6). Dennis Yu & Logan Young—How professors and students can build a personal brand on just $1 per day. *SlideShare.* Retrieved from https://www.slideshare.net/stukent/dennis-yu-logan-young-how-professors-and-students-can-build-a-personal-brand-on-just-1-per-day

Tesfatsion, M. (2018, July 23). JuJu Smith-Schuster is the NFL's most likable one-man brand: The B/R Mag Q&A. *Bleacher Report.* Retrieved from https://bleacherreport.com/articles/2787069-juju-smith-schuster-steelers-nfl-power-50

Tribbitt, M. (2019, April 2). Reese Witherspoon on why she self-funded her production company for five years. *Hollywood Reporter.* Retrieved from https://www.hollywoodreporter.com/rambling-reporter/reese-witherspoon-funding-hello-sunshine-1197920

Vaynerchuk, G. (2019a). The GaryVee content strategy: How to grow and distribute your brand's social media content. *GaryVee* [Blog post]. Retrieved from https://www.garyvaynerchuk.com/the-garyvee-content-strategy-how-to-grow-and-distribute-your-brands-social-media-content/

Vaynerchuk, G. (2019b). 9 strategies for personal branding online in 2019. *GaryVee* [Blog post]. Retrieved from https://www.garyvaynerchuk.com/5-strategies-for-personal-branding-online/

CHAPTER 7

Associated Press. (2020). *The Associated Press stylebook 2020 and briefing on media law.* New York, NY: Basic Books.

Canning, N. (2019, April 5). How to create an influencer media kit (+ free template!). Later. Retrieved from https://later.com/blog/influencer-media-kit/

Commission on Public Relations Education. (2018, April). *Fast forward: The 2017 report on undergraduate public relations education.* Retrieved from http://www.commissionpred.org/

Garrett, M. (2018, February 11). Pitching success stories from PR pros in the trenches. Meltwater. Retrieved from https://www.meltwater.com/blog/pitching-success-stories-from-pr-pros-in-the-trenches/

Giant Spoon. (2020). Uber driver stories. Retrieved from https://www.giantspoon.com/project/15181/uber-driver-stories

Jennings, H. (2018, June 21). 4 game-changing tips for pitching journalists. *PR News.* Retrieved from https://www.prnewsonline.com/4-game-changing-tips-for-pitching-journalists

Maxwell House is on a mission this Mother's Day to make Mom's invisible labor, visible. (2019, May 6). *Business Wire.* Retrieved from https://www.businesswire.com/news/home/20190506005367/en/Maxwell-House-Mission-Mother%E2%80%99s-Day-Mom%E2%80%99s-Invisible

Mireles, A. (2014, November 20). Persuasion: 6 principles that power PR success. Cision. Retrieved from https://www.cision.com/us/2014/11/persuasion-6-principles-that-power-pr-success/

Schick, S. (2018, January 17). What editors and writers want from PR pitches in 2018. Cision. Retrieved from https://www.cision.com/us/2018/01/pr-pitches-in-2018/

Shorty Awards. (n.d.). #FindMyiD. Retrieved from https://shortyawards.com/11th/findmyid

Sung, M. (2019, May 15). The Vita Coco pee jar was just another Brand Twitter stunt. *Mashable.* Retrieved from https://mashable.com/article/vita-coco-coconut-water-twitter-pee-in-jar/

Yonkman, D. (2017, June 1). Tips from PR pros for writing great press releases. *PR News.* Retrieved from https://www.prnewsonline.com/tips-from-pr-pros-for-writing-great-press-releases/

CHAPTER 8

Dietrich, G. (2020, February 27). PR pros must embrace the PESO model. *Spin Sucks.* Retrieved from https://spinsucks.com/communication/pr-pros-must-embrace-the-peso-model/

Griner, D. (2019, December 13). How Ryan Reynolds pulled off Aviation Gin's Peloton parody. *Adweek.* Retrieved from https://www.adweek.com/creativity/how-ryan-reynolds-pulled-off-aviation-gins-peloton-parody-capping-his-year-of-genius-ads/

Heat. (2020). Work: Wild Turkey. Retrieved from https://thisisheat.com/work

McAteer, O. (2019, February 5). Wild Turkey reaps rewards of "risky" spot with Deloitte's Heat. *Campaign US.* Retrieved from https://www.campaignlive.com/article/wild-turkey-reaps-rewards-risky-spot-deloittes-heat/1524906?utm_source=website&utm_medium=social

Ochieng, N. (2018, March 20). What the PESO model got wrong. *AXIA Public Relations.* Retrieved from https://www.axiapr.com/blog/what-the-peso-model-got-wrong

Waddington, S. (2020, February 14). PESO explained for marketing and public relations. Retrieved from https://wadds.co.uk/blog/peso-for-marketing-and-pr

CHAPTER 9

Broom, G. M., Casey, S., & Ritchey, J. (1997). Toward a concept and theory of organization public relationships. *Journal of Public Relations Research, 9*(2), 83–98.

Data Freaks. (2015, March 12). Brands take a stand: When speaking up about controversial issues hurts or helps business. *Forbes.* Retrieved from https://www.forbes.com/sites/datafreaks/2015/03/12/brands-take-a-stand-when

-speaking-up-about-controversial-issues-hurts-or-helps-business/#466f0193352d

Expert Commentator. (2018, June 6). Micro, macro, nano and hero creators: Whom to use and when? Smart Insights. Retrieved from https://www.smartinsights.com/online-pr/micro-macro-nano-hero-creators-influencers/Expert Panel, Forbes Agency Council. (2019, April 29). 12 agency pros share their favorite ways to Surprise and delight their clients. *Forbes*. Retrieved from https://www.forbes.com/sites/forbesagencycouncil/2019/04/29/12-agency-pros-share-their-favorite-ways-to-surprise-and-delight-their-clients/#4b71c55c53df

Ferguson, M. A. (2018). Building theory in public relations: Interorganizational relationships as a public relations paradigm. *Journal of Public Relations Research*, *30*(4), 164–178. https://doi.org/10.1080/1062726X.2018.1514810

Freberg, K., Graham, K., McGaughey, K., & Freberg, L. A. (2011). Who are the social media influencers? A study of public perceptions of personality. *Public Relations Review*, *37*(1), 90–92. https://doi.org/10.1016/j.pubrev.2010.11.001

Gee, C. (2017, June 20). The importance of audience insights for public relations. Affinio. Retrieved from https://www.affinio.com/blog/the-importance-of-audience-insights-for-public-relations-2/

Getting Gen Z primed to save the world. (n.d.). *The Atlantic*. Retrieved from https://www.theatlantic.com/sponsored/allstate/getting-gen-z-primed-to-save-the-world/747/

Goggin, B. (2019, December 10). 7,800 people lost their media jobs in a 2019 landslide. *Business Insider*. Retrieved from https://www.businessinsider.com/2019-media-layoffs-job-cuts-at-buzzfeed-huffpost-vice-details-2019-2

Goldberg, J. (2018, March 13). Creators are often influential but they hate being called "influencers." *Entrepreneur*. Retrieved from https://www.entrepreneur.com/article/309711

Hakim, A. (2015, August 3). Influencers vs. creators: How the landscape is changing. W2O. Retrieved from https://www.w2ogroup.com/influencers-vs-creators-how-the-landscape-is-changing/

Heald, E. (2017, December 16). Build an employee brand ambassador program. Meltwater. Retrieved from https://www.meltwater.com/blog/build-an-employee-brand-ambassador-program/

Hillman, A. J., & Keim, G. D. (2001). Shareholder value, stakeholder management, and social issues: What's the bottom line? *Strategic Management Journal*, *22*(2), 125–139. doi: 10.1002/1097-0266

Hon, L. C., & Grunig, J. E. (1999, November). Guidelines for measuring relationships in public relations. Institute for Public Relations. Retrieved from https://www.instituteforpr.org/wp-content/uploads/Guidelines_Measuring_Relationships.pdf

Joseph, S. (2019, May 23). "Believe in the brand": Kellogg's is now using influencers like creative agencies. *Digiday*. Retrieved from https://digiday.com/marketing/inside-kelloggs-influencer-marketing-strategy/

Kary, T., & Wagner, K. (2019, May 22). Philip Morris influencer tobacco ads on social media under fire. *Bloomberg*. Retrieved from https://www.bloomberg.com/news/articles/2019-05-22/philip-morris-influencer-tobacco-ads-on-social-media-under-fire

Kent, M. L., Taylor, M., & White, W. (2003). The relationship between web site design and organizational responsiveness to stakeholders. *Public Relations Review*, *29*(1), 66–77.

Lorenz, T. (2019, May 16). How tea accounts fuel the James Charles YouTube feud. *The Atlantic*. Retrieved from https://www.theatlantic.com/technology/archive/2019/05/how-tea-channels-feed-youtube-feuds/589618/

Maheshwari, S. (2018, November 11). Are you ready for the nanoinfluencers? *New York Times*. Retrieved from https://www.nytimes.com/2018/11/11/business/media/nanoinfluencers-instagram-influencers.html

Mailchimp. (n.d.). Marketing glossary: Audience segmentation. Retrieved from https://mailchimp.com/marketing-glossary/audience-segmentation/

Martin, E. (2015, July 29). A major airline says there's something it values more than its customers, and there's a good reason why. *Business Insider*. Retrieved from https://www.businessinsider.com/southwest-airlines-puts-employees-first-2015-7

Mediakix. (n.d.). Influencer tiers for the influencer marketing industry. Retrieved from http://mediakix.com/influencer-marketing-resources/influencer-tiers/

Parker, K., Graf, N., & Igielnik, R. (2019, January 17). Generation Z looks a lot like millennials on key social and political issues. Pew Research Center. Retrieved from https://www.pewsocialtrends.org/2019/01/17/generation-z-looks-a-lot-like-millennials-on-key-social-and-political-issues/

Patel, T. (2019, January 8). The beginner's guide to segmenting audiences for better PR results. Agility PR Solutions. Retrieved from https://www.agilitypr.com/pr-news/public-relations/the-beginners-guide-to-segmenting-audiences-for-better-pr-results/

Robehmed, N. (2018, July 13). Why The Rock's social media muscle made him Hollywood's highest-paid actor. *Forbes*. Retrieved from https://www.forbes.com/sites/forbesdigitalcovers/2018/07/12/why-the-rocks-social-media-muscle-made-him-hollywoods-highest-paid-actor/

Sabourin, T. (2014, April 17). Public relations and media relations: What's the difference? SHIFT Communications. Retrieved from https://www.shiftcomm.com/blog/public-relations-media-relations-whats-difference/

Safronova, V. (2019, May 27). James Charles, from "CoverBoy" to canceled. *New York Times*. Retrieved from https://www.nytimes.com/2019/05/14/style/james-charles-makeup-artist-youtube.html

Sands, M. (2019, May 24). The James Charles scandal was more than the "ugly" beauty community. *Forbes*. Retrieved from https://www.forbes.com/sites/masonsands/2019/05/24/the-james-charles-scandal-was-more-than-the-ugly-beauty-community/#16eb18866ae6

Schneider, M. (2018, September 19). Report: PR pros outnumber journalists by a 6-to-1 ratio. *PR Daily*. Retrieved from https://www.prdaily.com/report-pr-pros-outnumber-journalists-by-a-6-to-1-ratio/

Sharma, G. (2018, June 29). What you should look for in an influencer: 5 key characteristics. Business 2 Community. Retrieved from https://www.business2community.com/

marketing/what-you-should-look-for-in-an-influencer-5-key-characteristics-02084897

Solis, B. (2009, March 23). *Putting the Public Back in Public Relations* is now available. Retrieved from https://www.briansolis.com/2009/03/putting-public-back-in-public-relations/

Solis, B., & Breakenridge, D. (2009). *Putting the public back in public relations: How social media is reinventing the aging business of PR.* Upper Saddle River, NJ: Pearson Education.

Subramanian, K. (2019, April 3). Five influencer marketing trends for 2019. *Forbes.* Retrieved from https://www.forbes.com/sites/forbestechcouncil/2019/04/03/five-influencer-marketing-trends-for-2019/

Talkwalker. (2019, April 24). The global state of influencer marketing in 2019. Retrieved from https://www.talkwalker.com/case-studies/global-state-influencer-marketing

WestJet. (n.d.). Christmas miracle. Retrieved from https://www.westjet.com/en-us/about-us/christmas-miracle

YouGov. (2016, December 16). Four things every audience segmentation needs. *PR Week.* Retrieved from https://www.prweek.com/article/1418931/four-things-every-audience-segmentation-needs

Roberts-Islam, B. (2019, June 18). Accelerating the future of fashion: Creatives deliver much-needed tech disruption. *Forbes.* Retrieved from https://www.forbes.com/sites/brookerobertsislam/2019/06/18/accelerating-the-future-of-fashion-creatives-deliver-much-needed-tech-disruption/

Sehl, K. (2020, March 2). Everything brands need to know about TikTok in 2020. Retrieved from https://blog.hootsuite.com/what-is-tiktok/

Valat, P.-L. (2018, June 14). 6 good reasons to combine your PR and content marketing strategies. Meltwater. Retrieved from https://www.meltwater.com/uk/blog/6-good-reasons-combine-pr-content-marketing-strategies/

Vaynerchuk, G. (2019a). Announcing the GaryVee 004. *GaryVee.* Retrieved https://www.garyvaynerchuk.com/announcing-garyvee-004-sneakers/

Vaynerchuk, G. (2019b). The GaryVee content strategy: How to grow and distribute your brand's social media content. *GaryVee.* Retrieved from https://www.garyvaynerchuk.com/the-garyvee-content-strategy-how-to-grow-and-distribute-your-brands-social-media-content/

What is mixed reality? (2018, March 21). Retrieved from https://docs.microsoft.com/en-us/windows/mixed-reality/mixed-reality

CHAPTER 10

Cyca, M. (2019, July 9). What is social proof and how to use it in your marketing strategy. *Hootsuite Social.* Retrieved from https://blog.hootsuite.com/social-proof/

Expert Commentator. (2017, April 25). PR and content marketing: Two sides of the same coin. *Smart Insights.* Retrieved from https://www.smartinsights.com/content-management/content-marketing-strategy/pr-content-marketing-two-sides-coin/

Flywheel. (n.d.). Retrieved from http://view.ceros.com/ceros-marketing/hubspot-flywheel-vertical

Gynn, A. (2018, June 12). How to get content marketing wrong? Think like a PR person. Content Marketing Institute. Retrieved from https://contentmarketinginstitute.com/2018/06/content-marketing-wrong/

Koksal, I. (2018, December 11). How Alexa is changing the future of advertising. *Forbes.* Retrieved from https://www.forbes.com/sites/ilkerkoksal/2018/12/11/how-alexa-is-changing-the-future-of-advertising/#17f9bb061d4d

Lorenz, T. (2019, July 12). TikTok stars are preparing to take over the internet. *The Atlantic.* Retrieved from https://www.theatlantic.com/technology/archive/2019/07/tiktok-stars-are-preparing-take-over-internet/593878/

Odden, L. (2015, June 3). The evolution of public relations through content marketing. *TopRank Marketing.* Retrieved from https://www.toprankblog.com/2015/06/revolution-pr-content/

Pant, R. (2015, January 16). Visual marketing: A picture's worth 60,000 words. *Business2Community.* Retrieved from https://www.business2community.com/digital-marketing/visual-marketing-pictures-worth-60000-words-01126256#Uq8gT3hQ3ZJVevYC.97

Project Revoice. (n.d.). Retrieved from https://www.projectrevoice.org/

CHAPTER 11

Allison, M. (2014, December 29). The relationship between PR and marketing. *Trendkite.* Retrieved from https://blog.trendkite.com/trendkite-blog/the-relationship-between-pr-and-marketing

Avidar, R. (2017). Public relations and social businesses: The importance of enhancing engagement. *Public Relations Review, 43*(5), 955–962.

Brasche, R. (2017, March 2). Why communications teams have (finally) earned a seat at the C-suite table. Zignal Labs. Retrieved from https://zignallabs.com/why-communications-teams-have-finally-earned-a-seat-at-the-c-suite-table/

Commission on Public Relations Education. (2018, April). *Fast forward: The 2017 report on undergraduate public relations education.* Retrieved from http://www.commissionpred.org/

Duhé, S. (2013, December 12). Teaching business as a second language. Institute for Public Relations. Retrieved from https://instituteforpr.org/teaching-business-second-language/

Eisenmann, T. R. (2013, January 10). Entrepreneurship: A working definition. *Harvard Business Review.* Retrieved from https://hbr.org/2013/01/what-is-entrepreneurship

Frantz, C. (2018, June 14). The role of public relations in marketing. *Forbes.* Retrieved from https://www.forbes.com/sites/forbescommunicationscouncil/2018/06/14/the-role-of-public-relations-in-marketing/

Gillis, T. L. (2009). *It's your move: Communication competencies and expectations.* San Francisco, CA: IABC. Retrieved from https://www.iabc.com/wp-content/uploads/2014/11/It-is-Your-Move-Communication-Competencies-and-Expectations.pdf

Grunig, J. E. (2001, May 12). *The role of public relations in management and its contribution to organizational and societal effectiveness.* Speech delivered in Taipei, Taiwan. Retrieved from https://instituteforpr.org/wp-content/uploads/2001_PRManagement.pdf

Huntly, C. (2017, November 9). Does PR increase your sales or not? Business2Community. Retrieved from https://www.business2community.com/public-relations/pr-increase-sales-not-01955575

Jansen, K. (2017, August 9). Why communications needs a seat at the table. *Forbes.* Retrieved from https://www.forbes.com/sites/forbesagencycouncil/2017/08/09/why-communications-needs-a-seat-at-the-table/

Jones, J. (2016, March 11). Business acumen: More than just business knowledge. Society for Human Resource Management. Retrieved from https://www.shrm.org/resourcesandtools/hr-topics/organizational-and-employee-development/pages/business-acumen-more-than-business-knowledge.aspx

Lukitsch, C. (2016, February 5). PR professionals as leading entrepreneurs. *PR News.* Retrieved from https://www.prnewsonline.com/pr-as-entrepreneur

Midgley, B. (2018, September 26). The six reasons the fitness industry is booming. *Forbes.* Retrieved from https://www.forbes.com/sites/benmidgley/2018/09/26/the-six-reasons-the-fitness-industry-is-booming/#454a221506db

Monllos, K. (2018, January 4). Hyperlocal targeting and AI have made Orangetheory Fitness a nearly $1 billion business. *Adweek.* Retrieved from https://www.adweek.com/brand-marketing/hyperlocal-targeting-and-ai-have-made-orangetheory-fitness-a-nearly-1-billion-business/

Neill, M. S., & Lee, N. M. (2016). Roles in social media: How the practice of public relations is evolving. *Public Relations Journal, 10*(2), 1–25.

Penn, C. S. (2013, July 23). PR is a sales job. SHIFT Communications. Retrieved from https://www.shiftcomm.com/blog/pr-is-a-sales-job/

Ragas, M., & Culp, R. (2014, December 22). Public relations and business acumen: Closing the gap. Institute for Public Relations. Retrieved from https://instituteforpr.org/public-relations-business-acumen-closing-gap/

Ragas, M. W., Uysal, N., & Culp, R. (2015). "Business 101" in public relations education: An exploratory survey of senior communication executives. *Public Relations Review, 41*(3), 378–380.

Stone, T. (2019, April 25). Download free map, help charity: water. *Minecraft.* Retrieved from https://www.minecraft.net/en-us/article/download-free-map--help-charity-water

Warnick, J. (2019, March 20). Say hello to the lid that will replace a billion straws a year. Starbucks Stories & News. Retrieved from https://stories.starbucks.com/stories/2019/say-hello-to-the-lid-that-will-replace-a-billion-straws-a-year/

Wilden, M. (2017, November 27). CSR—Be the "employer of choice." Rencai Group. Retrieved from https://www.rencaigroup.com/corporate-social-responsibility-be-the-employer-of-choice/

Zundel, H. (2018, January 17). When PR meets entrepreneurship. *Progressions.* Retrieved from http://progressions.prssa.org/index.php/2018/01/17/when-pr-meets-entrepreneurship/

CHAPTER 12

AMEC. (2020). How the Barcelona Principles have been updated. Retrieved from https://amecorg.com/how-the-barcelona-principles-have-been-updated/

Aten, J. (2019, July 19). The internet is on fire over 2 movie trailers for completely different reasons and it's a perfect lesson in creating the right kind of buzz. *Inc.* Retrieved from https://www.inc.com/jason-aten/the-new-top-gun-maverick-cats-trailers-show-why-expectations-are-everything-in-creating-buzz-for-your-brand.html

Baer, J. (n.d.). Why is social media measurement so hard? Convince & Convert. Retrieved from https://www.convinceandconvert.com/social-media-strategy/why-is-social-media-measurement-so-hard/

Boyles, K. (2018, March 29). Why you should stop using AVEs to measure media coverage. AXIA Public Relations. Retrieved from https://www.axiapr.com/blog/why-you-should-stop-using-aves-to-measure-media-coverage

Commission on Public Relations Education. (2018, April). *Fast forward: The 2017 report on undergraduate public relations education.* Retrieved from http://www.commissionpred.org/

Lockie, A. (2019, July 20). Looks like the new Top Gun bows to China's communist party by censoring Maverick's jacket. *Business Insider.* Retrieved from https://www.businessinsider.com/top-guns-maverick-appears-changed-to-please-chinas-communist-party-2019-7

Meg. (2018, March 13). Definitive guide to PR measurement. Talkwalker. Retrieved from https://www.talkwalker.com/blog/definitive-guide-pr-measurement

PR 101: What is a media impression? (2017, September 4). SHIFT Communications. Retrieved from https://www.shiftcomm.com/blog/pr-101-what-is-a-media-impression/

PR Newswire. (2019, August 13). The Pittsburgh Knights team up with Zoomph to bring sponsorship analytics to esports. *Yahoo! Finance.* Retrieved from https://finance.yahoo.com/news/pittsburgh-knights-team-zoomph-bring-141000074.html

Public Relations Society of America. (2019). Measurement resources. Retrieved from http://apps.prsa.org/intelligence/businesscase/measurementresources

Wallace, C. (2019, May 6). The AVE debate: Measuring the value of PR. *PR Week.* Retrieved from https://www.prweek.com/article/903837/ave-debate-measuring-value-pr?utm_source=website&utm_medium=social

Watson, T. (2012). The evolution of public relations measurement and evaluation. *Public Relations History, 38*(3), 390–398. https://doi.org/10.1016/j.pubrev.2011.12.018

Wong, Q. (2019, August 14). Instagram is hiding likes. You may be happier in the end. *CNET.* Retrieved from https://www.cnet.com/news/instagram-is-hiding-likes-you-may-be-happier-in-the-end/

CHAPTER 13

EmployZone. (n.d.). Community manager—Financial technology: McCann. Retrieved from https://www.linkedin.com/jobs/view/strategy-director-at-mccann-new-york-1667294007/

Gary's Guide. (2019). Copywriter: VaynerMedia. Retrieved from https://www.garysguide.com/jobs/x7cz51c/ Copywriter-at-Vayner-Media-Singapore

HelpWanted.com. (2019). Public relations coordinator—Spartanburg: Denny's Restaurant. Retrieved from https:// www.helpwanted.com/6f209de8f0204-Public-Relations-Coordinator-Spartanburg-job-listings

Indeed. (2020, March 18). Public relations salaries in the United States. Retrieved from https://www.indeed.com/salaries/ public-relations-Salaries

Kasperkevic, J. (2016, March 15). Just saying no: US interns challenge employers over exploitation. *The Guardian*. Retrieved from https://www.theguardian.com/world/2016/ mar/15/just-saying-no-us-interns-challenge-employers-over-exploitation

LinkedIn. (2020). PR intern, corporate & public affairs: Edelman. Retrieved from https://www.linkedin.com/jobs/ view/1762415075/?alternateChannel=search

LinkedIn. (n.d.-a). Analyst (digital/social): Weber Shandwick. Retrieved from https://www.linkedin.com/jobs/view/ analyst-digital-social-at-weber-shandwick-1645037027/?or iginalSubdomain=uk

LinkedIn. (n.d.-b). Content coordinator: Uber. Retrieved from https://www.linkedin.com/jobs/view/content-coordinator-at-uber-1694005566/

LinkedIn. (n.d.-c). Executive leader, consumer PR, social & influencer marketing: Whole Foods Market. Retrieved from https://www.linkedin.com/jobs/view/executive-leader-consumer-pr-social-influencer-marketing-at-whole-foods-market-1330582828/

LinkedIn. (n.d.-d). Marketing and public relations account specialist: K Strategies Group. Retrieved from https://www.linkedin.com/jobs/view/marketing-and-public-relations-account-specialist-at-k-strategies-group-1331993788/

LinkedIn. (n.d.-e). Media relations associate: New York-Presbyterian Hospital. Retrieved from https://www .linkedin.com/jobs/view/media-relations-associate-at-new-york-presbyterian-hospital-1157717589/?trk=jobs_job_ title&originalSubdomain=qa

LinkedIn. (n.d.-f). Policy communications manager, EMEA: Twitter. Retrieved from https://www.linkedin.com/jobs/ view/policy-communications-manager-emea-at-twitter-1154246337/?originalSubdomain=ie

Monster. (n.d.). Senior account executive—Media relations: GolinHarris. Retrieved from https://job-openings.monster .com/senior-account-executive-%E2%80%93-media-relations-washington-dc-us-golinharris/5cd695af-b305-4bc0-b4f7-d2cffd976246

Peersight. (n.d.). Public relations account director at SutherlandGold Communications. Retrieved from https:// www.peersight.com/job/sutherlandgold-communications-public-relations-account-director-in-san-francisco-ca

CHAPTER 14

Adidas. (2019, August 19). Adidas unites the women breaking barriers in sport with "Change in Play" special. Retrieved from https://news.adidas.com/training/adidas-unites-the -women-breaking-barriers-in-sport-with--change-in-play--special/s/b162b86e-aa9d-493c-aa48-8a714009bdfe

Amarula. (n.d.). Let's make the ivory trade disappear, not our elephants. Retrieved from https://amarula.com/us/#!/ dontletthemdisappear

American Red Cross. (2019). Bleed for the Throne. Retrieved from https://www.redcrossblood.org/donate-blood/dlp/ hbogameofthrones.html

Arenstein, S. (2019, July 25). Boeing: Unhealthy leadership leads to crisis mismanagement. *PR News*. Retrieved from https://www.prnewsonline.com/prnewsblog/boeing-unhealthy-leadership-leads-to-crisis-mismanagement/

Asher. (n.d.). Fort Wayne International Airport: New York on United. Retrieved from https://asheragency.com/portfolio/ fort-wayne-international-airport-new-york-united/

Beer, J. (2019, August 28). The next phase of retail: Adidas is turning influencers into sneaker salespeople. *Fast Company*. Retrieved from https://www.fastcompany.com/90390629/ adidas-wants-you-to-be-its-next-sneaker-influencer

Blumberg, P. (2019, February 27). Nike women clear first hurdle in lawsuit over gender pay gap. *Bloomberg*. Retrieved from https://www.bloomberg.com/news/ articles/2019-02-27/nike-loses-initial-challenge-to-gender-bias-class-action-lawsuit

Burns, W. (2019, March 13). Qantas Airways proves a big marketing idea doesn't have to be expensive. *Forbes*. Retrieved from https://www.forbes.com/sites/ willburns/2019/03/13/qantas-airways-proves-a-big-marketing-idea-doesnt-have-to-be-expensive/

Coleman, L. (2019, August 7). Amarula partners with Heinemann to raise elephant conservation awareness. *The Moodie Davitt Report*. Retrieved from https:// www.moodiedavittreport.com/amarula-partners-with-heinemann-to-raise-elephant-conservation-awareness/

Coombs, T. (2013, October). *What zombies teach us about social media crises: Managing crises in the digital age*. Presented at the NEMO Conference, Lund University, Helsingborg.

Diaz, C. A. B. (2019, May 13). Stuck in traffic? Burger King sees a selling chance. *Bloomberg*. Retrieved from https:// www.bloomberg.com/news/articles/2019-05-13/stuck-in-traffic-burger-king-sees-a-selling-opportunity

Fleming, J. (2018, November 14). How the Flyers created Gritty, the internet's most beloved mascot. *Adweek*. Retrieved from https://www.adweek.com/creativity/ how-the-flyers-created-gritty-the-internets-most-beloved-mascot/

Fombrun, C. J., & Rindova, V. (2000). The road to transparency: Reputation management at Royal Dutch/Shell. In M. Schultz, M. J. Hatch, & M. H. Larsen (Eds.), *The expressive organization: Linking identity, reputation, and the corporate brand* (pp. 76–96). Oxford, UK: Oxford Business Press.

GivingTuesday. (n.d.). About GivingTuesday. Retrieved from https://www.givingtuesday.org/about

Gregg, A. (2019, July 24). Boeing reports its worst-ever financial losses as 737 Max crisis continues. *Washington Post*. Retrieved from https://www.washingtonpost.com/ business/2019/07/24/boeing-reports-its-worst-ever-quarterly-losses-max-crisis-continues/?arc404=true

Griner, D. (2019, August 23). Why Popeyes is positioned to be the next great brand marketer. *Adweek*. Retrieved from https://www.adweek.com/brand-marketing/why-popeyes-is-positioned-to-be-the-next-great-brand-marketer/

Hamblin, J. (2019, August 12). The hypocrisy of SoulCycle. *The Atlantic*. Retrieved from https://www.theatlantic.com/health/archive/2019/08/soulcycle-equinox-trump/595897/

Ingraham, C. (2019, August 13). Why SoulCycle and Equinox could be especially vulnerable to boycotts. *Washington Post*. Retrieved from https://www.washingtonpost.com/business/2019/08/13/why-soulcycle-equinox-could-be-especially-vulnerable-boycotts/?arc404=true

Jackson, K. T. (2004). *Building reputational capital: Strategies for integrity and fair play that improve the bottom line*. New York, NY: Oxford University Press.

Lipshutz, J. (2019, August 21). Lil Nas X's "Old Town Road": 5 things the music industry should learn from its record-setting run. *Billboard*. Retrieved from https://www.billboard.com/articles/columns/hip-hop/8527857/lil-nas-x-old-town-road-5-music-industry-takeaways

McAteer, O. (2019, August 8). U.S. Navy goes all in on influencer marketing with YouTube campaign. *Campaign US*. Retrieved from https://www.campaignlive.com/article/us-navy-goes-influencer-marketing-youtube-campaign/1593394

NBC Sports Philadelphia Staff. (2019, July 27). Flyers mascot Gritty makes his glorious video game debut in NHL 20. *NBC Sports Philadelphia*. Retrieved from https://www.nbcsports.com/philadelphia/flyers/flyers-mascot-gritty-makes-his-glorious-video-game-debut-nhl-20

Pike, N. (2019, May 1). Lizzo is out here making her own popstar pathway. *Vogue*. Retrieved from https://www.vogue.co.uk/article/lizzo-singer-interview-2019

Red Nose Day. (2018, June 8). Red Nose Day: The biggest celebrity trend. Retrieved from https://rednoseday.org/news/red-nose-day-biggest-celebrity-trend

Red Nose Day. (n.d.). What is Red Nose Day? Retrieved from https://rednoseday.org/what-is-red-nose-day

Reputation X. (2019, November 19). PR reputation management—Differences between PR and online reputation management. Retrieved from https://blog.reputationx.com/whats-the-difference-between-pr-and-online-reputation-management

Robehmed, N. (2018, July 13). Why The Rock's social media muscle made him Hollywood's highest-paid actor. *Forbes*. Retrieved from https://www.forbes.com/sites/forbesdigitalcovers/2018/07/12/why-the-rocks-social-media-muscle-made-him-hollywoods-highest-paid-actor/

Schomer, A. (2019, August 23). Samsung's sponsorship of a controversial Instagram influencer highlights the risk of misaligned partnerships. *Business Insider*. Retrieved from https://www.businessinsider.com/samsung-influencer-snafu-highlights-risks-of-misaligned-partnerships-2019-8

Setoodeh, R. (2019, June 27). Lizzo on being an LGBTQ ally, Rihanna and meeting Sandra Bullock. *Variety*. Retrieved from https://variety.com/2019/music/features/lizzo-lgbtq-ally-rihanna-sandra-bullock-1203255011/

Sheridan, I. (2019, April 8). What the rise of micro-influencers means for PR professionals. *PRLab*. Retrieved from https://www.bu.edu/prlab/2019/04/08/what-the-rise-of-micro-influencers-means-for-pr-professionals/

Sims, D. (2018, November 11). A Veterans Day apology from "Saturday Night Live" and Pete Davidson. *The Atlantic*. Retrieved from https://www.theatlantic.com/entertainment/archive/2018/11/saturday-night-live-pete-davidson-dan-crenshaw-veterans-day/575581/

Spilka, D. (2019, April 15). Why reputation management has become the most important facet of public relations. *Business 2 Community*. Retrieved from https://www.business2community.com/public-relations/why-reputation-management-has-become-the-most-important-facet-of-public-relations-02191214

Tassi, P. (2019, August 4). Microsoft's Ninja deal is likely about "Halo Infinite" and Xbox Scarlett as well as Mixer. *Forbes*. Retrieved from https://www.forbes.com/sites/paultassi/2019/08/04/microsofts-ninja-deal-is-likely-about-halo-infinite-and-xbox-scarlett-as-well-as-mixer/

Tobin, B. (2019, June 26). Catch this former Louisville basketball player in the new "Spider-Man" movie commercial. *Courier-Journal*. Retrieved from https://www.courier-journal.com/story/entertainment/2019/06/26/donovan-mitchell-appears-spider-man-far-from-home-commercial-with-tom-holland/1572692001/

Togoh, I. (2019, August 12). Coach and Givenchy join Versace in apologizing to China over controversial T-shirt. *Forbes*. Retrieved from https://www.forbes.com/sites/isabeltogoh/2019/08/12/coach-and-givenchy-join-versace-in-apologising-to-china-over-t-shirt-row/#1ad210b56942

West, J. (2018, June 27). Donovan Mitchell's "Spida" nickname is officially an entry on Dictionary.com. *Sports Illustrated*. Retrieved from https://www.si.com/nba/2018/06/27/donovan-mitchell-spida-dictionary-entry

Wong, Q. (2019, August 14). Instagram is hiding likes. You may be happier in the end. *CNET*. (n.d.). Retrieved from https://www.cnet.com/news/instagram-is-hiding-likes-you-may-be-happier-in-the-end/

CHAPTER 15

Abrahamson, R. P. (2019, September 9). Bullied boy's homemade Vols shirt raises nearly $1 million for charity. *Today*. Retrieved from https://www.today.com/parents/boy-s-homemade-ut-vols-shirt-sale-school-s-site-t162166

Entis, L. (2019, September 12). "We had to get ahead of skeptics thinking this was a joke": The inside story on Arby's Marrot. *PR Week*. Retrieved from https://www.prweek.com/article/1596583?utm_source=website&utm_medium=social

Fleming, J. (2019, September 13). Sexy Colonel Sanders; digital avatars for hire; how to creatively use slack: Friday's first things first. *Adweek*. Retrieved from https://www.adweek.com/creativity/sexy-colonel-sanders-digital-avatars-for-hire-how-to-creatively-use-slack-fridays-first-things-first/

Kitterman, T. (2019, December 31). PR crises that have defined 2019. *PR Daily*. Retrieved from https://www.prdaily.com/pr-crises-that-have-defined-2019/

Klein, A. (2019, September 12). Bullied boy who designed University of Tennessee T-shirt just got free tuition to the college. *Washington Post*. Retrieved from https://www.washingtonpost.com/lifestyle/2019/09/12/bullied-boy

-who-designed-university-tennessee-t-shirt-just-got-free-tuition-college/?arc404=true

Slotnick, D. (2020, March 5). Nearly a year after it began, the Boeing 737 Max crisis still drags on. Here's the complete history of the plane that's been grounded since 2 crashes killed 346 people 5 months apart. *Business Insider*. Retrieved from https://www.businessinsider.com/boeing-737-max-timeline-history-full-details-2019-9#the-plane-being-used-for-that-flight-a-737-max-8-had-given-incorrect-speed-and-altitude-readings-on-a-previous-trip-but-was-kept-in-service-anyway-37

Synder, L. (2019). Facebook updates. Retrieved from https://www.facebook.com/permalink.php?story_fbid=10114194128988573&id=5239432

Valinsky, J. (2019, June 27). Why Arby's is testing meat products that look like big carrots. *CNN Business*. Retrieved from https://www.cnn.com/2019/06/26/business/arbys-fake-meat-carrot-trnd/index.html

INDEX

Tinder, 250
Tiny House Nation, 34
Today show, 156
Tone, 204
Tonight Show, 116
Top Gun: Maverick, 245–246
Topic Wheel framework, 118–119
"Torches of Freedom" campaign, 28
Toyota, 251
TPB. *See* Theory of Planned Behavior (TPB)
TRA. *See* Theory of Reasoned Action (TRA)
"Trailblazers" campaign, 70
Transparency, 184
Treatment, 204
Trump, Donald, 38–39, 115, 120, 320
Twitter, 39, 49, 60, 103, 119, 129, 132, 136, 144–145, 167, 186, 192, 202, 206–207, 209, 211, 213, 245, 252, 254, 258, 276, 306, 308–309, 314, 331
Two-way asymmetrical communication model, 27–29, 36–38, 40
Two-way symmetrical communication model, 27, 29, 38–39, 40
Tyson Foods, 63

Uber, 19, 150, 279
United Airlines, 7, 202
Universal Love, 79
Universities, 107
University of California, Los Angeles (UCLA) vlogger, 136
University of Southern California (USC), 107
Uno, 79
USAA® Bank, 52
The U.S. Navy, 300–301

Validity, 98
Vanity metrics, 249
VanZant, Paige, 313
Varsity Blues, 326
Vaynerchuk, Gary (aka Gary Vee), 13, 38, 120–121, 189, 213–214, 220
VaynerMedia, 13, 120, 189
Versace, Donatella, 299
Virtual reality (VR) message strategy, 8–9, 13, 18, 214–215
Visual content, 210–211
Visual design principle, 111–112
Visual messaging, 111

Vita Coco, 129–130
Vitaminwater, 63
vlog, 213
"Voices," campaign, 60

Waddington, Stephen, 20
Wade, Dwyane, 157
Walmart, 6, 119
Warren, Elizabeth, 115
Warrior games, 79–80
"We All In," campaign, 79
Web analytics, 251–252
Weber Shandwick, 73
Website, 186, 208, 251–252
Wegmans, 114
Weinstein, Harvey, 65
Well Fargo crisis, 49
Wendy's campaign, 114, 167
Westminster Kennel Club Dog Show, 155
Wild Turkey bourbon company, 157–158
Williams, Serena, 6, 11, 166, 294
Wilson, Rebel, 61
Witherspoon, Reese, 117
Women Worldwide, 231
work environments, 284
World Record Egg Instagram campaign, 38
Writing content, 311
Writing skills, 266
Writing, 8–9. *See also* PR writing
  authenticity, 132
  consistency, 130
  social media content, ideas of, 144–145
  strong voice, 132
  traditional forms, 208
  types of, 9

Xbox Adaptive Controller, 79

YouTube, 35, 121, 186–187, 190, 192, 197, 250, 258
Yu, Dennis, 118, 260–261

Zignal Labs, 233
Zonozi, Amir, 315
Zoomph, 233
Zuckerberg, Mark, 59